THE DAMBUSTERS
'WAS THE RAID WORTHWHILE?'

BARNES WALLIS AND THE MEN BEHIND
THE OPERATION IN THEIR OWN WORDS

JOHN SWEETMAN

DAMBUSTERS: WAS THE RAID WORTHWHILE?
Barnes Wallis and the Men Behind the Operation in Their Own Words

First published in Great Britain in 2024 by
Airworld
An imprint of
Pen & Sword Books Ltd
Yorkshire – Philadelphia

Copyright © John Sweetman, 2024

ISBN 978 1 39906 381 4

The right of John Sweetman to be identified as Author of this work has been asserted by him in accordance with the Copyright, Designs and Patents Act 1988.

A CIP catalogue entry for this book is available from the British Library.

All rights reserved. No part of this book may be reproduced or transmitted in any form or by any means, electronic or mechanical including photocopying, recording or by any information storage and retrieval system, without permission from the Publisher in writing.

Typeset by SJmagic DESIGN SERVICES, India.

Printed and bound in the UK by CPI Group (UK) Ltd.

Pen & Sword Books Ltd includes the Imprints of Atlas, Archaeology, Aviation, Discovery, Family History, Fiction, History, Maritime, Military, After the Battle, Military Classics, Politics, Select, Airworld, Frontline Publishing, Leo Cooper, Remember When, Seaforth Publishing, The Praetorian Press, Wharncliffe Local History, Wharncliffe Transport, Wharncliffe True Crime and White Owl.

For a complete list of Pen & Sword titles please contact

PEN & SWORD BOOKS LTD
George House, Units 12 & 13, Beevor Street, Off Pontefract Road,
Barnsley, South Yorkshire, S71 1HN, England
E-mail: enquiries@pen-and-sword.co.uk
Website: www.pen-and-sword.co.uk

or
PEN AND SWORD BOOKS
1950 Lawrence Rd, Havertown, PA 19083, USA
E-mail: uspen-and-sword@casematepublishers.com
Website: www,penandswordbooks.com

Contents

Preface	Questions	vi
Chapter 1	Priority Targets, German Dams	1
Chapter 2	Enter Wallis	7
Chapter 3	Developing the Weapon	21
Chapter 4	Persuading the Doubtful	35
Chapter 5	Perfecting the Means	52
Chapter 6	617 Squadron Prepares	64
Chapter 7	Count-Down to Take-Off	99
Chapter 8	First Wave: Moehne and Eder	119
Chapter 9	Second Wave: The Sorpe	141
Chapter 10	Third Wave: Final Chance	156
Chapter 11	The Story Unfolds	171
Chapter 12	Impact – Germany	191
Chapter 13	Significant Outcomes	214
Chapter 14	Missing Aircraft	230
Conclusion	Some Answers	241
Acknowledgements		253
Appendix A		256
Appendix B		260
Bibliography		270
Glossary		278
Index		285

Preface

Questions

The Dambusters Raid has been covered exhaustively in print, on the cinema screen and on TV, often leading to searching doubts being raised about the operation. Was it well-planned, as successful as claimed, sound in concept, justified?

This collection of personal accounts comprises interviews and correspondence with those involved in the planning, preparation and execution of Operation Chastise. It includes contributions from civilian and military figures responsible for the reaction in Germany, eye witnesses and those who experienced the raid's impact. Material is drawn also from the records of authorities concerned with the construction, maintenance and repair of the dams, as well as British and German official documents.

Despite later research and analysis, popular perception of the operation remains largely fashioned by Wing Commander Guy Gibson's posthumous publication, *Enemy Coast Ahead,* and Paul Brickhill's *The Dam Busters,* which relied heavily upon it. Published two years after his death, Gibson's book was reputedly polished in the Air Ministry, which prompted navigator Sergeant D.P. Heal to muse, 'it didn't read like him'. Covering his whole RAF career, not just this raid, Gibson maintained: 'I have had to work without notes, and without the help from diaries.' As with Brickhill, recreated direct speech illustrates the tense atmosphere of action, but is factually suspect. Gibson asked forgiveness if he had 'put words into their own mouths which they never said. A memory is a short thing, and flak never does it much good'.

The producer of 'The Dam Busters', which successfully and dramatically drew on these sources, admitted to Barnes Wallis a 'somewhat simplified treatment of highly complicated issues … our film cannot hold interest unless we present "living" people … to an uninstructed audience'. There were, he added, 'many personal touches to this end'; tacit admission of fictional creativity.

QUESTIONS

There is need for caution, with other, ostensibly more reliable, sources. Official documents are not always accurate. One leg of the inward flight in the Operation Order was changed in the twenty-four hours before take-off without being altered in print. Furthermore, navigators' logs show that the locations of some turning points were amended during preparatory briefings.

Oral testimony, particularly with passing years, routinely requires careful attention, as flight engineer, Sergeant H.B. Feneron, conceded in 1977: 'It is a long time ago and one's memory can be a little uncertain.' Two crew members of a Lancaster severely damaged on the way to one dam later gave conflicting versions of the same incident. A civilian, closely associated with Wallis's experiments, was interviewed five years apart. On the second occasion, asked for confirmation of a previous assertion, he replied: 'Did I say that?'

Nevertheless, individual memories and written records offer an insight into the motives and feelings of people immersed in various aspects of the operation. They provide, likewise, an opportunity to re-assess it in the light, for example, of the revelation that Albert Speer, German Minister for Armaments and Munitions, believed the breaching of the Sorpe Dam would have shortened the war. He held, as well, that attacking the Eder Dam, unconnected with the Ruhr armament industries, undermined achievement of the primary aim of the operation. Closer to home, in April 1972 Sir Barnes Wallis asked Dr A.R. Collins, the scientist responsible for the model tests connected with his 'bouncing bomb', 'was the raid worthwhile?'

Contentious issues raised by these questions and other adverse judgements, which have gained momentum over time, merit re-consideration. The contemporary context is all-important.

Chapter 1

Priority Targets, German Dams

As conflict with Germany became increasingly likely, in 1937 a series of Western Air Plans was drawn up. One entailed bombing specific facilities servicing armament factories in the Ruhr, where Bomber Command held that '75–80 per cent ... of the war industries of Germany ... are situated'. If 45 individual power stations and coking plants were attacked over a fortnight in 3,000 sorties, 176 aircraft might be lost but the campaign would undermine, if not totally halt, the Ruhr's production capability. Sir Maurice Hankey, chairman of an Air Targets Sub-Committee, countered that a similar outcome could be achieved by breaching just two dams: the Moehne and Sorpe. Vast quantities of water, critical for processes like steel production, would be released from the adjacent reservoirs.

Before the close of the year, though, it had been established that creating 'fissures' in the structure would not breach the Moehne (a vast masonry construction essentially held in place by gravity and its own weight). No existing bombs nor torpedoes were likely to destroy it, even if the dam could be hit. Bombing trials suggested that from 10,000–15,000ft the average accuracy would be 102–113 yards. Although its triangular configuration did widen the potential target, the Moehne was only 21ft wide at the top. If pattern bombing were employed, assuming an average error of 200 yards, 750 bombs would have a 2 per cent chance of success. Recognising such an 'highly problematical' outcome, the Ordnance Board concluded: 'If the policy to attack the dams is accepted ... the development of a propelled, piercing bomb of high capacity would be essential to ensure the requisite velocity and flight approximately to the horizontal' for an attack on the face of the dam at right angles rather than bombing from above.

Despite the discouraging signs, in March 1938 Bomber Command Paper No. 16, *Air Attacks on Reservoirs and Dams,* was widely circulated within the Air Ministry. Although such an operation might seem at present 'uneconomic', re-examination of an attack 'with existing bombs or torpedoes or [significantly] with newly developed weapons', appeared warranted. On 26 July 1938, the Bombing Committee of the Air Ministry formally considered this analysis, noting that Hankey's sub-committee wanted dams and reservoirs 'treated as urgent and of pressing importance'.

Air Vice-Marshal William Sholto Douglas, Assistant Chief of the Air Staff, opened the meeting by stating that 'investigations' suggested certain reservoirs were the 'Achilles heel' of German industrial power, which was 'derived almost entirely from these sources'. Squadron Leader C.G. Burge, secretary of Hankey's sub-committee, maintained that this type of target was 'of very great intrinsic importance' and that the Moehne provided 'the bulk' of the Ruhr's water supply. Burge further held that 'enormous damage' would be wrought if that dam were breached, the 'low-lying Ruhr valley would be flooded, so that railways, important bridges, pumping stations and industrial chemical plants would be destroyed and rendered inoperative'. Douglas observed that a low-level attack would be needed to achieve the required accuracy. Dr Ferguson from the Research Department at Woolwich Arsenal explained that a typical gravity dam, like the Moehne, was 42ft thick, 40ft below the crest and available SAP (semi-armour piercing) bombs would only penetrate 5ft. Douglas therefore felt that a 'propelled bomb' might be necessary.

Burge then addressed the issue of earth dams, concluding that dropping high explosive (HE) bombs on top of the structure seemed the best option, although 'the prospect of success did not appear very favourable'. The Sorpe comprised a central, vertical concrete core stabilised by sloping banks of earth on either side. As a target, it bore no physical relation to the Moehne, which the Air Officer Commanding-in-Chief Bomber Command recognised. In his copy of the minutes, Air Chief Marshal Sir Edgar Ludlow-Hewitt scribbled in the margin: 'What about the Sorpetal, one of the most important in the Ruhr area?' – perceptive, but unavailing. Despite having been highlighted with the Moehne from the outset, the Sorpe would thereafter frequently evade the planner's attention as the project progressed.

Douglas's committee concluded that an attack on the Moehne from the water side, when the reservoir was full, would be 'feasible'. The use of 18in torpedoes was preferred, GP (general purpose) or semi-armour piercing bombs having less chance of success. Hence, on 28 July 1938, Ludlow-Hewitt could inform the Secretary of State for Air that 'the feasibility of attacking this form of objective is still under consideration'. In an appendix, the Eder Dam featured as a target due to its own two power stations and connection with an emergency pumping station at nearby Waldeck; six other important facilities were listed 'all in the industrial region of Kassel', below this dam. In January 1939, an 'Appreciation on the Attack of German War Industry' highlighted the importance of electricity generating stations. Nine months later, the Principal of Birmingham Central Technical College advised the Air Ministry: 'Cut off electrical supply and industry is paralysed, not one but dozens of factories would stand idle.' On 16 October, an appendix to 'Appreciation of Oil and Power Plans' pointed to the importance of the Mittelland Canal, which would later feature as another reason for attacking the Eder Dam.

Curiously, on 29 August 1939, Justus Dillgardt, Director of the Association of German Engineers, feared the threat to dams:

> not so much one of demolition due to direct hits by bombs on the wall, but of several bombs dropped 20 to 30 metres away from the dam, which explode below the water-line. The compressed effect of the water caused by the explosion could well cause the wall to collapse.

As a result of the 'vast outflow' following a breach:

> the entire industrial area [below it] ... would be completely paralysed ... not only would the population of four to five million [sic] be without water, but all mines and all coking plants would suddenly cease work owing to the lack of industrial water supply.

This was similar to Burge's prediction. Also concerned, the chief engineer of the power station beneath the Moehne Dam wall, Klemens Koehler, called for the volume of water in its adjacent reservoir to be reduced to 80 million cubic metres, a loss of roughly 50 million cubic metres. This was not done, but steps were taken to improve the defences in the short run. Twin torpedo nets were installed in front of the wall, balloons and multiple flak guns positioned around the dam. It would later emerge, though, that no dam was part of the air-raid warning network. In September 1942, Albert Speer, Minister for Armaments and Munitions, identified bottlenecks in the supply system including tanks at Friedrichshafen and ball-bearings at Schweinfurt, whose factories required special protection. Reservoirs and dams did not feature, which resulted in the withdrawal of heavy flak, searchlights and smoke canisters during the ensuing months to protect industrial targets already under direct bomber attack.

Meanwhile, in the wake of the various pre-war meetings and discussions in Britain, several other ways to attack the Moehne were examined and discarded, including air-launched rockets fired at the open side and a radio-controlled, explosive-packed drone across the water. The guidelines for such an operation were laid down in October 1938 by Group Captain J.C. Slessor, Deputy Director of Plans in the Air Ministry: '(i) Is it recognisable? (ii) Is it big enough to give us a reasonable chance of hitting it? (iii) Have we got the right sort of bomb to send it sky-high if we do hit it?'

In spite of failure to devise a satisfactory method of attack, the Moehne remained on the agenda. Prompted by his Senior Air Staff Officer, Air Vice-Marshal N.H. Bottomley, who would chair an influential inter-service committee in the immediate run-up to Operation Chastise and drafted this submission, on 3 July 1940, Ludlow-Hewitt's successor, Air Marshal Sir Charles Portal, resurrected the subject by sending a strong plea to the Under-Secretary of State for Air. Referring to the proceedings of the 1938 committee, he believed:

> that the time has arrived when we should make arrangements for the destruction of the Moehne Dam ... I am given to understand that almost all the industrial activity of the Ruhr depends on the water contained in and supplied by this dam, and that if it were destroyed not only would most of the industry in the Ruhr be brought to a standstill, but very great havoc would be wrought throughout the length of the water course.

He favoured a torpedo attack via the reservoir, envisaging 'at least twelve' Hampden bombers being taken from the production line to avoid depleting the existing main force and forming a specialised long-range unit.

Air Vice-Marshal Douglas, now Deputy Chief of the Air Staff, responded bleakly: 'Attacks on dams in general and the Moehne in particular have been the subject of exhaustive study since July 1938'. An 'elaborate series of tests' by Messrs Nobel had proved that 'thousands of pounds of explosive' would be required 'effectively' to damage a dam like the Moehne. There was an added problem. The pressure of water created by an explosion at a distance from it would tend to support and close cracks, and torpedoes fired at masonry jetties had caused only surface damage. It might be possible to drop 100 or more mines on the water and countermine with HE bombs, but 'the practical difficulties of this method are considered to be insuperable at present'. Nevertheless, the concept of attacking German dams remained active and elements of the ultimate plan – a special squadron of modified aircraft attacking across the reservoir at low-level – had been raised. In 1943 Portal would be Chief of the Air Staff.

PRIORITY TARGETS, GERMAN DAMS

A thorough re-examination of all the evidence available had been ordered on 2 May 1940 by the Chief Superintendent of the Woolwich Arsenal Research Department. The task to devise a viable way to destroy the Moehne and other gravity dams fell to Wing Commander C.R. Finch Noyes. He, in turn, revealed that Air Commodore Patrick Huskisson, Vice-President of the Ordnance Board, informed him that 'a sudden demand has arisen for an attack on the Moehne and a means evolved of carrying it out'. Huskinson emphasised 'that the greatest speed was necessary otherwise the attempt would be made with existing weapons'. This strongly suggests that the pressure led to Portal's initiative in July 1940 before Finch Noyes had completed his work.

His final report, 'The High Capacity Short Range Torpedo and Skimmer for Conveyance by Air and Other Craft' (he foresaw naval targets as well) was not submitted until 2 April 1941. Finch Noyes argued that if 20,000lbs of explosive were detonated 40ft below the crest of the Moehne, and crucially against it, 'there seems a probability that the dam will go' even if 2,000lb units were exploded 'at reasonably short intervals'. Acknowledging that the 1938 Bombing Committee had considered using 40 torpedoes each with 400lbs of explosive, Finch Noyes preferred a missile launched from an aircraft flying at 80mph 'very low over the surface of the water'.

He had designed such a missile to travel across the reservoir 'at a reasonable speed' in the form of a 'hydroplane-skimmer' or beneath the surface like a torpedo. The former would jump over protective nets, the torpedo proceed 'partly or wholly submerged' with its velocity allowing it to penetrate the netting. Each weapon would weigh 3,000lbs (2,000lbs explosive) and be driven by 'rocket-underwater plus steam jet propulsion'. Both would be directionally stable with buoyancy jackets designed to flood on striking the target, sink to the desired depth and be detonated by hydrostatic or other [unspecified] fuses. If either were used as a gliding weapon from an aircraft on touching the water it would shed its 'air-bearing surfaces and thereafter [be] driven by cordite explosion from the stern'.

To allow for losses or malfunctions, he recommended a moonlight attack at right angles to the Moehne over the reservoir by sixteen Wellingtons (32,000lbs of explosive) releasing their weapons 5½ miles from the dam at 5,500ft, so they would strike the water half a mile from the target and be self-propelled towards it by the special charge. He re-emphasised that 'the destruction of the Moehne Dam would flood the Ruhr valley and disorganise its industry. It is probably very heavily defended, so it is desirable to attack it from a distance and from a height'. 'Probably' anti-torpedo nets and possibly barges would screen the structure. Finch Noyes believed the skimmer to be particularly suitable for use against dam walls. Echoing Portal's suggestion, he proposed that a special Bomber Command squadron be formed. 'In determined hands, with singleness of purpose and free from disturbance, such a unit should in six months from the word "go" have effected its objectives given the necessary priority'.

Finch Noyes' ingenious plan was stillborn. Portal's successor at Bomber Command, Air Marshal Sir Richard Peirse, although admitting that the proposal 'attracts me', feared that the torpedo version travelling at 40 knots would bounce off the face of the dam 'before sinking in a docile manner alongside it'. Peirse asked his Senior Air Staff Officer, Air Vice-Marshal R.H.M.S. Saundby, for his opinion and Saundby instructed the Group Captain Operations to study Finch Noyes' submission. On 2 June, Mills reported dismissively. He agreed that destruction of the Moehne Dam 'would paralyse its [Ruhr] industry'. But a way of achieving this had been 'considered on many occasions' and discounted due to the 'enormous quantity of explosive' required. Therefore, he doubted whether a skimmer or torpedo, with such limited explosive content, would succeed; a conclusion which apparently did not acknowledge Finch Noyes' total of 20,000lbs of explosive in multiple missiles. Mills argued that 'big blast bombs' against either the water or air side 'might be possibilities'; despite previous calculations that such accuracy could not be guaranteed from the air. Another objection was that, 'once we use a gliding weapon, all sorts [of] errors in ranging and in line arise immediately, and are added to enormously when wind has to be taken into account'. Mills saw no future in the proposal, but suggested that it might be a 'better prospect' for the Royal Navy against ships.

So Finch Noyes' scheme was rejected by the RAF. However, like Portal's proposal, its influence would be detected in the evolution and execution of Operation Chastise: a weapon propelled across a reservoir designed to sink beside the target and explode at a predetermined depth, being delivered at right angles to the dam wall at low level on a moonlit night.

Destruction of the west German dams, and the Moehne in particular, had thus long been embedded in Air Ministry target files. Noting that 'the dams are always full in spring after the melting of snow and April rains', on 17 July 1939 the Air Staff drew up a list of seven target dams, five associated with the Ruhr: Moehne, Sorpe, Lister, Ennepe and Henne. Two others further east, Eder and Diemel, were connected to the inland waterway systems of the Weser Valley and Mittelland Canal. These seven would ultimately feature in the draft Operation Order for the Dambusters Raid.

Chapter 2

Enter Wallis

In retirement, Sir Barnes Wallis pondered, 'I had as many mad ideas as good ones'. R.C. (Bob) Handasyde, a Vickers test pilot involved in testing 'the bouncing bomb' during its development stage, declared Wallis's mind to be so agile that he needed somebody with a mallet 'to bonk him on the head, while engineers considered if his current notion would work. He had so many ideas that he was often away to Marks 2, 3 and 4 before the prototype was off the ground.' At first glance, Wallis's proposed way of destroying German dams qualified for 'mad' classification.

After his design work on the R.100 airship at Howden in Yorkshire ended, in 1929 Wallis was deployed to Southampton, home of Supermarine Aviation, which Vickers had recently acquired. There he was to co-operate with R.J. Mitchell in the design and production of flying boats. As Wallis's elder son, Barnes (junior), remarked: 'There was no place for two egotists in one office', and Wallis rapidly moved to Brooklands, Weybridge, as Chief Designer (Structures) Vickers Aviation Ltd. When Vickers Aviation was absorbed into Vickers-Armstrongs Ltd, he became Assistant Chief Designer (Aviation Sections). This meant, 'I now had the right to interest myself in the aerodynamic design of our aircraft', as well as structure. At Weybridge, the chief designer, R.K. 'Rex' Pierson, proved a wise and tolerant supervisor, the works manager, Tom Gammon, and managing director, Major Hew Kilner, equally supportive. It is worth noting that Wallis was frequently plagued by debilitating headaches, such as on 4, 12 and 20 April 1940, when diary entries simply read 'migraine'.

Significantly, he had the capacity to establish enduring professional relationships, which would be critical in the evolution of the Dams' Raid. Norbert Rowe, wartime Director of Technical Development at the Ministry of Aircraft Production, formed a friendship with Wallis during the construction of the R.100, when Rowe was the Resident Technical Officer on behalf of the Air Ministry. In 1981, reflecting that their association

THE DAMBUSTERS: 'WAS THE RAID WORTHWHILE?'

'survived throughout Wallis's life', Rowe explained: 'We respected one another as engineers, one essentially creative, the other critical in respect of specification standards.' Wing Commander (later Air Commodore) S.O. Bufton, who would become Director of Bomber Operations at the Air Ministry in 1943, had been impressed by 'Wally', when he gave a lecture on R.100 to the engineers' course at RAF Henlow in 1932, and was immediately sympathetic to his 'Big Bomb proposal', when Wallis sent details to him. Benjamin Lockspeiser, Deputy Director of Scientific Research at the Ministry of Aircraft Production had known Wallis pre-war when at the Royal Aircraft Establishment Farnborough and thought him 'an extraordinary man, a mechanical genius ... [with] abundant ability ... who always explained himself so well and so convincingly'; a valuable opinion when Lockspeiser became involved in the Dams' project. Wing Commander (later Group Captain) F.W. Winterbotham, chief of air intelligence in MI6, who first met Wallis at his Effingham home in 1940, was impressed and thereafter firmly backed his plans for both the 10-ton bomb and Dams' Raid. Possibly the most important senior officer, who would consistently support Wallis and command No.5 Bomber Group which launched Operation Chastise, was Air Vice-Marshal the Hon R.A. Cochrane. He first met Wallis in 1916, when he was working on military airships at Walney Island, Barrow-in-Furness. George Edwards, Experimental Manager at Weybridge, believed that 'Wally had the ability to persuade people in the Ministry to do what they did' and Bufton reflected that 'he was always in King Charles Street seeking advice'.

Wallis would certainly benefit from the support of influential civilian and Service figures and the Vickers' staff as he pursued his declared aim of undermining the enemy war effort. Reputedly after listening to Neville Chamberlain's dramatic broadcast on 3 September 1939, he mused, 'what can an engineer do to win the war?' Wallis reflected that his knowledge of the explosive effect of bombs was limited. The results of his extensive research, with the help of the librarians of professional bodies like the Institution of Civil Engineers, were illustrated in scores of sketches and diagrams. He used 'Military Engineering Data' to calculate the impact of different amounts of explosive dropped from varying heights, analysed a detailed paper, dated 18 August 1940, on 'Bombing Probabilities' compiled by the Directorate of Armament Development, a report from the ARP Department of the Ministry of Home Security and another more specific report on the damage caused by '100 kilos and a few 50 kilos' HE bombs dropped on 'Castle Bromwich Aeroplane Factory'. This, incidentally, confirmed his access to Air Ministry sources. Apart from information appearing in British publications, his files include translations from German printed sources, such as 'The Moehne Dam or barrage' composed by an Essen architect, and 'Dams and Their Influence on the Water Supply of the Ruhr' from *Das Gas Und Wasser* (No. 30, 1932).

Wallis's research led him to design the '22,400lb R.100 Shape' bomb, 19.85ft long, 3.72ft wide: an 'earthquake, 10-ton' weapon, whose points of delivery by a six-engine High Altitude Stratosphere or Victory bomber from 40,000ft were extensive including lock gates, harbours, coal mines and dams beside which it would burrow beneath the earth and explode underground causing the target to collapse. An entry in Wallis's diary, 22 July 1940, read: 'Started on Strato Bomber', with a top speed of 330mph and 4,000 mile range. The Vickers Company secretary, H.E. Scrope, though held that 'the six-engine bomber ... was a revamp of Rex Pierson's project of 1937 ... with a wing span of 235ft and a bomb load of 20 tons. Mr Pierson calculated that one of these machines would have the offensive power of a squadron of Wellingtons'.

Later summarising 'Important Dates' in his life, Wallis would write of this period: 'Autumn 1939 to Autumn 1940 spent learning about bombs, the behaviour, chemistry and elementary physics of High Explosives; the construction of the Winding Shafts of German Collieries; the Construction of Gravity, Multiple Arch and Earth Dams'. Without further comment, he continued: '19 July 1940. Disclosed scheme for 10ton bomb to [Lord] Beaverbrook'. His elaborate concept would be explained in a 117-page illustrated composition, 'A Note on a Method of Attacking the Axis Powers' [Germany and Italy], started in July 1940 and completed in March 1941.

Wallis circulated the paper for comment to chosen individuals, one of whom was the decorated First World pilot and editor of the journal *Aeronautics*, Major Oliver Stewart. On 22 April, Wallis appended a personal letter:

> I have long been wanting to have a talk with you over the various methods of development as regards air warfare, which have appeared from time to time in your most interesting paper, and for the last eight months I have been working hard on a method which is described in the accompanying Note. While the whole of the information is naturally secret, I feel that influential people such as yourself should have an opportunity of seeing such things, particularly as I know that you are on the opposite side, and I should be most grateful if you could find time to read my paper and let me have any criticisms that occur to you.

THE DAMBUSTERS: 'WAS THE RAID WORTHWHILE?'

Apart from consulting a vast quantity of written sources, Wallis's diaries show that he travelled extensively to consult scientific specialists; 13–14 August 1940, he drove a total of 256 miles to see professors G.I. Taylor, A.J. Sutton Pippard and J.D. Bernal. On 11 October, Wallis made the 100 miles round trip to Leigh Park, near Havant, Hampshire, to consult Captain Riley of the RN Admiralty Mine Department. During the week commencing 14 October, on successive days Wallis visited the Air Ministry, Ministry of Home Security at Princes Risborough, Institution of Civil Engineers in London, Woolwich Arsenal, Princes Risborough again and the Air Ministry once more. The following week saw visits to the Ministry of Aircraft Production in London, Road Research Laboratory at Harmondsworth and the Aeroplane and Armament Experimental Establishment at Boscombe Down. Routine design work was rarely detailed; just 'Burhill' or 'Works' entered.

In particular, Wallis secured the backing of Winterbotham and Dr W.H. Glanville, Director of the Road Research Laboratory (RRL). When Wallis's 'brilliant' proposal appeared in March 1941, Winterbotham immediately set out to circulate it with mixed results. Professor Frederick Lindemann (soon Lord Cherwell), the Prime Minister's scientific adviser, believed that no such project could be completed before the war ended, and the Air Ministry responded similarly. Wallis later reflected, not strictly correctly, that 'Lindemann was always against me' and demolished an associated legend: 'I never met Winston Churchill at all'. Winterbotham did, though, receive a sympathetic reaction from Lord Beaverbrook (Minister of Aircraft Production) and, through him, secured a meeting with Dr D.R. Pye, Director of Scientific Research at the Ministry of Aircraft Production. Pye pointed out that simultaneous detonation of a 19ft long weapon could not be guaranteed, which inevitably cast doubt on the whole idea. However, Glanville's interest had already been secured leading to a series of experiments, which would ultimately confirm the impracticality of the 'big bomb' at that time, but fortuitously lay the foundation for Operation Chastise.

Dr A.R. Collins, a scientific officer in the Concrete Section of the RRL, recalled returning by car to Harmondsworth from a meeting with Dr E.R. Stradling at the Ministry of Home Security site in Princes Risborough on a Friday in early October 1940 with the Assistant Director Dr A.H. Davis. Davis said that Glanville wanted to see him the following morning. Then, Collins was told to hand over his current task and be prepared 'to undertake some work on dams'. So, over the week-end he sought to familiarise

ENTER WALLIS

himself with this hitherto unknown subject. Collins believed that Glanville and Davis had decided jointly on the procedure, 'and I was given no formal authority beyond Dr Glanville's verbal instructions'. Collins discovered that, knowing him, the RRL director had offered to help, having become aware that Wallis was relying 'on theoretical calculations sometimes of doubtful validity especially in respect to the effects of explosions'.

At a subsequent meeting, Wallis explained his thoughts 'quoting the Moehne, Eder and [Italian] Tirso dams, and it was agreed that the Moehne and Eder were so similar that, using a 1/50th scale model, the Moehne alone would be tested as being the stronger of the two. The Tirso was entirely different and would be subject to separate tests ... Wallis said that the idea was to drop ten-ton bombs in the reservoirs and that he estimated that an attack by one squadron at high level provided a reasonable chance of getting one bomb 150ft from the dam. He brought with him and left with me a copy of N. Kelen *Gewichtsstaumauer* (Berlin, 1933) to provide details of the construction of the Moehne'. Collins wrote that 'the initial work started at once on some crude mock-ups of the Moehne', which he revealed had been chosen because a supportive earth bank stretching approximately 1/3 up the structure gave it added strength. With a team of four, during October and November 1940 Collins conducted tests with 2oz charges, based on Wallis's 7 tons of explosive in his massive weapon, detonated at varying distances from the 'rough' model of the Moehne Dam at Harmondsworth in an adjacent pool of water. He was aware that 'it appeared self-evident that the most effective place to drop a bomb would be in the reservoir as close as possible to the dam. With the available bomb sights, the nearest hit in a substantial raid might be as much as 30 or 45m away and anything closer than 15m would be just a matter of luck'.

Records show that government payments through the Ministry of Aircraft Production to the Road Research Laboratory for the work on dams began in November 1940 and were authorised to total £9,500 of which £4,317.16 would be spent by September 1942.

Cautioning that dates on the formal documents showed when they were typed, not when tests took place or decisions were made, Collins reported in November that scaled-down charges had been exploded at 4ft and 3ft from the Moehne model. 'Promising results' had been achieved and 'a more carefully prepared model' was to be constructed at the Building Research Station in Garston, on the outskirts of Watford, where Glanville had been director until 1936. A.J. 'Bill' Newman (Head of the Concrete Section) and his superior, Head of Structural Development and Principal

THE DAMBUSTERS: 'WAS THE RAID WORTHWHILE?'

Scientific Officer, Dr Norman Davey, designed the Moehne model 'from aerial photos and information gleaned from journals', unwittingly making an error: the measurements in the article were in metres, but the Garston design used yards. As Newman reflected, 'the painstaking model was actually wrong'; but, in practice, this was not a major drawback. Davey explained how he had become involved. Wallis and Glanville had come to his office at the Building Research Station, Garston 'one day before Christmas 1940'. Making clear that this was 'highly secret', they discussed an attack on the Moehne and Eder dams and asked him to design a model of the Moehne Dam.

For security, Davey and Newman laboriously carried material cast in the concrete laboratory in a wheelbarrow to a wooded area below the main building one Sunday morning, but found the work so exhausting that 'the heavy gang' was drafted in to complete the process. The labourers then cut a hole from the turf, Newman, A.B. Stapleton and Arthur Smith leading 'the tedious task' of laying 3 million blocks in the bitter cold. The structure, assembled between 25 November 1940 and 21 January 1941, was 42ft long, with 15ft between the two simulated towers, each block being 0.45 x 0.35 x 0.25in, and an adjacent small stream was dammed to create an imitation reservoir.

Collins later gave more details of the construction. There were 'four rows of blocks forming both the upstream and downstream faces, with the core filled with concrete. The rows of blocks on the downstream face were tilted back to simulate the coursing on the stone blocks in the real dam ... the cyclopean masonry of the Moehne was scaled for the main central section between model valve towers, with concrete for the wings'. Newman explained that to finish the complicated structure so quickly, they had worked seven days a week in all weathers. Post-war, Dr Davey would reflect that not until a letter from the Air Ministry on 24 September 1954 was his design work, the construction and existence of the model dam itself officially acknowledged. At some stage later, he explained 'somebody cut a V-shaped hole in the wall, possibly for an open day', which distorted the original appearance.

Newman recalled that Wallis often attended the tests on the model supervised by Collins, who produced illustrated results of ten uses of 2oz explosive charges on it. Disappointingly, the model was not breached, the best result being 'top portion of dam slightly dislodged with water leaking through' from an explosion 1ft from the face of the dam, 'relative accuracy believed unattainable operationally'.

ENTER WALLIS

A disused dam in Wales now came into the picture. Wallis explained that even before the Garston tests had been completed, he discussed with Sir Henry Tizard the need to check 'the validity of tests on small models by a large-scale test, if a suitable dam could be found'. Road Research Laboratory records confirm, 'fear that the models would not represent the full scale recurs throughout the [early] reports'. On 3 January 1941, Stradling reported that he had 'secured a real live dam at Elan Valley in Wales', owned by the Birmingham Water Company. Collins registered that it had been succeeded by the Caban Coch dam into whose reservoir water from it would flow if shattered. This was the disused Nant-y-Gro 1/5th the size of the Moehne, on which preparations were begun to carry out tests. Meanwhile, two 1/50th scale models of the Moehne and two 1/10th of the Nant-y-Gro (representing the same scaled version of the original) were used without significant success at Harmondsworth after the Garston model was abandoned.

Collins reflected that they could crack the models, but not destroy them. He observed that Wallis 'behaved very well', when attending tests and joining in subsequent discussions, always crediting Collins's team: 'You're the experts. I can't tell you what to do, you're telling me.' Collins revealed that Glanville was 'a bit cross' that subsequently 'Wallis got all the credit', but emphasised that at the time he always acknowledged the major contribution of him and his team. Collins whimsically reflected that, at Harmondsworth during 1941, they became known as 'The Dam Blasters'.

In 1977, Wallis admitted: 'I didn't know enough about the economic effects on the dams, what they were for, why required ... I was obsessed with volume, not use.' So the Sorpe 'didn't come into my calculations. Its volume was comparatively small and I didn't think it worth attacking'. This must be rationalisation in hindsight: several of the reservoirs abutting targeted gravity dams had much lower capacity (the Henne 11 million cubic metres to the Sorpe's 72 million cubic metres).

Wallis's preoccupation had been principally to prove his weapon capable of breaching the Moehne. He recorded, on 11 April 1941, an 'interview with Sir Henry Tizard's Committee', but on 31 May Tizard, acting in his Air Ministry advisory role, wrote discouragingly that 'your view that the single-purpose bomber offers a high probability of winning the war is not accepted'. Air Staff officers 'want not only to have the Wellington V in operation as soon as possible, but also want the utmost energy directed to the design and production of the high altitude Warwick'; indirect criticism that Wallis was not concentrating on his primary duties. Wallis himself admitted that 'this whole project was a sort of side-line'.

THE DAMBUSTERS: 'WAS THE RAID WORTHWHILE?'

H.E. Scrope, the Vickers Company secretary, thought the Air Ministry rejected the idea 'on the grounds of having too many eggs in one basket as well as the severe supporting drawbacks such as hangerage [sic] and the need for hard runways at a time when Bomber Command was operating from grass airfields'. Tizard, though, did hold out some hope: 'As for the big bomb itself, I am certainly in favour of the continuation of work.' So evaluation of Wallis's idea progressed, arrangements went ahead for the tests in Wales and further ones on the Harmondsworth models.

Encouragingly, re-examination of the Garston model and associated calculations, revealed that it had been more badly damaged than originally thought. In January 1942, a new system of constructing the gravity dam models at Harmondsworth was used 'with mortar layers placed using a sliding template'. One of these brought the decisive breakthrough. The possibility of a contact explosion had been discussed in mid-1941, presumably in the wake of Finch Noyes' identification of its need. Collins recalled, 'obtaining a direct hit on the water-face of a dam was, from the outset, considered as being too remote to warrant consideration'. However, 'in late February or early March 1942', at the end of one series of tests 'there was a slightly damaged model of the Nant-y-Gro which had to be demolished and the research team decided that this could be done most easily with a contact explosion'. Collins was astonished to see 'that the model was almost completely destroyed and some of the central parts were projected more than 20ft downstream'.

In 1981, Collins reflected: 'I still cannot understand why Wallis did not suggest a contact test earlier', especially as Collins had already concluded that a 15,500lb charge exploded 100ft from 'the face of a dam would cause severe damaged but not complete failure'. In retrospect, Wallis would assure Collins that 'the bouncing bomb was originated (invented?) solely to meet the requirement so convincingly demonstrated by your experiments that actual contact with the masonry of the dam was essential.' The importance of that quest was reinforced on 1 May 1942 after Wallis watched the first test on the Nant-y-Gro dam. Collins compared results there with similar ones on a Harmondsworth model. He concluded it 'unlikely' that a single charge of less than 30,000lbs detonated at a distance from a gravity dam would be required to breach it.

The test, therefore, seemed a disappointing failure, but Collins pointed out that it prompted decisive intervention from Glanville. His 'idea was a crucial turning point in the experimental work, because it gave us the confidence to undertake the second test on the Nant-y-Gro with a real hope of success'.

ENTER WALLIS

Collins explained that,

> Glanville's solution was really quite simple. We knew that a model test would indicate quite accurately the direct, immediate damage caused by an explosion such as cracking or cratering, but we also knew that it would not necessarily show the final effects on the structure as a whole. For example, a model would show whether an explosion would destroy a column in a building, but it would not show whether the building would collapse ... A gravity dam was a special case, because its stability depended on its own weight, which was in turn due to the force of gravity ... cracking and cratering the surface would not be enough, and to cause a breach the explosion would have to push a substantial part of the dam back far enough to make the fragments fall over the air face. We had, in effect, to use a battering ram rather than a hammer or pick-axe ... We could not rely on the pressure of the water because the pressure 100ft below the surface is only ten times that at a depth of 10ft. The energy had to be supplied by the explosive and this increased directly with its weight. If a test were made on a 1/10th scale model, both the model and the explosive would weigh only one thousandth of those of the prototype, so pieces of the dam would move the same distance in the model and the prototype. Thus, the damage to the model in relation to its size would be ten times that in the prototype. Glanville therefore suggested that the pieces in the model should be moved back 9/10ths of the distance to show what would happen on the larger scale.

That could not be done with the Nant-y-Gro (the prototype), but 'a visual inspection' would validate the results of a model test.

As these adjustments were underway, Wallis had already begun to investigate a way of detonating a charge in contact with a dam wall: 'the problem was therefore how to get the charge into position ... accuracy of this order was impossible with the usual method of bombing'. To solve the problem, he wryly reflected, 'took a bit of experimenting'. Wallis explained to Sydney Barratt at the Ministry of Aircraft Production: 'When working on the problem, I not unnaturally passed every alternative method of achieving this result under review.' In particular, it seems highly likely that he knew about the investigation carried out by Finch Noyes, culminating in his 1941 proposal to launch a missile across the surface of a reservoir towards a dam wall from low-flying bombers. On 13 December 1940, Wallis's diary shows that he visited the Armaments Research Department at Shrewsbury, where Finch Noyes worked, raising the intriguing possibility that they might have met and discussed the project.

Wallis recalled that, 'early in 1942 I had the idea of a missile, which if dropped in the water at a considerable distance upstream of the dam would reach the dam in a series of ricochets, and after impact against the crest of the dam would sink in close contact with the upstream face of the masonry'. Winterbotham recalled Wallis explaining that to ensure simultaneous explosion 'the obvious solution is to have a spherical bomb. Detonated from the centre, the explosion will reach all points of the surface at precisely the same moment'. He asked Winterbotham how such a weapon would behave if launched across the surface of a lake. After consulting an Air Staff officer, 'it would bounce like a football', Winterbotham replied. Wallis was delighted: 'But, my dear boy, splendid. Splendid!' However, Winterbotham urged him to come up with 'a properly baked pie – no under-cooked blackberries' this time and added that his Service contact believed that bouncing the bomb would achieve 'no accuracy at all – absolutely no accuracy'. Wallis retorted that 'there must be a law of ricochet' to counter this disadvantage.

To this end, in April 1942 he conducted his initial experiment involving projection of a collection of his younger daughter Elisabeth's marbles, replaced by 'half-inch diameter spheres of fibre and wood' when the supply ran out, over the surface of 'a tin bath full of water' placed on a wooden garden table at his Effingham home. All four Wallis children and their two McCormick cousins (John and Robert) witnessed the Easter display, which Mary declared 'exciting' and dubbed 'a marbles game with a wash tub'. Towards the end of the month, Wallis moved his experiment to Silvermere Lake, a pond sheltered from unauthorised view by trees between a golf club and the Vickers' experimental site called Foxwarren, whose sheds and equipment would afterwards play a critical role in the dams' project.

Herbert Jeffree, one of Wallis's experimental team, explained that the Foxwarren complex comprised three large structures on the Redhill Road, leading off the main Byfleet-Cobham road. Jeffree disarmingly observed that he had the designation 'Chief Physicist, a meaningless title, because I was actually a "loose number", a sort of odd job man'. Silvermere Lake was not Vickers' property, but part of an estate owned by Lady Seth Smith. As Experimental Manager, George Edwards visited her to seek permission for the planned further experiments. He found her 'sitting upright in a high-backed chair, perfectly attired in twin-set, pearls, blue rinse etc. I explained that I was unable to give her details of what was intended. "Dear boy, what are you waiting for? Anything to get rid of that man Hitler." I was dismissed as if I was wasting time not getting on with it'.

Wallis had not yet settled on the precise shape of the weapon, spherical or oblong, or how it would be projected: without spin, forward spin or back-spin. A catapult mounted on the bank of the lake fired the different types of missile across the water, where in a boat a stalwart of Weybridge Ladies' Rowing Club, Amy Gentry, indicated the distance reached. Edwards explained that he 'rigged up the catapult which had a tube attached for the balls to run down … The balls fired had two indentations linked with a trigger top and bottom on the apparatus. If neither trigger were engaged, there would be no spin. If the top trigger were used, top spin; the bottom, back-spin'. Before starting, Wallis was convinced that top spin would prevail, whereas Edwards favoured back-spin, 'and so it proved … Top spin went into the water, non-spin bounced an average seven times, back-spin fourteen'. 'Wallis', Edwards recalled, 'was dumbfounded'. Previously, he had declared, 'you can produce no scientific evidence that top spin is wrong and any other spin will be better'. Edwards concluded that 'the value of back-spin was that it allowed the plane to drop from higher and further away'.

On 29 April, Wallis concluded that 'golf balls' (spheres) had better 'ballistic properties' for aerial bombing. Understandably, he opted for back-spin, which has generated considerable controversy. Wallis merely recalled that 'I had the idea of back-spin' without describing how the thought developed. His son, Barnes, suggested that it might have come from chipping a golf ball onto a green or using back-spin on a tennis court. Collins speculated that need to provide stability in flight (failure to guarantee being a major criticism of Finch Noyes' air-launched missile) led Wallis to back-spin, crawling down the face of the dam being an unexpected bonus. Edwards was more specific. He explained that, as an amateur leg-spin bowler for Guildford Cricket Club, he had dismissed the legendary West Indian cricketer Learie Constantine. Following two orthodox leg-breaks, he bowled a 'flipper' with the same action by turning his wrist over, so that the ball back-spun and skidded through. Knowing that this worked on a hard surface, 'I thought it worth trying on water'.

Winterbotham recalled, 'I never heard Edwards' name mentioned … However, Barnes was always rather over insistent that every detail of the "invention" and "development" came from himself, which is not strictly true'. Dr Collins thought that 'the story of Wallis and the cricketer can have little substance ... [because] Wallis was well informed on aerodynamics'. Nevertheless, it is likely that, as Wallis implied, he decided on back-spin through a combination of sources, and Edwards' input was part of that process.

Wallis was firm, though, about the suggestion that knowing Nelson's sailors had bounced cannon balls off the water to gain distance affected his thinking: 'I was delighted to discover this afterwards. It confirmed my theory.' He explained how the spinning weapon would, indeed, crawl down the dam wall, acknowledging that it would initially rebound after contact, because of 'the great momentum of the weapon at high speed'. 'After the bounce back ... the spin, acting in conjunction with the vertical velocity of the sink (the density of the weapon being greater than that of water) would cause the weapon to continue forward in the water until it reached the face of the dam, down which it would roll in close contact, until it reached the critical depth for explosion.'

The encouraging results at Effingham and Silvermere prompted Wallis, without revealing back-spin, to outline in 'Spherical Bomb – Surface Torpedo', dated 14 May 1942, his new proposal for attacking 'the hydro-electric dams on reservoirs and floating vessels moored in calm waters, such as the Norwegian fjords ... By approaching the target in a fast glide and flattening out, the bomb should be dropped from a height not greater than 26ft when travelling at a speed of 470ft/sec in order that the impact angle shall not exceed 5 deg .... If released in smooth water 3,500ft (2/3ml) from the target, that distance would be 'covered in five bounces, the height at the fifth bounce just over 4ft, while the first bounce rises to only ½ the height of the initial drop'.

Wallis recorded that:

> I felt anxious as to the possibilities of the extraordinary weapon which I seemed to have put my finger on. Having great confidence in the intellectual power of my friend, Professor P.M.S. Blackett, I disclosed my new idea to him in the presence of Group Captain Winterbotham, who introduced me to the Admiralty building where Blackett was based. Blackett, having received my paper, passed it straight to Sir Henry Tizard, who within two days made available to me the William Froude Tank at the National Physical Laboratory (NPL) ... for a series of more elaborate experiments than had been [previously] possible.

He placed the visit to Blackett on 22 April and noted that Tizard met him at Burhill the following day. On 21 May, Tizard informed Wallis that the

ENTER WALLIS

Head of the Aerodynamics Department 'agrees that it is well worthwhile to try a few experiments in the tank at the NPL to establish the fundamentals of the problem'. Wallis regarded Tizard as 'my best advocate, my principal supporter ... [who] fully understood what I was trying to do. Very pleasant and easy to get on with, he came to see me and I went to London to meet him several times ... very knowledgeable, very kindly'. But Collins was right to credit Blackett with giving much-needed official impetus to the project.

Between 9 June and 22 September 1942, Wallis and his team used the indoor tank facilities at the NPL, Teddington, on 22 occasions. The William Froude Laboratory comprised two indoor tanks: No.1 (or Alfred Yarrow) 550ft long and utilised by the Vickers' team only once, and then after fierce debate. Herbert Jeffree revealed that it was 'dirtier than the other tank and had two eels in it'. No.2, 640ft long, 23ft wide and 9ft deep, decreasing to 2ft over the final 200ft, was used on all other occasions. From a specially rigged catapult on a raised platform, 2in-diameter spheres made of material ranging from lead to balsawood were projected, in the words of A.D. Grant who timed the bounces, 'to kiss, kiss, kiss the water'. Grant explained that he and Jeffree were part of the small group chosen by Wallis 'to man the Froude tank and from then on were involved virtually full time on his weapon work and test programmes'.

An NPL employee, Fred Rayment, working in the adjacent tank, thought Wallis 'the perfect scientist ... [who] rolled up his sleeves and joined in'. Not all the experiments went smoothly. Once, a sphere strayed off course to shatter a side window. Jeffree explained that to ensure consistency of results, the water was skimmed regularly with a stick stretched across the tank and drawn from the far end towards the gantry. Sometimes 'the depressions in the dimpled balls were partly filled with plasticine', one of which proved 'the prize performer'. For images of the underwater tests connected with anti-ship operations, two domestic geysers with windows were lowered into the water with ballast. Their tops were open, 'with enough free-loading not to flood'. Positioned either side of the far end of the tank, close to the simulated target, one contained photographic lights, the other an RAE cameraman. To the Road Research Laboratory scientist, Dr A.R. Collins, Wallis observed: 'I was conducting a lengthy series of experiments ... to establish the empirical constants in the mathematical formula.'

Tizard remained an active promoter. After a visit to the National Physical Laboratory, he declared the results 'very promising' and concluded 'that a full-scale test is desirable with a Wellington'. But Wallis recognised the importance of continued naval support, especially from Rear-Admiral Edward de Faye Renouf of the RN, involved with Amphibious Warfare at

THE DAMBUSTERS: 'WAS THE RAID WORTHWHILE?'

the Admiralty, with whom Wallis's diary showed he kept in close touch, his home being in Dorking within easy reach of Effingham. Renouf led a party of senior officers to Teddington and, Wallis noted, was *tremendously impressed*. He explained: 'For their benefit I moored a wax model of a battleship several hundred feet up the tank, broadside on. We then fired 2in diameter balls at it, which of course after hitting the freeboard of the ship the sinking velocity of the ball combined with the back-spin to move towards the ship ... [and] pass right under "the soft underbelly" of the hull.'

Wallis wrote, 'it was due to the enthusiasm shown by him [Renouf] and Admiral McGrigor that the anti-ships weapon as fitted in Mosquito bombers went ahead'. (618 Squadron would be formed to deliver a smaller version of the dams' 'bouncing bomb' against the battleship *Tirpitz*). This, Wallis would recall to Dr Collins, 'was at a time when the Air Ministry would have nothing to do with my idea ... You must remember that Halcrow [W.T. later Sir William, civil engineer] had sent in a written report to the Air Staff [in 1939] stating that the dams were absolutely impregnable'. On 2 June, prior to the Teddington tests, Winterbotham had warned Wallis that the Air Staff thought that his bomb was 'liable to blow up an aircraft'. In addition to Tizard, among those to make the trek to the NPL were Air Vice-Marshal the Hon R.A. Cochrane, Norbert Rowe, Group Captain S.O. Bufton, Deputy Director of Bomber Operations, and Air Vice-Marshal F.J. Linnell (Controller of Research and Development at the Ministry of Aircraft Production), who on 25 June 1942 informed Wallis that he was 'impressed by the tests'. He had, therefore, given orders 'to use a Wellington for full-scale trials when you are ready'.

Even as the Teddington experiments went ahead, Collins supervised the second and pivotal Nant-y Gro test on Friday 24 July at 17.00 hours. He recalled that if 'the dam had been severely damaged but not breached, the case for an attack would have been seriously weakened'. A 500lb anti-submarine mine containing the appropriate scaled-up weight of 279lbs of explosive was suspended in contact with the face 7½ft from the crest. After the mine was detonated under the surface, a bubble of white disturbed the water followed by a giant spout. When it cleared the centre of the dam had been punched out. Wallis, who was present, justifiably declared the result 'spectacular'. Collins calculated that, if 7,500lbs of explosive were detonated in contact with a gravity dam 30ft from the top, a 50ft deep breach would be caused. 'Such a breach would allow approximately 70 per cent of the water in the reservoir to escape.'

The way ahead, though, remained dismal: '22 September 1942, 11.30am – I see Lord Cherwell, and find him very unresponsive.'

Chapter 3

Developing the Weapon

Allocation of a Wellington on 25 June 1942 for dropping trials proved an important step towards developing a weapon for the RAF to attack German dams and the Admiralty enemy ships. Barnes Wallis was searching for a similar weapon of different size to meet these twin requirements.

By now, the main Vickers' design team had moved from Brooklands to nearby Burhill Golf Club for security reasons. At lunch time on 4 September 1940, without warning, an air raid killed 83 and injured 419 from the workshops and offices. In his diary, Wallis wrote 'works bombed – 1.24pm', followed by another entry two days later, 'works bombed 9.15am'.

In mid-1942, Wallis foresaw a weapon of 7ft 6in diameter but believed extrapolation from the Teddington tests with 2in spheres 'beyond the bounds of reason'. He therefore welcomed the opportunity to test 'an intermediate 4ft 6ins sphere'. The necessary modifications to allow dropping trials from the Wellington were made by Vickers at Brooklands. On 20 October, Wallis witnessed one of these spheres being rotated in the aircraft in the former Hawker shed, where more static, spinning tests were thereafter conducted. On 2 December 1942, Captain Joseph 'Mutt' Summers, Vickers' chief test pilot, took the Wellington into the air from the Brooklands grass airstrip, as Wallis recalled, 'over the sewage works north to the Queen Mary reservoir, where Mutt did several low runs to judge distances in the air'. Summers was unaware when four practice spheres were spun simultaneously.

The way was now clear for the beginning of dropping trials. On 25 August 1942, at a meeting in Vickers House, London, government and Service representatives agreed that trials of 'the Spherical Bomb' would take place in Dorset close to Weymouth between Chesil Beach and the mainland 'known as East and West Fleet'. Before then, Wallis consulted Dr Purcell, Professor of Concrete Technology at Imperial College London, about the composition of the filling in the test spheres. Wallis's diary shows that he was also in regular contact with A.J. Pippard Sutton, Professor of

THE DAMBUSTERS: 'WAS THE RAID WORTHWHILE?'

Civil Engineering at Imperial College, who had been a consultant during the construction of the R.100 airship at Howden in the 1920s.

Summers took off at 13.40 hours on 4 December from Brooklands in Wellington BJ 895/G to fly directly to the south coast bombing range. He had Wallis as bomb-aimer with Bob Handasyde second pilot and 'flight test observer'. The bomb bay doors had been removed and apparatus constructed internally for two practice bombs, mounted one behind the other, to be spun and released. Wallis recorded that one dimpled ball was released at 224mph, spinning at 220rpm from 200ft at 15.54 hours. The second smooth one was dropped at 16.00 hours also from 200ft, spinning at 475rpm with the aircraft flying at 233mph. 'Both balls broke on impact', but Wallis declared the exercise 'exciting' and arranged for the outer casings to be reinforced. Handasyde was adamant that a story of naval gunners, misled by the strange outline of the aircraft, opening fire on it during this first trial was a myth. A.D. Grant, one of the test team, believed that by now 'Wallis was so involved with ballistics and his special weapons that he was very much on his own, although I imagine he discussed his ideas with Pierson [Vickers' chief designer].'

No camera had been carried in the aircraft, though one did photograph this trial from the ground. In future, Wallis explained, one would also be installed 'on the floor above the bomb-bay' of the Wellington to record the first bounce, with the ground operator reacting to a flash from the aircraft as the weapon was released. On 11 December, Summers and Handasyde flew the Wellington to RAF Warmwell, 10 miles north-east of Chesil Beach. From there, all following flights would be made, and necessary adjustments to the practice weapons take place. Clement Shaw, a technical officer in the Royal Aircraft Establishment (RAE) Armaments Department remembered spheres being routinely spun there. The Second Trial with the reinforced spheres was planned for 12.30 hours on 13 December, but stormy weather prevented flying that day at the close of which Wallis had dinner with Admiral Renouf. The occasion, Wallis reflected, was memorable because, as a waiter lifted a tankard from his tray, the bottom fell out and deposited beer over the senior naval officer. Not until 11.00 hours on 15 December, with Handasyde as co-pilot, an RAE cameraman on board and with Wallis this time on the ground did Summers take off from RAF Warmwell.

He dived over the water behind Chesil Beach to release one smooth and one dimpled sphere. Wallis noted that the smooth one was dropped at 11.24 hours from 45ft at 255mph, spinning at 725rpm. The dimpled 'steel ball' was released at 11.30 hours from 39ft at 240mph, spinning at

DEVELOPING THE WEAPON

430rpm. Once more, 'both balls broke up'. Undeterred, Wallis spent two hours in a rowing boat before recovering one sphere from 5ft of icy water. To his relief, although damaged, it was not broken. Chesil Beach was an RAE range, 'tasked by the Air Ministry to evaluate new schemes', so its scientists analysed the drops and concluded that the weapons had speeded up during them. Herbert Jeffree declared this 'rubbish' and by painstakingly hand-copying enlarged projected images of frames from the film, he proved that the theodolite sighting rods were sticking. Thereafter, he analysed the results of all the airborne trials.

Of the practice weapons dropped at Chesil Beach, A.D. Grant explained: 'The original spheres were made of relatively thin steel pressing welded together and stiffened with diaphragms. The earliest trials were carried out with the spheres empty so that they floated and were readily recovered. But the impact on the water dented them so severely that a number were filled with concrete and served to demonstrate that non-floaters ran almost as far.'

On 17 December, Renouf chaired a meeting at the Ministry of Aircraft Production in London, which included Government and Service personnel, representatives from the Oxley Engineering Co., manufacturers of the bomb casings, Wallis and Summers. The ciné films of the two trials showed that the release height varied between 45 and 220ft, the speed between 230 and 255mph, the practice weapons spinning between 250 and 750rpm; slightly, but not significantly, different from Wallis's figures. Renouf pointed out the trials were 'primarily to ensure the safety of the aircraft when releasing the rotating bombs'. Although the casings had undoubtedly 'failed badly', further strengthening would take place before the next trial for which Vickers would provide two wooden spheres as back-up, in case the Oxley metal ones were not ready. A separate meeting, on 23 December 1942, laid down guidelines for future trials. Safety of the aircraft remained fundamental, 'resistance to impact on the water of the strengthened' spheres and 'length of travel over the water, height of bounces and angles of incidence and reflection' of major interest. A phone call to Wallis from the Ministry of Aircraft Production (MAP) on 31 December made the facilities at the National Physical Laboratory (NPL), Teddington, once more available, although no further tests took place there immediately.

With the Admiralty keen to develop an anti-ship weapon, another trial was scheduled for Monday 28 December at Chesil Beach. Three variations of Wallis's proposed weapon were to be tested: smooth and dimpled stores strengthened by extra welding, the same configuration with additional ribs and, thirdly, wooden ones with equipment to record impact forces. Bad

THE DAMBUSTERS: 'WAS THE RAID WORTHWHILE?'

weather postponed this third trial until 9 January 1943, when Summers once more took off from RAF Warmwell, the spheres 'rewelded but not strengthened' according to Wallis. At 12.13 hours a smooth sphere was released from 80ft at 278mph and spinning at 800rpm. It 'broke up immediately, but ran about 1,400ft'. The dimpled sphere was dropped at 12.18 hours from 50ft at 285mph, spinning at 860rpm. Wallis noted that it 'did not drop when release pressed, but subsequently dropped over land [due to] electrical trouble'. 'One bomb only was rewelded at the forward station [Warmwell] but not strengthened.' This smooth sphere was released on 10 January at 15.21 hours from 10ft at 289mph and spinning at 980rpm. It, too, broke, but to Wallis's delight 'did one enormous bounce to a height of 55ft'; the first practice weapon to do so. 'I was immensely encouraged by that'.

On 21–22 January, Wallis found 'aerodrome US'; Warmwell's grass runway out of action. Instead, 'worked on bomb', the result being a dated series of calculations, illustrated by diagrams and mathematical formulae, in his distinctive clear script. So the fourth trial took place on Saturday 23 January. Flying east to west, at 10.45 hours, the Wellington released the sphere at 283mph from 42ft and spinning at 485rpm. It bounced 13 times. The release flash was missed 'due to approach behind C G [coast guard] station ... [so] distance unknown'. No further drops were possible that day, causing Wallis to complain of 'blisters on bottom!' On the Sunday morning, a wooden sphere released at 10.33 hours from 48ft at 311mph and spinning at 525rpm bounced '20–22' times. At 16.45 hours, Summers dropped the third from 108ft at 322mph, spinning at 740rpm to bounce over a special boom defence erected on the range. Writing to Dr W.H. Glanville at the Road Research Laboratory on 3 February, Wallis thanked him for helping to calibrate the copper discs used and informed him how 'very successful' had been 'the full scale trials at Weymouth'.

The fifth trial, on 5 February involved smooth wooden balls. Instructions read: 'The Wellington with 3ft 10in [sic] sphere can be used as a direct example of a Lancaster working at the same speed and height or as a scale model working at scale speed and height in which case the range will of course be multiplied by the scale number.' Wallis recorded that the 'black and white smooth wood ball', dropped at 17.32 hours from 144ft at 310mph achieved a range of 1,316 yards, though not without some alarm: 'Fabric tore off wing [as] A/C pulled out of dive'. Writing to Winterbotham on 12 February, Wallis expressed delight that the Chesil Beach trials thus far had achieved longer ranges 'than forecast through the tank experiments'.

DEVELOPING THE WEAPON

Barnes Wallis's large diary. January 1943 showing extent of meetings connected with development of separate versions of his bouncing bomb for the RAF and Royal Navy. Note meeting with Admiral Renouf, a firm supporter.

Moreover, he was satisfied 'the bomb will operate in smooth water so that no rough weather trials are required, and impact with the target can be made at extreme range'. He then revealed that he was already considering the operation itself, though seemingly only against the selected Ruhr dams, including the Sorpe. If 'thirty machines [Lancasters] were to be used to destroy simultaneously five dams, this is six machines per dam to make certain of doing it'. Wallis noted that, on 30 January, the Ministry of Aircraft Production had allocated two Mosquito IV machines to be 'on loan' to Vickers with authority to modify them, so emphasising that the twin concepts of attacking the dams and capital ships remained very much alive.

Wallis's diary entry for 20 February shows a 'joint meeting [Flight Lieutenant] Green, Summers, Handasyde, Jeffree' to fix programme for

THE DAMBUSTERS: 'WAS THE RAID WORTHWHILE?'

next week at Weymouth'. However, four planned drops at Chesil Beach on 22 February, at speeds of 240–300mph and heights of 200–400ft, do not appear to have gone ahead. Handasyde did record five flights, 24–25 February, which Wallis independently confirmed. On 24 February, three drops occurred at speeds of 238–295mph and heights between 140 and 360ft with all the spheres spinning at 500rpm. Wallis added that the third drop had been planned for 1,000rpm, but ground tests had revealed 'severe vibration at 700rpm, therefore revs were reduced to 500'. During one drop, the sphere 'lost a retaining band' and another was 'badly damaged and lost metal band'.

In between the Chesil Beach trials, 'crushing tests' were conducted at Porton Down with inert-filled spheres 'dropped directly on to concrete' from the Wellington. On 11 February 1943, Wallis instructed Summers to release two spheres, both spinning at 500rpm, one from 67ft, the other 268ft. Two days later, entries in Wallis's diary show that he had lunch at Boscombe Down and travelled that afternoon to Porton, where 'two drops both missed target 1st 6ft too early, 2nd 30–50 yards too late'.

Wallis was incapacitated with a migraine when Summers carried out two more drops at Porton on Sunday 21 February. Both 'missed the concrete apron', according to Major Kilner at Weybridge, after which one of the damaged spheres went to RAF Warmwell, the other Foxwarren. Two successful drops did occur, though, on 25 February, at 110mph from a height of 70–80ft and spinning at 500rpm; one wood and one steel sphere. Wallis wrote: 'Test run was made with wing tip just above 50ft wall, estimated height by crew 55–60ft, radio altimeter indicating 80ft.' During the actual drops, 'both balls hit centre of target'.

On Sunday 7 March, Wallis noted: 'Proceeded to Weymouth 3.30pm', in preparation for the following day's programme. '1st Run' would involve one high density dimpled and one low density smooth sphere being released from 50ft at 300mph and spinning at 500rpm. '2nd Run' would be with one high density dimpled and one smooth low density sphere under the same conditions except that this low density sphere should be spun at 1,000rpm. Wallis emphasised 'both trials to be done inside [sic] in smooth water. If there is not enough water – say 4 to 5ft – drops to be done outside if the sea is calm'.

On 8 March, therefore, he was at 'Langton Herring 11am' to witness the final set of trials at Chesil Beach 'test range of the high density spheres [and] to test range of low density spheres in open sea'. Spheres, 3ft 10in diameter, in 'welded steel, one smooth, one dimpled, filled with cork and cement to give approximately 75lbs per cubic foot, the anticipated density' of the final weapon would be used. In his diary, Wallis wrote, 'Summers dropped

DEVELOPING THE WEAPON

2 balls 12.30pm. Back to Hotel 6pm'. There were further trials on 9 March. As Admiral Renouf looked on, without elaboration Wallis recorded that 'Summers dropped 2 11.30am'. Two days later, 11 March, Wallis visited the RAE, Farnborough, 'to see films of last drops'.

Wallis's reference to the depth of water at Chesil Beach underscores concern about its unsuitability for further trials. On 7 March, Group Captain Wilfred Wynter-Morgan at the Ministry of Aircraft Production informed Wallis that he had chosen a site (Reculver Bay on the north coast of Kent) for continuation of the trials and had heard 'unofficially' that 'your group' would be able to supply five stores 'for inert filling' by 7 April. Two modified Lancasters would be allocated for these further trials.

On 7 April, after spinning tests at Foxwarren, Jeffree allayed Wallis's fears that the planned weapon would leap clear of its retaining arms if spun above 400rpm. That morning, Wallis met the Avro chief designer Roy Chadwick and Captain H.A. 'Sam' Brown, the Avro chief test pilot, at Farnborough to discuss progress and recorded that in the afternoon they watched Upkeep being spun on the ground at 320rpm. On 7 April, too, Air Commodore S.O. Bufton (Deputy Director of Bomber Operations) sent Wallis 'two photos and two interpretation reports of a certain objective' (the Moehne Dam) following reconnaissance flights.

Meanwhile, Handasyde flew Wellington BJ 885/G (used at Chesil Beach) to RAF Manston, where ten inert, cement-filled weapons had already arrived. A meeting in the Air Ministry on 25 March, chaired by Air Vice-Marshal Bottomley, had instructed Summers to inspect its runways for suitability with RAF Bradwell Bay as an alternative. The secluded dropping zone to the west at Reculver Bay, overlooked by the ruins of an old Norman abbey on a promontory, had its beach sloping towards a raised earth path beyond which lay agricultural land. No private dwellings were in the vicinity. These trials aimed to determine 'the range and the trajectory of the large store with particular reference to the heights and speeds considered suitable by the Air Staff'. Initially 200mph, release at 100ft and weapon spinning at 300rpm was planned. When the flights commenced the full-size Upkeep had not been completed, so a scaled-down version was used. Interspersed with dams-related flights were others in a Mosquito connected with the smaller, anti-ship version of Wallis's weapon.

On 9 April, Handasyde flew the Wellington from Manston to survey the Donna Brook bombing range at Reculver. One modified Lancaster (ED 765/G), which had tested 'the carrying and launching gear' at Farnborough, piloted by Mutt Summers and with Wallis on board, reached RAF Manston

THE DAMBUSTERS: 'WAS THE RAID WORTHWHILE?'

at 18.00 hours the following day. Wallis recorded that on Sunday 11 April, he met 'all Vickers staff and arranged a programme of work'. Firstly, the Wellington had to be made ready: 'on completion of repairs to the rear bulkhead S/L Longbottom [Squadron Leader M.V. 'Shorty' Longbottom on secondment to Vickers] will do a test flight, with no balls on board, diving up to 320mph IAS [indicated air speed]. If OK, load up two balls, one heavy in front, one light in rear. Carry out dropping tests as laid down at pilot's discretion. Release of 2nd pair (1 heavy, 1 light) and drop as convenient. Light wooden balls should be recovered in each case'. Wallis added that 'during previous flights the rear bulkhead of the Wellington had again failed and that the failure on this occasion followed temporary repairs which had been carried out at Warmwell Aerodrome earlier in the year'. This might explain why a single thirty minute flight comprised the final Chesil Beach trial on 9 March, according to Handasyde's log book. Presumably, the latest problem had occurred during Handasyde's preliminary flight over Reculver on 9 April.

At the 11 April meeting, detailed instructions concerning the Lancaster were also laid down. The 'hydraulic system is to be flight tested for 30mins with spinning in operation, <u>without ball in position</u>: 6 drops electrical release, 6 drops hand release … When not otherwise engaged, Vickers Armstrongs' staff to continue balancing both Mosquito and Lancaster balls when gear is to hand. Air Force personnel to be shown all parts of routine'. Late in the afternoon, the 'Lancaster ball was put in place and spun up, using the two inboard engines only. During this test, it was found that the rev counters were not indicating correctly and steps were taken to replace the rev counters with a pair taken out of the [two of four] unused stations in the Wellington'. The next day, Wallis noted that this had been successfully achieved. During that afternoon (12 April), 'a further spin on the ground was carried out on the Lancaster up to 310 rpm'.

Unlike the Wellington, where it was electronically spun, in the Lancaster the weapon was hydraulically rotated. 'Rev counters indicated satisfactory and all OK. By Monday evening all tests laid down in the Sunday programme were completed and all aircraft were ready for flight.' Wallis explained that 'the bomb was carried in the aircraft with its axis athwartships. Two circular pads, attached to movable arms on the aircraft, engaged with the flanged ends of the cylinder by means of a hydraulic motor and as the bomb was set rotating before being released. The bomb was released by opening the arms'. Its central metal cylinder was packed out to form a sphere fashioned by wooden staves held in position with metal bands.

DEVELOPING THE WEAPON

Wallis recorded, 'the weather on Monday evening was unfortunately unsuitable, being generally overcast and hazy'. So he took the opportunity to write a letter to his wife from Hotel Miramar:

> Just a brief line to tell you that I am alive and well. I arrived by air late on Sat [sic] and had great difficulty in getting a room, as the whole coast is more or less deserted – shops boarded up and so on. Then I only got a rather uncomfortable bedroom, and had meals at a pub. Now I have found a room miles away here: all a bit trying to the old, but we survive. I don't think it is worth writing to me here, as I may return at any time – quite uncertain. I do hope you and the children are all fit, and that young C [Christopher, their youngest child] has duly obliged by measling. Oh my poor cold feet, where is thy hot bottle? Oh my faithful pen, where thine ink?

On the back of the envelope, for economy 'made from a Tate and Lyle sugar bag', he added:

> Oh Censor! Should thy steely Eye/Upon this missive chance to prey,/Then prithee for the Writer weep, His feet are COLD; He cannot SLEEP. Spokeshave-on Spur.

Eventually, with visibility and tide favourable, flying east to west parallel to the beach towards two white buoys bobbing in the water, at 09.20 hours on 13 April Handasyde released the heavy sphere. Wallis recorded that he did so at 277mph from 81ft with the store spinning at 520rpm: 'woodwork broke up on impact, cylinder ran on, remaining stable until the extreme end of run', which he proclaimed 'excellent'. Ten minutes later, 09.30 hours, the light sphere was released with 'no flash' at 275mph from 90ft and spinning at 500rpm; 'a good average run' and the Wellington's last active participation in the trials. Handasyde recalled that thereafter he and Summers used it as 'a fish van' to deliver Dover sole to Manston. At 11.08 hours that day, Squadron Leader Longbottom released his first store from 230ft, spinning at 300rpm from the Lancaster flying at 210mph. This sphere also shattered, but at low tide in the afternoon Wallis waded in to recover the remains, having already required the next one to be strengthened at Manston.

He wrote that 'the ball entered the water at an angle which, from previous experiments, would have been considered too steep for any run to be obtained. However, the film shows that the ball rose above the surface until approximately three-quarters of its diameter was above the water and ran in this condition for a short distance. There was evidence from the splash that the bottom was struck at considerable violence'. Wallis reasoned that Longbottom had dropped from too high, so his second release at 19.07 hours, as dusk approached, was from 50ft, a height at which the Lancaster's elevator was damaged so that Longbottom had difficulty in landing at Manston. Spinning at 300rpm and dropped at 232mph, after the outer casing failed 'the cylinder continued running for a distance of approximately 700 yards' (elsewhere, Wallis quoted 950 yards). He maintained that yet further strengthening of the metal strips holding the wooden casing would solve the problem, and that was done at RAF Manston prior to the next trial. On 14 April, he wrote: 'It having been noticed that in certain cases wood segments were loose, tests were made to determine how much the bands could be tightened.'

A.D. Grant explained that for the 13 April and all future flights he was stationed on the shore with four stopwatches. One he activated when a flash from the aircraft signalled release, the others to time the first three bounces. He pointed out, too, that the recording technique varied from that employed at Chesil Beach. No photographic equipment was mounted in the aircraft. A 'theodolite, high-speed cine camera' was located on the shore, broadside to the aircraft's path, to register range. A second 'normal speed' camera stood on the promontory below the abbey towers approximately 1 mile ahead of the anticipated point of release to record line. Grant further explained that another device on the shore was mounted on a tripod with a peephole at its apex through which the operator peered to track the store from its release. To do so, he rotated the apparatus 180° as the number of bounces was also drawn on the wood attachment covered in perspex. The progress of each run was then copied onto tracing paper and the perspex wiped clean for the next release.

The second trial, scheduled for 12.45 hours on Saturday 17 April, was to be watched by Ministry of Aircraft Production officers and civilian departmental heads, including Norbert Rowe together with the distinguished scientist Professor G.I. Taylor and Wallis. Setting out at 09.30 hours in 'own car', Wallis arrived at 12.20 hours to discover that overcast conditions prevented flying. The bevy of disappointed spectators was provided with a less conventional spectacle. Wallis noted that the water seemed 'so inviting' that, at Rowe's suggestion, he, Taylor and Rowe plunged in for a nude bathe before lunching at Manston. On re-emerging, they dried themselves with

DEVELOPING THE WEAPON

handkerchiefs to a chorus of 'delighted hoots'; 'a relaxed occasion, one might say', according to Rowe. After flying for the day had been ruled out, at 17.15 hours Wallis returned to Reculver. Here he, Taylor and Vickers staff members more conventionally rolled up their trousers and ventured once more into the Thames estuary. They sought to recover more fragments from the 13 April trial – unsuccessfully. Wallis admitted, 'water too deep and cold'. That evening, after dinner at the Miramar, he and Taylor discussed developments until 23.00 hours. Once during the Reculver trials, he could not pinpoint precisely, Handasyde recalled that Summers was watching through the glass panel, which replaced the under turret in the Lancaster just forward of the tail. He 'was almost killed when the wooden casing splintered and the panel disintegrated' during a low-level release.

At 11.00 hours on 18 April, Summers dropped the first of three spheres: 'varnished – held up and sank complete', Wallis wrote. The second 'plain – exploded and sank complete'. The third, at 13.30 hours, 'varnished and filled – held up but cylinder came out'; the wooden casing again broke off. The cylinder bounced on for an estimated 700 yds; the third time this had happened. That it 'went on hopping', Wallis reflected, 'gave a ray of hope'. He explained to the Road Research Laboratory scientist, Dr A.R. Collins: 'Alas, so great was the pressure generated on the first impact with the water, that the bands in an axial length of some 7 or 8ft snapped like so much pack thread.'

Over a late sandwich lunch, Wallis and Taylor decided that 'the fairings' should be removed from all the inert-filled stores at Manston. In future only the inner metal cylinder would be dropped. Thus was the shape of Upkeep (the anti-dams bomb) determined. This development was unknown to Air Vice-Marshal R.H.M.S. Saundby at HQ Bomber Command, who on 20 April produced a 'most secret ... Report on the State of Preparedness of Upkeep' declaring the Reculver trials 'very disappointing'.

On Wednesday 21 April, Wallis did not see Sam Brown, the Avro chief test pilot, with Handasyde as observer, drop the first bare cylinder from low-level ('too low' for Handasyde) without success. Wallis and Taylor had been at a planning meeting during the morning in the Air Ministry, where the 'inconclusive' Reculver trials were discussed. After lunch with Winterbotham at the Royal Aero Club, he met Group Captain Wynter-Morgan 'to discuss supply of materials supplied by sub-contractors'. In view of security concerns about disclosure of information contained in Wallis's 'Air Attack On Dams' paper, which was now well-known in the UK and USA, at 15.30 hours he called on Winterbotham 'to discuss the rate

THE DAMBUSTERS: 'WAS THE RAID WORTHWHILE?'

of leakage of news from USA to Germany. He [Winterbotham] says he does not think any news of spheres has escaped'.

Next day, back at Reculver, he saw Brown drop '1 bare cylinder height 185ft speed 260mph', but it, too, sank; 'a complete failure'. The Dams' Raid was three weeks away. Wallis claimed that he lost 'not a wink of sleep' over the project, which never became 'an obsession'. Handasyde was not so sure. He recalled that with the deadline for success rapidly approaching and 'the bloody thing didn't work, Wally was tearing his hair out'.

Hitherto, scaled versions of Upkeep had been used, but on 29 April Wallis noted that at 09.15 hours Longbottom with Handasyde dropped a full-size cylinder on 'troubled sea', spinning at 500rpm from 60ft at 258mph 'less about 5mph head wind'. It bounced six times over 670 yards, although deviating 30ft to the left towards the end.

The following day, Friday 30 April, he wrote: 'Reculver awaiting trials, rain and overcast'. Not until 10.30 hours with Longbottom flying and Handasyde as observer, 'Lanc dropped bare cylinder'; another cylindrical Upkeep spinning at 520rpm from 65ft at 218mph in calm water, similar to that expected in a reservoir. It bounced four times, ran 435yds, deviating left 50ft: 'a very good show', enthused Wallis. Curiously, in his diary as distinct from this later report, Wallis wrote 'ht 60ft rpm 500 Speed 218mph Cylinder ran about 480 yards', though he agreed 'flat calm'. On 1 May at 11.30 hours, Longbottom and Handasyde dropped yet another bare cylinder, spinning at 680rpm from 80ft at 190mph in choppy water with 2–3ft waves ('very rough sea. Cylinder just seen'). Predictably, it was less successful: three bounces, 360yds distance and 40ft variation. Nonetheless, Wallis wrote that he was now convinced that the cylindrical Upkeep would 'do the job'.

Early spinning tests, in autumn 1942, had been carried out in the Wellington on the ground at Brooklands. Wallis's diary showed that in the New Year the exercise was moved 2 miles south-east to the Foxwarren complex by Silvermere Lake. One rig dealt with vibration and the effectiveness of the release gear by dropping an inert-filled store onto plates to roll between sand-bags. Another focused on spinning and balancing data. Norbert Rowe from the Ministry of Aircraft Production noted that at Foxwarren Herbert Jeffree solved balancing problems by devising a pendulum system with a sensitive galvanometer. Jeffree himself explained that the deviations at Reculver hastened that process. His initial effort was rejected by Wallis, because it could not be used for live versions. So Jeffree 'went back to first principles' to develop the pendulum arrangement. With that he and Grant balanced the practice weapons by fitting plates behind

DEVELOPING THE WEAPON

the screws in the recess at the end of each store; 'a somewhat tedious business' to Grant. Only one live-filled cylinder was spun without mishap in Richmond Park, as Grant recalled 'controlled at a distance from behind a sandbag emplacement'. Wallis's fear was that, spinning at 500rpm, 'would cause the explosive in the casing to expand and split it'.

In the first week of May, the direction of the flights at Reculver altered dramatically to simulate the operation. Handasyde explained that two poles, set apart on the beach below the promenade had flags attached to represent the towers on the Moehne Dam. Pilots now flew at right angles towards them, below the ruined towers, instead of parallel to the shore. The aim was that all the stores would come to rest on the shingle short of the flag-poles, though they frequently cleared the embankment. Mischievously, Handasyde hoped that one would set off a mine buried to hinder invaders.

Two modified Lancasters (ED 765/G and ED 817/G) were at Manston. On 6 May, with Handasyde as observer, Longbottom successively flew four times to drop a store at right-angles to the shore, but Wallis declared only one 'shot' satisfactory. The following day, 7 May, Wallis's diary shows him during the morning at Reculver searching successfully for a 'Mos plated store [with] little damage'. Then 'pm to Manston to supervise adjustment of calliper arms on Avro Lanc. Found them badly out'. At 15.30 hours, Longbottom returned more successfully to Reculver, where Wallis recorded: 'Shorty did two good drops – direct hits.' Having travelled home overnight, on 8 May Wallis wrote in his diary, 'weather too bad to go to Manston'. Instead he drew up a list of names of those to whom he sent 'Air Attack on Dams' and entered mysteriously 'pm Diag of Target Z' (Sorpe Dam). On Sunday 9 May 'weather still too bad to go to Manston' and inclement conditions continued the following day.

However, on 11 May, this time flying parallel to the shore, Longbottom released two more inert-filled Upkeeps, one from each of the Lancasters. Both were spun at 500rpm, the first dropped from 75ft at 230mph, the second from 50ft at 245mph. Neither deviated from track. The first bounced five times over 430yds, the second six times over 450yds. On 12 May, Handasyde did a similar drop. Wallis declared himself completely confident that his 'bouncing bomb' would work in action. There was precisely one week left before the operation would be postponed, or even cancelled.

Although one had been spun on the ground, no live Upkeep had yet been dropped, so there was no proof that it would function as predicted. Wallis recorded that 'live bombs had four devices. One self-destructive to operate one minute after arming, if none of the three Admiralty Mark XIV depth charge pistols functioned. All would be armed on release.' So, on 13 May, Longbottom completed the most significant test thus far. Instead of Reculver, flying south-west to north-east 5 miles off Broadstairs on the east Kent coast, he released an Upkeep filled with Torpex underwater explosive, spinning at 500rpm from 75ft. It bounced seven times 'almost 800yds' without deviation. In the rear turret, Group Captain W. Wynter-Morgan watched the weapon bounce as it slowed to 55mph, well behind the Lancaster.

With two cameramen on board to operate a normal speed cine camera, Handasyde followed in the other Lancaster 1,000yds behind at 1,000ft. The film showed a water spout 500ft above the height of Handasyde's aircraft and an explosion estimated at 33ft beneath the surface. Without having seen this film, and relying on equipment mounted on shore, Wallis (who witnessed the trial from the ground) wrote: 'We obtained a "dome" or rise in water about 20 feet in height 200 to 300 yards in diameter at the instant of detonation. This was followed by the "plume", which rose to a height of about 750 feet and was probably between 100 and 200 feet in diameter'. Herbert Jeffree added an interesting postscript. He had seen the drop from the North Foreland lighthouse. As Upkeep was released, he contrived to 'borrow' the keeper's binoculars. Without their magnifying effect, the owner declared it 'a beautiful explosion' and 'terrific' to get 'eight bombs to explode simultaneously under the water'. That same day, a progress meeting at the MAP in London was warned that trials had shown that if Wallis's weapon were dropped 'below 50ft' an aircraft would be damaged.

On 15 May, Jeffree was on board when Handasyde carried out another critical trial. Torpex was a comparatively new explosive (42 per cent RDX, 40 per cent TNT, 18 per cent powdered aluminium) and fear persisted that it might detonate on contact with the surface. Official records show from 500ft, Handasyde was adamant at 4,000ft, Jeffree 5,000ft, the second live Upkeep, fitted neither with hydrostatic nor self-destructive pistols, was dropped directly below the aircraft without bouncing. No explosion occurred, and another fear was erased. Upkeep left the Lancaster immediately the release mechanism was activated, the sharp jolt being confirmed by Jeffree.

The 'bouncing bomb' had proved itself. The very next day, Sunday 16 May, it would be used operationally.

Chapter 4

Persuading the Doubtful

Even while the model experiments were in progress at Garston and Harmondsworth, Air Commodore P. Huskinson at the Ministry of Aircraft Production remained 'very sceptical' about upgrading the data obtained. He was not alone.

In the wake of the 'Note', outlining Wallis's 'big bomb' theory in 1941, a body had been created 'to advise the Director of Scientific Research, Ministry of Aircraft Production [Dr D.R. Pye], on the experimental work to establish the technical possibilities of aerial attack on dams'. It acquired the designation 'Air Attack on Dams Committee'. Its first meeting, on 10 March 1941, agreed that specific mention of the Moehne Dam should be excluded from these and subsequent minutes. Mr R.S. Capon reminded the Committee that attacking gravity dams had been under consideration 'for many years' and several suggestions had been rejected by the Air Staff 'just before the war'. Following the meeting another member, Professor E.N. da C. Andrade, like Huskinson, queried the ability satisfactorily to upgrade small-scale experiments and, more broadly, cast doubt on the soundness of Wallis's whole proposal.

Andrade's negative 'Notes on Mr B.N. Wallis's "Method of Attack on the Axis Powers"' was potentially terminal. He accepted that a large bomb, rather than a cluster of small ones, 'might be more effective, but Mr Wallis gives simple calculations, which are impaired by misprints. They are based upon empirical relations mostly obtained in air and at fair distances from the explosion ... I very much doubt if these calculations are valid; they seem much too favourable on the information which I have available'. Quoting details of the explosion of mines beneath German positions on the Messines Ridge near Ypres in 1917, he attacked Wallis's claim of the camouflet effect of underground detonation: 'His theoretical work is, to say the least, not convincing in its present form.' Andrade queried, too, Wallis's contention 'that the bomb will pursue a more or less straight path in the earth' to a depth in excess of 64ft. Referring to the bomb landing 40 yards from a target having been released at 40,000ft using a Sperry 01 bomb sight, 'to me the accuracy claimed seems on general grounds impossibly high'.

On 10 April 1941, Wallis circulated a lengthy retort. He acknowledged Andrade's 'criticism of my failure to produce any authority for the statements in my paper' and indirectly confirmed the nature of the assistance given to him. 'The omission is due to anxiety not to commit any indiscretions as all my information comes from serving officers or others in government departments and from secret papers.' Furthermore, 'I disclaim also any attempt to write a scientific paper. To some extent, it has been based upon the numerous objections to the use of a large bomb which were raised by many officers, with whom I first discussed the matter about a year ago.' The general opinion 'held in the Naval and Air Services' was 'anyone who explodes more than 1,500lbs of HE is merely wasting good explosives'.

'Chapter 4 in which the calculations referred to by Professor Andrade occur has been checked and re-checked, but we cannot locate the misprints... The empirical relations referred to were given me by the Superintendent of Mine Design, Admiralty, and are obtained from experiments in water, not air.' Wallis rebutted other aspects of Andrade's critique with detailed analysis. He therefore vigorously contested Andrade's objections, but in doing so exposed the dilemma of having to persuade Service decision-makers, who relied on their scientific advisers for professional guidance.

Undeterred, on 11 April Wallis recorded that a separate gathering, which he termed 'Tizard's committee', assembled 'to consider the soundness of the suggestions by Mr Wallis'. The minutes of this meeting focused on 'the two most important dams vulnerable to attack in Germany are the Moehne and Eder. There is a third important dam, the Sorpe, which although important we would rule out as being unsuitable for attack for tactical and technical reasons. Of the other two dams, the Moehne is much the more important, is tactically more suitable for attack, and its destruction would have far reaching effects on the enemy's war economy'.

Once more, the Sorpe slipped beneath the administrative radar. The work of this body seems to have been overtaken by the Air Attack on Dams (AAD) Committee, but through 'Tizard's Committee' a channel of communication had been opened up between Wallis and Sir Henry, for whose support he would consistently express gratitude.

Ministry files show Wallis's extensive correspondence 1940–41 seeking the interest and support of influential scientific figures. At a crucial moment, Dr D.R. Pye proved invaluable. The 'big bomb' proposal had been recently rejected and Wallis feared that the whole idea of attacking the German dams would be jettisoned. Before the second meeting of the AAD Committee on 19 June 1941 at ICI House, London, the wartime location of the Ministry of Aircraft Production, Wallis arranged to meet Pye and secured his active support. So the project remained alive even after the third AAD Committee meeting on 10 December 1941, from which Pye was absent. Members showed their disquiet, though, by re-exploring several old ideas like a stick of small bombs providing a 'greater statistical possibility of a direct hit'. Nevertheless, further model tests at Harmondsworth were approved. On 9 July 1942, in effect Pye reinforced his support, 'I think we can safely say that the gravity dam is a hopeless proposition', using conventional methods.

RAF opinion remained uncertain, though Admiral Renouf kept faith. Wallis somewhat bitterly wrote, the potential of his idea 'has not yet been realised by the Air Force, but is now much appreciated by the Admiralty'. That position began to change in mid-1942 with Air Commodore G.A.H. Pidcock replacing Huskinson as Director of Armament Development at the Ministry of Aircraft Production and his deputy, Group Captain W. Wynter-Morgan, taking active interest in the National Physical Laboratory experiments.

Winterbotham continued to rally political support, too. On 26 August 1942, he wrote to G.M. Garro-Jones, Parliamentary Private Secretary to the Minister of Production, about Wallis's frustration: '... I feel that you should know personally about the apparent "blocking" of developments in a certain sphere, which in my own view, might very well have a decisive effect on this war'. On 14 September he went further, sending the Parliamentary Private Secretary a summary, 'Notes on the Work of Mr B.N. Wallis', supported by diagrams. Winterbotham referred to the 'comprehensive proposals for the construction of a Stratosphere Bomber to carry a 10 ton bomb for destruction of Axis primary sources of power – coalmines, water power dams and oil refinery and storage plants – by utilisation of new and hitherto unrealised potentiality of the "shock wave" of large bombs'. Lord Beaverbrook, he wrote, 'favourably viewed ... the proposition ... and its possibilities were admitted by a technical committee set up by Sir Henry Tizard'. However, it was 'turned down by the Air Staff, in spite of this resulting in the formation of an Air Attack on Dams Committee'.

During 1941–42, Wallis had:

> continued to press forward with methods of destroying enemy water dams ... Experiments have shown that the destruction of large dams required bombs at least of the size forecast by

Wallis, and even larger when they are dropped in the usual way and explode in the water as "near misses". This is presumably the reason why the project has not been favourably received by the Air Staff, but experiments have also shown that large dams can be destroyed by much smaller charges than those required above, provided that the charge is detonated in actual contact with the masonry of the dam on the water side at a considerable depth below the surface ... Wallis has accordingly invented a "surface torpedo" which when dropped by a low-flying aircraft will travel a considerable distance (estimated at about one mile) along the surface of the water.

Winterbotham asked Garro-Jones to:

excuse me for speaking rather plainly ... In my whole experience of aeronautical engineers and inventors, I have never come across one more able, and it seems a pity that such a man whose brain is probably worth four or five thousand a year should be baulked so consistently by a Civil Service mind, whose maximum value is probably six hundred per annum.

The second Nant-y-Gro test of 24 July, Winterbotham explained, had proved Wallis's 'Rota-mine [with] 8000lb charge' would destroy 'the largest dam in Europe'. Optimistically, he held: 'If this new weapon is intelligently used e.g. for simultaneous attacks on all German capital ships and main hydro-electric power dams ... industry in Germany would be so crippled as to have decisive effect on the duration of the war. ... To attain this result much preparation and careful planning are clearly required and meanwhile I repeat <u>nothing is being done</u>'. On 30 September, Sir Henry Tizard, coining the term which would henceforth be applied to Wallis's weapon, independently wrote. 'I should myself be inclined to advise that Wallis be instructed straight away to submit an opinion as to whether a bouncing bomb of this size could be fitted to a Stirling or a Lancaster.'

The AAD Committee met for the fourth time on 12 October 1942. It rejected use of multiple charges to destroy a dam, but gave no positive encouragement to Wallis. The following month, Winterbotham recalled, Garro-Jones arranged for Wallis to address the newly-created Tribunal of Scientific Advisers to the Ministry of Production, chaired by Dr T.R. Merton. After 'a long and interesting examination', Winterbotham recorded that Wallis was encouraged 'to go ahead with his experiments'. He acknowledged that 'my own active part in the Wallis bomb ceased after I piloted him through the Merton Committee'.

Towards the close of 1942, Wallis completed his most influential paper, 'Air Attack on Dams'. Renouf received a copy on 9 January 1943 and copies were also despatched to RAF officers, including Air Vice-Marshal R.S. Sorley, Assistant Chief of the Air Staff Technical Requirements, Group Captain S.O. Bufton, who would become Director of Bomber Operations on 10 March, other RAF, RN and MAP authorities. Some went to scientists and journalists like Major Oliver Stewart. In his paper, Wallis explained that he was describing 'the effect of destroying large barrage dams in the Ruhr Valley, together with some account of the means of doing it'. He argued that the results of the Chesil Beach trials had 'more than justified' hopes raised by the Teddington tests with 2in spheres. 'Large scale experiments carried out against similar dams [sic] in Wales have shown that it is possible to destroy German dams, if the attack is made at a time when these are full of water (May or June).'

He was now confident that his novel way of placing a charge against a gravity dam face would achieve success. Wallis accepted that the Sorpe, with concrete core and supporting earth supports, 'at first sight' appeared invulnerable. Historical evidence suggested otherwise. This sort of construction 'became practically self-destroying if a substantial leak can be established within the water-tight core'. He believed that a dam could be destroyed by a detonation on the water side 'at a suitable distance below the surface'. In support, he quoted evidence of the collapse of the Bradfield Dam, near Sheffield. In three quarters of an hour, 3.5 million tons of water poured out 'caused by a small crack which started on the crest of the dam'. If an attacking aircraft released its unique weapon 'at extreme range' so that it reached the sloping support as it was virtually spent, 'it would drop back into the water rather than leap over the crest'. An alternative would be that at the end of its run, it would sink within lethal range of the slope 'without actually having made contact while above the surface'. Both options relied on the energy from the explosion being transmitted laterally to crack the core, through which water would seep to build up pressure and cause the structure to collapse. The Road Research Laboratory scientist, Dr Collins, was doubtful about 'the [Bradfield] dam near Sheffield, which failed in the 19th century [1864] because of a crack in the core wall ... this was of clay rather concrete as in the Sorpe, and I feel that he made too little allowance for the difference'.

THE DAMBUSTERS: 'WAS THE RAID WORTHWHILE?'

The five main Ruhr dams (Moehne, Sorpe, Lister, Ennepe, Henne), Wallis explained, held back 254 million cubic metres of water, whereas seven smaller ones totalled just 12 million cubic metres. The primary function of them all was to provide the 'domestic and industrial water supply of the Ruhr district'. A breach would empty the Moehne in ten hours and that alone would 'cause a disaster of the first magnitude even in the lower reaches of the Ruhr'. Furthermore, flood water would fundamentally disrupt river, road and rail traffic, as well as thirteen electricity stations. Referring to the Weser Valley, Wallis noted that the Eder and Diemel dams held back 222 million cubic metres of water of water. Their 'principal function' was to 'provide a regular supply of water for pumping from the Weser into the Mittelland Canal', a major artery for transporting industrial supplies across Germany and a major designated target in its own right. Several power stations, including two at Hemfurth below the Eder with a combined output of 44,000hp, boosted electricity supplies and would be inundated.

Summing up, Wallis maintained that 'in the Ruhr district the destruction of the Moehne Dam alone would bring about a serious shortage of water for drinking purposes and industrial supplies … in the Weser district the destruction of the Eder and Diemel dams would seriously hamper the transport in the Mittelland Canal and in the Weser, and would probably lead to an almost immediate cessation of traffic'.

The final section of the paper focused on 'the Spherical Torpedo'. Once it struck the target, it would rebound and sink at 10–20ft/sec, being held in contact with the surface by lateral force. Detonation would be attained by a pistol activated by water pressure. With the technique proposed, no air bubble would be formed, so the depth of explosion could be 'controlled within satisfactory limits'. Finally, experiments had proved that 'massive gravity dams' were 'invulnerable' to any charge within the carrying capacity of existing aircraft unless exploded at lethal depth below the surface of the water in contact with the dam wall. Inability to achieve the required accuracy using conventional bombing techniques and 'erratic flight path' of bombs under water meant that only the proposed spinning weapon could obtain success.

On 30 January 1943, Wallis sent a copy by hand to Lord Cherwell with a detailed covering letter hoping to prompt a more favourable response than hitherto. He explained that his paper considered 'the effect of destroying the large barrage dams in the Ruhr Valley, together with some of the means of doing it'. He mentioned that the results of the Chesil Beach trials, so far carried out, 'more than justify' hopes raised after the 2in sphere experiments. The Admiralty had now given 'full priority' to developing the weapon, which was expected 'to be available for operations in 6–8 weeks'. 'Unfortunately, the possibilities of this new weapon against naval targets appear to have overshadowed the question of the destruction of the major German dams.' He contended that his proposal 'clearly shows that the destruction of the five major dams in the Ruhr district would have a powerful effect on the Ruhr industry ... Unless the operations against the dams are carried out simultaneously with naval operations, preventative measures will make the dam project unworkable'.

Wallis declared that if 'a high level decision' were taken to give equal priority to the two weapons, 'we could develop the larger sphere to be dropped from a Lancaster bomber within a period of two months'. Modifications to the Lancaster would be 'small...and the aircraft can be returned to their original use after having achieved their particular object in a few days'. Reacting swiftly, Cherwell saw Wallis on 2 February, watched a film of the NPL experiments and proved infinitely less antagonistic. Possibly, he recalled a scheme put to him in October 1939, which involved the impact of flooding: 'Plan for Inundation of Siegfried Line...by blasting the left bank of the Rhine'. Furthermore, in a proposal to Churchill on 30 March 1942, he himself had advanced the concept of concentrating on fifty-eight urban centres, which contained a third of the German population. 'There is little doubt that this would break the spirit of the people... Nor has regard been paid to the inevitable damage to factories, communications etc in these towns and the damage by fire, probably accentuated by breakdown of public services'. Wallis's idea met these criteria.

That same day, Wallis visited Benjamin Lockspeiser, now Director of Scientific Research at the Ministry of Aircraft Production in succession to Pye, gave him a copy of 'Air Attack on Dams' and sought permission to begin preliminary design work on 'Big Highball' (Upkeep, the anti-dams weapon). Subsequent phone calls established that the Ministry approved, but not of progression to development. The Controller of Research and Development, Air Vice-Marshal F.J. Linnell, feared that Wallis's commitment to the B.3/42 (Windsor) four-engine bomber would be compromised.

When Wallis sent a copy of 'Air Attack on Dams' to Air Vice-Marshal Sorley on 5 February, he acknowledged the help of Winterbotham, Squadron Leader C. Verity, Squadron Leader Wigglesworth and Professor Baker from Oxford University, 'an authority on German inland waterways'. Verity recalled that, in October 1942, 'there came into my office a tall man with grey hair and a charming smile, who shook me warmly by the hand as he

THE DAMBUSTERS: 'WAS THE RAID WORTHWHILE?'

introduced himself ... He asked me to obtain for him a lot of information – geographic, engineering and economic – about the various large dams in Germany'. During the meeting he produced a sketch of how his 'bouncing bomb' would work. In his covering letter to Sorley, Wallis wrote:

> I can find no authority to dispute the supreme importance of either the Ruhr or Weser groups of dams, and do not think that the immense extension of German territory during the present war has done anything to modify their importance ... We have got an exceedingly simple and practical design of bomb which can be carried by Lancaster aircraft having a charge weight of just under 7,000lbs and an all-up weight of about 10,000lbs and we only await the necessary authority to go ahead. I am quite satisfied that, given the necessary authority, we could be ready to carry out an attack in the month of May this year.

During the morning of 1 February, Wallis met the Weybridge Works Manager, Major Kilner, 'on bomb. Arranged to make 3 test bombs for dropping trials'. The following day, Wallis had a meeting at 11.00 hours at the MAP in London 're explosives. New wood packed design of Bomb approved ... annular type if necessary will not be difficult to explode ... Showed film to Sorley and Baker'. At a 16.15 hours meeting with the Director of Scientific Research, 'received authority to proceed with Lancaster Bomb installation as far as designs are concerned. Asked for written confirmation. Handed Director copy of Dam Paper [sic]'. On 3 February, he recorded: 'Phone from DDSR [Deputy Director of Scientific Research] to say that CRD approves prelim'y design work on Big Highball', which seemed clear.

However, the following morning, without further explanation, a diary entry read: 'Rang DSR's office to ask for decision re Big Highball'; perhaps a plea for development beyond the design phase approved on 3 February. He received a rapid, dispiriting, response: 'pm DSR states CRD is considering delay to B 3/42 (Windsor) and wishes a file to be prepared and circulated !!!' Nevertheless, the entry concluded: 'Started work on Lancaster Bomb and evolved plain cylinder + wood sheathing. 7pm Saw Gammon on new wood balls for Wellington'.

On Friday 5 February 1943, 'arranged Tank Sunday am. Grooved models', indicating another session at Teddington. The following day, he and A.D. Grant discussed 'new depth pistol'. A full diary for 8 February included '11am Kilner's Meeting – 1pm' and 'FWW re Linnell and Ld

PERSUADING THE DOUBTFUL

C – he advised weekly reports'. At 10.00 hours on 9 February, Wallis left Burhill for 'tests at NPL till 6.30pm'. There was no hint of the impending bombshell.

On 10 February, conceding that Highball work should continue, Linnell ruled that work on the Lancaster project must cease. In his diary, Wallis simply wrote: 'FWW on new types and CRD's decision not to act re Lancasters'. Two days later, Linnell outlined his reasons to Assistant Chief of the Air Staff (TR), Sorley. He admitted that 'model experiments, mathematical analysis and full-scale drops of a smaller weapon, all indicated that Upkeep is technically feasible'. But Vickers-Armstrongs was about four to six weeks behind schedule with the B.3/42 project and Lancaster production at Avro would also suffer. He did not rule out an anti-dams operation, but wanted to wait for completion of Highball tests. Linnell, therefore, implied that with the amount of work still to be done, a dams' operation should more reasonably be planned for 1944.

However, Wallis's diary shows that work on the dams' project did not slacken (on 16 February he was at Teddington for further tests). Writing to Cherwell on 20 February, Wallis explained that 'no opportunity' had arisen to carry out 'full scale tests with rotating spheres', so concentration had been on 'getting some underwater photography showing the behaviour of spheres after striking the target ... some remarkable pictures ... confirm the theory that the sphere will develop a horizontal force directing it towards the target'. Having studied this 'secret and confidential' communication on 24 February, Cherwell arranged to meet 'DSR [Director of Scientific Research] 10.30 morning'.

The fortnight ending 26 February 1943 proved much more decisive than Linnell envisaged. On 13 February, Sorley chaired a meeting at the Air Ministry of Air Staff, Bomber Command and Admiralty representatives 'to discuss the development and possible operational use of the spherical bomb' for use against ships and dams. After outlining the results of tests at Teddington and Chesil Beach, Lockspeiser explained that two bombs were planned: Upkeep (11,000lbs, including 7,500lb explosive, 84ins diameter) and Highball (950lbs, same charge/weight ratio, 35ins diameter). Acknowledging the success of the Chesil Beach trials, Air Commodore Pidcock, Director of Armament Development at the Ministry of Aircraft Production, nevertheless noted that there was no proof that the bomb would function after striking a target. Air Vice-Marshal H.M. Bottomley, Assistant Chief of the Air Staff (Ops), observed that now the spherical bomb 'had been brought to the attention of the Air Staff', its development and trials connected with it should be watched and Bomber Command must also keep in touch with Highball development.

Bottomley cautioned that independent use against a ship would 'give away the idea and that it was a small step to imagine the use of such a weapon against a dam'. In summary, Sorley forecast that 'the earliest possible date' for Upkeep to be available seemed 'six months' hence. He did not appear to have grasped that the water would be too low for success from June. Bomber Command would now officially be briefed and Group Captain S.C. Elworthy was detailed to make the Air Officer Commanding-in-Chief Sir Arthur Harris personally aware. Sorley ruled that, if further advice from experts like Wallis proved satisfactory, despite the reservations so far expressed, development of Upkeep should go ahead. Hence, he wrote to Wallis: 'I have started the operational people off on the subject.'

Unknown to Wallis, the next day, 14 February, presumably after being briefed by Elworthy, Air Vice-Marshal R.H.M.S. Saundby, Senior Air Staff Officer at HQ Bomber Command, attaching a copy of Wallis's 'Air Attack on Dams', summarised the position for Harris; in some instances using figures slightly different to those studied in Sorley's meeting. Saundby explained that Highball was being developed to attack capital ships, and a 'similar weapon' was being considered 'for the special purpose of destroying dams, the Moehne Dam in particular'. It would weigh 10,000lbs with a 6,500lb charge and be dropped from a 'specially modified Lancaster' at 80–120ft and 220mph, spinning at 500rpm, and travel 1,200yds over the water. The attack would have to be made when the reservoir was full 'or nearly full' on the 'up-stream side of the dam' and exploded 'at a depth of 30ft' below the surface of the water. Time was of an essence, because Sorley wanted to make a decision on 15 February. Saundby concluded that one squadron would need to be diverted from Main Force duties for 'two to three weeks'. The operation should take place in clear moonlight using radio altimeters.

Harris proved scathing in a hand-written appendix to Saundby's minute. 'This is tripe of the wildest description. There are so many ifs and buts that there is not the smallest chance of its working. Unless *"perfectly* balanced", spun at 500 rpm it would either "wreck" the aircraft or "tear the bomb loose" ... I don't believe a word of its supposed ballistics on the surface ... At all costs stop them putting aside Lancasters and reducing our bombing effort on this wild goose chase ... The war will be over before it works – and it never will'. At first sight, under pressure to attack Germany in force and believing this scheme to be as unworkable as the Toraplane (a gliding

PERSUADING THE DOUBTFUL

torpedo fitted with wings and tail designed by Sir Dennis Burney compared to which he thought Wallis's concept 'madder'), Harris's reaction did not seem unreasonable.

The meeting on 15 February was chaired by Group Captain J.W. Baker, currently Director of Bomber Operations, not Sorley. Wallis and Summers were present, Wallis noting in his diary, '2.30pm. Air Miny King Charles St meeting with Air Staff to discuss Highball'. Baker would have been well prepared by his then deputy, Group Captain S.O. Bufton, who had long been familiar with Wallis's proposal. Baker decided that a single Upkeep should be produced and installed in one modified Lancaster for experimental purposes.

The very next day, 16 February, Winterbotham complained to Air Vice-Marshal F.F. Inglis, Assistant Chief of the Air Staff (Intelligence) that despite naval commitment, 'little enthusiasm appears to have been shown by the RAF in the Ministry of Aircraft Production. My fear is that a formidable strategic weapon will be spoiled by premature use against a few ships instead of being developed and used in a properly co-ordinated plan'.

Unknown to Winterbotham and Wallis, beyond Baker RAF interest had begun to quicken. On 18 February, Saundby summarised the outcome of Baker's meeting three days earlier for Harris. He emphasised that it had been decided to develop 'the large sphere' and that the Minister of Aircraft Production would allocate one Lancaster to be modified and used in trials. If successful, modifications would be made to other Lancasters to drop the weapon ¼ - ½ mile from a target dam. Air Chief Marshal Sir Arthur Harris promptly despatched a furious personal letter to the Chief of the Air Staff (Portal), and added further weight to his objections. 'Linnell rang me up this morning about the Highball proposition'; a generic term in use for both versions. 'He [Linnell] is as worried as I am about it ... all sorts of enthusiasts and panacea mongers [are] careering around the Ministry suggesting the taking of 30 Lancasters off the line to rig them up for this weapon, when the weapon itself exists so far only within the imagination of those who conceived it'. He 'strongly' condemned diversion of Lancasters 'at this critical moment in our affairs' on the off-chance that 'some entirely new weapon, totally untried, is going to be a success ... I am now prepared to bet that the Highball is just about the maddest proposition as a weapon that we have yet come across – and that is saying something'.

He continued: 'The job of rotating some 1,200lbs of material at 500rpm on an aircraft is in itself fraught with difficulty. The slightest lack of balance will tear the aircraft to pieces, and in the packing of the explosive, let alone in retaining it packed in balance during rotation, are obvious technical difficulties.' With mounting anger, Harris went on: 'I am prepared to bet my shirt (a) that the weapon itself cannot be passed as a prototype for trials inside six months; (b) that its ballistics will in no way resemble those claimed for it; (c) that it will not work, when we have got it.'

His closing remarks were caustic: '... we have made attempt after attempt to pull off successful low attacks with heavy bombers. They have been, almost without exception, costly failures ... while nobody would object to the Highball enthusiasts being given one aeroplane and told to go away and play while we get on with the war, I hope you will do your utmost to keep these mistaken enthusiasts within the bounds of reason and certainly to prevent them setting aside any number of our precious Lancasters for immediate modification.' An unsigned handwritten comment attached to a note to Portal from the Air Ministry revealed that Harris had already expressed his views more widely to Air Staff officers, whose opinions would be conveyed to the Chief of Air Staff by Assistant Chief of the Air Staff (TR), Sorley.

Not knowing about Harris's outburst to Portal, Wallis was encouraged by Lockspeiser informing him on 20 February that Renouf and the Admiralty wanted 'this smaller version of your toy to be brought into operational use as quickly as possible'. Linnell had agreed that 'a small body ... of all interested parties', including Wallis, should convene under Lockspeiser to pursue this aim. Six days later, Wallis learnt that the First Sea Lord, Admiral Sir Dudley Pound, believed Highball 'the most promising secret weapon yet produced by any belligerent'.

Independently, Combined Operations (Ops) had been planning 'the demolition of the Moehne Dam', which its commander Lord Louis Mountbatten termed 'one of the great strategic targets'. As early as 29 August 1942, through contact with the Ministry of Home Security, Combined Ops had been aware of the German dams as a target. Not until 2 February 1943, though, was it asked formally to investigate the destruction of dams with special reference to the Moehne. Ten days later, Mountbatten was supplied with information 'gleaned' from the Road Research Laboratory, which could lead to 'a large breach in a masonry dam by means of a charge, which it is assumed will be carried in one or more flying boats which will land on the surface of the reservoir'. The proposal contained surprising statistics. Explosion of a 5,000lb charge in contact with a masonry dam 26ft below the crest, when the reservoir was full, would cause a breach 39ft deep and 156ft wide leading to an 80 per cent leakage of water. If the charge were

PERSUADING THE DOUBTFUL

in a cylindrical container of 1/8in steel plate, the total weight would be 5,750lbs. A flying boat could land on the reservoir and be settled 'in the desired position' or have the charge released 'to float in position and sink to the appropriate depth ... The accurate placing of such a charge should be relatively simple to arrange as it can be gently sunk to the desired depth on a suitable suspension rope by reducing the buoyancy to a slightly negative value'. No mention of defences, and the communication closed with a recommendation that the Air Ministry be contacted.

On 26 February, an alternative plan was considered involving four paratroopers dropping from high altitude each with ten charges. After setting the charges in place, they would be recovered by flying boats. This appears to have been a modification of a plan advocated on 27 January by Major H. de Bruyne of the Special Operations Executive for 30 paratroopers to attack the Moehne Dam, which was discussed with Flight Lieutenant D. Verschoyle of Combined Ops during February. Both schemes coincided with the RAF's decision to mount Operation Chastise and Mountbatten revealed that neither was discarded but 'held in abeyance when Wallis came along with his rolling bomb'.

On 20 February, Wallis had written to Cherwell, noting that since they had met almost three weeks earlier 'no opportunity' had arisen to carry out 'full-scale tests with rotating spheres'. But there were 'some remarkable pictures ... showing the behaviour of spheres striking the target' underwater at the NPL. 'They confirm the theory that the sphere will develop a horizontal force directing it towards the target.'

Wallis's most optimistic and daunting trip was to HQ Bomber Command at High Wycombe on 22 February. Air Vice-Marshal Cochrane, after visiting Teddington and explanatory discussions with Wallis, had persuaded Harris to see the films. Wallis recorded: 'To High Wycombe with Summers. 3.30pm showed film to Sir Arthur Harris C in C Bomber Command and AVM Saundby SASO. H. had letter from CAS authorising 3 Ls. H very much misinformed re job. Saw photos of M dam with booms in position.'

Years afterwards, Wallis rather more colourfully recalled the scene. As he and Summers entered the room, Harris roared: 'What the hell do you damned inventors want?' Wallis held his nerve, explained the scope of his scheme, the two types of bomb, different targets and aircraft involved (Mosquito as well as Lancaster). Harris retorted fiercely that he had heard about destroying the Moehne Dam before, but agreed to watch the NPL and Chesil Beach films with Saundby as projectionist for security reasons. The AOC-in-C gave no overt encouragement, as Cochrane reflected: 'Wally was proposing to project a five-ton lump of iron across a lake.' Harris's reluctance was set against need to step up the bomber campaign in the face of Germany's formidable aerial defences, spearheaded by a sophisticated combination of ground and airborne radar, searchlight belts and well-equipped night fighters. To do so, he had 33½ heavy bomber squadrons, only 15½ of them with Lancasters. The forecast production total for this four-engine machine in April was 123. Wallis's scheme thus required roughly a quarter of the monthly output.

Almost forty years later, contrary to Wallis's feeling, Harris implied that this meeting had been decisive. He admitted that, prior to it, he had confused the different targets:

> What I was adamantly opposed to was the <u>original</u> idea to use such a bomb from Lancasters to attack capital ships !! and I said so in no uncertain terms. It would have out-Kamikasied the Kamikases bringing a Lanc down to surface level 2 or 3 hundred yards from a capital ship and, at that, probably over dockyard or escort destroyer guns!! Nothing doing!! ... Only then [22 February] did Wallis say it was also for attacking the dams – and produced photos of his working model of the whole idea in action!! It was then that I immediately told him that I would raise a special squadron of thoroughly experienced warriors, who had finished a whole tour of operations and put Gibson in charge of it.

He added, with a dash of hindsight: 'That was my "negative reaction" reinforced by proven fact that bombs could deal with battleships without suicide squads!! As they did! Bombs destroyed twice as many as the Navy did!' Despite recognising the potential of Wallis's weapon against gravity dams, 'I knew, and asserted from the start, that the Sorpe dam was the wrong construction to collapse from the bouncing bomb, though there was a faint chance that it might [*sic*] start a leak, crack the concrete "blade" and then escaping water <u>might</u> do the rest.'

To Wallis, the meeting was much less positive. He maintained that he left it unaware of Harris's change of heart or that broader RAF opinion was softening. After viewing the test films at Vickers House on 19 February, Portal had written to Harris informing him that Wallis's scheme could not be summarily dismissed. He was anxious for the concept's feasibility to deal with the German dams to be fully investigated. 'No more than three of your precious Lancasters' were to be 'diverted' for this purpose. The implication was that if those trials proved successful an operation was likely. Portal, unlike Harris, did not confuse the two weapons, their different targets or the separate type of aircraft involved. Quaintly, Wallis mused that Portal had been influenced by a friend of his, Egerton Cooper, who had painted the AOC-in-C's portrait and in whose studio Wallis had met Portal. Dr A.R. Collins, though, felt that Tizard and Glanville were particularly influential. Harris recalled that Portal told him; 'If you want to win the war, bust the dams'.

Any dismay felt at Harris's brusque treatment was almost immediately countered by formal notification that the Ministry of Aircraft Production had approved modification of two Mosquitoes for Highball trials. Then, on 23 February, Wallis and Summers were summoned to the office of the Weybridge works manager, and 'at 12 noon proceeded to Town and saw Sir Charles Craven, Vickers Armstrongs' chairman, with [Major Hew] Kilner'. Wallis was utterly deflated when Craven told him emphatically that he must cease all work on Upkeep. He was making a thorough nuisance of himself at the Ministry of Aircraft Production, had upset the Air Staff and, moreover, was in danger of damaging the reputation and commercial interests of Vickers Armstrongs. Craven quoted Air Vice-Marshal Linnell, who had urged him 'to stop his [Wallis's] silly nonsense about the destruction of the dams'.

Thoroughly shaken by this 'bad row', Wallis offered to resign, which provoked a volcanic response from the imposing Craven. Crashing his fist onto the table, he erupted: 'Mutiny!' Wallis noted 'private interview afterwards with K and told him again anxious to go'. He wrote in his diary: 'What happened on the Golf Links at Ulverston', close to Vickers-Armstrongs' Barrow-in-Furness site, to harden Craven's opinion. Following his ordeal he had lunch with Winterbotham and in the afternoon met Sydney Barratt and Dr T.R. Merton, who expressed sympathy but were powerless to be more positive.

In fact, Wallis neither resigned nor ceased work on Upkeep. Quite possibly his two hours' meeting with Admiral Renouf in the late afternoon of 24 February stiffened his resolution. Then, on 25 February, just two days after the traumatic encounter at Vickers House, he received a letter from Lockspeiser confirming that a planning conference about the project would take place the following morning as previously arranged.

In the event, the meeting commenced at 15.00, not 11.00 hours as planned, chaired by Linnell. In addition to Roy Chadwick (the Lancaster designer), two Air Ministry and five MAP representatives with three from

THE DAMBUSTERS: 'WAS THE RAID WORTHWHILE?'

Vickers-Armstongs, including Craven and Wallis, were present. Chadwick's presence was highly significant, as Wallis would later stress. Like Cochrane, he had long known Wallis, which served as a reminder that, with his lengthy involvement in airship and aeroplane design, Wallis was no anonymous crank. Chadwick's elder daughter, Margaret, recalled several references in which her father revealed that 'he had assisted Sir Barnes with one of his airships, the R.100' and, on more than one occasion, 'he mentioned his admiration for Sir Barnes' geodetic construction [used in the Wellington] ... So they knew one another from the early days'.

Linnell opened the 26 February meeting by emphasising 'that the Chief of Air Staff had now instructed that every endeavour was to be made to complete the aircraft and bombs, so as to allow them to be used during the spring of 1943. For this purpose, the CAS has allotted priority to UPKEEP over work on the B. 3/42 aircraft at Vickers, and over other projects on the Lancaster at Avros'; reversal of Craven's diktat three days earlier. 'The requirement was for three LANCASTERS to be prepared as quickly as possible with full UPKEEP apparatus for trial purposes. These to be followed by conversion sets to complete 30 aircraft. The requirement for bombs had been stated as 150 to cover trials and operations [*sic*]'.

The Director of Bomber Operations (Baker) noted that 26 May would be the latest date possible that year: thereafter, the water in the reservoir would be too low to guarantee success. Although 19 May would be full moon over Germany, 13–26 May represented the moon period that month. The meeting agreed that 'full delivery of aircraft and bombs must aim at the 1st May in order to allow a reasonable period of training and experiments'. Wallis explained that 'no detailed scheme had been agreed for the LANCASTER. After general discussion it was agreed that the line of demarcation between the two firms should be for Avros to be responsible for the strong point attachments to the airframe, for the bombcell fairings, electrical bomb release wiring and the hydraulic power point for the rotating motor. Vickers would be responsible for the attachment arms carrying the bomb (including the driving mechanism) and for the bomb itself'. To expedite the process, Avro would send draughtsmen to Weybridge 'at once'.

Wallis confirmed that no 'detailed drawings' of a full-size Upkeep yet existed, but promised to send them to Vickers-Armstrongs works at Newcastle, where Upkeep would be manufactured, 'in ten days to a fortnight'. On his copy of the minutes, Wallis wrote: '<u>Actual</u> – 100% complete in 6 days'.

In summary, Linnell 'emphasised the extremely tight programme ... of the 8 weeks available, at least 4 were already bespoken for the completion of the drawings and filling of the bombs'. This timeframe would, in practice, be complicated by parallel development of the anti-ship version of Wallis's bomb and associated trials with a modified Mosquito, which the meeting acknowledged. At 17.45, Wallis once more showed his films to a captive audience in the 'Admiralty cinema'.

Wallis admitted that he had, in the past – not least to Lord Cherwell on 30 January –declared that eight weeks would be sufficient, but felt 'physically sick' as he left the conference room. Knowing that 'somebody had called my bluff ... I had the terrible responsibility of making good all my claims'. Norbert Rowe recalled: 'I well remember leaving the meeting in company with him [Wallis] when he made the remark, "where can I turn for help?" I offered to send him a prayer to St Joseph, which gave me solace in times of stress. I knew Wallis had spiritual depths and I felt he needed spiritual help then, more than anything else, to strengthen and reinforce his own powers to enable him to do what he alone could do, and to carry an enormous load'. Wallis acknowledged being not only deeply touched by Rowe's gesture, but that he did make frequent use of the prayer in the weeks ahead.

In a 'secret' covering letter to a copy of the minutes subsequently sent to Wallis, Sir Charles Craven wrote: 'Personally, I think this time we have been set an impossible problem and I have told Sir Stafford Cripps [now minister in charge of the Ministry of Aircraft Production] this, but on the other hand, I have assured him we are going to do everything humanly possible.' Ominously, he concluded: 'I do want to be assured that this is being done, please.'

On the morning following the decisive meeting, Wallis recorded: 'Meeting of all staff concerned to formulate plans for Upkeep. Full Size dwgs of Store in hand'. Less positively, also on 27 February, Wallis wrote to Air Commodore R. Mansell at Boscombe Down, where a modified Lancaster would carry out important tests in connection with the dams operation. 'It appears that we are to go ahead at full steam, and my only fear now is that this important decision may have been arrived at too late.' Nevertheless, the die had been cast.

Chapter 5

Perfecting the Means

Wallis was wise to express concern about the limited time available with so much still to be done in terms of the weapon and the aircraft to deliver it. G.M. Garro-Jones warned Winterbotham that Wallis's troubles had only just begun.

The final design comprised a near-spherical shape, with its poles flattened to accommodate the retaining and rotating mechanisms, thus allowing Upkeep to be back-spun before release. Wallis recalled that 'the Ministry gave two years as the time required to get steel to make pressed dies for the 7ft 6ins dia, of the semi-spherical bomb cases ... The original design of the weapon was spherical, but this had to be given up and a cylindrical container substituted owing to the impossibility of obtaining the steel billets for the dies that would be required to make spherical casings, in the time available'. The required diameter would be obtained by packing 'roughly welded steel girders' around it to form 'a double skin', held in position by 'great staves of wood' bound by six 1½ in diameter metal bands sunk in grooves'. Wallis revealed to Dr Collins that he was initially committed to a spherical weapon 'as spheres run much further and truer than any other shape'.

Shortly before noon on 27 February, Wallis began the full drawings of Upkeep. A preliminary draft was ready for a meeting at Burhill the following evening, chaired by Group Captain W. Wynter-Morgan and attended by RAF officers and civilian representatives from the Royal Ordnance Factory, Woolwich, and Vickers-Armstrongs works at Crayford and Weybridge. Wallis explained that, in view of the restricted availability of steel, the casing of the core cylinder containing the charge would be 3/8in thick. To achieve detonation, three standard Admiralty hydrostatic pistol pots with twice the normal number of CE (composition explosive) pellets of the powerful Tetryl detonator would be installed and armed by removing the horseshoe washers immediately before take-off. A fourth, self-destructive fuse, armed 'when the store [Upkeep] leaves the aircraft', was to be added

PERFECTING THE MEANS

to destroy the weapon and prevent it falling into enemy hands should the other three fail to work. It would be positioned 'at the same end of the store as the hydrostatic pistols'.

Correspondence, meetings and associated telephone communications now escalated. Wallis recorded that at 15.30 hours on 1 March, Roy Chadwick 'and party' arrived at Weybridge from Manchester for discussion with Wallis and his staff, which continued into the evening. Next morning, at Burhill, Chadwick chaired a meeting whose members included Wynter-Morgan, to whom Wallis had sent six copies of the 'preliminary Upkeep sketches', four other Ministry of Aircraft Production representatives, two from the Ministry of Supply and four Vickers-Armstrongs staff (including Wallis and Summers). Arrangements for the 'filling and handling Upkeep stores' topped the agenda. It was agreed that production of the core cylinders and wooden casings be allocated to the Vickers-Armstrongs works at Elswick, Newcastle-upon-Tyne, and Barrow-in-Furness, while Crayford concentrated on Highball. The Royal Ordnance factory at Chorley would fill cylinders with live charges, Woolwich deal with inert filling ('aerated concrete', according to Wallis). Avros planned to have the first modified Lancaster at the RAE, Farnborough, by the end of the first week in April. There, Vickers-Armstrongs' personnel would test the balancing, hoisting, spinning and dropping equipment on the ground using an inert-filled Upkeep. To reduce drag, increase speed and save fuel, bearing in mind that a large, ungainly weapon would be suspended below the fuselage, Chadwick suggested that the mid-upper turret be removed. This had defensive implications by taking away one of the aircraft's two main gun positions. Wynter-Morgan undertook to refer the matter to the Air Staff for a ruling, which proved favourable and the distinctive profile of the Dambuster Lancaster was born: Type 464 Provisioning.

Wallis explained in more detail the arrangement required to install Upkeep in the modified Lancasters:

> This consisted of two V-shaped arms each hinged about a fore and aft axis, and so arranged that by means of the disc-wheels, the cylindrical case of the weapon could be rotatably held between them, the wheels being mounted on ball bearings. The external diameter of the discs was very slightly smaller than the internal dia. of the circular tracks at the ends of the weapon, and rotation was imparted by means of a V.S.G. Hydraulic Motor and belt drive to one of the discs, the desired spin being

thus transmitted to the weapon by frictional contact between the internal track and driven disc ... The calliper arms were held inwards against stops (to prevent actual clamping of the cylinder), by a straining system retained by a bomb-slip. On the release of this, the arms were instantaneously forced outwards by powerful springs thus leaving the spinning weapon unsupported.

Speaking to Norbert Rowe, Wallis paid tribute to 'the wonderful co-operation' that he received from Chadwick, not least 'in working out the design and installation of controls and gear for the carriage and release of the bomb in the Lancaster aircraft'. Chadwick's daughter, Margaret, revealed that her father, like Wallis, did not confine his work to the office. Chadwick had a liking for 'State Express 555 [cigarettes] in pale, lemon-coloured boxes'. They provided space on which to write when at home. 'The insides of the lids were covered in calculations and at the end of the evening – these and *The Manchester Evening News* with calculations all round the margins – were items my mother did not know whether to throw away in the morning!'

The Newcastle and Barrow works expressed concern about ability to deliver more than 20–25 cylinders and wooden casings in the time available. On 4 March, Wallis wrote formally to both 'about the manufacture of 100 4ft diameter steel cylinders and wood casings for a special purpose ... I am afraid that you may have received the impression that we require this to be a good mechanical engineering job, but ... the workmanship required is of the mine class, produced by rolling and welding. No machining whatsoever is required'.

The following day, Wallis sent to Wynter-Morgan further technical details about the lifting and spinning of the 'Lancaster golf mine'; 'golf mine' being the generic term for all forms of Wallis's weapon, which included the still-born Baseball to be fired from a forward-facing mortar on a motor torpedo boat or motor gunboat. He also confirmed that the belt drive to rotate Upkeep would be on the starboard side of the fuselage, the belt itself 195ins inside measurement. It would go round Upkeep and the spinning mechanism be mounted in the aircraft, where a hydraulic control valve would permit the operator to regulate the speed. Wallis wrote as well to Squadron Leader C.T. Freeman at the Ministry of Supply research centre, Fort Halstead, Kent, with drawings of the modified Lancaster's hub and an explanation of how the spinning mechanism would work to allow him to design the self-destructive device.

Writing to the Vickers-Armstrongs' chairman, Sir Charles Craven, on 6 March Wallis confirmed that drawings of 'the big bomb' had been

PERFECTING THE MEANS

completed 'on Thursday 4 March' and despatched to the Newcastle and Barrow sites. Wallis explained that he was now 'in touch with Avros' and hoped to redesign the cylinder by the end of the week. 'My impression is that we shall come through all right as things are going far better than I thought would be possible.'

Having now secured details of the Lancaster's construction, hitherto unknown to him for security reasons, Wallis intended to reduce the length of the Upkeep cylinder, whose diameter was 50in, from 61 to 59 7/8ins. Craven replied expressing his satisfaction at the rate of progress, adding: 'I have seen the Chief of the Air Staff twice in the last week, and also Sir Wilfrid Freeman [Chief Executive of the Ministry of Aircraft Production]. They are taking intense interest in the whole scheme.' Group Captain Winterbotham provided an interesting, explanatory footnote to this episode. 'After I had told him [Wallis] of the Air Ministry's scorn of a circular bomb and his tin bath experiments at Effingham, he asked me to get him the most secret plans of the Lancaster bomber. I did in fact get the loan of these from the Air Ministry and he based the size and weight of the bouncing bomb on this.'

The Newcastle works then raised an important issue. If the steel cylinder and wooden casing were separated for transportation and filling, the cylinder

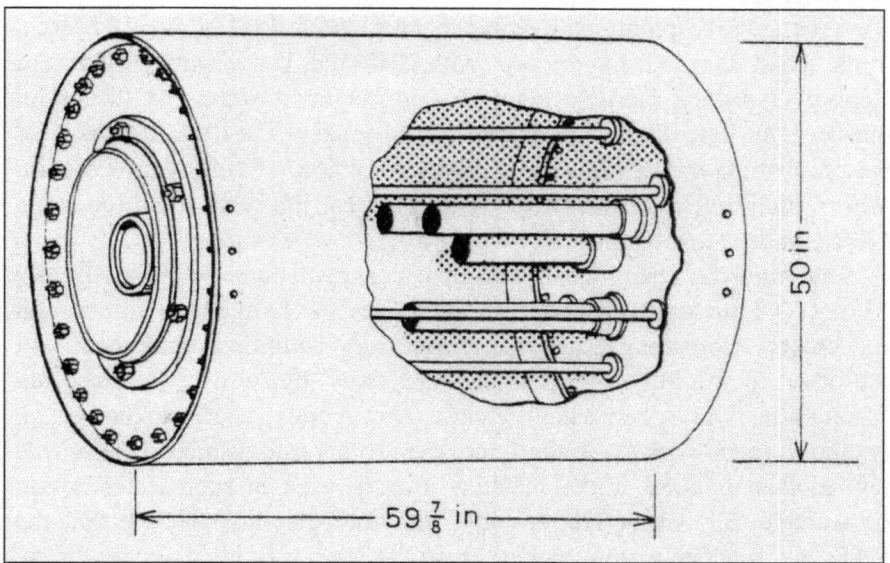

Upkeep. The cylindrical weapon, which breached the Moehne and Eder dams. Known as 'the bouncing bomb', but more accurately by the Germans as 'a revolving depth charge'.

would be liable to a 0.25in plus or minus variation. This meant that perfect reassembly at the operational station could not be guaranteed. Wynter-Morgan, therefore, reversed the original instruction: assembly should occur at the manufacturing works. On 8 March, Squadron Leader Freeman wrote to Wallis from Fort Halstead. He had nearly finished the electrical ignition of the self-destructive device, which would form a separate unit and not affect Wallis's design. However, he was concerned that Wallis wanted 'to pull out the arming forks of the hydrostatic valves' after the machine was in position. He thought this unwise, as they might twist around the operating wire of the destructive device 'with awkward results'.

On Saturday 13 March, Wallis telephoned Barrow to confirm an Air Ministry decision that live Upkeeps should be painted dark green, inert-filled grey. In practice, possibly due to lack of time, some of both variety left the factories with a red oxide undercoat. On 17 March, Wallis informed Craven that the Barrow and Newcastle works were 'performing miracles' with five Upkeeps ready to leave each of them immediately. At 15.00 hours, 'Air V M Bottomley' was at Burhill for 'discussion on targets for new weapon. Asked for New RECCO'. They then drove to Weybridge (6 miles), where 'introduced B to Kilner and Gammon'. That day, too, Freeman revealed that, as requested, the fusing equipment would be on the starboard side and was quite safe to arm in the air.

A particularly important meeting occurred the following day, 18 March, at the Road Research Laboratory 'with Glanville, Davies and Collins and Renouf to discuss possible allowance in height of water for successful attack. After long discussion, it was agreed to leave the RRL to think over the problem. G thinks we could safely allow a drop of 10ft.' On 19 March, Wallis complimented Barrow on 'a magnificent job' with the three inert-filled Upkeeps that had reached Weybridge.

That same day changes to the original arrangements were outlined. Only 23, not 30, Lancasters would be modified. Three were to go to Farnborough for Vickers-Armstrongs' staff to fit necessary additional equipment, but the other 20 would be modified 'in every way' by Avros in Manchester. Meanwhile, Wallis had asked Vickers-Armstrongs' works to design an engine to rotate Upkeep in the Lancaster. To his astonishment, Newcastle replied that a four-cylinder machine already used in submarines would be suitable. Sir Arthur Harris could therefore gleefully declare that the RAF 'had pinched a small engine from the Navy'. In his diary on Friday 19 March, Wallis noted that 'Air Cdre Gray Bomber Command asks me to go to Knapp Hill [the High Wycombe HQ] Sat 4pm to meet AOC 5 Group'.

PERFECTING THE MEANS

The meeting did not work out as expected. 'Kept waiting for 1½ hrs!' and, instead of seeing Cochrane, 'met Gray, Sealy, Oxland'; the matters discussed not being recorded. In his small diary for 20 March in addition to note of the Knapp Hill meeting is a single word 'Gibson', which is intriguing given that the large diary puts 23 March as the day that he learnt that Gibson would be leading the operation.

On 22 March, Wallis was at the Air Ministry to consult Captain R.N. Liptrot 're Lancaster heights and range'. He learnt '1700 miles still air – 12,000lbs bombs ... Target distance = 430 miles OK'. Chadwick rang Wallis on 23 March 're altimeters', there was a conference at Burhill 're supply of ball races' and at 16.00 hours Wallis and Jeffree drove to the National Physical Laboratory for a meeting 're thermal cond [*sic*] of steel textile'. He was at Foxwarren the following morning 're balance' and investigation of the 'gyroscopic effect of Upkeep', which was declared 'OK'. In the afternoon of 25 March, Wallis went to London to meet Sir Alexander Dunbar, seconded from Vickers-Armstrongs to the Ministry of Aircraft Production to whom he 'gave copy of Dam paper', and attended an 'Air Council Room Mtg' at 15.00 hours before travelling back to Foxwarren. There he 'arranged to visit Grantham to discuss stowage and balancing of Upkeeps' via 'wire to Cochrane'. He was at the MAP again on Friday 26 March to see 'Pidcock re additional Large Stores – advised 20 more filled inert'.

The Air Ministry confirmed on 25 March the target for delivery of the modified Lancasters: two by 21 April, six more by 28 April, a further eight by 5 May and the final four of the 20 operational machines by 8 May. Avro records would confirm that all were subsequently delivered directly to RAF Scampton from the Woodford works. However, on 27 March, Chadwick informed Wallis that, unfortunately, the first modified Lancaster would be a week later than planned, adding a 'rather amusing' postscript. He had just received a telephone call cancelling an order for radio altimeters to be installed following a letter received that morning requesting them. On 29 March, Wallis was at the Admiralty to consult Professor Blackett and Dr E.C. Bullard about wave behaviour after an explosion in water. The following day, Bullard answered Wallis's query. Acknowledging that a 6,600lb charge of Torpex had now been settled, Bullard calculated that its detonation would create waves a foot high over 7.5 square miles. Even allowing for reflection from a dam wall or banks of an inlet, he felt 'there is nothing to fear from the direct wave ... I feel confident that after five minutes the height of the wave will be measured in inches not feet'.

THE DAMBUSTERS: 'WAS THE RAID WORTHWHILE?'

On 3 April, a progress meeting at the MAP learnt that 'ten inert-filled stores' were now at RAF Manston (for the Reculver trials), and live filling had begun at Chorley where 40 were on order and destined for the designated operational station. A further 20 inert-filled Upkeeps were set for Manston. That day, Wallis had 'CRD and D/CRD to lunch' prior to watching insertion of 'big ball in arms for 1st time. Run up to 150 rpm. All OK'. He noted, also, 'decided to increase width bands to 5/8 ins'. On 5 April, 'Spun Lanc store up to 400 rpm OK ran for 30 mins at that speed. Limit of rig power ... Notified CRD all OK'. Five days later, Wallis received news that Barrow had completed its complement of 50 cylinders and wooden casings.

Preparations had become so advanced that, on 12 April, Air Chief Marshal Portal sent a 'most secret private and personal' cypher message to Air Vice-Marshal W.F. MacNeece Foster in the office of the Combined Chiefs of Staff in Washington outlining progress. 'A spherical bomb which will be dropped from a low flying aircraft and act in the nature of a surface torpedo' would be suspended under the bomb-bay. 'Balanced spin of about 500 rpm ... [which] lengthens initial flight before impact on the water, increases the angle of incidence of ricochet and serves to control the action of the water drag and the tendency of the sphere to roll under water.' It could be used 'on capital ships' and 'against important enemy dams ... Experiments up-to-date indicate that the weapons are technically feasible but we cannot guarantee success until we have seen results of the trials. The potentialities, however, are so great that we have taken a gamble and pressed on with development of the weapon as quickly as possible ... Intended to launch major operations simultaneously so as to exploit surprise and avoid possible counter measures.'

Writing to Collins, Wallis later revealed that he was not entirely happy about Upkeep's ultimate version. 'The cylinder had a <u>great</u> disadvantage in that while a slight degree of roll on the aircraft at the instant of release had no perceptible effect on the directional accuracy of the run, the result of the roll on a cylinder was disastrous in that one end striking the water before the other caused the cylinder to run on the arc of a circle'. Two practice Upkeeps certainly veered to port at Reculver and one would do so in the attack on the Moehne.

Important as the development of Upkeep was, without the 464 Provisioning modification the operation could not be mounted. Almost certainly following discussions with Chadwick that day, on 1 March Wallis wrote to C.H. Smith, chief engineer of The Hoffman Manufacturing Co.

PERFECTING THE MEANS

Ltd, Chelmsford, referring to 'Type 464 Aircraft (Lancaster)', noting that 30 sets of LS 221/2 AC bearings were required 'for a special job' and ready to be installed in the aircraft by 1 May. Further details of the modified machine began to emerge during the morning meeting at Burhill on 2 March. It was ruled that Messrs A.V. Roe and Co (under Chadwick's direction) would install 'hydraulic piping, fairing and electrical wiring', Vickers-Armstrongs Ltd, Weybridge (designed by Wallis's team) the calliper arms to be attached to the fuselage to carry Upkeep, four hydraulic pumps per aircraft, one 15hp hydraulic engine per aircraft (for spinning Upkeep), hoisting slings and balancing gear. The following day, Chadwick confirmed to Wallis that the 'Type 464 (Provisioning)' aircraft would be a Lancaster III, powered by Merlin 28 engines manufactured under licence by the Packard Motor Company of Detroit. The crew of seven would be retained with the mid-upper gunner manning the two guns in the bomb-aimer's forward compartment beneath the cockpit, which on a normal operation would be operated by the bomb-aimer. A minor absentee on this operation would be the rest bed usually put between the mid-upper and rear turrets.

Avro records show that 20 of the modified Lancasters were, as planned, delivered to Scampton by Air Transport Auxiliary (ATA) pilots. In addition, ED765 went to Farnborough on 6 April, ED817 left Woodford on 15 April and appears also to have gone to Farnborough. Both would move on to Manston for the Reculver trials. ED825 reached the Aeroplane and Armament Experimental Establishment at Boscombe Down, 'for handling and performance trials' on 17 April. After removal of the mid-upper turret, the Lancaster had two machine guns in the nose, four in the rear turret and 'one free ball-mounted in the ventral position [later removed] ... The bomb-bay doors have been removed and the fuselage modified, and two external carrier [calliper] arms, one on each side of the fuselage'.

The normal 'saucer-shaped transparent bomb-aimer's window' had been replaced 'by a more nearly hemispherical type'. No de-icing nor barrage balloon cutters were fitted. Details and sketches of their construction appear in Wallis's files, but A.D. Grant felt sure that they were drafted by Herbert Jeffree. Lockspeiser, rather extravagantly, credited Wallis with responsibility for 'the bomb, fuses and storage in the Lancasters'. 'A one man band', he claimed. Wallis noted the arrival of the modified Lancaster at Farnborough 'late' on 6 April and the following day, 'am Conference re Lancaster with Chadwick, Capt Brown, Gammon, Edwards (at Burhill). Early lunch, proceed Farnborough. All pm inserting store. Spun in ground

THE DAMBUSTERS: 'WAS THE RAID WORTHWHILE?'

rig to 320 rpm witnessed by Chadwick. All OK'. On 8 April, there was another morning 'conference re hydraulic system with Chadwick'.

617 Squadron's bomb-aimer, Sergeant J.H. Clay, recalled that arrival of the modified aircraft at Scampton 'caused some consternation. The belly of the plane had been cut away to accommodate the bomb, mine or whatever. We christened the planes "abortions", two cymbal-like contraptions on either side of the cut-away became known as "clappers"'.

Determining the spot at which to release Upkeep onto the reservoir in front of the dam proved complicated. Drop too soon and it would sink short of the wall; drop too late and it would bounce over. An unmarked and undated paper in Wallis's files, clearly in his writing, summarised the dimensions of the Moehne and, using a line between the two towers as a base, formed a triangle whose point was reached over the reservoir with the calculation 'range at release 380yds ... speed 220mph over ground'. In retrospect, a bomb-aimer on the operation, Flight Sergeant L.J. Sumpter, thought 'the point of impact was 350 to 400 yards from the dam', and, in a post-war document, Wallis showed 'point of release – about 400–450 yds upstream'. This roughly coincides with his estimate at a meeting in the Air Ministry on 5 May 1943. The minutes recorded: 'Mr. Wallis said that with the cylinder alone at air speeds between 210 and 220mph ... a range of 450 to 500 yards could be obtained, of which 250 yards would be travel along the surface of the water.'

To Dr Collins in April 1972, Wallis reflected that 'so great was the pressure generated on the first impact with the water ... we had to ask Gibson to shorten his release range from about 650 yards to about 450 yards'; the precise figure quoted by Air Commodore Bufton on 13 May 1943 in a signal to Portal in Washington. Flying Officer E.C. Johnson recalled 425–475 yards at the pre-operational briefing, which would allow reasonable leeway either side of this ideal spot. Wallis explained:

> The distance was critical, firstly to ensure that the height of the bounces should have diminished to a dimension less than the freeboard of the dam, a matter of only a few feet when the lake was full, [to ensure Upkeep did not bounce over the dam wall] and, secondly, that the impact with the dam should not be so great as to detonate or unduly damage the weapon – in particular the pistols and the fuse ... It was found during trials that it was difficult to dive the Lancaster at such a low altitude beyond a speed of 240–250mph and the range was determined by this limiting value.

PERFECTING THE MEANS

Once the dropping zone had been established, how to achieve it must be determined. In *Enemy Coast Ahead,* Gibson wrote that, 'one fine day in April' a wing commander from the Ministry of Aircraft Production visited his office at Scampton to sketch out 'a very simple bomb-sight using the age-old range-finding principles', which the instrument section 'knocked up ... within half an hour' and Gibson tested 'over our dam in Sheffield'. The RAF officer was Wing Commander C.L. Dann, an armaments specialist and since October 1942 on the technical staff of the Ministry. Gibson explained that the bomb-aimers then constructed their own sights. Hence the hand-held wooden triangle with, in Sir Arthur Harris's words, 'two rusty nails' at the base to coincide with the towers and a peep hole at the apex for the bomb-aimers to hold and operate, which appeared in the celebrated film.

However, Dann seems to have been presenting a proposal from elsewhere that had been approved by the Ministry and its evolution was not so straightforward. On 2 April, Dann met Air Vice Marshal Cochrane and Gibson at HQ 5 Group in Grantham, which predated his visit to Scampton. That day, an RAE document suggests that use of chinagraph marks on the clear vision panel with string attached to the retaining nuts and drawn back to the bomb-aimer's eye was favoured. This is supported by Benjamin Lockspeiser's belief that Dr T.R. Merton, who in November 1942 had chaired the body of scientists advising the Ministry of Production to which Wallis explained his idea, first realised that the Moehne Dam towers could be used to gauge the necessary release spot. According to Lockspeiser, Merton thought that pieces of tape 'inside the windscreen' would suffice. Evidently, the triangular contraption came later. A curious sketch appears in Wallis's diary on 11 May 1943, which looks like a variation of the so-called Dann Sight with the caption, 'Invented range finder'. Bill Startup, a Vickers' draughtsman, believed Herbert Jeffree thought of this solution and Wallis perfected his draft. Possibly, known to be in contact with Merton, Wallis had rather instructed Jeffree to tidy up Merton's idea. However, 11 May is too late for introduction to training. Whatever its origin the triangular sight was certainly made available to bomb-aimers during pre-operational exercises.

With the means of achieving the required dropping point solved, ensuring release at 60ft remained a puzzle. Originally, when the height had been 150ft, Gibson suggested trailing a wire of that length with a heavy weight attached. This is where Lockspeiser came into the picture, because at speed however weighted the wire stretched out behind the aircraft. Gibson's log book suggests that this failed experiment took place over the Derwent reservoir on 4 April. Discussing the problem with a colleague,

THE DAMBUSTERS: 'WAS THE RAID WORTHWHILE?'

Lockspeiser recalled use of 'double converging beams in an anti-submarine experiment', aimed at catching a U-boat on the surface, which failed due to choppy water. He remembered this exercise involving Hudson aircraft; Stanley Wright, a fitter at the RAE, held there were similar experiments with Lysanders.

Reviewing the Hudson experiment, Lockspeiser wondered whether such an arrangement would work over a placid lake. He travelled to Grantham to see Cochrane, admitted that he could not guarantee success, 'but pleaded successfully to be given a chance'. Making use of contacts at Farnborough, who had worked on the failed scheme, an Aldis lamp, the most powerful such device available, was installed 'on the underside of each wing' angled inwards to meet. But, in practice, the intersection could not be seen from the cockpit. One lamp was then placed in the front camera spot, by the bomb-aimer's position aft of the clear vision panel in the nose, as at low level and high speed no camera would be carried on this operation. The downward firing gun forward of the tail having been removed, he tried unsuccessfully the second lamp in that position. Eventually, with the bomb-bay doors removed on the 464 (Provisioning) Lancaster, the rear lamp was secured at the back of the bomb-bay and beams from the two Aldis lamps set to meet in touching circles to form a figure of eight, forward of the leading edge of the starboard wing. Detailed instructions for installation of the lamps, complete with explanatory diagrams, drawn up by Lockspeiser show that the distance between the front lamp, port of centre, and rear lamp on the centre line was 20ft, each 'held in position by brackets'. The front lamp was to be set 30 degrees from the vertical out to starboard, the rear one similarly 40 degrees and angled forward. However, another document held by The Barnes Wallis Memorial Trust suggests that they were fitted 'pointing 80deg from the vertical out to starboard, level fore and aft' and 'pointing 40deg from the vertical out to starboard and [slanted] 15deg forward'.

When Cochrane described the proposal to Harris, who had commanded a flying boat squadron in the 1930s, he was unimpressed: 'I tried that with flying boats [to assist landing] and it didn't work because the spotlight went through the water.' Nevertheless, this system would be fitted to modified Lancasters for the operation. In a hand-written comment attached to a summary of progress from the Air Ministry, on 15 April 1943 Harris signalled his enduring scepticism. 'As I always thought the weapon is balmy [*sic*]. I will not have aircraft flying about with spotlights on in defended areas.'

PERFECTING THE MEANS

When the commercial film was being made, the producer rang to ask whether, as there were too many in the cast, the lamp configuration could be attributed to Gibson. Lockspeiser considered Gibson 'a very brave man, who had given his life for his country'. So the legend of the high-kicking chorus girls illuminated by theatre spotlights entered folklore; dismissed by Lockspeiser as 'a lot of balls'. He maintained that he and Cochrane 'fixed it up between us'.

Curiously, in view of the detachment of Vickers and Avro civilian staff to help with local work on the modified Lancasters and Wallis's involvement in the design of apparatus like the calliper arms to retain Upkeep, there is no record of a visit to Scampton during the run-up to the operation. Leading Aircraftman Victor Gill, an engine mechanic who looked after the Lancasters of Squadron Leader Young and Flight Lieutenant Astell, maintained otherwise. 'A white-haired civilian' visited A Flight 'on two or three occasions and spoke to me'. He seemed particularly interested in the bomb-bay, and by implication the calliper arms. Gill found him 'interesting and knowledgeable', but at the time he was unaware of his identity. Only after the raid did he identify Wallis.

Prior to 15 May, the station is only briefly mentioned by Wallis twice. On 20 March, when he visited Bomber Command HQ at High Wycombe, the last diary entry was a single word, 'Scampton', and on 6 April, Wallis noted a phone message concerning handling of the 'Big Store' to the RAE and 'Armament Officer RAF Scampton'. Apart from Easter Sunday (25 April) and 13–14 May, which are blank, all other dates show a full diary. The absence of an entry for 14 May, though, indirectly points to the unreliability of Wallis's diaries as comprehensive proof of his activity. That day, undoubtedly, he attended a lengthy meeting at Weybridge, chaired by Air Commodore B. McEntegart from the Ministry of Aircraft Production and including twelve other serving officers and Vickers representatives, to discuss 'release failures which occurred during HIGHBALL trials in Scotland'.

As the means to carry out an operation against the German dams was still being finalised, the Squadron that would deliver Upkeep had already begun a demanding training programme.

Chapter 6

617 Squadron Prepares

On 15 March 1943, AOC-in-C Bomber Command (Harris) informed Air Vice-Marshal the Hon R.A. Cochrane, AOC 5 (Bomber) Group at Grantham, Lincolnshire, that he was to form a new squadron to carry out the operation.

Four days earlier, on 11 March, Wing Commander G.P. Gibson DSO DFC optimistically wrote in his log book, 'My last trip'. He was due to relinquish command of 106 Squadron at RAF Syerston after 170 bomber or night fighter operations over 3½ years. Instead of a sailing holiday, he found himself posted to HQ 5 Group for administrative duties, including to his dismay writing a book. Shortly after he reached Grantham, Cochrane asked him without elaboration to do one more raid and he agreed. At a second meeting, with Group Captain J.N.H. 'Charles' Whitworth present, Cochrane revealed that it would be 'no ordinary sortie' and that he would lead a newly-formed squadron to carry out a low-level operation at night in two months' time. On learning about it, Whitworth thought the dams' concept 'rather fantastic'.

Squadron X nominally came into existence on 17 March, when Cochrane learnt that it would be armed with a unique, spherical bomb ('Up-keep') [sic], which would be spun, dropped from a mere 100ft at 200mph and travel 1,200yds. 'It is proposed to use this weapon … against a large dam in Germany, which, if breached, will have serious consequences in the neighbouring industrial area … The operation against this dam [the Moehne] will not, it is thought, prove particularly dangerous, but it will undoubtedly require skilled crews. Volunteer crews will, therefore, have to be carefully selected from the squadrons in your Group'. Air Vice-Marshal R.D. Oxland, Senior Air Staff Officer at Bomber Command, added, 'some training will no doubt be required' and speculated that this might initially include demonstrations to the crews at Chesil Beach.

Whitworth's presence at Gibson's meeting with Cochrane was explained as the Commanding Officer of RAF Scampton destined to be the operational

617 SQUADRON PREPARES

station, from which Gibson had previously flown with 83 Squadron. On 21 March, Gibson arrived to take over his new charge, which would only gradually take shape. Not every pilot was known personally to him, aircrew ages ranged from 20 to 32 and the bulk (including six pilots) contrary to legend were not decorated. Far from seasoned veterans, many who would attack the dams had completed fewer than ten operations and by no means all were volunteers. Wireless operator, Sergeant H.J. Hewstone, having been assured that his crew with a handful of operations over Germany would be 'the backbone of the new squadron', aware of its inexperience on arrival at the new venue, allegedly remarked that it must be 'at the arse end' of the spine.

In a letter dated 28 April 1978, Sir Arthur Harris strenuously rejected the suggestion that he had not favoured formation of the new squadron:

'Some "smear" mongers assert that I was against Wallis's dambusting idea. Totally untrue. In fact, I immediately offered to raise a special Sqn to do the job.' Harris insisted that he had 'never heard of the dams' before meeting Wallis on 22 February 1943 and clearly 'immense [operational] difficulties' were involved. 'That's why I believed highly experienced and skilled crews' would be required. Harris affirmed that he chose Cochrane, 'the most brilliant officer in the Service' in whom he had immense faith since their time together in Iraq during the inter-war years, and Gibson, 'a very able, incredibly brave youngster', familiar to him from Harris's time commanding 5 Group earlier in the war.

Flight Sergeant K.W. Brown's navigator, Sergeant D.P. Heal, recalled that four of the crew had flown with Brown in Whitleys on anti-submarine sweeps before going to a Heavy Conversion Unit, where 'we qualified to fly Lancasters and picked up a flight engineer and another gunner'. Posted to 44 Squadron at RAF Waddington, Brown's Lancaster crew had flown only 14 operations over enemy territory, the last to Berlin. Heal reflected: 'I couldn't understand why we were selected to join 617 Squadron'. Due to a faulty compass, 'once we arrived over Munich ¾hr after everybody else. Next morning the Squadron navigation officer remarked that "Heal had clearly done an aerial tour to most of the cities in Germany". I did wonder whether 44 Sqn wanted to get rid of an unwanted navigator'.

Brown and his crew reached Scampton on 30 March, with the understanding 'that five operations would count as a tour'. The bomb-aimer Sergeant S. Oancia wryly mused, 'I do not recall volunteering for this transfer.' Brown, revealing that he had 'not previously met Wing Commander Gibson', and that, when he protested about wanting to complete his tour with 44 Squadron, had been peremptorily told there was no choice. That was true of the four crews, including those of Squadron Leader H.M. Young DFC and Bar, Flight Lieutenant W. Astell DFC and Pilot Officer G. Rice, which comprised C Flight of 57 Squadron already at Scampton. They were simply posted across the station.

Rice reflected, 'having flown eight operations and settled into 57 Squadron, I protested in vain'. The Squadron Officer Commanding, Wing Commander F.C. Hopcroft, said, 'you'd better go'. Rice had previously flown a tour on Whitleys and picked up his additional two crews members at 1660 Heavy Conversion Unit at Swinderby. Young, who had done a Whitley tour over Germany and another with Wellingtons in the Near East, gathered five of his crew at Swinderby, all on their first tour, and he did not settle his bomb-aimer until 14 April. Three days later, Flying Officer V.S. MacCausland RCAF sought to reassure his family about returning to operations: 'We are on a revision course for the next month before going over with a few bundles for the squareheads.'

The crew of Pilot Officer L.G. Knight RAAF did volunteer. The wireless operator, Sergeant R.G.T. Kellow, recalled that, after twenty-two operations with 50 Squadron at RAF Skellingthorpe:

> we were called into the office of the commanding officer and offered the opportunity of moving over to a special squadron which was being formed the purpose of which was not made known to us. The policy at this period was to break up an operational crew after they had completed thirty trips and we all had twenty-three completed and wanted to continue together, completing our first tour and then, if fortunate, complete a second tour together. The offer presented to us sounded interesting and with our faith in each member's ability made up our minds there and then that we would accept the offer and move over as a crew to this new squadron.

The navigator, Flying Officer H.S. Hobday, agreed only after 'twelve hours or so of soul searching'. He had been nominated for a special navigation course and his acceptance of the 617 Squadron opportunity made 50 Squadron's navigation officer 'livid'. Hobday felt that Knight's crew might have been selected because it took part in the low-level (max 7,500ft) raid on the Schneider armaments factory at Le Creusot in October 1942, in which Gibson flew with 106 Squadron. To the rear-gunner, Sergeant

H.E. O'Brien, 'Les Knight was the coolest and quickest thinking person I have ever met. And, in my opinion, the most knowledgeable person in the squadron with respect to his job. Our crew addressed Les Knight as Les, in the air or on the ground. In the air there was no rank distinction.' He added: 'Les did spend time in our Sergeants' Mess ... We were happy to see him, because among other things, Les did not drink or smoke, so he always had money for beer or so when we reminded him it was his turn every other round.' To Kellow, he was 'a young steady pilot, respected by everyone'.

Hearing that Gibson was forming the new outfit, Pilot Officer W.H.T. Ottley DFC organised a transfer to Scampton (arriving 6 April) and his whole crew agreed to go with him. Sergeant F. Tees explained that, then with 207 Squadron, the crew were due to finish a tour at different times but Ottley was keen to keep them together. 'Bill heard of a new squadron being formed under Gibson, whom he knew, and said we'd stay together if we went. We had to take our own aircraft.' This briefly raised the number of crews with 617 Squadron to 22. Flight Lieutenant J.C. McCarthy DFC RCAF, an American who had crossed the Canadian border to volunteer before Pearl Harbor, responded positively to a phone call from Gibson to him at 97 Squadron, RAF Woodhall Spa, and took his crew with him. As the bomb-aimer, Sergeant G.L. Johnson, remarked, 'it seemed an interesting venture'. He had enormous respect for McCarthy, 'who had the largest hands I've ever seen'. At 6ft 3in, 'he had great presence and confidence' and Johnson would fly 40 operations with him 'unscathed'.

Flight Lieutenant J.L. Munro RNZAF, like Flight Lieutenant D.H. Maltby DFC, reached Scampton on 25 March from 97 Squadron. Not all of his regular crew went with him. Bomb-aimer, Sergeant J.H. Clay, explained: 'I had just carried out a raid on St Nazaire and this ended my first tour of operations. Shortly after this, Les Munro who was not my pilot asked Harvey Weeks and me if we would like to join him on another squadron just forming. Harvey was rear gunner in my crew. Les let us know that the new squadron would probably be special, probably dangerous. He was a tall New Zealander, somewhat dour, so we christened him "Happy Munro". Les was a first class pilot and besides didn't object when we raided his hoard of parcels from New Zealand! ... I think we were the third or fourth crew to arrive at Scampton and consequently had little to do until things got a bit more organised'.

The front gunner, Sergeant W. Howarth, explained further: 'On the last few operations at 97 Squadron we had several different bomb-aimers, because our regular one had some stomach trouble. We also lost our regular rear gunner, who was called to take a pilot's course. So we were joined by Jim Clay and Harvey Weeks. I believe we took our aircraft from 97 Squadron and, when we arrived at Scampton, it was strange to see aircraft of several squadrons parked together as our first training aircraft'.

Flight Lieutenant H.B. Martin DFC, an Australian in the RAF, was another who responded to a telephone request from Gibson and put together his crew while at 1654 Heavy Conversion Unit where he was an instructor, arriving at Scampton on 31 March. His chosen flight engineer, Sergeant I. Whittaker (commissioned Pilot Officer, 5 April), had completed a tour with 97 Squadron. The rear gunner, Flight Sergeant T.D. Simpson, joined the crew in a roundabout way. 'On 23 March 1943, I journeyed down from Lossiemouth in Invernesshire to Wigsley in Lincolnshire. I had written to Mick prior to this saying I was not happy where I was and asking if he could do anything about having me posted back to Lincolnshire. When I met Mick he said he was going back on Ops shortly and I could join him and I jumped at the opportunity. I arrived at Scampton on 5th April 1943.'

In some crews, individuals did decline the move; one was that of Sergeant (promoted Flight Sergeant 1 April) W.C. Townsend DFM, an experienced pilot, who had flown a twin-engine Hampden on the May 1942 1,000 bomber raid against Cologne. His front gunner on the Dams Raid, Sergeant D.E. Webb, explained that the crew had moved with 49 Squadron from Scampton to RAF Fiskerton on 13 January 1943 to facilitate the building of hard runways. Townsend's crew had the best bombing record in the squadron and the pilot became restless so vainly applied to join the Pathfinders. The crew was about to fly on another operation from Fiskerton, when called to the squadron commander's office to be told that their tour had been completed: Townsend and Webb thought that the original 200 hours of operational time still applied, but a tour now comprised 30 operations and those had been flown. The following day, after the traditional celebratory party, the crew was again called to the OC's office and asked whether, like Brown's, it would join a new squadron for a five operations' tour. Webb recalled that they went outside to discuss the proposition. All agreed, except the wireless operator, who was about to get married.

With the depleted crew, Townsend flew his own Lancaster to Scampton, where Gibson greeted them with 'welcome to the squadron – whatever it's going to be'. This was one of the first crews to arrive and Townsend asked for end of tour leave, which was granted. Webb reflected years later that 'Bill was the best pilot I flew with in every way.' On their return from leave,

617 SQUADRON PREPARES

a replacement wireless operator, Flight Sergeant G.A. Chalmers, who had requested a return to operational duties, joined the crew. Like him and the navigator himself its members did not know that Pilot Officer C.L. Howard had been commissioned in January. The inevitable administrative time-lag during wartime would result in some of the Squadron flying to the Dams unaware that they, too, had been commissioned. Chalmers:

> found on my arrival that security was to be of great importance, my first act having to report to the Security Office and seeing the Service Police guarding our hangar. At my interview with Wing Commander Guy Gibson, the Squadron Commander, he told me that 617 Squadron was a newly formed one consisting of experienced crews being gathered for a special mission and special training more of which I would learn later. I did. My Flight Commander, Flight Lieutenant Martin, said I could choose a crew that required a wireless operator and I chose Bill Townsend who had [he thought] an all NCO crew.

Several other crews formed at Scampton; Gibson's being one. Only the navigator, who had flown occasionally but not regularly with him at Syerston, came from 106 Squadron. As squadron commander, though, he had the pick of unattached flying personnel. It is, therefore, strange that later he would refer to his front gunner, Flight Sergeant George Andrew Deering RCAF, as 'Jim' and 'a sprog', suggesting youthful inexperience. Deering joined 617 Squadron on 29 March 1943, having completed a tour with 103 Squadron. He was posted, while instructing at an Operational Training Unit (OTU). Unknown to him or Gibson, he had been commissioned on 14 February (notified 18 May) and would be one of those to fly to the dams without that knowledge. Like Gibson, just his navigator agreed to go with Flight Lieutenant D.J. Shannon DFC RAAF. After a tour with him on 106 Squadron, during which initially he flew operations as Gibson's co-pilot, Shannon had secured a posting to 83 (Pathfinder) Squadron. He had been there 'for two or three days, when I got a phone call from Guy Gibson, who asked me to join him on a special squadron for a special operation. I had no idea what was in the offing, but was happy to join him ... He was a fantastic character, one of the finest leaders of men I've ever met. He wouldn't ask anybody to do something he didn't.' So 'the appropriate strings were pulled and I was on my way to Scampton'.

After reaching there on 28 March, he completed his crew in an odd way. The pilot of bomb-aimer, Flight Sergeant L.J. Sumpter, and flight engineer,

THE DAMBUSTERS: 'WAS THE RAID WORTHWHILE?'

Sergeant R.J. Henderson, had been grounded for medical reasons. Sumpter recalled: 'We had heard about the new squadron forming on the other side of the station and wandered over to have a look.' Clearly they liked what they saw, and so did Shannon, for they duly joined him from 57 Squadron. Sumpter found Shannon's crew informal, but efficient and disciplined. The pilot was called 'skipper' in the air and 'shearer' off duty. He addressed Sumpter as 'Satan' because as a keen motorcyclist he had that on the back of his flying jacket.

Contrary to Gibson's original intention, the more experienced gunner was in the rear turret for this operation, not necessarily the taller. Before joining 617 Squadron, Sumpter had completed only 13 Lancaster operations, the last to Berlin on 29 March. Shannon's crew was not finalised until 22 April, when wireless operator Flying Officer B. Goodale arrived from 10 OTU. Two other crews from 106 Squadron, those of Pilot Officer L.J. Burpee DFM RCAF and Flight Lieutenant J.V. Hopgood DFC & Bar, reached Scampton incomplete. Flying Officer K. Earnshaw RCAF, Hopgood's navigator, did not arrive from 50 Squadron until 29 April. The Australian pilot, Flight Lieutenant R.N.G. Barlow, arrived at Scampton with his crew on 7 April. His wireless operator, Flying Officer C.R. Williams DFC, also an Australian, found 'things a bit of a mess here', severe overcrowding and a gale blowing 'with dust flying everywhere'.

Squadron Leader H.M. Young, a former Oxford rowing blue nicknamed 'Dinghy' for twice having survived ditching in the sea, who according to Pilot Officer Rice 'lived with a typewriter, a fantastic administrator, industrious and professional', became one flight commander and Gibson's deputy. That Group Captain Whitworth had been an instructor with the Oxford University Air Squadron pre-war when Young was learning to fly might have influenced this appointment. Sergeant G.L. Johnson, McCarthy's bomb-aimer, recalled that Young ran the squadron 'very efficiently' during Gibson's many absences. According to Flight Lieutenant Shannon, 'he had a habit of taking snuff, practising yoga and often sitting cross-legged on his desk'.

B Flight commander, Squadron Leader H.E. Maudslay DFC, although only 21 years old, had completed one tour with 44 Squadron and been flying operationally with 50 Squadron since January 1943. He had arrived with Young from Skellingthorpe on 25 March. Pilot Officer Whittaker (Martin's flight engineer) considered Maudslay 'a gentleman ... quiet, kind and purposeful, somebody for whom nothing was too much trouble'. Flight Lieutenant Munro agreed that Maudslay was 'extremely well-liked'.

Nor was the number of crews rapidly settled. After a short period, Gibson decided that one ex-57 Squadron crew 'did not come up to the standard required for this squadron' and it was replaced by that of Sergeant

617 SQUADRON PREPARES

W.G. Divall from the same squadron. Following a night exercise on 16 April, Gibson proposed to replace Flight Sergeant Lancaster's navigator so that whole crew opted to leave 617 Squadron, which now had its scheduled 21 crews. Officially, surplus aircrew and one with a medical condition were posted out by 24 April. Thirty years after the operation, a navigator who flew on the raid, was shocked to receive a letter from his pilot, who mentioned in passing that he was 'glad' that he had resisted Gibson's attempt to replace him during the training period.

Meanwhile, as aircrew began to assemble, non-flying personnel gathered to be scrutinised by Flight Sergeant G.P. Powell; according to Gibson, 'a great little man, and a king in his own way'. In November 1940 he had been posted to 57 Squadron as a sergeant air gunner and remained with it until the move to Scampton, having progressed to Flight Sergeant (Discip) on the administrative staff. When his posting with Sergeant J. Heveron (orderly room clerk) to 617 came through, the OC ignored it and sent Powell's replacement away. 'Then 617 screamed', Wing Commander Hopcroft had to wire the replacement to return and Powell and Hevron duly crossed the station. There Powell drew up the ground staff newcomers in a hollow square, suspecting rightly that other squadrons had off-loaded 'scruffy buggers', who were swiftly replaced.

Other more worthy recruits experienced a different shock. RCAF radar specialist, Leading Aircraftman H.K. Munro, 'received my posting to Scampton from 97 with consternation. Because of the urgency I was to move within 48 hours. I remember thinking that I was leaving the best Squadron for an unknown quantity. When I arrived at the Guardhouse at Scampton, I was still in the dark because on 23 March we were not even organized with a Squadron number.' He was directed to one of a collection of First World War wooden huts, which he later discovered had been condemned as unfit for human occupation. Each housed 24 men, his full of 'Rhodesians, Canadians, Scots, Welsh, Geordies and English personnel'. To improve the bonding process, he convinced them 'to do callisthenics for fitness before retiring each night'. A signals specialist newcomer stumbling across 'one of these limb-jerking exercises' was alarmed that he had drifted into the annex of a mental institution. Munro proudly reflected that 'he soon joined our lunatic activities'.

Aircraftwoman Class 2 Morfydd Jane Gronland's experience of her arrival following transfer from RAF Waddington was similarly daunting:

> My first glimpse of Scampton filled me with the deepest gloom. It was a raw, windy day in March, when I and five

young WAAFs huddled together in the back of an RAF van which trundled into camp. We lurched along uneven roads, then as we passed the huge hangars we could see on the rain swept runways the shapes of five Lancasters. They looked formidable yet they had an air of vulnerability. I was suddenly glad that I was only a WAAF and would never have to fly in them. The van pulled up at some Nissen huts. We clambered out and stood in a line our kitbags by our sides. A WAAF sergeant led us into one of the huts where a pot-bellied stove gave off a comforting warmth. The sergeant smiled at us and said, "put your gear on your beds and I'll march you to the Mess for tea". The next morning we went on parade. A young P/O [pilot officer] welcomed all the new arrivals and told us about the new squadron. It was being formed for a very special operation, which was to be kept a complete secret. Whatever information we might overhear in the course of our duties was under no circumstances to be repeated or spoken of to anyone. He went on to say that our squadron commander was Wing Commander Gibson and warned us to be very particular about our dress and appearance as he was a stickler for neatness. The P/O wished us 'good morning' and walked away. The WAAF sergeant then took over and gave us our designated jobs. Two of the WAAFs and myself were sent to the Sergeants' Mess, the other three were to serve in the Officers' Mess.

By now, Powell was grappling with serious practical difficulties. When 49 Squadron moved out the furniture had been stripped from much of its accommodation. Raiding parties were despatched to all quarters of the station, leading the Flight Sergeant (Discip) to remark: 'Nobody knew were the chairs for the crew room came from, but I know'. The quarters of his former squadron provided a fruitful source, 'we robbed 57', he smiled. Beds for 700 men created a particular headache – that is until 'an 'erk' mentioned that three-tier bunks had been just replaced at another station. A quick phone call, deployment of a 'Queen Mary' lorry and 617 could sleep 66 men in a space designed for 22. In theory, securing administrative and technical stores should have been easier as the Group's handling centre was located at Scampton. But when he formally submitted a list of requirements, Powell was brusquely informed, 'you won't get 'em'. The stores officer had clearly not come across the OC 617 Squadron. As Powell observed, 'although a

617 SQUADRON PREPARES

small man, he could bark'. After a sharp phone call from Gibson, orders arrived from the Air Ministry that his squadron should have priority. So the required uniforms, blankets, paper, spare spark plugs, tools, starter motors and winches rapidly appeared.

Facilities like workshops, signals section and armoury also began to take shape. Such was the pressure that neither Powell nor any of the ground crew lived off station. He admitted to being too busy to visit his wife, when she travelled to Lincoln to see him. Sergeant Clay, Munro's bomb-aimer, explained that, parallel to these efforts, air crew 'did manage to get our flight offices into some sort of shape by putting up blackboards with rawl plugs and scraping old tables clean with bits of broken glass'.

Clay recalled Gibson's introduction 'standing on the bonnet of a station wagon, [he] addressed the assembled squadron. He seemed very young indeed to lead such an experienced mob, like the saturnine Les Munro, the hefty and exuberant Joe McCarthy and moustachioed Micky Martin. The general tenor of Guy's address was 1) keep your mouths shut 2) we've a pretty tough job and if anyone wants to leave they may do so without any imputation of L.M.F. To the best of my knowledge no one left'.

On 24 March, the Squadron officially 'formed on ordinary Lancasters' and Flight Lieutenant H.R. Humphries, secured from 106 Squadron by Gibson, arrived to replace the designated adjutant because 'the officer selected by Bomber Command for that duty was found to be unsuitable'; a married man, who wished to live off base. Pilot Officer Rice reflected: 'It cannot be stressed too highly the great contribution he made to the smooth running of the administration of the Squadron, starting from scratch, in conjunction with Flight Sergeant Powell. "Hump" was Guy Gibson's right hand man, and he did an invaluable job.'

The following day, 25 March, when a Bar to Gibson's DFC was announced, Humphries declared Squadron X ready to fly. On 27 March 1943, Group Captain H.V. Satterly, Senior Air Staff Officer at 5 Group HQ, issued Gibson with 'most secret orders' and the squadron with an identity. 'No 617 Squadron will be required to attack a number of lightly defended special targets.' Although some details differed from Air Vice-Marshal Oxland's communication to Cochrane, Satterly's outline would prove remarkably accurate. 'These attacks will necessitate low-level navigation over enemy territory in moonlight with a final approach to the target at 100ft at a precise speed, which will be about 240mph', though records show that many practice flights were at 150ft. The exact speed, Satterly noted, would be determined later and visibility at the target might well 'not exceed one mile'. He expected aircraft to attack Target A at ten-minute intervals. Once this had been destroyed, aircraft would be directed to 'Target B, Target C and so on'. In preparation, Gibson must ensure accurate navigation in moonlight or simulated moonlight 'at a height which will best afford security against fighter attack'. Without revealing the targets, Satterly recommended that 'it will be convenient to practise over water' and that all crews be able to drop their 'mine' within 40 yards of a specified release point. During daylight training, he advised pilot and bomb-aimer to wear dark goggles to simulate moonlight and that a second pilot be carried in case of emergency. He concluded by listing several lakes and reservoirs deemed suitable for practice in Wales, Yorkshire and Leicestershire.

Immediately, on 27 March, Flight Lieutenant Astell set out to photograph them. Not until 31 March, however, were any of the long cross-country routes involving the lakes, none under three hour duration, flown to commence the demanding training programme in earnest. That day, five A Flight crews led by Young (with Sergeant Byers as second pilot) carried out 'X country and bombing' flights. Meanwhile, lack of available aircraft had allowed McCarthy, like Townsend, to secure leave for his crew for a specific reason. His bomb-aimer, Sergeant G.L. Johnson, was due to be married on 3 April. When warned that, in view of his posting, this would not be possible, his fiancée made clear that 'if he did not turn up then, it was all off'. As George Johnson remarked, 'Joe came up trumps'.

On 4 April, despite the lack of aircraft, Gibson revealed that 'to date' 26 low-level daylight cross-country flights had been completed, 204 practice bombs had been dropped from 100ft at an indicated air speed of 240mph with an average error below 40yds. Later that month, another aircrew member, Flight Lieutenant Hopgood's Canadian bomb aimer, Flight Sergeant J.W. Fraser, was given permission by Gibson to get married. After completing a tour with No.50 Squadron, Fraser's leave had been cut short to join 617 Squadron. He had, though, already arranged to marry 'a striking honey blonde English girl' Doris Wilkinson in Doncaster and Gibson allowed the wedding to go ahead on 28 April during a two-day leave pass.

The low-level training did come as something of a shock to crews, as Townsend's navigator, Pilot Officer Howard recalled:

> When we joined 617 at the end of March 1943, low-level cross country was the order of the day and night from there on, and was a big change from our previous operations with 49 Squadron, when we flew at an average of 20,000 feet. It can

truthfully be called hard work – the low level was 150 feet (often a matter of guess and by God) and at that height on spring days in England, the aircraft bumped mercilessly as it encountered warm air rising from the ground. We had been briefed to maintain this height and speed of 240mph and navigation was pure map reading, in which the bomb-aimer in the nose and I behind the pilot read directly from the ground to the maps. As you can imagine, the speed brought up features and turning points at a dizzy rate and I still marvel that we returned safely to base ... Of course, ... we did not know the target ... and visualised either the *Tirpitz* or the submarine pens on the French Atlantic coast ... Having attacked the latter shortly before joining 617 we knew their defences frightening enough at 20,000ft, but at 150!

Howard further explained that:

it soon became obvious that the operation would involve flying over water and to this end we flew over lakes and along canals over much of England and used twists and turns of rivers as turning points. I often think of the beautiful scenery I missed in those cross-countries – looking only at the country in close proximity to the aircraft and striving desperately to keep on track ... Progress in flying to the required limits soon became evident with a self-indulgent, smug satisfaction at flying at low level all over England, a crime in the orders of all other Bomber Command aircraft.

Even as the crews began to practise, Group Captain Satterly was working on the plan of attack. He must have started to do so as soon as he knew the targets. For, on 7 April, RAF Tempsford responded with requested comments on three detailed routes suggested by him for the inward track to the Moehne, which all aircraft would initially make for. The first, involving crossing the enemy coast over the Frisian Island of Vlieland, would be used for aircraft ultimately bound for the Sorpe Dam. The third via the Scheldt delta would be chosen for the rest of the operational force. The second, south of the Frisians and across the Zuider Zee, would entail crossing the Helder peninsula between Egmond and Ijmuiden aiming for Akersloot on the mainland. It would become one of the three designated exit routes.

THE DAMBUSTERS: 'WAS THE RAID WORTHWHILE?'

Before receiving Satterly's instructions, Gibson had learnt something about the task ahead. On 23 March, Barnes Wallis wrote in his diary: 'a.m. Group Capt. H V Satterly SASO No 5 Group Grantham 200 to introduce Wing C Gibson who is doing the big job'. Gibson recorded that next day he travelled south to meet 'a scientist' in connection with his squadron's targets. After going by rail, he was picked up at Weybridge station by 'Mutt' Summers, who drove him to Wallis's office at Burhill golf club. There Gibson was shown the practice films and given a general overview of Upkeep and its performance, incredibly because the squadron commander did not have full security clearance for more specific information. In his diary for 24 March, Wallis simply entered: '4.20 W/C Gibson and Summers'.

Gibson noted that, due to various other commitments including meetings like that with Wallis, he was only able to fly irregularly with his new crew. His log book shows their first flight was on 1 April, followed by three more up to 9 April, including one lasting four hours and five minutes entered as 'Scottish X Country'. Gibson does not record the date in his log book, but between 12 and 14 April, he noted 'local Manston' in a Magister followed by 'crashed in a field'. That is known to have occurred on a return flight, so it seems reasonable to assume that Gibson (and the Squadron bombing leader, Flight Lieutenant R.C. Hay DFC RAAF) witnessed the trials on 13 April and had the mishap involving a field wired to deter enemy parachutists and gliders the following day.

On 15 April, after being briefed by Cochrane more fully and now knowing the targets, his log book shows that he flew an Oxford aircraft to and from Fairoaks airfield, near Chobham in Surrey, from which Squadron Leader Longbottom took him to Weybridge in a Mosquito. Presumably this was prior to another meeting with Wallis, not confirmed in Wallis's diary which is blank for that afternoon. The next day, 16 April, Gibson and his crew flew a 5hr 10mins 'Cornish X Country at low-level with dummy attacks on lakes'. On 20 April, with Section Officer Fay Gillan a Scampton intelligence officer on board, Gibson and his crew carried out a 'Night X Country to many reservoirs with dummy attacks'.

The Reculver trials showed that the height of release caused an acute problem leading to Wallis meeting Gibson again for an urgent discussion. He explained that analysis of the data suggested that, for success, Upkeep would have to be dropped from just 60ft at a speed of 232mph. Gibson's agreement was critical. Wallis recalled that 'Gibby complied without a murmur whatsoever', though, in reality, he did so a week later after trials by the squadron. The meeting, on 24 April, did not apparently involve just

617 SQUADRON PREPARES

the two men. Wallis's diary records a 15.00 hours meeting at Burhill with Gibson, Summers, Longbottom and Renouf 'to discuss height and speed' of bare cylinders (Upkeep) and spheres (Highball).

By the end of the month, Gibson and his crew had carried out four long cross-country practices but only eight exercises in total, and were about to move into the final phase of exercises specifically designed to prepare for Operation Chastise. All were with a standard Lancaster, as none of the 464 (Provisioning) aircraft arrived for almost three weeks and, at the end of March, the Squadron Operations Record Book admitted that '617 is not, as yet, a complete Squadron'.

Flight Lieutenant J.L. Munro flew a 2hr 5mins 'low level X country' day exercise on 31 March, which the front gunner Sergeant Howarth noted was 'the first of 31 training flights carried out before the raid itself'. Between 1 and 6 April, five 'low level X country and bombing' exercises lasting between 3hrs 25 mins and 5 hrs 25mins were undertaken. Munro's first night 'low level X country' took 4hrs 35 mins on 11 April. Interspersed with short 'air firing and bombing', 'bombing' and 'night tactics' exercises before the end of the month, Munro and his crew flew six cross country exercises, two of them at night, the longest being 5hrs 15mins.

Sergeant D.P. Heal, Brown's navigator, recorded that his crew flew its first exercise on 31 March, and, using six different aircraft, during April completed a total of 38hrs 10mins by day and 12 hours at night in 18 training flights. During April, Pilot Officer G. Rice carried out 19 practice flights, twice with 'boffins on board to carry out R/T tests'. The log book of Sergeant C. Brennan, Flight Lieutenant J.V. Hopgood's flight engineer, reveals that between 21 and 30 April that crew flew four day and two night exercises. The Squadron medical officer, Flying Officer M.W. Arthurton, 'quickly' became aware that 617 was 'very different from that of the other night bomber squadrons. It involved a tremendous amount of low flying all over the country, whereas normal bomber squadrons flew at considerably greater heights ... I knew that apart from learning to fly at very low levels over water and land it was most important that they learned ... to maintain a very steady height of 50ft [sic] above the water'.

Pilot Officer Rice remembered particularly what he called 'the Scottish cross-country run'. It involved flying eastwards from Scampton to Mablethorpe on the North Sea coast, north-west to Montrose, Inverness, down the Caledonian Canal to the Mull of Kintyre, Rathin Island off the north coast of Northern Ireland, Isle of Man, Shrewsbury and back to Scampton. McCarthy's bomb-aimer, Sergeant Oancia, using his log book entries, reflected: 'Referring to the cross country exercises, I note that they are numbered and each exercise had a different number which confirms my recollections that they were over different routes and I do recall these routes covered flying over dams and lakes and including some exercises of low level flying over the Welsh Mountains on the sea coast.'

Flight Sergeant W.C. Townsend flew his first 'low level cross-country – bombing' flight with 617 Squadron on 4 April and during that month the crew completed 19 exercises. In May before Operation Chastise, he and his crew flew 12 more apart from 12 May, when Townsend went on 'exercise' with Flight Lieutenant Munro; in reality, to drop a practice Upkeep at Reculver.

Between 6 and 21 April, Flight Lieutenant Shannon and his crew flew seven lengthy cross-country exercises, varying in length between 4hrs 5 mins and 5hrs 25mins; that on 21 April 'night as day'. In addition, one 'fighter affiliation' session and a low-level flight to Wainfleet bombing range occurred.

After the operation itself, Flying Officer B.T. Foxlee DFM RAAF, Martin's front gunner, declared, 'don't forget the "penguins"', the non-flyers, 'who made the whole operation successful' and crucially 'the ground staff'. Leading Aircraftman Victor Gill, who had serviced McCarthy's Lancaster at Woodhall Spa, was a mechanic who survived Powell's clear-out, having arrived at Scampton on 26 March. He was, like Leading Aircraftman Munro, accommodated in a wooden hut and had to walk in all weathers to a detached hut for washing facilities, which was 'normal'. The following day, 27 March, Gibson addressed the ground crew in a hangar, 'laying down fairly heavily about rumour and speculation'. Emphasising need for absolute security, he expected '100% commitment and dedication'. Gill recalled that ground crew were allocated to the two flights on an alphabetical bases. He therefore found himself attached to A Flight, stationed closer to the hangar, south of the perimeter track, where the hard stands for the aircraft were situated. B Flight was about ½ mile to the left or west.

Leading Aircraftman Munro, the radar specialist who had organised daily keep-fit sessions in his hut, summarised his contribution, indirectly underlining the administrative disorder discovered by Flight Sergeant Powell: 'We were finally able to locate the area designated for airborne radar in a barren room about 18ft long by 5ft wide inside the N E corner of the Squadron hangar. Our work area was a bench about 6ft long. Our tool kits, I recall, consisted of a large wrench and an oversized screwdriver.

617 SQUADRON PREPARES

This was useless for our needs. We had a couple of Petrol-Electric generator sets we could wheel around to the different aircraft. We were able to do "D[aily] I[nspection]s" by running up the equipment to the aircraft ... It was our constant hope on each run-up that nothing of a major nature would "go on the fritz" since we were not in a position to rectify it. However, within a matter of a few days the spares and tools began to arrive. This situation was repeated in all ground trades – making do – until the arrival of supplies. The efficiency and tempo picked up as more equipment and parts arrived'.

Munro noted:

> The work was indeed unique. Instead of the normal Squadron routine where you phone through at 8am to see if you were on "ops" – if the answer was "yes" you'd quickly go about your D.I. routine, if "no", your approach hadn't the sense of urgency about it. We were required not to do just a regular D.I., but a continuous round of maintenance before and after day and night flying. In other words, ground maintenance took place all through the hours of daylight under the constant feeling of deadlines. A side effect of the seemingly perpetual activity was the extremely rapid build-up of a camaraderie between the ground and air crew. Our original aircraft were flown so steadily that there was a feeling that they were being flown into total fatigue. This was borne out by discovery of an air frame mechanic, while making a routine inspection, that a crack had developed in the main spar of Les Munro's aircraft. The comment was made at the time that if he had taken off once more on a low-level practice, the aircraft would not have returned.

Munro's aircraft appears to have had other structural adventures. The bomb-aimer, Sergeant Clay, recalled that, 'when landing at Scampton after an early morning training session, the undercarriage collapsed and we slid along on our belly. I was sitting in the nose at the time, but no one was hurt'.

The low-level exercises intrigued LAC Munro. 'Coming from a no-nonsense Squadron [97], where I recall they demoted a Sergeant Pilot to LAC and grounded him for two weeks because he flew around his girlfriend's house in Carlisle, it was quite exhilarating to realize that our boys were flying at ground-level with official sanction. If any of the crew in a particular aircraft were unable to fly, we were able at times to be included

THE DAMBUSTERS: 'WAS THE RAID WORTHWHILE?'

in their cross-country navigational practices. I was flying with Mickey Martin on one particular day that I remember. We passed what seemed to be an ancestral home, on the brow of a gently rising hill, at such low level that I was able to look almost directly into the drawing-room windows. I believe this was somewhere in the Yorkshire Wold'.

'Off duty, a popular meeting place of both ground crew and air crew was the Salvation Army Canteen that was situated on the grounds south of the guard house. There was quite a lively exchange of conversation between the personnel of 57 Squadron [on regular ops] and our own. "57" would insist that they were carrying on the war effort, while our non-operation was totally suspect. It was quite frustrating to keep calm throughout, without revealing the Squadron's actions. This was accentuated by Gibson himself who, as I recall, assembled us in the hangar on a frequency of about twice a week. He would address us regarding security and made "no bones about it", in his statements. I remember him saying "if any personnel is caught talking about anything that was taking place on the Squadron, he would be court-martialled and shot"'.

Flight mechanic Leading Aircraftman Arthur Drury recalled that due to his 'knowledge of machine work, I was put to work on a lathe and did the station turning ... in the station workshops'. This brought him into direct contact with 617 Squadron once the Upkeeps began to arrive:

> My work involved machine work on the bouncing bombs. These appear to have been brought onto the station from the place of manufacture, as each bomb was complete. When they arrived on the station, work began on them to get each one operationally ready for the raid. This involved centrifugally balancing the bombs as they were hung under a modified Lancaster, in a frame which held two bearings on which the bomb was revolved prior to dropping into the dam. The first I remember of this work, I was given an order for the requisition of steel plate from Ruston Hornsby's Boiler Works in Lincoln. As far as I can remember, they measured about 8ins x 6ins x 1¼ ins thick. On arrival at the station, I had to mark out and drill two holes in each piece of plate. The plate was then taken and bolted on to the lighter side of the bomb. If the plate proved too heavy to balance the bomb centrifugally, the plate was taken off, brought back into the machine shop and I had the job of machining metal off the plate to reduce weight.

617 SQUADRON PREPARES

> This was done a number of times until the bomb was correctly balanced. No matter what time of day the bomb arrived, this operation was started immediately, and whatever job I had in the lathe, this had to be stopped and the plates machined – much to my annoyance. Along with the plates, I had to machine a few one thousandth part of an inch off a brass cup, which was part of the fuse gear to these bombs.

Once the need for haste almost landed Drury in disciplinary trouble:

> Not knowing the urgency of this work, I almost got myself on a technical charge for refusing to carry out an order from a senior NCO. One of these brass cups was brought into the machine shop, just as I was about to go to lunch, by the Sergeant Armourer. He asked me to start on the machine work and I told him that it could wait until after lunch, to which he replied that I had a choice of doing the machining at once or be escorted to the guard room and be locked up awaiting a technical charge. I chose the former and had a late lunch!

Due to the pressure of time, civilian employees of Vickers and Avro were deployed to Scampton to carry out some of the work originally allocated to the firms' own facilities. Writing to Margaret Dove, Chadwick's daughter, forty years later a Rolls-Royce supervisor, C.E. Brennan, revealed that workmen from that firm were also sent to the RAF station to deal with engine adjustments. For 'about three weeks' before the raid, Brennan was detached to Scampton 'modifying and bringing the Lancasters up to scratch'; the 464 (Provisioning) aircraft which arrived at intervals between 8 April and 13 May. 'It was a really hectic time.'

Noting that the third week of training, ending 15 April, had 'seen the end of most teething troubles', Gibson nevertheless highlighted a particular peril of low flying. One aircraft had been grounded for a week for repairs after 'collision with a bird' had 'smashed the perspex panel of the Bomb Aimer's compartment'. Indeed, smooth running of the training programme could not always be achieved. On 22 April, cross country exercises had to be curtailed, 'weather hopeless', and the following day all flying was cancelled for the same reason. In Gibson's summary of the fourth week of training, apart from detailing the nature and number of exercises carried out, he explained that with one of the two gunners deployed in the front turret throughout the operation, a stirrup system would be devised to keep his legs from obstructing the bomb-aimer positioned below him. Gibson also assured Whitworth that crews were now proficient at map reading by night, flying over water at 150ft and carrying out 'the special type of attack'. So, on 24 April, Cochrane informed HQ Bomber Command that the 617 Squadron training programme had been so successful that 'it is not considered that the operation will present any special difficulties'.

Six days later, Gibson confirmed once more to Whitworth, that all crews were able to navigate from pinpoint to pinpoint at low level at night, bomb accurately and fly safely over water at 150ft. More than 1,000 hours had been flown in training and the Squadron's complement was now 58 officers and 481 other ranks. However, due to need for 'local modifications to the new aircraft' only nine of the twelve so far received were currently available. He emphasised that the precise form of Upkeep was not yet known to the Squadron.

There had been complications other than adverse weather and availability of aircraft. Initially, crews used the normal ground targets at the Wainfleet bombing range. Sergeant D.E. Webb recalled bombing a yellow triangle target on the ground, while three startled men were still on it. Flight Sergeant Sumpter remembered that often a single pole was used. On 11 April Gibson reported that 'two white cricket boards' (30ft x 20ft) to represent towers on a dam would be erected 'to promote range sighting by day and night'. Sergeant S. Oancia recalled that, on 25 April, Flight Lieutenant McCarthy's crew carried out 'the first practice bombing run on the "sighting boards".' The very next day, a gale blew them down, and they were replaced by flags. Gibson informed Whitworth on 7 May, that this had resulted in bombing accuracy being reduced to 52 per cent, and steps would be taken to re-erect 'the boards' without delay.

During training, individual crews developed their own method of operation. Sergeant J.H. Clay, Flight Lieutenant Munro's bomb-aimer, who like all other bomb-aimers on this operation would assist the navigator with map reading, swiftly realised that to identify a feature 'immediately below' was 'well nigh impossible ... The trick was 1) to keep your map(s) orientated, 2) pick out salient features ahead, 3) pass the pinpoint to the pilot and navigator, 4) mark your map and check back'. Clay and Flying Officer F.G. Rumbles (the navigator) maintained that, due to the peculiar circumstances, 'it was more of a team effort' with the gunners also helping out. Stories of horses bolting and cyclists being deposited in thorny hedgerows in terror were possibly fanciful, but there is no doubt that the Lancasters were flown unusually low. Clay explained:

617 SQUADRON PREPARES

> Some of us, most likely all, had done some low level training in the normal course of our education ... but low level with 617 was really low and dicey. I have seen people working in Lincolnshire fields lie flat as we passed ... The exercises took us along various canals and many a time whilst lying in the nose, I have looked to port and starboard wing tip to see by how much they were missing the embankment and looking ahead for high-tension cables to climb up over. But Les Munro was unbelievable and steady as a rock.

On one occasion, Squadron Leader Maudslay returned from an exercise 'with foliage somewhere under the rear of his undercarriage', according to Clay. Rice recalled that, apart from the initial crew interview with him, as Gibson was away from the squadron so much, 'I saw very little of him until near the end.' But once, in the hangar they were both shown a Lancaster, which had returned from an exercise with four bolts meant to secure the outer panels of the centre section sheered off. Rice thought it 'probably due to stress caused by constant buffeting at low-level'. Both Flight Sergeant L.J. Sumpter and Sergeant F. Tees confirmed that 'thermals at low-level led to unpleasant turbulence'. In a letter to his girlfriend in Nottingham, Flying Officer C.R. Williams illustrated the perils of 'flying low' in recounting that Flight Lieutenant Barlow's aircraft ran 'into a flock of birds, some of which came through the windscreen of the plane and caused the pilot to lose control of the plane for a few seconds. We hit the top of a tree, but it did not do any damage and we were able to continue our journey'; seemingly not the incident referred to by Gibson.

Flight Sergeant G.A. Chalmers, Flight Sergeant Townsend's wireless operator, explained that:

> at the outset life was a bit boring. With no set aircraft to fly, we just hung about getting to know one another, discussing the kind of target it might be. Even when we saw our first modified Lancaster, we never came close to guessing the right answer. Soon flying started at low-level and take-offs in a Vic formation of three. Maintaining Vs in flight was a new experience for us and required a great deal of skill by our pilot. Altogether, I found it quite exciting. We flew practice low-level flights all over the country and the North Sea and became quite used to it. There were some hilarious and dangerous moments flying at around 100 feet above the ground. It soon appeared that this

was not low enough for the purpose of our mission and we had radio altimeters fitted ... During all this training, we were often called to the Ops Room by the station tannoy and each time I thought tonight's the night. But it was more and more lectures about security.

Sergeant G.L. Johnson also found the low-level flying 'exhilarating', though admitted that in the process tulips were often flattened. He recalled an unauthorised manoeuvre at Sutton Bridge, where crews 'flew under cables and over the bridge'. The exuberance of Townsend, though, gained him a reprimand: 'I once took off very low over the Officers' Mess and did a split-arse turn over Group Captain Whitworth's house. Almost immediately, I was ordered to land and report to the Control Tower. There I was sent to the OC's office, where Gibson really tore me off a strip. Then he said, "good show, keep it up"'. During one exercise, which entailed flying over the North Sea, Sergeant G.L. Johnson, McCarthy's bomb aimer, spotted a dinghy with men in it. RAF Scampton was alerted and Air Sea Rescue duly informed. Johnson subsequently had the satisfaction of learning that the three occupants of the dinghy had been brought to safety.

Creating artificial darkness during daytime flights proved hard. Satterly's suggestion on 27 March of wearing dark glasses was not successful. Nor was the issue of tinted, wire-framed Livingston goggles to bomb-aimers 'to accustom them to map reading in synthetic moonlight', noted by Gibson in his report to Whitworth for the week-ending 8 April. The Air Ministry, therefore, decided to install an adaptation of USAAF (United States Army Air Force) equipment to simulate darkness during the day. This lengthy process involved clipping tinted celluloid panels inside the framework of the cockpit windows and, Sergeant G.L. Johnson confirmed, the bomb-aimer's compartment. The first 617 Squadron flight with the new arrangement occurred on 11 April and Gibson reported: 'There is no doubt that this equipment is the answer to all night map reading problems'. By 16 April, the adapted Lancaster had been flown for 25 hours and Gibson enthused that, 'the system is most efficient'. Reflecting the Air Ministry's intention, he added, 'it is hoped to equip five more aircraft by the end of the next fortnight'.

Gibson himself does not appear to have made use of this equipment until 21 April for a 'local' one-hour test and, four days later, during an extended cross-country exercise attacking Welsh dams. On 30 April, Gibson informed Whitworth that two adapted standard Lancasters were

617 SQUADRON PREPARES

now in regular use and it seems doubtful whether any more were modified. In his post-operational summary on 7 June 1943, Cochrane referred to two 'normal' Lancasters being fitted with Bexoid night-day synthetic equipment. The Air Officer Commanding had been impressed from an early stage, on 17 April informing Sir Arthur Harris: 'We have developed special coloured Perspex for the Lancasters in No 617 Squadron, which simulates moonlight conditions with great success and I feel that after a month's training the Squadron should be able to find its way to any reasonable landmark within range, and do so with less than the normal risk of casualties.'

Flight Lieutenant Shannon's bomb-aimer, Flight Sergeant L.J. Sumpter, found that on removing the coloured goggles outside the aircraft 'everything was red', so he learnt to put on dark glasses until he felt comfortable. Nevertheless, he blamed this exercise for permanently damaging his eyesight. On 27 April, Munro flew for 1hr 55mins 'X country' in daylight, with 'blue perspex and glasses'. In Flight Lieutenant McCarthy's machine, Sergeant G.L. Johnson experienced 'a glare' when the goggles were removed and, like Sumpter, quickly learnt to put on sun glasses. Post-war, Munro elaborated intriguingly on the installation of the equipment, revealing that this was the second version. 'In the first, amber screens were fitted round the cockpit with the crew members wearing blue goggles', which proved 'unsatisfactory ... [and] caused headaches ... The change to blue screens and amber goggles proved a better combination'. He recalled that 'the whole cockpit canopy was fitted with the blue screens'. He held that the system was 'reasonably effective in simulating moonlight conditions and did, I believe, prove a satisfactory transition from daylight to night time conditions'. Many years later, Pilot Officer Rice reflected on 'The Bexold Day-Night Synthetic Equipment', but seemed only to remember the first arrangement, 'Two Stage Amber'. 'The system using coloured screens and goggles ... consisted of amber screens on the windows and side windows, and the crew wore blue tinted goggles, with three grades of tint in interchangeable lenses to give varying degrees of intensity.' When flying with this arrangement during training, Rice always took a second pilot and not every time his whole crew. Similarly, Flight Lieutenant Munro's front gunner, Sergeant W. Howarth, recalled: 'For daytime flights we progressed to flying with the windows covered with orange coloured perspex and the pilot wearing blue goggles to simulate moonlight.'

Quite who was responsible for installing aspects of the equipment remains obscure. Retrospectively engine fitter, Corporal J. Bryden, wrote that blue celluloid was fitted in the Scampton workshops, which might suggest that it replaced the amber screens on the original two aircraft.

Another arrangement, which caused problems during training was the so-called Dann Sight. Because at low-level thermals caused severe buffeting and Sumpter required one hand to activate the bomb-release mechanism, he could not use two to steady the sight: 'those wooden handmade sights with nails for sighting, I thought very chancy. A good thick line of chinagraph was, in my eyes, much easier to line up on.' So he and the navigator, Flying Officer D.R. Walker DFC RCAF, worked out a system involving two chinagraph marks on the clear vision panel with string attached to the retaining screws on each side drawn back to the bridge of Sumpter's nose. Lying full length on the floor, he could thus achieve a stable position during the bombing run. Pilot Officer L.G. Knight's bomb-aimer, Flying Officer E.C. Johnson, devised a similar arrangement, as the navigator Pilot Officer H.S. Hobday recalled: 'Johnny was very proud of the special bomb-sight we invented. Instead of the one provided, which was in the form of a small wooden triangle sighted on the dam towers to get the correct distance, he used a piece of string for an "eyepiece" and grease-pencil lines on the front perspex of his compartment, which gave a larger triangle with very much greater accuracy'.

Johnson himself explained: 'I didn't decide the hand-held sight was useless, but I did decide that a more practical device was possible with the chance of more accuracy under operational conditions. The principle was the same of reproducing inside the aircraft a proportional triangle of the one to be attained externally. But mine could be much larger and in my opinion much more easily managed.' Clay, Munro's bomb-aimer, used the retaining screws of the clear vision panel and held the attached string at a predetermined length to his right eye. He released practice weapons, when eye, screws and target were in line. Nevertheless, some crews, retained the triangular contraption. In Hopgood's Lancaster, Flight Sergeant J.W. Fraser described it as 'a wooden box with two points on it, which moved outwards as the aircraft approached the target and when they coincided with the two practice structures, I pressed the tit'. He calculated that the base of the isosceles triangle was 6in wide, the height of the peep-hole and two nails was 9in.

In acknowledging that the Dann Sight had not been altogether successful, on 7 May in his weekly report to Whitworth, Gibson gave the impression that it had been abandoned by all crews. 'A new and simpler form of range

617 SQUADRON PREPARES

finding sight had been adopted, this within the sides of the clear vision panel (or marks adjacent to it) as the foresight and two pieces of string ... which are stretched to the eye ... This has proved more accurate and easier to use at night than the small hand-held range finder.' On 30 April, he had informed Whitworth that 'from 5 May onwards' exercises involving ten aircraft at a time would be carried out at 60ft. On the day that Gibson phoned Wallis to inform him that this height could be achieved, 1 May, an entry in his log book recorded that he and Squadron Leader Young flew from Scampton to Manston, suggesting that the two officers witnessed the trial that day.

Between 30 April and 6 May, 31 exercises were flown involving 168 bombing attacks at Wainfleet. Twenty live cylindrical Upkeeps would be ready for balancing within three days and more practice ones had been stripped and balanced for use by the Squadron at Reculver 'on or about 10, 12 and 13 May'. All leave would be stopped from 12.00 hours on Friday 7 May.

On 14 April, the civilian scientist, Benjamin Lockspeiser, had told a progress meeting at the Ministry of Aircraft Production in London that six sets of 'spotlight altimeters' (Aldis lamps) would be installed 'under RAE guidance' by 16 April. He hoped that the balance would be ready for fitting by 'about 25 April' and noted that installation of each would require two man-days of work. On 7 April, Squadron Leader Maudslay had flown a 464 (Provisioning) Lancaster to Farnborough for the lamps to be fitted. After testing them over The Wash, he demonstrated the system to a sceptical audience at Scampton. But he convinced Gibson that it should be fitted to all 617 Squadron Lancasters; hence Lockspeiser's announcement a week later.

Gibson informed Whitworth, on 22 April, that only four aircraft had been equipped with the new apparatus and ten crews were 'proficient in its use ... Trials have been carried out in all conditions of weather, but it is not yet possible to find a glass calm'. A week later, at a meeting attended by Wallis, he revealed that 'the fitting and positioning' of the lamps, under RAE supervision, was being undertaken in the Squadron workshops at Scampton. The plan was for all the operational aircraft to be suitably modified by 10 May, just nine days before the cut-off date, which had been advanced from 26 May. Navigator, Pilot Officer Howard, was not initially impressed, registering that 'horror came with the arrival of a simple device to get the correct height – two lights under the fuselage angled down'.

THE DAMBUSTERS: 'WAS THE RAID WORTHWHILE?'

A special exercise connected with the Spotlight Altimeter took place at Scampton. Lockspeiser explained that crews would be required to dive their Lancasters at a predetermined spot short of a target dam to acquire an attacking speed, 40mph in excess of that flown on the approach over enemy territory. So white lines were drawn on the grass runway area to show where crews would dive, level out and pull up at a second set to represent climbing steeply after dropping Upkeep. The lines proved difficult to identify, so large tarpaulins were substituted. Flight engineer, Pilot Officer Whittaker, recalled that it was his task to supervise these activities armed with a theodolite. Once Aldis lamps had been fitted, this process was adapted to practise their use before setting off on exercises over canals, lakes or The Wash. Sergeant R.E. Grayston, Pilot Officer Knight's flight engineer, reflected on a particular complication early in the diving exercises: 'The engines of the Mk I Lancasters tended to cut out, but the problem disappeared with the arrival of the Mk III fitted with an American carburettor.' Flight Sergeant Townsend's front gunner, Sergeant D.E. Webb, remembered diving from 1,500–60ft and the pilot having to watch he did not sink to the ground as he straightened out. Sergeant J.H. Clay thought this 'a particularly nasty type of exercise'.

Arrangements were also made to devise practice locations to prepare crews more specifically for both the routes to and from the targets and the targets themselves. 'Uppingham Lake', the Eyebrook reservoir with a straight wall at its southern end and supplying water for the Stewart and Lloyd steel works at Corby, was chosen to represent the Moehne. Years later, Sir Ralph Cochrane revealed, slightly inaccurately, that its use had been secured 'by taking the manager of the local steel works out for a slap up lunch'. On learning belatedly of this subterfuge, the manager of the Corby (Northants) and District Water Company, Mr G.C.S. Oliver and directly responsible for the reservoir, deeply regretted that he had not been the beneficiary of such 'bribery and corruption'. On 3 May 1943, Mr G. Le Mare, director of the water company, met RAF representatives, who 'explained that they wanted a sheet of water for special and urgent tests for some new device during the next three weeks. On their assurance that they would drop nothing, fire nothing and damage nothing, I said we would do anything they wanted'. So the following day, a Service party erected 'four special canvas targets, approximately 20ft x 12ft ... on the top of the dam on poles fixed in barrels of concrete'. The four 'targets' were grouped in two linked together by camouflage 'scrim', unknown to Le Mare, Oliver or any other employee representing the two towers on the Moehne. At

617 SQUADRON PREPARES

16.00 hours on 4 May, the first low-level attack on the simulated towers took place. The next day, Oliver recorded: 'Lancaster bombers have been flying low over the reservoir last night and to-day. They fly between two targets which are put up on the dam. The targets are light structures and are in no way doing any harm'.

Local residents were not so relaxed at the regular interruptions to their night's sleep, as the columns of the local press demonstrated. 'The house shook as the plane, making a deafening noise, passed overhead' and caused his wife to dive under the table, complained one correspondent. Another dubbed 'the roar' of the aircraft 'frightening'. Spectators, however, gathered in the road to witness the flying displays during which 'purple flares' were discharged as each machine cleared the dam wall. When one of the targets was blown down, it was re-erected by water company personnel under RAF direction.

No similar negotiations appear to have occurred concerning the Abberton reservoir, in relevant documents described as 'Colchester Lake', situated three miles south of Colchester, Essex. Its dam, carrying the Abberton to Maldon Road, lay just south of the Layer-de-la-Haye pumping station. It had no towers, but in relation geographically to the Eyebrook as the Moehne proved an ideal substitute for the Eder Dam. Local resident, Mr A.A. Lowes, recalled that the road was closed for night time, low-level flights. From a distance, aircraft could be seen firing 'a flare' as they crossed the dam before climbing steeply beyond.

The pace of practice did not flag in May. In the first week, A Flight flew 39hrs 35 mins by day, 34hrs 15mins at night, during which 50 practice bombs were dropped, often at the end of a cross-country run. Following exercises with the Aldis lamps over The Wash in April, on 3 May 'all pilots' carried out 'spotlight runs over aerodrome'. The following day, Gibson flew to Manston, almost certainly to discuss the test pilots' change of direction to attack the Reculver promenade at right angles. Three days later, he took his own crew to Manston to familiarise it with the procedure. Apart from these administrative flights, he and his crew completed four exercises. The entry in his log book for 5 May notes a three-hour long 'Special Night Attack' using the simulated 'blue yellow' equipment. The previous day, he had declared the TR 1196 R/T set 'completely unsatisfactory' at low-level. Air-to-ground reception had proved satisfactory, but air-to-air, especially at night, despite adjustments had not. Following contact from 5 Group, HQ Bomber Command recommended Type TR 1143 used in fighters. Cochrane, paying tribute to the RAE Radio Department and No 26 (Signals) Group, would reveal, 'the fact that all aircraft were fitted with VHF by 1730hrs in Sunday 9 May indicates the drive and enthusiasm with which this apparently impossible task was handled'. That evening, flying separately, Maudslay and Young verified the set's suitability, although Cochrane acknowledged that 'some modifications' were subsequently necessary.

On 1 May, Flight Lieutenant Munro and his crew undertook an interesting 3hr 15mins daylight exercise: 'Wings for Victory beat up of Horncastle-X country-bombing'. The following day came a 'night tactics' flight, repeated on 5 May, following a 2hr 'X country – bombing' exercise. A 1hr 40mins daylight 'X country-bombing' excursion the next day was followed by 2hrs 15mins night 'bombing-X country-tactics'. Munro carried out a daylight 'air firing – bombing' exercise on 8 May. Meanwhile, on 4 May, Flight Sergeant Brown and Pilot Officer Divall completed 'blue yellow' flights and on 6 May, it was Shannon's turn during a 2hrs 50 mins 'X country' flight. The day, 5 May, that he flew with Gibson on a 'blue yellow' exercise, Young covered a prolonged cross-country route culminating in 'bombing and spotlight runs' and the following night covered the Midlands area, while Divall went to Wainfleet and Colchester.

Flight Lieutenant R.N.G. Barlow, recorded a lengthy flight on 7 May, which included both Uppingham and Colchester lakes; the same day that Pilot Officer W.H.T. Ottley flew over 'Uppingham Lake'. Pilot Officer Rice's crew, undertook 7 exercises 3-14 May, between 1 and 14 May, Flight Lieutenant Hopgood fourteen. His navigator's log book showed that Flight Sergeant Brown carried out 8 flights between 3 and 14 May, 12hrs 10mins by day and 12hrs 55 mins at night, on 11 May flying ED 918 (his raid machine) for the first time. Gibson's log book records that, on 8 May, he was flown to Manston in an Airspeed Oxford, presumably to discuss progress.

Flight Sergeant T.D. Simpson, Martin's rear gunner, emphasised that 'the training was very intensive and security very tight'. In his diary on 22 April he wrote: 'Bags of security gen and various threats to those who are found from now on speaking or writing about our job'. The medical officer, Flying Officer M.W. Arthurton, agreed that security was 'very rigid as I can remember when I endeavoured to phone a member of my family who was ill, I think on the actual night of the operation'. Section Officer Ann Fowler recalled that she had arrived at Scampton with incomplete documentation and 'under suspicion' confined to the station until the omission had been rectified. Section Officer Fay Gillan, who would deal with complaints from civilians and be responsible for informing 5 Group HQ of training

617 SQUADRON PREPARES

programme details, was initially confronted by Gibson with 'can you keep a secret?' At one point she was obliged to warn Gibson that another new intelligence officer had returned from a visit to the Air Ministry and stated that he knew the target. He was strangely reticent after a visit to the OC's office.

An incandescent Gibson filed an official complaint, on 2 May, after the Squadron armament officer Pilot Officer H. Watson returned from a prolonged visit to RAF Manston, where he had seen 'sectional drawings of certain objectives, a map of the Ruhr showing these objectives and various secret sketches in connection with Upkeep'. He, therefore, knew more about the impending operation than Gibson himself. Moreover, he understood that Squadron Leader Rose, who was flying Mosquito trials connected with Highball, and an officer from the Marine Aircraft Experimental Establishment (MAEE) also shared this information, which heightened the risk of a security breach with 'most distressing results'. In forwarding the complaint formally to Bomber Command, Cochrane underlined that only he, Satterly, Whitworth and Gibson knew any details of the operation: 'No other member of the Squadron has been told, nor will they know until they are briefed for the operation'. He was extremely concerned that the MAEE officer had 'a most secret file, which he has been showing to Junior Officers'. The AOC 5 Group thought this 'criminal'. In forwarding Cochrane's furious reaction to Air Vice-Marshal Bottomley at the Air Ministry, Saundby emphasised that, 'incidents such as this let down those of us, who are trying to "play the game" by drastically restricting the number of people in the know and make our preservation look absurd'. On 6 May, Bottomley assured Saundby that 'appropriate action' had been taken. Thus Gibson had full support for his insistence on tight security.

Within 617 Squadron, Pilot Officer C.L. Howard agreed that such measures were 'absolutely justified' and Pilot Officer I. Whittaker insisted that with so much at stake Gibson could 'neither tolerate inefficiency nor any hint of slackness'. But he also 'fiercely defended' members of the Squadron, co-operating with the medical staff to post as 'sick' anybody suspected of 'lack of moral fibre', which Flying Officer M.W. Arthurton, the 617 Squadron medical officer, confirmed: 'I remember one member of the air crew who reported sick and was obviously unable to contemplate taking the strain of this particular type of work and with his permission I approached Wing Commander Gibson. He immediately had this officer posted to another unit and there was no ill feeling on either side, as far as I could tell.'

THE DAMBUSTERS: 'WAS THE RAID WORTHWHILE?'

Pilot Officer T. Bennett, in the Operations Room at 5 Group HQ in Grantham, revealed how tight security concerning the operation was there. Bennett recalled:

> We were aware that "Gibby" was forming a new squadron ... [but] not one word of the Dams' Raid leaked into any section of the Headquarters. Group Captain Satterly was Senior Air Staff Officer at the time and, quite often, Air Vice-Marshal Cochrane, Satterley and "Gibby" were closeted together ... the general assumption was that "Gibby" was helping form a new Main Force squadron, and was being given a leavening of really experienced personnel to help get it off on the right foot ... Even during the actual raid, the target was referred to solely by its code name. Wing Commander "Mary" Tudor was absolutely flabbergasted when the operation was all over and the actual scope was revealed. I am sure that he felt a little aggrieved to think that even his standing as Officer Commanding Operations Room had not entitled him to be on the "inside". However, he was but one of many senior officers somewhat chagrined by the whole affair.

In the Air Ministry, aware that details of at least some of the experiments might leak out, the Director of Intelligence (Security) had concocted an inventive cover story, which hinted at overseas use by multiple units. 'The weapon is a special type of mine and the wooden casing surrounding it is provided for protection in handling. This is particularly necessary as the mine is designed for use in localities where it will be manhandled by native labour. The spinning device is in connection with the fusing, which is effected by centrifugal action. The uses of the weapon are in the main anti-submarine, but it will also function against shipping. Units armed with the weapon are to be known as Special Mining Squadrons.'

In the second week of May, at 5 Group HQ Satterly put the finishing touches to the Operation Order. On the 10th, Squadron Leader F. Fawssett from Bomber Command sent information about the Eder Dam. A satellite station of RAF Medmenham at Phyllis Court, Henley, had constructed models of the Moehne and Sorpe dams, which reached Grantham by mid-April and would be transported to Scampton before the final briefings. Unfortunately, the Eder model would not be finished until 17 May, twenty-four hours too late. So Fawssett's data became crucial. He placed the towers

617 SQUADRON PREPARES

at the Eder 750ft apart, 639ft at the Moehne. There were no detectable defences at the Eder, but the 'tent-shaped' roofs of the Moehne towers had been removed for the installation of a platform approximately 20 x 15ft on which a single light flak gun had been mounted. A third 20m gun was positioned on the flat surface of a buttress to the right of the right-hand tower for an aircraft approaching over the reservoir. Beyond the dam and north of the equalising basin, three more light flak guns were located, each on a 'slightly raised square' roughly 18 x 18ft and surrounded by a wall of sandbags. Although they could not be entirely ruled out, no searchlights had been detected. A double-line boom with timber spreaders, possibly attached to the north shore but not 'visibly' the southern one, floated on the reservoir 100–300ft from the dam. The distance between the two lines with their underwater anti-torpedo nets varied between 10 and 12ft.

Armed with this and all other available details, including that from reconnaissance flights, Satterly completed his draft operation order and despatched it that day, 10 May, to Whitworth at RAF Scampton. It was, he explained, the only copy in existence 'written as you can see in my own fair hand'. He would later reveal that he had gradually composed it over a period of time and locked the uncompleted version in a safe, when not being worked on. Satterly further asked Whitworth: 'Will you please get down to it right away with Gibson and either re-write it completely to suit yourselves or pin on it slips of paper giving any amendments you want to suggest?' He did not want the original draft altered, so that it could be more easily compared to the proposals. So that sufficient time could be allowed for typing and distribution, the draft order and comments should be returned to him 'personally' no later than 14.00 hours on Wednesday 12 May. This was a tight schedule considering that Gibson and his crew were committed to dropping a practice Upkeep at Reculver on 11 May.

In a typed response, further amended by hand, Gibson did suggest a number of changes and additions, not all of which were accepted. He also laid out his proposed order of battle, which would be changed significantly before the raid mainly due to the unavailability of two pilots. The first nine, led by him, would take off in sections of three at 21.55, 22.05 and 22.15 hours and each set course 5 minutes later. The second wave, designed to back-up the first and be prepared to attack all the designated targets, comprising Nos. 10–15, would take off singly at three minute intervals between 22.18 and 22.33 hours, setting course at 22.21 to 22.36 hours. In the event, this wave would leave after the other two and act as a mobile reserve. The third wave (second on the night), Nos. 16–20, would attack

'Target C (Sorpe) only' and take off between 22.05 and 22.25 hours. This complicated, overlapping take-off procedure would be simplified before the operation.

The line-up envisaged 20 attacking aircraft with one in reserve. The unavailability of two crews allocated to the back-up wave led to a reshuffle with two of that wave moved into the first wave, two from the draft first wave into the Sorpe wave and two from the Sorpe (2nd) wave into the 3rd back-up one. The crews of both Flight Lieutenant Wilson and Pilot Officer Divall featured in Gibson's draft line of battle on 12 May, which indicates that the changes became necessary at a very late stage. Divall flew three exercises 4–6 May, Wilson five 1–5 May. However, Wilson's inclusion at all puzzled the medical officer Flying Officer M.W. Arthurton. 'I do not remember the sickness details relating to Pilot Officer Divall's crew, but Flight Lieutenant Wilson himself had not been well for some considerable time prior to the raid ... [and] my only "brush" with Wing Commander Gibson resulted from his suggestion that Flight Lieutenant Wilson and his crew should spend a fortnight on a destroyer for convalescence! I disagreed and I am glad to say my opinion was respected.'

The intensity of activity in the immediate run-up to the operation was such that, apart from the final night exercise on 14 May and dropping Upkeep at Reculver, from the beginning of May Flight Lieutenant Shannon's crew carried out eight 'cross country + bombing' exercises and one air test. During the second week of May, several crews practised at Reculver. Before he responded to Satterly, flying G for George his raid aircraft, on 11 May Gibson was one of three crews (with Hopgood and Martin) to attack the simulated targets at right angles like Longbottom and Handasyde earlier. He recorded: 'Upkeep dropped at 60ft. Good run of 600yds.' In his diary, Wallis wrote: '3.30pm proceeded Reculver to see 3 Squadron m/cs drop on range at 6pm. 100% successful'.

Possibly, Air Commodore S.O. Bufton was also present, for Wallis and he dined together that evening and 'discussed method of attack'. Early the next morning, 12 May, Wallis 'left for London' to discuss problems with the release of Highball by Mosquitoes, so missed Shannon (with Barlow as second pilot), Knight and Munro (with Townsend) similarly exercising at Reculver. The sight of Upkeep, described by an unidentified Canadian as 'an oversized tomato can', bouncing over the water and rolling up the beach remained vividly thereafter with navigator, Flying Officer Hobday, and the fight engineer, Sergeant Grayston, had even sharper memories: 'We thought we were flying at 30–50 feet but were actually below that and

617 SQUADRON PREPARES

the splash badly damaged our machine. The tailplane and back end looked like a sardine can where the water had hit it', which appears excessively colourful as the Lancaster was not extensively damaged.

Shannon's bomb-aimer remembered the occasion for a different reason. At 18.15 hours, according to his log book, Flight Sergeant Sumpter released Upkeep, which fell 20yds short, and the next morning, as he put it, 'the error of my ways' was forcefully made clear to him by his commanding officer. It was the only time that Gibson and Sumpter spoke before the operation. Flight Lieutenant Maltby dropped an inert-filled Upkeep on 12 May and suffered minor damage to his aircraft from water splashing up. Relying on an altimeter, like the others, to judge height in daylight, Flight Lieutenant Munro dropped Upkeep from below 60ft and damaged the tail plane of ED 921/G more severely than Knight, though his log book simply read: 'Exercise dropped Upkeep'. Fortunately, that machine could be repaired.

Full details of B Flight's activity at this time have not survived, though Squadron Leader H.E. Maudslay unquestionably 'badly damaged' ED 933/G at Reculver. Wallis's diary is blank for 13 and 14 May, but he certainly witnessed the live drop off Broadstairs and appears to have been at Reculver the following day. Flight Lieutenant H.B. Martin's rear gunner confirmed that on 13 May that crew dropped 'a dummy store' there and a second on 14 May, the fourth day running 617 crews had practised at Reculver, when Wallis expressed delight at the crews' ability ... to put stores on the beach with remarkable accuracy'.

Munro recalled that, exclusive of other pilots flying with one of them, 12 crews dropped Upkeep at Reculver and, logically, as deputy leader Young would have been one. 'Remember that six aircraft were damaged at Reculver on the 12th and were not available for training over the next couple of days, in my case ED 921 was not ready until the 16th.'

Of the aircraft damaged in this exercise, only Maudslay's would not be ready for the operation. Hence, hours before the raid there would be only 19 Lancasters available for 19 crews; no reserve in case of emergency. On 13 May a meeting at ICI House in London was attended by Gibson, which underlined the pressure that he was under during those last frantic days of preparation. Earlier in the day, he had flown as Handasyde's observer to witness Longbottom's live drop off Broadstairs. The full extent of the damage to aircraft at Reculver was unclear, though Satterly still envisaged 20 crews flying to the dams. So to provide a back-up, 'it was decided to transfer one of the three prototypes to the squadron ... and the aircraft at

THE DAMBUSTERS: 'WAS THE RAID WORTHWHILE?'

Boscombe Down was selected for transfer. The Squadron undertook to prepare the aircraft for operations.' In the event, this decision would be critical.

The day after the live drop and ICI House meeting, 14 May, Gibson and his crew carried out local bombing and VHF tests, prior to a 'full dress rehearsal on Uppingham Lake and Colchester reservoir' that evening. The station commander, Whitworth, flew with him on the exercise, which Gibson declared 'completely successful'. This might be true of direction and organisation of the crews at the simulated targets and in terms of navigation, but not every available crew took part. There was also at least one guest, who flew with Maudslay. The medical officer, Flying Officer M.W. Arthurton, had done so with that crew on 25 April 'and I was air sick after ½ hour, so on this second trip I took some appropriate medication, which was most effective ... We took off at 2100 hrs and flew for four hours. I have not the foggiest notion where we were nor exactly what we were doing except that we were doing low flying ... People said very little and I did not embarrass them with very difficult questions, as I realised that there was something in the wind.'

Possibly due to lack of serviceable aircraft, apart from Wilson and Divall who were sick, Flight Lieutenant D.H. Maltby (his repaired aircraft did not return to Scampton until 20.00 hours), Pilot Officer L.J. Burpee and Flight Sergeant W.C. Townsend did not fly, and only 14 aircraft appear to have been involved. Furthermore, not all of the original ten standard Lancasters had left the Squadron. Earlier that day, Shannon flew one to Manston and back and Sergeant V.W. Byers (notified of promotion to Pilot Officer the following day) piloted one during the dress rehearsal. After the damage to his aircraft at Reculver on 12 May, Munro flew a standard Lancaster the following day. On the final exercise, he took the aircraft Townsend would fly to the dams and not all crews matched Gibson's 3hrs 5 mins in the air. Gibson's was among those to fly to Uppingham and Colchester replicating the whole operation, but others went only to Uppingham for the Moehne simulation.

Unknown to any of the crews and Gibson himself only forty-eight remained before the operation would be launched. That was almost prevented at the last minute by a serious administrative hurdle. Parallel to the Dams' Raid preparations, Wallis had been working on 'Upkeep's little brother' – the smaller Highball weapon destined for use by Mosquitoes of No. 618 against German capital ships and specifically *Tirpitz*. With the similarity of technique self-evident, simultaneous attacks had been anticipated to avoid one being compromised if the other went ahead independently. On 18 March, it had been affirmed that 'the use of the one vitally affects the successful use of the other ... It may be necessary for the Chiefs of Staff to decide whether or not to release the weapon for the Moehne Dam and the Eder Dam to the prejudice of possible later attacks on capital ships'.

The Chiefs of Staff were in Washington for a conference with their American counterparts, so their deputies in London faced a tricky decision on 13 May. Air Chief Marshal Sir Douglas Evill explained that, whereas Upkeep trials had proved successful, those involving Highball had not. He argued that, if the Germans did recover an intact Upkeep, 'the particular characteristics of this type of weapon' would be revealed, but Highball would not, he believed, be compromised. Stressing that the window of opportunity that year was rapidly closing, he pressed for authority to go ahead immediately. The Vice Chief of the Naval Staff, having been instructed by the First Sea Lord not to make a decision without his express permission, insisted that the matter be referred to their superiors in the USA.

Therefore, an encoded signal was despatched to the Chiefs of Staff at 18.55 hours (Double British Summer Time) on 13 May, drafted by the Director of Bomber Operations at the Air Ministry, Air Commodore S.O. Bufton. He maintained that the cylindrical nature of Upkeep and its release 450yds from a target could not be compared with Highball. Moreover, 'method of attack might well engender belief that special form of depth charge had been dropped between the boom and dam. This would be confirmed by attack on target Z (Sorpe) in which aircraft will fly close and parallel to the dam face'. Bufton suggested that bounces at short range, especially considering the distance in the air (approximately 250yds) before striking the water, would create the impression of a normal skip bomb dropped short. Disingenuously, considering that 617 Squadron had been formed to attack special targets, Bufton held that to postpone the dams raid would be to deny its participation in main force operations. Finally, he thought it 'improbable' that the enemy would associate Upkeep with a 'spherical weapon against ships'. To support this contention, he added that the joint service committee, set up under Air Vice-Marshal N.H. Bottomley to oversee evolution of the two projects, agreed that the dams' attacks should proceed without delay.

At 10.40 hours (DBST) the following day, 14 May, Evill sent a 'most immediate and personal' cypher message to the Chief of Air Staff, Sir Charles Portal, in Washington. Also quoting support of the Bottomley committee, he asserted: 'We are fully convinced that balance of factors is strongly in favour of disassociating the two operations and getting on with the heavy'. The trial on 13 May (Longbottom's live drop) had been 'entirely satisfactory technically and tactically': 'immediate action' would be taken if approval were gained. At 14.40 hours (DBST) on 14 May (decoded in London at 15.55 hours) a signal to the Air Ministry read: 'For reasons stated by you, Chiefs of Staff agree to immediate use of Upkeep without waiting for Highball.'

A ruling made 3,000 miles away from RAF Scampton forty-eight hours before take-off thus determined that Operation Chastise would proceed.

Chapter 7

Count-Down to Take-Off

At 09.00 hours on 15 May, the Assistant Chief of the Air Staff (Ops) in the Air Ministry sent a 'most immediate most secret' signal to HQ Bomber Command: 'Op CHASTISE. Immediate attack of targets "X" "Y" "Z" approved. Execute at first suitable opportunity.'

This was then conveyed informally to HQ 5 Group. Group Captain H.V. Satterly recalled Air Chief Marshal Harris during a phone call to Air Vice-Marshal Cochrane as he listened on an extension saying: 'It's Chastise'. This was the cue for him to take the hand-written Operation (Op) Order from his office safe and prepare it for typing as Squadron Leader Fawsett from Bomber Command signalled he calculated water in the Moehne reservoir was 2ft from the crest of the dam. Satterly instructed the Group's chief signals officer, Wing Commander W.E. Dunn, to read the document and devise appropriate procedures for the operation. Meanwhile, Cochrane prepared to travel to Scampton to tell Whitworth and Gibson that the raid would take place next day, Sunday 16 May.

During 15 May, most 617 Lancasters were grounded for maintenance work or fitting of Upkeep, a process taking approximately half an hour. No Lancaster, though, was bombed up before Cochrane reached Scampton. Martin's was one of those loaded on 15 May. The rear gunner, Flight Sergeant T.D. Simpson, recalled that 'after tea ... we were all out at the aircraft' and saw 'the store slung under P for Popsie'. With him were Martin, Flying Officer L. Chambers (wireless operator) and Flight Lieutenant J. Leggo (navigator), together with 'Blondie ... a WAAF Intelligence Officer, who formed an attachment with our crew and used to paddle about with Mick and Bob [Flight Lieutenant R.C. Hay, the bomb-aimer] when she was able.' Previously that day, some crews had taken their aircraft up. Barlow went with Byers as his second pilot to the Wainfleet bombing range and Astell carried out an air test on AJ-B.

In mid-afternoon, HQ 5 Group received the results of Photographic Reconnaissance Unit flights from RAF Benson over the target area from the previous day and that morning, as well as interpretation reports of the findings from RAF Medmenham. No unusual activity had been detected. At 15.40 hours, the Air Ministry signal sent that morning to High Wycombe was formally forwarded to Grantham.

Wallis recorded landing at 16.00 hours in an uncamouflaged Wellington having been flown from Weybridge by 'Mutt' Summers. Quite why he was there is unclear, but it seems probable that Cochrane had made him aware of the ensuing operation and he would be on hand for last-minute technical queries. 'Met Gibson. Inspected a/c', he wrote in his diary. It seems likely that the meeting was brief and the Officer Commanding travelled back to HQ 5 Group either with Cochrane or shortly after him, for Satterly wrote that he, Gibson, Cochrane and the signals officer, Dunn, discussed the draft Operation Order at Grantham 'later that day'. An important adjustment would be made overnight, presumably because Satterly learnt that two 617 crews could not fly. A copy dated 15 May lists the seven target dams always under consideration, with the Diemel Target G, the Henne dam Target F. The version typed on 16 May evidently finalised the previous evening, and the draft with which Gibson returned to Scampton, promoted the Diemel to Target F and omitted the Henne. This had the smallest reservoir capacity, involved a difficult approach in hilly country and, after the attack, meant aircraft having to clear the adjacent, defended Ruhr riverside town of Meschede.

Wallis entered in his diary for 15 May: '6pm Addressed crews – Captains only on object of raid'. This meeting would have been more restricted. Cochrane had insisted that only the two flight commanders (Young and Maudslay) be briefed before the day of the operation. The Op Order included: 'Secrecy is VITAL. Knowledge of this operation is to be confined to the Station Commander, Officer Commanding 617 Squadron and his two Flight Commanders until receipt of the Executive signal'. However, almost certainly during Cochrane's visit to Scampton on the afternoon of 15 May, Hopgood (deputy leader at the Moehne) and Hay were cleared to attend the meeting addressed by Wallis. The reference of Simpson, Martin's rear gunner, to the crew's inspection of its Lancaster 'after tea' mentioned Flight Lieutenant J.F. Leggo (Squadron navigation officer) being present and not Hay (Squadron bombing leader), suggesting that the bomb-aimer was at Wallis's meeting, but not the navigator.

Pilots ('captains') from the different waves later confirmed that they were not briefed on 15 May and knew nothing of the targets until the morning of the operation. Flight Lieutenant Shannon verbally stressed this, Flight Lieutenant Munro wrote simply, 'pilots did not attend the briefing on the Saturday evening'. Years later, he reflected: 'I was unaware that there had been a separate briefing on the Saturday including Flight Commanders, Nav [sic] and Bombing leaders until after the war'; although doubt must remain that Leggo was there. Flight Sergeant Brown, too, revealed that, 'I knew nothing about the target until the day of the operation'. Years later, Sir Ralph Cochrane was adamant that to have revealed details on the eve of the operation to all the pilots would have been 'a grave breach of security'.

Possibly, Wallis used his film to explain to the restricted group the method and purpose of Upkeep's delivery before Gibson returned with a copy of the Op Order. Subsequent discussion of this led to a major route adjustment. A section of the planned, inward route ran between Rees on the Rhine and Ahsen, 38 miles almost due east. Hopgood realised this was close to a heavily defended factory at Huels, where he had previously encountered flak. Frantic work must now have taken place involving the squadron navigation leader, Leggo, and detailed communication with Grantham. For instead of flying via Ahsen, on a distinctive bend of the Lippe River, to the next turning point a road, rail and canal intersection close to Ahlen, crews would be briefed to fly roughly parallel to this track north of the Wesel River from Rees to a group of five lakes south west of Duelmen (identified by the coordinates of the southernmost Vogelvenn) before turning eastwards to Ahlen, 21 miles north of the Moehne. Hobday (Knight's navigator) believed that 'the change of route gave us more safety and better pinpoints'. This important adjustment to the inward route for all three waves was not something suddenly thought up. It was a reversal of the third planned exit (homeward) route between Ahlen and Rees via the Duelmen lakes; a deft solution.

The alteration was completed in time for a '10pm meeting in CO's [Whitworth's] office to finalise method of attack' attended by Wallis and noted in his diary. It lasted approximately two hours as Wallis then wrote, '12.30 Bed', with a sad postscript: 'Nigger Killed'. As the gathering dispersed, Whitworth gave Gibson that distressing news. Flight Sergeant Powell recalled that early on the evening of 15 May, he had been summoned to the Guard Room by a phone call from the Service police. Eve Gibson would later explain that the labrador, Gibson's faithful companion, had dashed out of the main gate and been struck by a passing car, which crashed trying to avoid him and whose driver and passenger were injured in the attempt. The dog's body was put in a detention cell in the Guard Room,

THE DAMBUSTERS: 'WAS THE RAID WORTHWHILE?'

where Powell identified it and informed the adjutant, Humphries, who in turn told Whitworth.

The following morning, 16 May, activity began early in the Squadron offices, workshops and on the hard stands as Upkeep was loaded into aircraft not bombed up the day before. Alerted by Gibson, 'just after 9.30am', Humphries drew up the Order of Battle, disguised as 'Night Flying Programme'. On his orders, Powell quietly arranged for coffee, sandwiches and fruit to be placed in each Lancaster and Humphries himself organised a traditional pre-operational evening meal for the crews. Elsewhere, panic occurred, when the Upkeep in Martin's aircraft dropped from its calliper arms onto the tarmac. Fearing that it had been armed and would explode, a flurry of bodies dashed for cover while Martin sped off to find the armament officer. Pilot Officer I. Whittaker, the flight engineer, recalled that 'we were all just pottering around, when we suddenly had to break into a sprint'. On arrival Watson somewhat dismissively declared the weapon safe, sheepish figures emerged from their hiding places and Whittaker recalled that 'once hoisted into position again' the crew made sure that the green Upkeep was painted black to blend with the fuselage. As Upkeep had been installed the previous evening, something extraordinary must have occurred to cause it to fall off. A rumour that it resulted from a curious WAAF pulling a lever in the cockpit is delightful but scarcely credible. Returning from lunch on 16 May, Leading Aircraftman Victor Gill, one of the maintenance team servicing the Lancasters of Squadron Leader Young and Flight Lieutenant Astell found that both aircraft had been bombed up with Upkeep, still with their 'oxide red' undercoat. Those, too, were painted black, though Gill did remark that one on a nearby Lancaster was dark green as scheduled.

While this activity was in progress, at the Air Ministry Air Commodore S.O. Bufton laid down procedures for handling of the press once the operation had taken place. No reporters were to get information from 5 Group sources or the aircrew involved; a forlorn hope, it turned out. He drew attention to the cover story originally circulated on 25 March. Official communiqués were to note that 'a mine of great size' had been used by a number of experienced crews, which had been carefully selected. They had been 'specially and rigorously trained' for an operation 'which commanded an extremely high standard of flying and the highest degree of accuracy in dropping the mines sufficiently close to the target to be effective'. It should be emphasised that 'crews displayed the greatest skill in executing the operation as planned'.

COUNT-DOWN TO TAKE-OFF

During the morning at Scampton, Gibson allegedly suffered a personal rebuff. Leading Aircraftman Arthur Drury recalled that the squadron commander asked a busy Flight Sergeant F.O. Brown in the station workshop to make a coffin in which to bury Nigger, which the NCO refused to do. As Drury recalled: 'With that the Wing Commander lost his temper, there were high words with very little wisdom, and the Wing Commander went on his way without getting a coffin made for his dog.' However, 'Chiefy' Powell claimed that Brown did comply with Gibson's request when less busy later in the day. The coffin, according to Powell, was inscribed with the dog's name and the date of his burial. During the afternoon, an armoury officer went into the machine shop to collect a grease gun, which Drury had modified for use with Upkeep. Realising that Drury 'had been put to a great deal of trouble and had shown a great deal of patience', he asked him if he would like to see the weapon which he had been producing parts for. The flight lieutenant added that, if he did not see it now, he never would. Drury was led into the Squadron hangar, where a Lancaster stood 'with what appeared to be a large steel drum hanging underneath the fuselage and a chain drive to revolve it'. Looking at the 'massive object', Drury had no idea of its nature or purpose; further confirmation of tight security.

That morning, dated 16 May 1943, 'No 5 Group Order No B. 976' with three appendices - A 'Routes and Timings'; B 'Signals Procedures for Target Diversions etc'. C 'Light and Moon Tables' – minus the course adjustments including the new Rees-Ahlen leg and readjustment of the final turning point at Ahlen before the Moehne made at Scampton – was distributed. Of the twelve numbered 'most secret' copies, two went to Scampton, three to Bomber Command. The remaining seven, destined for officers and files within 5 Group, would not be distributed until the executive signal for the operation had been issued that afternoon. Although the practice designations A, B and C for the Moehne, Eder and Sorpe would be used verbally and in navigators' logs on the night, the Op Order retained the draft X, Y and Z.

It maintained that: 'Destruction of TARGET X [Moehne] alone would bring about a serious shortage of water for drinking purposes and industrial supplies ... in the Ruhr District'. This would cause 'considerable local flooding' and 'a large loss of electrical capacity in the Ruhr'. Satterly explained that 'additional destruction of one or more of the five major dams in the Ruhr area would greatly increase the effect and hasten the resulting damage ... Target Z [Sorpe] is next in importance'. Breaching of Target D [Lister] and Target E [Ennepe] completed the western group of four target dams; 'havoc in the Ruhr valley' being the objective.

THE DAMBUSTERS: 'WAS THE RAID WORTHWHILE?'

Separately to the east, 'in the Weser District the destruction of TARGET Y [Eder] would seriously hamper transport in the Mittelland Canal and in the Weser [river], and would probably lead to an almost complete cessation of the great volume of [industrial and military supply] traffic using these waterways'. Destruction of the nearby Target F [Diemel] would enhance this devastation.

Aircraft would fly from base to the target area 'in moonlight at low level' and be divided into three waves. The first comprising three sections [each of three machines] would take off at ten-minute intervals, cross the North Sea and the enemy coast via the Scheldt estuary to Target X. There, unlike the draft which designated five minutes, 'spinning of the special store is to be started ten minutes before each aircraft attacks'.

Meanwhile, the second wave of five aircraft, 'manned by specially trained crews ... to attack Target Z', would fly a more northerly route over the North Sea to cross the island of Vlieland, turn to starboard over the Ijsselmeer [Zuider Zee] and enemy territory to connect with the southern route at Rees. The aircraft would then follow the first wave route to the Moehne Dam and on to the Sorpe. Lancasters of this wave were to fly singly and 'are to cross the enemy coast at the same time as the leading section of the 1st wave'; 120 miles north-north-east aiming to confuse the enemy defences. Cochrane later explained, underlining the importance of the Sorpe, taking into account its different structure and the hope that a maximum of six Upkeeps would be required to breach the Moehne and Eder, that he planned for 'about half' of the combined first and second waves to deal with the Sorpe, from a total of 14 Lancasters.

The third wave of six (reduced to five on the night due to the two crews being unavailable), flying the southern route via the Scheldt estuary, would form 'an airborne reserve under the control of Group HQ ... Orders will be passed to the aircraft on the special Group [W/T] frequency, if possible before they cross the enemy coast instructing them which target to attack'. 'The time of take-off is to be such that they may be recalled before crossing the enemy coast if the 1st and 2nd waves have breached all the targets'. If no message were received, they would proceed to X, Y, D, E and F in that order, 'attacking any which are not breached'.

Caution is necessary when studying this document. Apart from the major and minor route variations not being shown, the altitudes depicted not only differ from those in the original draft sent to Gibson for comment, but the optimum word would be 'maximum'. Navigators' logs and oral evidence confirm that on the night heights of 100–150ft were flown for much of the way in and out. The printed order required aircraft not to exceed 1,500ft over England before crossing the North Sea coast. From there all the way to

COUNT-DOWN TO TAKE-OFF

Ahlen, the maximum height should be 500ft, rising to 1,000ft from Ahlen to the target areas. The true air speed to the targets would be 180mph, after the attacks increasing to 220mph via three designated exit routes except for the last phase over the North Sea to base at 180mph. A maximum 500ft would be flown on all exit routes.

'The detailed plan' included in the Operation Order required aircraft to 'fly to the target at low level', over the North Sea 'set their altimeters to 60ft using the Spotlight Altimeters for calibration' and cross the enemy coast 'as low as possible ... An accurate landfall on the enemy coast is important, but on no account should aircraft turn back if their landfall is not quite accurate. The routes selected should be free from all major opposition from flak, but good map reading and crew co-operation is essential to keep aircraft on track'.

'The leader [Gibson] is to attack first and is then to control the attack on Targets X and Y by all other aircraft', using the signals procedure laid down and practised:

> The direction of attack of Target X is to be at right angles to the length of the target. The general direction of attack is, therefore, to be SE to NW. Aircraft are not to be diverted to Target Y until Target X has been breached. If Target X is breached, up to two additional aircraft may be used, at the discretion of the leader, to widen the breach in Target X providing at least three aircraft are diverted to attack Target Y ... When Target X is seen to be breached beyond all possible doubt, the leader is to divert the remainder of the First Wave to Target Y ... where similar tactics are to be used for the attack on this target. The general direction of attack of Target Y is to be from NW to SE. If Target Y is seen to be breached beyond all possible doubt, all remaining aircraft [still with Upkeep] are to be diverted by the leader to attack Target Z independently using the same tactics as the 2nd Wave.

The first three aircraft were to take exit Route 1, the next three Route 2 and the final three Route 3. The Op Order emphasised that 'for the attacks of both Targets X and Y, the special range finder is to be used, the height of attack is to be 60 feet and the ground speed 220mph'.

Bound for the Sorpe, 'the 2nd Wave ... aircraft are to cross the enemy coast in close concentration, but not in formation ... [and] aircraft of this wave will be controlled on the alternative VHF channel. The special stores are not to be spun for the attack on Target Z. Aircraft are to attack this target

THE DAMBUSTERS: 'WAS THE RAID WORTHWHILE?'

from NW to SE parallel to the length of the dam and are to aim [Upkeep] to hit the water just short of the centre point of the dam about 15–20 feet out from the edge of the water. Attacks are to be made from the lowest practicable height at a speed of 180mph IAS'. The first two would take exit Route 1, the next two Route 2 and the fifth Route 3.

Aircraft of the 3rd Wave 'are to use tactics of attack similar to those used by the 1st wave when attacking Targets X and Y', but those on the other targets 'are to be made independently ... After attacking, aircraft are to return to base independently at low level by any of the three return routes'.

Further instructions were included on the 'Method of Attack ... already practised ... The pilot being responsible for line, the Navigator for height, the Air Bomber for range and the Flight Engineer for speed ... The interval between attacking aircraft is to be not less than three minutes on all targets ... On all targets except Target Z each aircraft is to fire a red verey cartridge immediately over the dam during the attack'; that is, after releasing Upkeep. 'Aircraft attacking Target Z are each to fire a red verey cartridge as they release their special store'. Then, crucially for safety purposes, 'all aircraft are to fly left hand circuits in each target area keeping as low as possible when waiting their turn to attack'.

With reference to navigators, 'the route is to be carefully studied before flight and all the outstanding features, obstructions and pinpoints noted, particularly water pinpoints ... if any pinpoint is not found on ETAs [estimated times of arrival] a search is to be made before proceeding to the next pinpoint'. Crews were advised that 'all watches are to be synchronised with BBC before take-off'; DBST coinciding with that in the Low Countries and Germany, which were one hour ahead of Central European time. 'Secrecy is VITAL' was yet once more emphasised. 'After crews are briefed they are to be impressed with the need for the utmost secrecy because of the possibility that the operation may be postponed should weather reconnaissance prove the weather to be unsuitable.'

Op Order No. B 976 and its subsequent formally unrecorded amendments provided the basis for the different briefings at Scampton prior to take-off on Sunday 16 May. Models of the Moehne and Sorpe dams were available, but only photos of the other four targets, including the Eder. The Moehne (Target X), 7 miles south of Soest and 26 miles east of Dortmund, lay at the convergence of the Moehne and Heve rivers. A curved gravity dam, it held back 134 million cubic metres of water, was 40.3m (132ft) high, 650m (2,133ft) long, 34.02m (112ft) thick at the base, narrowing to 6.25m (21ft) at the top; wide enough for a roadway.

COUNT-DOWN TO TAKE-OFF

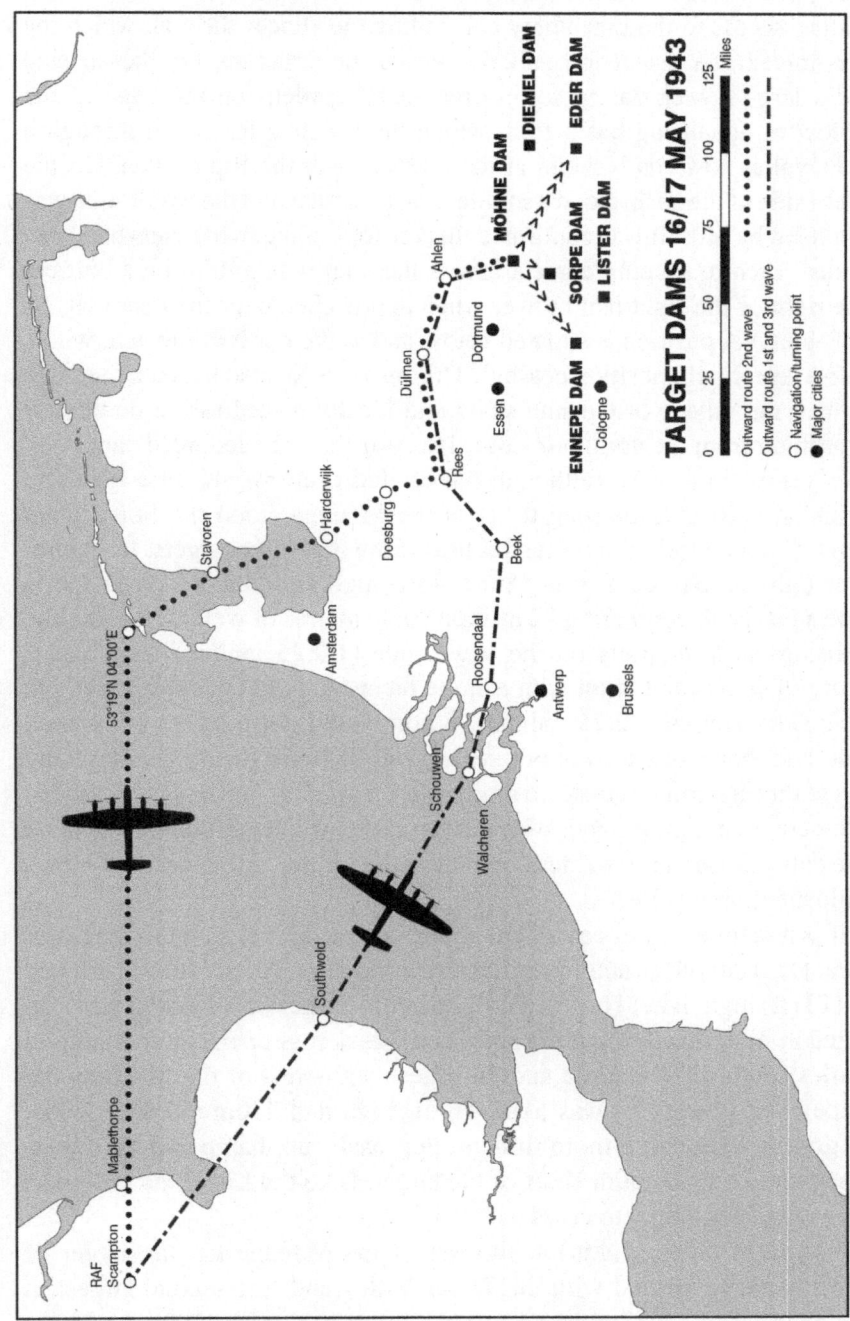

Inward Routes. Showing that all aircraft aiming for the six designated targets made initially for the Moehne.

THE DAMBUSTERS: 'WAS THE RAID WORTHWHILE?'

Protruding above the structure, 196m (639ft) apart were two towers shielding access to the machinery controlling the sluices through which the water flowed and inspection galleries inside the structure. On the air side stood a large power station set in ornamental gardens on the edge of the overflow or equalising basin from which the Moehne River ran through a narrow valley towards Neheim at its junction with the Ruhr River. On the western side of the basin stood a smaller power station and the whole area was surrounded by hills. It was confirmed that the tops of the two towers had been flattened, each to accommodate a 20mm flak gun with a third on a buttress to the right of the right-hand tower when approached over the reservoir. 'A light 3-gun A A position is situated below and to the north of the dam with a possible searchlight position nearby'. This unit was located beneath the ridge on which the village of Guenne stood and ideally placed to fire on aircraft approaching from the north (air side). This was the only defended dam.

Six miles south-west (although the briefed route would take attacking aircraft on a 10 mile dog-leg to it) of the Moehne stood the Sorpe Dam (Target Z), an entirely different structure to the other five targets. Its central 'water tight cement core' was 58m (190ft) high and 600m (1,965ft) long beside a reservoir containing 72 million cubic metres of water. The sloping, stabilising earth supports on the water side (1:2.25 incline) contained a mixture of stones and loam with a stone facing to hold back the water. On the air side (similar 1:2.25 incline), a non-watertight mixture of 'gravel, rubble and stone waste' was not sealed with a stone facing to allow any seepage through minor cracks to drain away. This dam, too, was surrounded by tree-covered high ground, with a steep rise exceeding 300m at each end of the dam. Close to the western one stood the village of Langscheid with a prominent church spire.

Fifty-five miles south-east of Duisburg, lay the third Ruhr dam, the Lister (Target D); a curved structure similar to the Moehne: 264m (866ft) long and 40m (131ft) high. It held back 22 million cubic metres of water and was also situated in hilly country, but the approach was across open water. Standing 20 miles south of Dortmund and 30 miles south-west of the Moehne, the Ennepe Dam (Target E) was 51m (165ft) high and 330m (1,083ft) wide. This gravity dam had a more difficult approach run, hampered by a tree-covered spit of land 300m short of the target. Like the Lister, its crest was wide enough for a road to cross.

Forty-eight miles (80km) south-east of the Moehne lay the larger of the two dams connected with the Weser Valley and 'the second largest in Germany'. The Eder (Target Y) was 42.4m (139ft) high, 399m (1,309ft)

COUNT-DOWN TO TAKE-OFF

long, 35m (115ft) thick at the bottom tapering to 58m (19ft) at the top. Its two towers, similar to those at the Moehne, were 238m (781ft) apart. Close to the village of Hemfurth, 20 miles south-west of Kassel and 2 miles south-south-east of Waldeck Castle perched high on a hill, it too was surrounded by high ground and at the end of a winding reservoir containing 202.4 million cubic metres of water. Two power stations were at the extremities of the dam on the air side and 350m directly beyond was a 343m high hill. Cochrane rightly described the attack run as 'very confined, very tricky'.

The second dam in this area, the Diemel (Target F), stood 20 miles north-west of the Eder and 30 miles west of Kassel. Close to the village of Helminghausen, 194m (637ft) long and 40m (131ft) high, it nestled between hills 557m and 596m high and held back 20 million cubic metres of water.

Flight Sergeant Powell reflected that, after the early flurry of activity, the hangars and offices became 'very quiet, like a morgue'. Leading Aircraftman Victor Gill, maintenance mechanic with A Flight, recalled that it was 'hot and sunny all day'. Although the unusual activity strongly suggested the operation was pending, he saw very little of the crews that day and when he did, 'I sensed that questions would not be welcome'. The adjutant, Flight Lieutenant Humphries, similarly recorded that 'all through the day preparations proceeded quietly and efficiently'. During the morning, he received a hand-written note from Gibson, delivered by a 'runner', indicating the anticipated take-off and return times. This allowed him to arrange transport to the aircraft and to be ready to pick up crews on landing and ferry them to de-briefing. Arrangements for the pre-operational meal did cause a temporary headache. Aware of the continued need for secrecy, he was unable formally to request it and had to persuade the WAAF sergeant by insisting that this was a special and arduous flight. Meanwhile, Powell had arranged with the help of Corporal J. Bryden to bury Nigger outside Gibson's office at midnight, as requested by the OC.

Gibson recorded that, without formally breaking for lunch, a series of briefings took place from late morning onwards; in his post-operational report, Cochrane agreed that specialist briefings commenced 'early on the day'. Wallis rose later than usual ('a.m. rested'), but was then involved in the briefing of different groups using his film and diagrams on a blackboard to explain the performance and purpose of Upkeep. Prior to the final briefing, his diary showed, 'p.m. Inspected A/C and Stores'. This must have been when, as Gibson recalled, he rushed up to the OC worried about the absence of special oil without which Upkeep rotation would not function; a false alarm.

THE DAMBUSTERS: 'WAS THE RAID WORTHWHILE?'

Wing Commander Dunn at 5 Group HQ was warned at 10.00 hours that the operation was on that night. He made his way, according to Satterly, 'at once' to Scampton and at about 11.30 hours began a lengthy session to instruct the wireless operators on the procedures and code words laid down in App B of the Op Order. He recorded that 'all W/Ops [wireless operators] were carefully instructed in the W/T procedure to be followed, and the actual specimen messages were transmitted on a buzzer circuit and each aircraft was given its particular signals role'. Satterly agreed that, after briefing the wireless operators together, Dunn had 'a final talk with W/T operators wave by wave', as each had 'a different signals role'.

Simultaneously, pilots and navigators were briefed separately. Flight Sergeant L.J. Sumpter and Sergeant S. Oancia recalled that they and other bomb-aimers joined them in the early afternoon; the different briefings independently confirmed by pilots Townsend and Rice as well as navigators Hobday, Heal and Howard. Heal acknowledged that they were briefed on all the target dams, 'but mainly the first three'. He underlined the tightness of security. Referring to the two models, 'I cannot recall anything more clearly than my reaction when we attended the first briefing to see these objects covered up and then exposed for our inspection – Dams!' Howard emphasised that he, too, had no knowledge of the target before 16 May and that 'the revelation of the dams in Germany as such brought what sounded like a sigh of relief ... No Tirpitz, no submarine pens! The models of the dams were a great idea.'

Hobday's log shows that he plotted a course in sequence to the Moehne, Eder, and Sorpe. Flight Sergeant K. Brown remembered that 'there were briefings of various kinds and I do remember my radio operator binding about not being included in a briefing but be damned if I can remember which one!' Flight Sergeant G.A .Chalmers recalled that, concentrating on their procedures, the wireless operators did not learn of the targets until the final briefing. Brown did, though, recollect that at one stage, first and second wave personnel were briefed separately from those of the third wave. As a third wave pilot, he was 'briefed on the three main targets and others including the Ennepe'. He recalled that they were told 'the Sorpe had a concrete core with earth on each side, (and) the idea was to crack the core and the water would wash away the earth and the dam collapse ... the drop point was to be the middle point in the dam as our run was along the face and approx. 40ft [sic] out'.

Pilot Officer G. Rice agreed about these details and emphasised that pilots were notified of their targets at the first specialist briefing and, despite

COUNT-DOWN TO TAKE-OFF

the Sorpe's unexpected nature, was 'glad that I now knew what to do'. Sergeant G.L. Johnson (McCarthy's bomb-aimer) was 'surprised' at being sent to this target, 'as we had practised like the others with the special bomb sight at Wainfleet and Joe [McCarthy] had flown as second pilot in one of the Lancasters at Reculver'. Furthermore, the crew had 'mainly practised at Uppingham and Colchester'. Pilot Flight Lieutenant J.L. Munro agreed, in retrospect, that 'I don't remember flying along the crest of the Derwent or any of the other practice dams ... it was not until briefing that we were directed to attack the Sorpe by flying along the crest of the dam'.

Flying Officer H.S. Hobday (Knight's navigator), reprising Howard, was 'very relieved it wasn't battleships'. When these groups broke for tea, NCOs sharing a house with rear gunner, Sergeant Tees, remained tight-lipped, causing him to ponder, 'well it can't be any worse than others'. Similarly, Sergeant D.E. Webb recalled Flight Sergeant Townsend and his bomb-aimer demanding refreshment without 'giving away anything'. Tees wrote specifically: 'Only pilots and navigators attended the first briefing as to target familiarisation and best method of attack, the rest of us a general briefing a few hours before take-off. The Lister [Ottley's designated target] doesn't ring any bells with me'. Webb and Knight's rear gunner (O'Brien) confirmed that they, too, did not learn details of the operation until the final general briefing. Nor did flight engineers Feneron and Grayston.

While the various briefings were in progress, it became apparent that ED 933/G, damaged by Maudslay at Reculver, could not be repaired. So only 19 Lancasters were available for 19 crews with no reserve machine in case of a pre-operational malfunction. Belatedly, therefore, the decision made on 13 May to fly up from Boscombe Down the Type 464 (Provisioning) Lancaster aircraft used there for range trials was implemented. Shortly after lunch on 16 May, Central Flying Control ordered Commander H.C. Bergel of No 9 Ferry Pilots' Pool to fly ED 825/G to Scampton immediately. With some dismay, he surveyed the 'gutted fish ... with bomb-bay doors faired over and its doors removed'. He was even more puzzled by 'the hefty metal arms with small wheels at their extremities, the driving belt from the starboard side to a pulley attached to a hydraulic motor bolted to the cabin floor, and the instructions connected with it in the cockpit'. One more unpleasant surprise greeted him. During the tests prior to take-off, he discovered that 'No 3 engine would not run at full throttle with the full booster pump off.' In view of the urgency impressed on him, he decided to 'ignore' this problem, which would normally have rendered the machine unserviceable.

THE DAMBUSTERS: 'WAS THE RAID WORTHWHILE?'

At 15.30 hours, he landed at Scampton to discover 'a large number of other gutted aircraft' carrying objects 'about the size and shape of the front wheel of a stream roller in vast claws', similar to those attached to his Lancaster. Bergel noticed that the strange contraption was slowly rotating on one of them and set off for a closer look. He was forcefully intercepted and persuaded to beat a swift retreat to a waiting Anson. During his return flight, he reflected that 'I had no idea what this peculiarly modified aeroplane was required to do, and it was made clear that curiosity was unwelcome.' Unknown to Bergel, without his arrival, 617 Squadron would have only able to put 18, not 19, aircraft in the air that night.

As Bergel left, maintenance personnel converged on ED 825/G, soon to become AJ-T. LAC Munro, the erstwhile gymnast, discovered that a 16-strand coaxial cable had a bakelite insert missing from the end, which fitted into the Gee navigational aid box. No spares were available, so Munro gambled that he could solve the problem, otherwise the aircraft would be unserviceable. 'I carefully spaced out 16 small wire-end sockets, lined them up with the male plugs and pressed them together. I then held my breath when the engines were tested. Fortunately no shorting occurred.' After the raid, Munro wrote that 'Joe McCarthy flew close to Hamm with more than just a poor compass swing'; reference to a navigational problem over Germany during AJ-T's return flight.

Another of the modified Lancasters, ED 817/G, which had been used at Reculver, was flown to Scampton by the test pilots Longbottom and Handaysde late on the afternoon of 16 May. Never having visited Scampton, Herbert Jeffree, one of Wallis's team, 'hitched a lift'. On landing, Handasyde realised 'a flap was on and tight security about to close the station and we had work to do at Manston', so he and Longbottom, like Bergel, opted for a rapid withdrawal. With neither instruction nor authority, Jeffree stayed on. Years later, Handasyde could not recall why that Lancaster had flown to Scampton, but the timing suggests that it was a back-up in case the engine problem identified by Bergel could not be fixed.

At 16.15 hours, Group HQ at Grantham sent a 'secret and immediate' telex message to Scampton: 'Code name for 5 Group Operation Order B.976 is Chastise'. A half an hour later came 'Execute Operation Chastise 16/5/43 zero hour 2248'. The way was now clear for the final briefing, though air crew recalled that it had already begun and this must therefore have been formal confirmation of a verbal communication. Flight Lieutenant Munro judged the time to be around 16.00 hours, Sergeant G.L. Johnson 'about

COUNT-DOWN TO TAKE-OFF

3.30' and Flight Sergeant K. Brown wrote: 'Main briefing Sunday at approx. 15.00hrs, ended 17.30'.

With take-off shortly before 21.30 hours, after the final briefing crews would return to their quarters and have a pre-operational meal before going to the flight rooms to get their equipment prior to being transported to the hard stands for pre-flight checks. Martin's rear gunner, Flight Sergeant T.D. Simpson, remarked 'it was the longest briefing I ever attended'. So a mid-afternoon start does seem feasible, which makes the entry in Wallis's diary, '6pm Briefed the Crews', puzzling. In his log book, navigator Flight Sergeant D.A. MacLean, wrote '18.08' under 'Watches Synchronised', which would suggest perhaps that the briefing ended about 18.00 hours. This would fit in roughly with the start time suggested by Munro, Johnson and Brown, Simpson's memory of a long briefing and a lengthy period before crews made their way to pick up their flight equipment. It also allows time for crews to look more closely at the models, as indicated by some aircrew.

The final gathering took place in the upstairs briefing room, whose closed door was guarded by Service police. They did not prevent an interloper. Learning that the session was in progress, Herbert Jeffree produced a numbered pass which only authorised access to Reculver and RAF Manston and bluffed his way in. Sitting at the back, he saw Wallis with senior officers beside a raised area immediately opposite the door with their backs to a window. Sunlight streamed in through a row of windows along the side and he noted how hot the room was. There were at the front the large models of the dams, enlarged reconnaissance photos, a map of Europe displayed with red tape pressed on it to indicate the various routes and, as Jeffree put it, 'all the trappings of an operational briefing'. He had not attended one before, was 'surprised to see so many "brass hats"' and was intrigued to hear instructions about 'survival rations, escape silk maps and button compasses with left-hand thread to confuse the enemy if captured'.

Flying Officer E.C. Johnson, Knight's bomb-aimer, recalled that 'Gibson spoke first and introduced Barnes Wallis, who from large drawings explained the principles of the "bomb" and what it was hoped it would do'. One of these was a cross-section of the Moehne Dam, with blue crayon showing the reservoir and the bounces of Upkeep over the surface in pencil. The weapon was depicted hitting the wall then crawling down it to a point where it would explode. Jeffree recalled that Wallis emphasised that the loss of water would gravely affect steel production in the Ruhr and strike a major blow to the enemy war effort. He raised a nervous laugh, as he recalled later to the scientist Dr Collins, when he observed that 'in 1913,

THE DAMBUSTERS: 'WAS THE RAID WORTHWHILE?'

Kaiser Wilhelm II declared the Moehne Dam open amid much flag wagging and brass bands', so it must be a valuable target. Wireless operator Flight Sergeant G.A. Chalmers found Wallis's sketch of the anticipated destructive effect of the raid 'lasting and impressive'. Bomb-aimer, Sergeant J.H. Clay, thought Wallis's presentation 'detailed and clear', but could not avoid feeling that 'it seemed incongruous that this kindly and quietly spoken white-haired man should be involved with devastation'.

Wallis was followed by Cochrane, who assured crews that they would cause 'a tremendous amount of damage' during this 'historic' operation. 'I know this attack will succeed'. Sergeant Grayston was impressed by the massive impact that loss of water from the reservoirs on the German war effort, but also that 'we had to hug the ground so the Germans couldn't vector us with their radar, otherwise they would have picked us off like flies'. Sergeant G.L. Johnson clearly recalled the two models, photos and target map, but also 'deep disappointment to realise that all our practices had been worthless ... We hadn't practised this type of attack at all. It wasn't brought up in training in any way. We had to do it all from scratch'. Johnson remembered that Sorpe crews were advised to use the church steeple as a marker. He emphasised that 'I didn't know about the attack until the afternoon of the raid, not until briefing', and recalled, too, that Barnes Wallis believed 'it would need 4–6 bombs to crack the Sorpe'. Johnson, like so many others, only saw Upkeep on the day of the operation.

Sergeant Webb, Townsend's front gunner, had slightly different memories of the final briefing, although he agreed that crews had been assured that 'the actual dam itself would shield us from the explosion and water spout'. He recalled that 'there seemed to be an opinion that one bomb would suffice for each target, and this is rather qualified by the reactions of those of us who did bomb. Remember that we had no practical experience of the actual explosive effect. Nothing of this size had been dropped before ... We were given a list of targets at briefing and I do remember that the Sorpe and Ennepe were among them'.

After the briefing ended, Sergeant J. Clay was one to recall that individual crews crowded round the models or formed isolated groups. Knight's rear gunner, O'Brien, admitted to being 'more curious than studious ... my job probably had something to do with my attitude'. Although this operation would clearly be even more dangerous than a normal Main Force attack on the Ruhr, due to its unique nature, Clay recorded, 'everyone was in high spirits and eager to go'. Flight Lieutenant Shannon agreed: 'We were all dying to go'.

COUNT-DOWN TO TAKE-OFF

Security remained tight. Section Officer Ann Fowler only sensed that the raid was on, when she noticed two eggs being served for the evening meal. Yet she was not altogether sure 'as 617 Squadron was always doing strange things'. The medical officer Flying Officer M.W. Arthurton, who shared a room with Flying Officer J. Buckley, Shannon's rear gunner, asked him whether he could fly with him on that evening's practice flight and received an evasive answer. Only then did he suspect that the operation was on. Arthurton later disputed the assertion ('I think this is mentioned in Wing Commander Gibson's book') that sleeping pills had been handed out prior to the raid: 'I would have been rather worried lest the drugs prescribed produced any untoward reactions'. He wondered whether this was actually a confusion with the provision of air-sickness pills, which solved 'a problem in the Squadron' during training.

As crews drifted away from the Briefing Room, the enthusiasm identified by Clay was tempered as individuals thought more soberly about the reality of the task ahead. Pilot Officer G. Rice, destined to attack the Sorpe, was concerned about the unpractised method of delivery and awkward approach to the dam there. Having to drop Upkeep 'at a relatively low speed without spinning' after diving over a steep hill meant that he would need to put the Lancaster's flaps down and 'wriggle round the church steeple' of the village of Langscheid. Flight Sergeant W.C. Townsend confessed to 'feeling sick, as I was convinced we were all for the chop'. Pilot Officer A.F. Burcher considered the time between briefing and take-off 'like waiting for an exam paper to be handed out'. Flight Lieutenant D.J. Shannon recalled that Flight Lieutenant J.V. Hopgood, unfortunately correctly, told him that he would not come back. Sergeant H.E. O'Brien, Pilot Officer Knight's rear gunner, noted the varied reactions of crew members. Some talked quietly together, but others laughed and joked in unusually loud voices. After the meal, a few made unscheduled and premature visits to the hard stands.

Sergeant H.B. Feneron, the flight engineer, tried to lift the Upkeep on Flight Sergeant Brown's Lancaster and Warrant Officer A.A. Garshowitz, Flight Lieutenant Astell's wireless operator, chalked on AJ-B's Upkeep: 'Never has so much been expected of so few'. Poignantly, Garshowitz's aircraft would not return. Flying Officer K. Earnshaw, Hopgood's navigator, eerily and accurately mused, 'perhaps we might lose eight tonight and maybe we might go ourselves'. Flight Sergeant D.A. MacLean, McCarthy's navigator, believed 'only a 50/50 chance of coming back'. Sergeant J.H. Clay remembered that 'in the mess, there was no ribaldry from our 57 Squadron comrades. They obviously sensed that something was afoot with 617'. Sergeant G.L. Johnson remembered that, when somebody made 'a vague remark that could have given a hint of what lay ahead, he was swiftly told, "For heaven's sake, keep your mouth shut"'. At 19.30 hours, Barlow's wireless operator, Flying Officer C.R. Williams, wrote what would be his last letter to his girlfriend, Gwen Parfitt, in Nottingham: 'I'm almost sure I will be in Monday or Tuesday night, but will phone you and try to let you know.' He felt that there was 'quite a chance that I may get leave sooner than I expect ... I will have a lot to tell you when I do see you'.

Gradually, as the sun settled in the west, crews began to converge on the Squadron hangar below Gibson's office to collect their parachutes and other equipment. Flight Lieutenant Munro explained: 'Our flying gear was kept in the crew rooms and after kitting up we would be picked up outside these rooms and that practice was followed on the night of the Dams' Raid'. The adjutant, Flight Lieutenant Humphries, recorded: 'This was Der Tag for 617 Squadron ... [and] from eight o'clock onwards the scenes outside the crew rooms were something to remember'. He added that Gibson arrived with his whole crew crammed into his car, to Humphries looking 'fit and well and quite unperturbed', which the squadron commander later declared 'a lie'. The adjutant remarked that others arrived by bicycle or on foot and was relieved to have confirmed that the transport was standing by. Flight Lieutenant Shannon remembered that Wallis 'walked backwards and forwards among the crew members expressing confidence that all had been arranged and the raid would be successful'. Humphries recalled individuals 'lying around on the grass surrounded by Mae Wests, parachute harnesses and other items of flying equipment'. He noticed Squadron Leader Maudslay talking to his crew and Flight Lieutenant Munro 'sprawled in a chair' reading an RAF magazine. Gibson urged Humphries to arrange 'plenty of beer in the Mess when we return'.

After a short while, crews piled into buses and trucks to be ferried to their aircraft. Many, like O'Brien, saw Upkeep for the first time and were 'astounded to see the massive object beneath the bomb bay'. As their crews clambered on board for the final pre-flight checks, each captain formally took possession of the machine by signing a Form 700 produced by the maintenance NCO. Several individuals performed superstitious rituals. Martin tucked a toy koala bear into his tunic as a good luck charm. His flight engineer, Pilot Officer Whittaker, watered the tail wheel. Officially, each Lancaster carried '1 UPKEEP; 6 loose 4lb INC; Pyros'.

Just after 21.00 hours, Gibson's wireless operator, Flight Lieutenant R.E.G. Hutchison, fired a red verey cartridge, the signal for engines of

COUNT-DOWN TO TAKE-OFF

all first and second wave machines, which had been switched off after the pre-flight tests, to be restarted. In a prearranged order, the aircraft made their way onto the perimeter track and towards the head of the runway. At 21.28 hours, a green light flashed from a lamp at the control caravan and Flight Lieutenant R.N.G. Barlow edged AJ-E, the first Second Wave aircraft, down the runway before lifting off and turning eastwards towards the North Sea. Operation Chastise had begun.

After the operation, the sequence of signals for take-off was queried. However, the Flying Control Officer on duty, Flight Lieutenant J. Frisby, confirmed that no variation in the normal procedure occurred that night. 'The Tower maintained silence at take-off, but were in touch by TR9 with the caravan. In the caravan the time of moving off was noted and take-off time was plus one minute. These times were transferred to the Ops Board in the Intelligence section'.

Outside the Squadron hangar to the east of the runway, Flight Sergeant Powell, office staff, civilian workers and maintenance staff together with senior and junior uniformed personnel watched. Sergeants Mess waitress, ACW2 Morfydd Jane Gronland, recalled: 'It was late evening. All the WAAFs and all the ground crew not on duty watched the great planes prepare to depart. The planes' engines had been warming up and now they began to roar. The first wave sped down the runway and heaved themselves into the sky and headed off. They were quickly followed by the second wave ... We watched with heavy hearts, because we knew that many of our young friends might never return.'

Wallis, too, was there. In his diary, he wrote, '9pm Take-off', which must be the time he moved to take up position to witness it. Herbert Jeffree, the final briefing gate-crasher, noted the long run needed to get the heavily-laden bombers off the ground against a background of 'a beautiful sunset'. He reflected that 'my job was over, theirs about to begin'. Leading Aircraftman Victor Gill watched aircraft of the first wave make their way 'round the peri [perimeter] track and away to the left before forming threes and taking off on the north-east runway to clear the boundary'. He then went 'to have something to eat and wait for them to return'. Many years later, Corporal J. Bryden wrote: 'I can still picture that Sunday night as the sun set the aircraft taking off ... and each of us saying to the other "where are they going?"'. Humphries, the adjutant, who had returned to his office after the crew buses departed for the hard stands and watched the take-off through the window, reflected that 'Lancasters always reminded me of ducks. They seemed to waddle'. After watching the aircraft away, he made his way to the

THE DAMBUSTERS: 'WAS THE RAID WORTHWHILE?'

Officers' Mess ante-room, where other administrative staff, like Caple and Watson, the engineering and armament officers, gathered. So did Section Officer Fay Gillan, the intelligence officer who sometimes flew with Martin's crew during practice. In conversation with her, Humphries realised that she, and not he, knew the targets. He was not surprised that, when she recognised his ignorance, she said: 'You know I can't say anything don't you?'

After watching the first two waves take off, many uniformed personnel and senior civilians gathered in the Officers' Mess, some to have supper and most to await the Lancasters' return. Jeffree, the final briefing gate crasher was one, Rolls Royce supervisor, C.E. Brennan, who had spent three weeks at Scampton working on the engines, another. Brennan would raise doubts that, contrary to published assumption, Roy Chadwick went with Wallis to Grantham. Brennan knew Chadwick well having spent part of his working life at Avro's in Chadderton, where he reminded Chadwick's daughter, Margaret Dove, that he saw him 'almost every day'. Although Brennan had been closely involved with preparing the aircraft, he went to the Mess 'still not knowing for certain the destination of the departed "Lancs" only rumours at this stage ... I believe about 11pm I spotted Mr Chadwick among the "brass hats" and I caught his eye. He came across and asked how I was, and did I miss dear old Stockport. We had quite a conversation. I left the Mess at about 2.30am. Mr Chadwick was still there and I was to see him no more'. This seems to prove that Chadwick remained at Scampton until he flew back to Ringwood a few hours later.

Leading Aircraftman Drury recalled: 'I was cycling into Lincoln, as I lived out of camp with my wife and family, and the Lancasters took off and flew at low level'. Referring to the second wave, which took of first and singly, he did not realise then that they were departing on the operation. For they were 'not as on other bombing missions circling to gain height before setting course for their target'. 'The evening', he remarked, 'was beautiful, without cloud.'

Back at Scampton, as the aircraft faded into the distance, the five Third Wave crews dispersed to await their delayed departure. Some passed the time throwing dice or playing cards. Sergeant D.P. Heal recalled sitting on the grass to see the first two waves away, then going back to the married quarter he shared with NCO members of his crew. 'Three were Canadian, so naturally we played poker'. Sergeant Webb, convinced that he would not survive the night, determined to 'die clean' and took a bath. As he did so, a 617 Squadron Lancaster brought down by flak was plunging into the sea off the Dutch island of Texel.

Chapter 8

First Wave: Moehne and Eder

As the sun dipped in the west, Gibson in AJ-G (ED 932/G) began to move down the south-west to north-east runway from the edge of the airfield to give the maximum distance on the ground. Unusually for a heavy bomber squadron, with Hopgood in AJ-M (ED 925/G) on his right and Martin in AJ-P (ED 909/G) on his left, Gibson did so in a vic-3 formation. Flight Lieutenant J.F. Leggo, Martin's navigator, recorded 'airborne' at 21.39 hours and at 21.48 ½ hours the three aircraft 'set course' south-eastwards to cross The Wash near King's Lynn and fly west of Norwich towards a prominent lighthouse at Southwold. Leggo estimated a 2hrs 20mins flight to the Moehne, and soon realised that his compass read 5 degrees low so made the necessary adjustment. A Gee fix at 22.17 hours confirmed they were on track and AJ-P duly crossed the Suffolk coast at 22.29 ¼ hours.

Flying over the North Sea at 200ft and 180mph, Leggo noted 'calm' conditions. Flame floats were dropped to allow estimation of drift, which proved negligible. Martin's rear gunner, Flight Sergeant T.D. Simpson, squinted down his gun sight at a second flame float to verify the first reading but did not test his guns, arguing that it was a waste of ammunition: 'I did my testing on the ground and in the butts.' The three aircraft did test the Aldis lamps, and at one point a friendly convoy flashed a recognition signal. Approaching the enemy coast, stronger winds than forecast were encountered and they made landfall at 23.06 hours, four minutes late and off course in the Scheldt estuary. Instead of passing between the islands of Shouwen and Walcheren, they found themselves crossing heavily-defended Walcheren, which fortunately caught the enemy gunners by surprise. Simpson noted AJ-P 'crossed Dutch coast ... in formation with Wingco and Hopgood'. Clear of the estuary, Gibson climbed to 300ft to identify an anticipated windmill and wireless masts. With the bomb-aimer, Spafford, using maps on a roller, rather like 'a roll of lavatory paper', assisting Flying Officer H.T. Taerum the navigator by looking out for landmarks and unexpected obstacles like high-tension cables, the leading section of the First Wave made for Roosendaal and the intersection of three railway lines, 25km west of Breda. They then picked up the Wilhelmina canal 10km east of Goirle and south-east of Tilburg having flown between Gilze-Rijen to port and Eindhoven starboard, fighter bases highlighted in the Op Order.

Reaching the junction with the Zuid Willens canal at right angles 2km south-east of Beek at 23.31 hours, the aircraft set course for a distinctive bend in the Rhine river at Rees an estimated 12½ minutes away. The Operation Order put this turning point 1 mile south-west of Rees, which would allow crews to avoid the defended port following the planned route via Ahsen, but over it for the new track: hence the amendment to 2km north-north-west of Rees. With the Rhine ahead glistening in the moonlight, the crews realised that they were too far south, a detour costing almost seven minutes. After turning to port along the river, the Lancasters ran into a barrage from barges and flak posts on shore. The aircraft reached the bend unscathed at 23.51 hours to pick up the briefed route to the lakes 2 miles south-west of Duelmen, reached according to Leggo at 00.04 ½ hours.

At 00.07 hours, Gibson's wireless operator, Hutchison, warned 5 Group of flak just short of Duelmen at 51°48N 07°12E. Received at Grantham a 00.11 hours, it was re-broadcast to the all operational Lancasters a minute afterwards. Gibson later explained that the unexpected defences close to 'lakes north of Haltern' (Duelmen) comprised 12 searchlights and light flak. An even stronger concentration of flak was encountered east of Duelmen in the vicinity of Luedinghausen, which caused the first damage to this trio of aircraft. Shortly afterwards, Flight Sergeant T.D. Simpson, the rear gunner, noted with some trepidation that Martin's Lancaster went under high-tension wires, and he recalled that 'Toby [front gunner Pilot Officer B.T. Foxlee] and I had some hectic moments engaging ground flak all the way in.' A post-war analysis of his leadership on the night claimed Gibson alerted 5 Group to flak concentrations other than near Duelmen. 'He took the same action on approaching Hamm where he saw great defensive activity, with the result that the following aircraft were enabled to avoid these areas, with consequent diminution of risk to themselves.'

Flying north of Hamm, whose railway marshalling yards were strongly defended with expanding belts of flak, Gibson made for the final turning point, where the Operation Order advised 'the high ground near Ahlen should be seen'. However, there seems to have been another agreed variation from the printed Order, which indicated a location '1 mile E.N.E. of Ahlen (5146N 0756E)'. The planned route of Taerum had '1½ M S/E Ahlen'

FIRST WAVE: MOEHNE AND EDER

without co-ordinates. Flying Officer H.S. Hobday (Knight) more precisely identified 'S. Ahlen 5140 0756E'; both Leggo (Martin) and Sergeant V. Nicholson (Maltby) put this turning point at 51°44.5N 07°22.5E. This reinforces the impression that an amendment to the Op Order, as with Rees, was agreed by navigators at a specialist briefing on 16 May. A starboard turn was then required to take the aircraft between Werl and Soest almost due south 21 miles and an estimated 6 mins (7 mins in the Op Order, based on the printed co-ordinates) to the Moehne Dam.

Warned by the order that 'the ridge of high ground running EAST to WEST should be a good indication of position', breasting this north of the equalising basin, the power station and the dam wall, they would glimpse the main reservoir beyond and fly towards the rallying point to the south over the water. The words of a post-operational report laconically sketched this inward flight: 'Various small flak posts opened up and as the aircraft flew over a defended area they were caught in the beam of searchlights while flying at very low level, but their low level and high speed helped them escape the searchlights and flak. Several searchlights were shot out of action.'

The impression gained from official accounts of the operation and attached maps, bolstered by the commercial film, is that Gibson successfully and triumphantly led his section to the Moehne. Simpson's diary tells a different story. After crossing the Dutch coast in formation, 'Lost Hoppy! Later picked up some searchlights near Rhine – shot some out somewhere – bit off track over some town – bags of shooting – lost Wingco – arrived Moehne. Hoppy and Wingco turned up.' Martin's was the first Chastise aircraft to reach the Moehne Dam at 00.15 hours on the morning of 17 May 1943.

Meanwhile, the second section of the First Wave led by Squadron Leader H.M. Young in AJ-A (ED 877/G) with Flight Lieutenant D.J. Maltby in AJ-J (ED 906/G) to starboard and Flight Lieutenant D.J. Shannon (ED 929/G) to port had left Scampton. Nicholson (Maltby's navigator), who noted the Lister as the last resort target, recorded 'chocks away' at 21.44 hours and 'airborne base' four minutes later, eventually setting course for Southwold at 21.58 hours at 150ft; an altitude maintained throughout the fight to and from the target area except for the final return phase across the North Sea. Maltby's Lancaster flew over Woodhall Spa, a future 617 Squadron base (22.05 hours), and at 22.10 hours the northern shore of The Wash, where the Aldis lamps were tested. West Raynham was reached at 22.20 ½ hours and Southwold at 22.38 ½ hours. IFF (identification friend or foe device) was turned off at 22.47 hours and three Gee fixes confirmed the Lancaster was on track over the North Sea. Crossing the enemy coast as planned in the Scheldt estuary at 23.12 hours, 'bomb fused' appeared followed by 'evasive action'; notifying trouble in the coastal region.

Roosendaal, 36 miles away, was reached at 23.25 hours, where 'leader turns too soon' for Beek, 51 miles ahead. Maltby arrived at the canal junction at 23.42 hours and began the 37 mile leg to Rees. Six minutes later, Nicholson recorded 'Gee jammed something chronic'; normal action by German defences to nullify the navigational aid. The bend in the Rhine was located at 23.56 hours and the aircraft set course for Duelmen. At 00.00 hours, Nicholson wrote: 'Flak fired at a/c. Evasive taken' and nine minutes later the lakes were reached. Shortly afterwards, more 'evasive action' was necessary, probably at the concentration met by Gibson at Luedinghausen 25km south-west of Muenster. After turning at the amended Ahlen position at 00.19 ½ hours, AJ-J arrived at the Moehne at 00.26 hours.

Shannon's bomb-aimer, Flight Sergeant L.J. Sumpter, did not use a roller, but folded 1: 250,000 maps with high-tension cables etched in red. He recalled that the turning points, illuminated in the bright moonlight, were easily identified and he was able to pick out obstacles in time to warn his pilot. At low level there was so much to do that there was no opportunity to worry about flak, 'at 20,000ft more time to think'. Shannon revealed that he and Maltby were concerned that Young persisted in gaining height, particularly at turning points, to confirm their position and were not slow to make their feelings known. Shannon recalled that, while he and Maltby flew at 150ft, Young tended to be at 500ft. Young, though, as section leader was responsible for keeping them all on track. Neither did these three reach the Moehne together, Shannon admitting to having arrived after the others to a hot reception. Sumpter recalled being 'hose-piped' flying over the dam wall towards the reservoir. His pilot remembered being advised by his bomb-aimer 'to get bloody well out of here'.

The third section of the First Wave, Squadron Leader H.E. Maudslay in AJ-Z (ED 937/G) with Flight Lieutenant W. Astell in AJ-B (ED 854/G) to starboard and Pilot Officer L.G. Knight in AJ-N (ED 912/G) to port according to Knight's navigator (Hobday) became airborne at 22.00 hours. Eight minutes later, the three aircraft set course for Southwold, where the English coast was crossed at 22.48 ½ hours and Upkeep fused. Like Simpson, Martin's rear gunner, Sergeant H.E. O'Brien, did not test his guns over the water nor did Hobday ask him to judge drift from released flame floats. Stronger winds than forecast over the North Sea, already experienced by preceding aircraft, meant that Hobday recorded the enemy coast crossed at 23.21 hours and Roosendaal reached at 23.34 ½ hours.

FIRST WAVE: MOEHNE AND EDER

O'Brien marvelled at the effect of the moon on the countryside below. 'Farm houses, canals, some people, rivers, roads, hay stacks, gun positons were easily seen.' Rather wistfully, he reminisced, 'I would like to do it all again, now that I can enjoy the thrill ... I also recall the men at the ground gun positions in Holland and Germany running from their positions when Fred Sutherland and I fired at them. I believe it was the tracers they were running from.' In the bomb-aimer's compartment, Flying Officer E.C. Johnson carried out 'super map reading' with a roller map, feeding information to Hobday, who checked pinpoints. Fortunately, this navigator recalled 'extraordinarily good Gee ... well beyond normal range ... almost to the German border': his log entries suggest this might actually have been inside it between Rees and Duelmen.

Johnson and O'Brien agreed that for AJ-N there was 'no real trouble – some flak, some searchlights'; not enough for Hobday to enter in his log. Sergeant F.E. Sutherland, the front gunner, did recall taking evasive action 'when we came up to power lines and that was a hairy ride'. The turning point at Beek was reached at 23.52 ½ hours, where the aircraft appear to have become separated. Flight Sergeant R.G.T. Kellow, Knight's wireless operator, reflected that 'Astell did not turn with us and did something of which I'm not sure, which put him behind us.' The flight engineer, Sergeant R.E. Grayston, more specifically recalled: 'Bill Astell was on our starboard side one minute and the next moment he'd gone. Just like that, gone.' No contact would be regained with AJ-B. 617 Squadron's Operations Record Book (ORB) believed Astell 'appeared uncertain of his whereabouts, and on reaching a canal crossing actually crossed at the correct place, and turned down the canal as if searching for a pinpoint. He fell about ½ mile behind his accompanying aircraft doing this and got slightly off track'.

There is no canal junction in the area where Astell would undoubtedly later be lost, and it seems logical that he became detached near the designated intersection at Beek in The Netherlands, east of Eindhoven. If, as the Operations Record Book maintains, AJ-B did cross at the correct intersection point, the crew might have thought that wrong and the briefed one was another similar, though in truth minor, intersection to the south near Helmond. This would have entailed turning to starboard, as Grayston recalled.

The picture is further obscured by Knight's front gunner, Sutherland, asserting that AJ-N parted company with Maudslay 'soon after crossing the Dutch coast. We didn't see or hear from him again until the Eder'. An unidentified handwritten note in Air Ministry files held that Maudslay's machine was 'believed damaged between Scheldt and Rhine ... something seen hanging down'; an observation that can only have come from Knight's crew. The fact that in the vicinity of Beek Knight climbed to 270ft is not significant, because Hobday planned to attain that height there before take-off. Nor does it indicate that he was specifically searching for Maudslay or Astell.

Hobday recorded that Knight arrived at Rees at 00.04 hours, where Sutherland remembered Johnson saying, 'Hobby you're bang on course'. At 00.12 hours, the navigator entered 5 Group's re-broadcast of Gibson's warning of flak ahead (51°48N 07°12E) and the Lancaster reached Duelmen at 00.19 hours, three minutes later than estimated. No opposition was identified before Knight reached the Ahlen turning point at 00.28 hours. Four minutes earlier, though, Hobday wrote in his log 'a/c to maintain track,' which might suggest a problem with an outer belt of the Hamm flak defences. AJ-N reached 'Target A' (Moehne) at 00.34 hours, where 'standing by', as the dam was already under attack.

Once Gibson, Martin and Hopgood gathered at the Moehne, they circled to assess the situation. Gibson remarked how 'grey and solid ... squat and heavy and unconquerable' the dam looked in the moonlight. But briefing had been accurate, the defences spiteful. They appeared, according to Gibson, either 37 or 20mm. More guns active in the meadowland below the Guenne ridge caused Gibson to report 'two positions on the north bank of the Lake on each side of the dam'. He estimated up to 12 guns (actually six) and correctly that, from their elevated positions, three would be able to fire almost horizontally at the Lancasters as they attacked over the final, open stretch of the reservoir. At least, there were neither balloons nor searchlights. Gibson was heard to say over the R/T, 'stand by, chaps, I'm going to look the place over', before making a dummy run.

As he prepared to attack in earnest after this exercise, the second section of the First Wave arrived. Maltby's navigator, Nicholson, recording the time as 00.26 hours, added, 'contact OK – circling ... flak none too light'. Reaching the area slightly later, Shannon's bomb-aimer, Sumpter, noticed the height of the surrounding hills and the navigator, Flying Officer D.R. Walker, mused that the light flak would be 'beautiful in all its different colours' under different circumstances. Shannon confirmed that, waiting for the order to attack, 'the aircraft circled in the hills'. He added all crews were aware that the longer they remained near the dam, the greater was the chance of night fighters appearing.

The agreed procedure involved the flight engineer taking care of the speed and the navigator looking out of the perspex blister on the starboard side of the cockpit to ensure that the beams met in a figure of eight forward of the leading edge of the starboard wing (Hobday immediately ordered 'up' to ensure that the intersection was not under the water). As Knight's bomb-aimer explained, 'the navigator ... was responsible for switching on [the lamps] and providing verbal indication to the pilot and all crew on the intercom about the action to be taken to put the light reflections into the correct position on the water'. The wireless operator with the aid of a valve and gauge set in motion the hydraulic motor to activate the belt for rotating Upkeep. The tactic, laid down at briefing and mentioned in the Op Order, was for individual attacks to be directed by Gibson.

With the weapon already spinning at 500rpm, each nominated aircraft would dive over the Koerbecke bridge crossing the Moehne sleeve of the reservoir, 2,800 yards from a tree-covered spit of land at the tip of the peninsula dividing the two arms of the reservoir, which up to that point had concealed the aircraft on its attack run. The aim was to obtain the 220mph ground speed and a height of 60ft by use of the converging Aldis lamps before reaching the spit, which lay 1,600 yards from the dam wall and at a slight angle to it. An added difficulty after clearing the spit to line up on the dam was another prominent strip of land to starboard jutting into the reservoir 900 yards from the wall. Having dropped Upkeep roughly half that distance from the target, the aircraft would climb swiftly over the dam and turn to port across the equalising basin and 255m high ground containing the village of Bruenningsen. That would expose them to fire from both the flak guns on the dam wall and those in the meadow below Guenne. That the attack was carried out as planned was subsequently confirmed by crew members and witnesses quoted in an official German report.

As Gibson cleared the spit where the Moehne sleeve met the main reservoir on his attack run, Flight Sergeant G.A. Deering in the front turret sprayed the active defences. This time the gunners were not confused by the low-level approach from an unexpected direction. Gibson would confess to spasms of fear, but determinedly pressed on and again the aircraft emerged unscathed. Upkeep was released at 00.28 hours at a ground speed of 230mph on a bearing of 330 degrees M (magnetic) in 'bright moon, no cloud, very good visibility'. Looking back from the rear turret, Flight Lieutenant R.D. Trevor-Roper DFM saw Upkeep bounce three times and, after about ten seconds delay as it sank, a sheet of water rose high and swamped the wall. Shannon's navigator, Walker, watched from afar as flak tracer increased in intensity when Gibson neared the dam and wondered 'will he make it?' Then 'a great spout of water went up following a terrific explosion' and Walker felt sure that a breach had been achieved. But after

THE DAMBUSTERS: 'WAS THE RAID WORTHWHILE?'

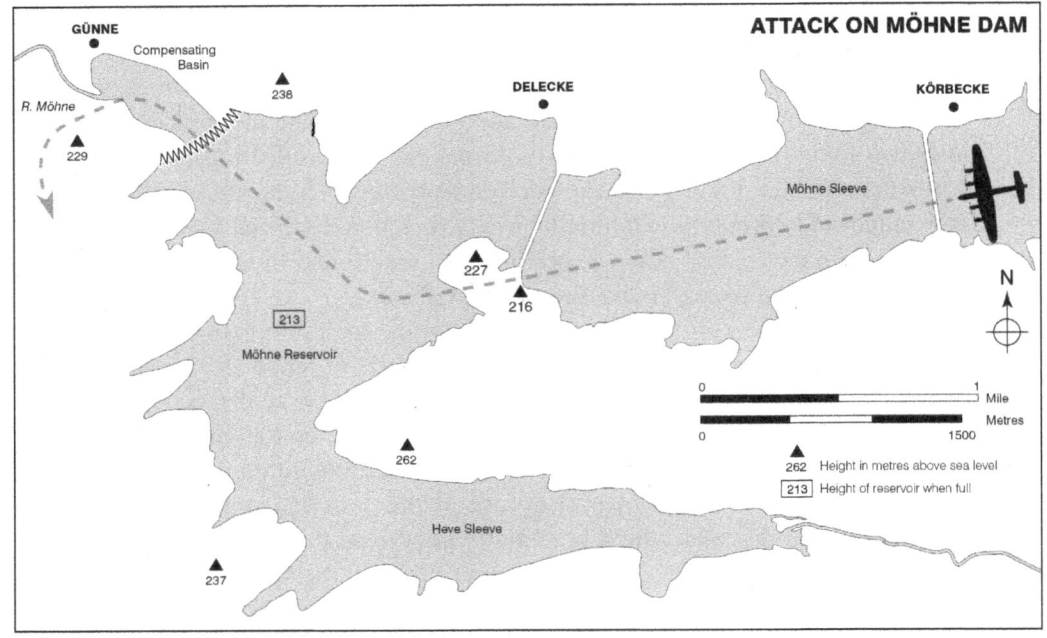

Moehne Dam Attack. Designated attack run along the Moehne sleeve of the reservoir and turn across the prominent spit of land short of the target.

the water subsided the wall remained firm. At 00.37 hours, Flight Lieutenant R.E.G. Hutchison [Gibson's wireless operator] signalled to 5 Group that Upkeep had exploded 5 yards from the dam with 'no apparent breach'; short of the left-hand tower.

Once the water had settled and the spray cleared, Gibson called in Hopgood. As AJ-M crossed the open water, the flak gunners heavily engaged an aircraft already damaged on the inward leg. Gibson noted another hit on the port wing, which Pilot Officer A.F. Burcher DFM RAAF found disabled his power-operated rear turret. The starboard wing was also hit and amid the confusion Upkeep was dropped late. So instead of striking the dam wall, it bounced over to land close to the large power station beyond. In accordance with orders, Hopgood's wireless operator fired a red signal crossing the dam with the aircraft already well alight.

FIRST WAVE: MOEHNE AND EDER

Simpson, Martin's rear gunner, observed: 'I saw Hopgood catch a packet. They must have hit a petrol tank as he was in flames as he passed over the top.' Similarly, Walker in Shannon's Lancaster recalled, 'a short sheet of orange flame coming out of the side of the aircraft – he'd been hit ... [and I] watched the aircraft crash in the valley beyond'. Sumpter, Shannon's bomb-aimer, saw the stricken Lancaster struggle to about 500ft before exploding. One wing fell off as the remains plunged to the ground near the village of Ostoennen, 6km north of the dam. In his post-operational report, Gibson suggested that some of the crew might have baled out following Hopgood's gallant effort to gain height. Three did, but only two survived to be taken prisoner.

With the loss of hydraulic power, the rear gunner Burcher had to crank his turret by hand so that he could get back into the fuselage and find the parachute stacked there. Although officially discouraged, because of likely injury caused by the tail plane, he intended to exit via the rear entrance on the starboard side just forward of his turret. He had realised that the aircraft was on fire about the time that Upkeep was released and registered the flight engineer's confirmation of the seriousness of the situation through the exchanges with the pilot over the intercom. Sergeant C. Brennan could not quell the flames and the last words Burcher heard from Hopgood was 'for Christ's sake get out of here'. In 1955, he recounted what happened to him. 'As soon as I realised what was happening, I came out of the turret. As I entered the fuselage, I saw the wireless operator [Sergeant J.W. Minchin] crawling towards me. He had been wounded. I gathered him in my arms, knowing he had a parachute buckled on, and managed to throw him out of the plane.' Burcher opened his own parachute, which billowed in his arms, when 'there was a tremendous explosion and I found myself on the ground'. The tail plane had badly damaged his back and, immobilised, he was captured.

The bomb-aimer, Canadian Flight Sergeant J.W. Fraser, also managed to bale out and survive. He recalled that, approaching the dam, he waited for the 'two points' on his version of the Dann sight to coincide with the towers, when he would 'press the tit' to release Upkeep. Before doing so, he had time to reflect that, with the aircraft illuminated by the Aldis lamps, it was 'pretty simple duck shooting' for the flak gunners. Gibson's words seems distinctly optimistic: 'Cooler 2, it's your turn to attack. It's a piece of cake'. In reality, alerted by Gibson's two runs, the weapons on the towers 'crossed up on us', reinforced by the third gun on the right. Fire was 'intense', with 'no alternative but to fly through the middle of

THE DAMBUSTERS: 'WAS THE RAID WORTHWHILE?'

it'. Orders were that, if Upkeep could not be dropped accurately, aircraft should overshoot, do a circuit and try again. Fraser was about to abort the release when AJ-M was hit severely, so he let Upkeep go knowing that he had done so fractionally late. Like Burcher, he heard the tense exchanges between Brennan and Hopgood, by which he understood that the starboard wing had been hit and one engine was alight. The flight engineer quelled the fire 'for an instant', but 'it burst out again'. About 25 seconds after crossing the dam came Hopgood's urgent order to bale out. In his forward department, Fraser had no idea of the extent of the damage or who might have been wounded behind him. Strangely, he made no reference to Pilot Officer G. Gregory the front gunner in the nose of the aircraft with him. Lying over the escape hatch, he reached to clip his parachute on, pulled the hatch open and, as the manual advised knelt facing forward. Peering down through the hole, 'the trees looked awfully damned close'. Similar to Burcher, because of the low altitude, he pulled the ripcord and let the parachute billow in from front of him and effectively pull him out. 'The tail wheel then whizzed by my ear', before he swung into a vertical position and two or three seconds later touched the ground without injury. Ahead, he saw Hopgood's Lancaster explode as it hit the ground, '1,500–2,000m away'. Behind him, the self-destructive fuse had detonated and the power station went up with 'a gigantic flash'. The wall, though, survived.

Ten minutes after Gibson, Martin launched the third attack. As he did so, Gibson displayed courageous leadership by flying beside him slightly ahead to starboard to engage the gunners and distract from Martin's approach. The right-hand tower was clearly visible, but smoke from the burning power station obscured the one on the left. AJ-P flew in at a ground speed of 217mph and bearing of 335 deg M. The Lancaster was hit, but the flight engineer, Whittaker, knew that none of the tanks carrying fuel had been holed. With Upkeep spinning at 480rpm, the bomb-aimer, Flight Lieutenant R.C. Hay, released Upkeep at 00.38 hours. The wireless operator, Flying Officer L. Chambers RNZAF, fired the required red verey as the machine crossed the wall before Martin turned to port and Simpson, in the rear turret, engaged the flak positions beneath Guenne. Martin noticed a large column of water rising above the pall of smoke, which prevented Simpson from seeing how many times Upkeep had bounced. In reality, the weapon had veered to the left after release and exploded close to the western bank of the reservoir. It swamped the left-hand tower and, unknown to the attackers,

FIRST WAVE: MOEHNE AND EDER

disabled the flak gun. Wireless operator, Chambers, signalled explosion 50 yards from the wall, like Hutchison with 'no apparent breach'.

In his diary, Simpson wrote: 'Hoppy shot down. We were next – shot up badly, got through however.' A tendency to veer left towards the end of its run had been noted during trials at Reculver, possibly because the weapon did not hit the water precisely horizontal so pivoted on its rim. An alternative cause might have been the unscheduled visit to the Scampton tarmac adversely affecting the balance. Writing to Dr Collins in 1972, Wallis chose the first option. 'The cylinder had a <u>great</u> disadvantage in that while a slight degree of roll on the aircraft at the instant of release had no perceptible effect on the directional accuracy of the run, the result of the roll of the cylinder was disastrous in that one end striking the water before the other caused the cylinder to run on the arc of a circle.'

Three Lancasters had now attacked and the Moehne remained intact. Gibson called in Young in AJ-A. This time, Gibson patrolled the air (far) side of the dam in an attempt to draw the flak fire on the wall and in the meadow beyond. As further distraction, Martin bravely flew in on Young's left. Gibson recorded that Young's Upkeep made 'three good bounces', hit the dam and exploded in contact with it, and at 00.50 hours Young's wireless operator (Sergeant L.W. Nichols) informed Grantham that Upkeep had achieved 'contact with dam', though 'no apparent breach'. Gibson, too, was convinced, that the wall had been hit. Nevertheless, at 00.44 hours he had called in Maltby, the fifth aircraft, Nicholson recording 'receive OK. Flak'. This time, Gibson and Martin orbited to starboard and port respectively in front of the dam to distract the gunners. The smoke had now largely dispersed and visibility was good, though Maltby reflected that his machine was highlighted by the moon for the gunners. He would have preferred to be running into it. As AJ-J neared the target at a ground speed of 232mph on a course of 330 deg M, Maltby realised that 'the crown of the wall was already crumbling ... [with] a tremendous amount of debris on top'. Young had been successful after all. Maltby therefore moved slightly to port and at 00.49 hours released Upkeep, which bounced four times. The pilot recorded: 'Our load sent up water and mud to a height of a thousand feet ... It rose with tremendous speed and then gently fell back. You could see the shock wave at the base of the jet.'

Nicholson wrote in his log: 'Bomb dropped. Wizard. Send Message'. Despite Maltby's observation of crumbling along the top of the dam and Gibson's feeling that Young's Upkeep had hit it, there was no clear evidence yet of a breach: at 00.55 hours Maltby's wireless operator, Sergeant

THE DAMBUSTERS: 'WAS THE RAID WORTHWHILE?'

A.J.B. Stone, sent the same message as Young's wireless operator: contact with the dam with 'no apparent breach'. So Gibson called in Shannon. As AJ-L prepared to attack and the water subsided, a gap appeared through which surged a torrent, to Gibson 'looking like porridge in the moonlight'.

Quickly, Gibson told Shannon not to proceed and all the aircraft circled to witness the spectacle. Meanwhile, at 00.56 hours, Hutchison signalled 'Nigger' to Grantham, signifying success at the Moehne. Shannon recalled 'a most fabulous sight ... it was almost impossible to describe the elation in success, as he watched more and more water pour through the shattered wall'. Gibson similarly noted: 'This was a tremendous sight which no man will probably see again,' and Simpson, Martin's rear gunner, later wrote: 'I have vivid memories of seeing a huge sheet of water as the dam gave way.'

The seven aircraft orbited before the next phase, Hopgood and Astell not there, with Martin and Maltby about to fly back to Scampton. Maudslay, Shannon and Knight with Upkeep, Gibson and Young without the weapon, but designated leader and deputy leader, were left to go on to the Eder Dam. Walker, Shannon's navigator, remembered Gibson ordering 'B Target' before the five aircraft set off south-eastwards from the southern tip of the Moehne reservoir. Hobday, Knight's navigator, noted that they did so at 00.58 hours for the estimated 14 mins flight.

Meanwhile, the 5 Group Ops Room was digesting the implications of the various W/T messages from the attacking aircraft, not least Hutchison's last communication. Harris admitted that, as the operation got underway, those present were 'in a considerable state of excitement' and Satterly agreed that 'it was very exciting'. Cochrane and Wallis had seen the first two waves off from Scampton, before leaving for Grantham shortly after 23.00 hours. They were joined by Harris and the duty staff including the chief signals officer, Wing Commander W.E. Dunn, who had direct radio contact with the Chastise aircraft. As senior officers talked quietly together, Cochrane observed that, pacing up and down, Wallis appeared to be 'having kittens'.

For those aware of the distribution of the aircraft and order of attack, the fragmentary sequence of messages caused further anxiety. Transmission itself proved clear and questions from Grantham could, in Cochrane's words, 'be answered in a minute'. When, at 00.37 hours, Hutchison reported that Gibson had dropped Upkeep without success, Wallis muttered 'it's no good' and buried his head in his hands. Thirteen minutes later, at 00.50 hours, came Young's message again apparently reporting lack of success. Satterly recalled alarm among the Service personnel, who knew that Hopgood and Martin (message not received until 00.53 hours) were scheduled to attack

FIRST WAVE: MOEHNE AND EDER

before him. He had a mental image of disaster especially after Sergeant Nichols and Sergeant Stone, Young's and Maltby's wireless operators, indicated that their Upkeeps had hit the dam 'with no apparent breach'. However, a minute after Stone Hutchison's message that the Moehne had been breached was sent, the mood changed rapidly. Satterly saw Wallis leap in the air and pump his arms violently as elation replaced despair. Both he and Wallis later recalled vividly Harris's congratulatory remark: 'Wallis, I didn't at first believe a word you said when you came to see me. But now you could sell me a pink elephant'. It was a scene which remained with Cochrane, too. The primary target had been destroyed.

Back in Germany, the five Lancasters after leaving the Moehne met no opposition on their way to the Eder. They did not, though, find it easily due to the terrain as explained by Knight's bomb-aimer, Johnson. 'It was formed in a lengthy very winding valley with steep sides and quite high pieces of land alongside ... tending to keep available light out of the valley'. Gibson reached the reservoir too far west and took time to locate the dam, nestling beneath high hills and at the end of the sharp bend in the winding lake. He found that early morning mist had begun to gather and mingle in the surrounding trees to give an eerie atmosphere, although the neighbourhood of the dam itself was clear. Only Young appears to have been with Gibson.

Shannon also reached the reservoir too far west and compounded the error by flying initially in the wrong direction, before being corrected by his navigator onto an easterly course. Although puzzled by the absence of others, 'in very, very foggy conditions', confirmed by his bomb-aimer, Sumpter, Shannon identified what he thought was the target at Rebach, 2.5km west of the actual dam, on a sharp bend and roughly along the briefed line of attack. He was about to begin this attack, when Gibson's voice came over the R/T. After establishing that AJ-L was in the vicinity, Gibson arranged to fire red verey cartridges as a guide to joining the others. Shannon was emphatic that this was the only time that Gibson fired them and that subsequent reports he did so beyond the dam during the attacks are inaccurate.

Hobday's log recorded 'Target B standing by' at 01.12 hours, precisely the estimated 14 mins from the Moehne, suggesting that Knight and possibly Maudslay flew straight to the rendezvous point, Waldeck Castle. This medieval structure perched high over the village overlooked the final twist in the reservoir leading to the dam. As they circled preparatory to launching their attacks, with relief the crews noted no flak, searchlights nor balloon defences, and no nets in advance of the wall. The enemy relied on the natural terrain to deter or frustrate aerial attack.

THE DAMBUSTERS: 'WAS THE RAID WORTHWHILE?'

As 01.30 hours neared and darkness began to ebb, directing the proceedings from the right-hand side of the reservoir, with the attacking aircraft due to fly port circuits on the other, Gibson ordered in Shannon. The pilot recalled diving 'from 1,000ft over the castle and doing a split arse turn cross a spit of land and heading for the target' (banking to port across a prominent stretch of land extending into the reservoir below and almost opposite before lining up on the dam). 'Three or four times' (neither Shannon nor bomb-aimer Sumpter could remember precisely) he tried in vain to secure the correct approach and each time had to pull up sharply over a 343m high hill scarcely 400m beyond the dam wall before circling to try again. At 01.47 and 01.50 hours, in vain Gibson attempted to raise Astell via W/T, presumably already having tried R/T. Maudslay now tried twice unsuccessfully before Shannon made two further attempts. On the third, Sumpter said 'everything all right' and dropped Upkeep, which navigator Walker declared 'hit spot on'. Flying Officer B. Goodale, the wireless operator, signalled a small breach, the message curiously not recorded at Grantham until 02.06 hours after messages from Maudslay, Knight and Gibson.

Although damaged, the dam still stood, and Maudslay made his third attack. Gibson confirmed something hanging down beneath the fuselage, the reported damage on the inward flight. He and other watching crews saw the bomb-aimer, like Fraser at the Moehne, drop Upkeep late. On this occasion, instead of clearing the dam, it struck the parapet 'with a cordite flash', as predicted by Wallis if hit at speed. Significantly, a red verey light was fired before the explosion, suggesting that the aircraft was intact as it crossed the dam, which Johnson and Hobday in Knight's Lancaster believed. They were adamant that Upkeep detonated after Maudslay crossed the dam, though to them the aircraft itself was obscured by the lurid after-effects of the detonation. Gibson observed that the weapon had struck the top of the dam and exploded 'with a slow, yellow, vivid flame which lit up the whole valley like daylight for just a few seconds', and that he saw the aircraft 'banking steeply a few feet above it'. Members of Knight and Shannon's crews supported Gibson's contention that following a second enquiry via R/T 'are you all right, Henry?', the pilot said 'OK, leader'.

Knight's rear gunner, Sergeant H.E. O'Brien, thought Maudslay's voice 'very faint' and unnatural, but was certain he heard it. Johnson, the bomb-aimer, agreed, adding, 'I saw the aircraft quite clearly silhouetted against the explosion' – beyond it. Undoubtedly, too, at 01.57 hours Warrant Officer A.P. Cottam sent a W/T message to Grantham reporting AJ-Z's attack and indicating that it had not breached the dam. In his post-operational report,

Gibson held that 'the mine overshot and struck the parapet, detonating instantaneously. The pilot was spoken to afterwards by R/T and was heard to reply once, when he sounded very weak.' So one undated and unidentified note in Air Ministry files concluded, 'believed damaged by own mine after hitting target (probably faulty release)'. Nor does the official verdict that the aircraft had 'probably' been blown up by the explosion of Upkeep at 01.56 hours make sense, being four minutes after Knight's attack, and a minute before Cottam's signal. For some time, Maudslay's fate would remain a mystery.

If Shannon's oral testimony be accepted, backed by Sumpter who recalled 'going down by the castle ... [was] very difficult', initially the aircraft dived over or possibly close to Waldeck Castle and, therefore, had great difficulty in lining up accurately on the dam after banking sharply to port over the spit below. Sumpter remembered distinctly, like his pilot, 'us doing a sharp bank to port on the way in'. Later evidence from Knight's front gunner, Sutherland, strongly suggests that for their final attempt his crew tried a different approach, diving down a gully 1,300m north-west of the spit to gain the necessary speed and execute a gentler port turn to clear that feature. Independently, the bomb-aimer, Johnson, supported this contention in sketching the approach over the spit below the castle. Using a line crossing it from the area of Sutherland's gulley, he described as 'ideal ... but high ground, rising steeply [243m] from the lake surface, so close to the dam made getting down to dropping height almost impossible'. The course taken, he showed, was therefore much closer to the base than the tip of the spit, which made the final approach so tricky. O'Brien commented on 'the steep drop to the water surface' and of 'Les having difficulty in aligning the aircraft perfectly'.

Encouraged by Gibson's terse comment, 'make it good', Knight failed to release Upkeep on another attack run, during which O'Brien 'never thought we would get over the mountain' beyond the dam. He noted, too, 'that the aircraft had a tremor when the bomb was rotating, but this tremor did not affect my position or job'. As AJ-N carried out this manoeuvre, distracted by well-meaning comments from the other crews, Knight told Kellow to switch off the R/T. Johnson, the bomb-aimer, remarked that 'by now, of course, [we were] fully aware of the difficulty involved in mounting an attack due to the difficult position of the dam and surrounding terrain'.

O'Brien, Kellow and Hobday recalled how meticulous Knight was in his approach at a ground speed of 222mph and a course of 135 deg M, 15 degrees to the left of Shannon in 'perfect visibility' with a bright moon on the starboard beam. After clearing the spit, the Lancaster closed on the dam, O'Brien heard the navigator watching the Aldis lamps saying, 'lower, lower, lower, OK'. Upkeep was released at 00.52 hours, and from his rear turret O'Brien saw Upkeep bounce three times to strike the wall slightly to the right of centre. He 'waited for it to explode like Maudslay's, but nothing happened until the Lancaster had cleared the mountain', then he had a grandstand view of the outcome. 'I was the only one of our crew to have a front centre seat at the breaching of the Eder as our aircraft was standing on its tail for the climb-out. Simultaneously, the dam broke and a column of water rose vertically behind us. It is the column of water that I remember most vividly … it was like a plume. I exaggerate when I say it rose to 1,000ft, it only seemed like it.' In fact, O'Brien was not alone in witnessing the scene. Kellow, the wireless operator, was looking behind from the astrodome. 'When we passed over the dam wall at the Eder we had to clear a large hill directly ahead of us. After the mine had been dropped, Les pulled the nose up quite sharply in order to clear the hill and in doing so I could look back and down at the dam wall. It was still intact for a short while, then as if some huge fist had jabbed at the wall a large almost round black hole appeared and water gushed as from a large hose.'

Further forward, Knight, Grayston, the flight engineer, Hobday, the navigator, Sutherland and Johnson in the nose were in no position to see what happened to the dam. They were preoccupied with self-preservation. Johnson recalled:

> The recovery from low level as the bomb was released to clear the large hill immediately facing the dam wall was quite hair raising and required the full attention of the pilot and engineer to lay on emergency power for the engines and climbing attitude not approved in any flying manual and a period of nail biting from the rest of us, not least me who was getting too close a view of the approaching terra firma from my position in the bomb-aimer's compartment. By the time we had recovered a normal flying position and circled back, the dam had gone much to our delight … in our excitement we began to follow the tidal wave released from the dam until Gibson called us up to say it was time we left the area and set course for home.

In Shannon's Lancaster, Sumpter heard 'a hell of a bang' and almost immediately the rear gunner, Flying Officer J. Buckley, 'yelled over the

FIRST WAVE: MOEHNE AND EDER

intercom, "it's gone"'. By the time Knight had cleared the hill and circled to port to get a better view of the destruction, the bridge that had remained above the hole had collapsed. O'Brien thought the murky flood resembled treacle and many of the exclamations over the R/T, he recalled, were somewhat colourful. He experienced 'great joy. We felt the exquisite pleasure one feels when he had completed a difficult task perfectly'. Sutherland believed the result 'a terrific sight' and was relieved that they would not have to return to finish the job. He recalled that Cochrane had said: 'If you don't do it to-night, you're going back again.' The following day, 'a pilot', who was unidentified, confirmed that the dam had been breached in two places: 30ft below the top and a second break 'towards the eastern end of the dam'. He added that a 30ft wave then 'surged through the valley'.

Undeterred by the ecstatic outbursts, at 01.54 hours Hutchison sent 'Dinghy', notification of success at the Eder. Six minutes later, Kellow in AJ-N confirmed a large breach in the dam. Now came the sobering thought

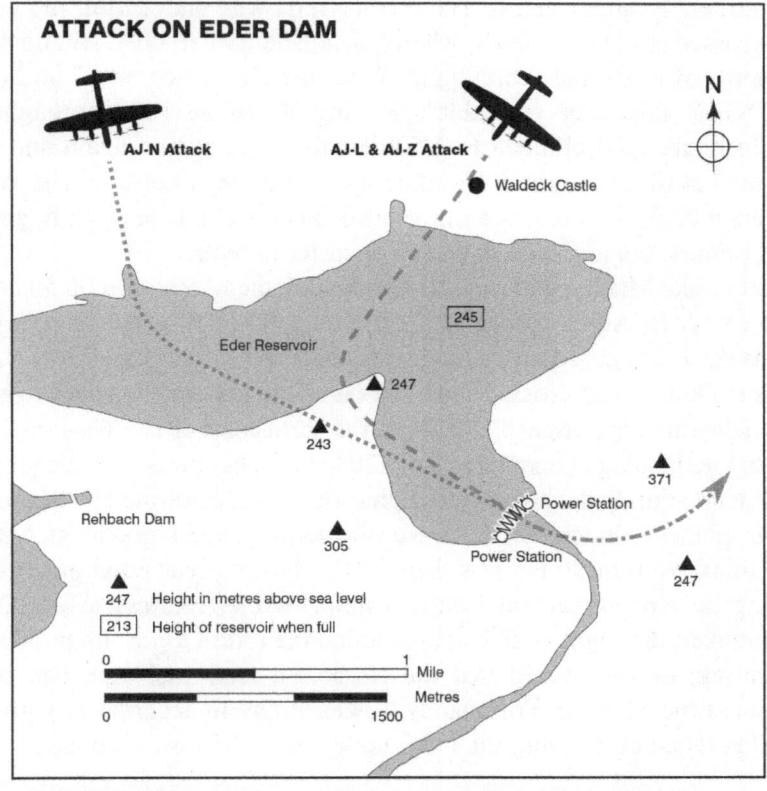

Eder Dam Attack. Sketch of the attack runs of AJ-L, AJ-Z and AJ-N.

THE DAMBUSTERS: 'WAS THE RAID WORTHWHILE?'

of having to get back safely, particularly fearing night fighters. Gibson said, 'good shooting boys', and ordered the aircraft to follow the briefed return routes. O'Brien agreed, 'we didn't stick around too long'. The feeling of 'elation ... was short lived, as we then faced the journey to base.'

Receipt of 'Dinghy' triggered renewed excitement at Grantham. Harris immediately phoned Portal in Washington and received warm congratulations. He firmly dismissed the delightful rumour that a Lincolnshire operator had first of all connected him to the local White House hostelry. Portal undertook to inform Prime Minister Winston Churchill. But Operation Chastise was still not over. At 02.10 hours, 5 Group asked Gibson how many aircraft of the First Wave remained to attack the Sorpe. 'None' came the reply.

Maltby had already made his way back from the Moehne, leaving the target area at 00.53 ½ hours. Flying via Ahlen to Duelmen, no opposition was noted in Nicholson's log, but shortly afterwards 'evasive action' occurred before Nordhorn, just inside the German border, 85km north-west of Muenster. Progress across The Netherlands was uneventful, the coast being crossed at 01.53 ½ hours, where Nicholson wrote: 'GEE still no dice. Flak north of coast and searchlight'. Over the North Sea, at 02.06 hours came 'GEE faint but workable'. Having flown at 100ft throughout, at 02.26 hours AJ-J climbed to 1,500ft only to go 'down again and test spotlights' at 02.36 ½ hours. Wainfleet bombing range north of The Wash came up at 02.53 ½ hours, Scampton at 03.06 hours and the aircraft landed at 03.11 hours, the initial First Wave Lancaster to return.

Martin, like Maltby, flew back after bombing the Moehne, at 00.56 hours setting course for Ahlen, reached at 01.03 hours. AJ-P followed the same exit route as AJ-J. Leggo, Martin's navigator, recorded 'flight plan flown ... on all legs to Dutch coast' crossed at 01.46 hours. The Lancaster appears to have reached the English coast at 02.35 hours, the north coast of The Wash at 03.05 hours before landing at Scampton at 03.20 hours. There was no indication of enemy action during the homeward flight, which was confirmed by Simpson, the rear gunner. 'On the way back we saw nothing, thank goodness, but by then I think we were flying less than 50ft'; Martin's celebrated practice of brushing the tree tops paid off. Simpson simply wrote, 'returned to base OK'.

Whittaker, the flight engineer, also found the return flight 'no problem'. On landing, he discovered that the starboard outer fuel tank had been ruptured at the Moehne. Fortunately, it was empty in accordance with the normal practice of draining the outer tanks first. There was damage to the

FIRST WAVE: MOEHNE AND EDER

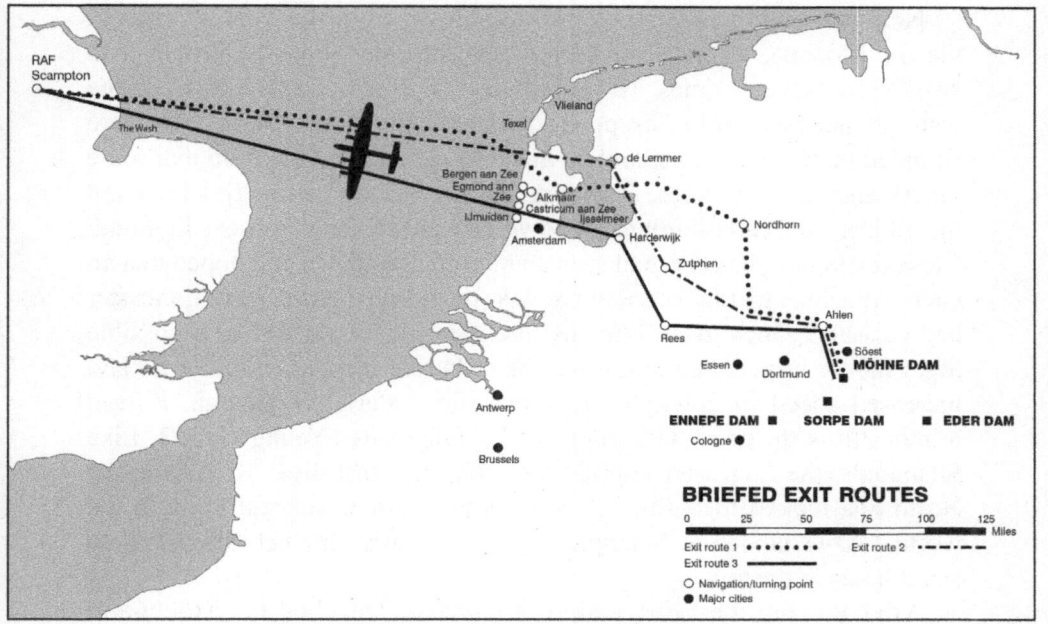

Exit Routes. Eight of the surviving Lancasters flew right to left over the Helder Peninsula towards the North Sea. Some encountered heavy flak and AJ-A was shot down off Castricum. Three others returned via the Frisian Islands to the north, two certainly using the gap between Texel and Vlieland.

starboard aileron, as well, and Whittaker was relieved that none of this was serious. Martin reacted less calmly. When the test pilot, Summers, arrived he complained bitterly that the flak gunners had the gall to hole 'Popsie', his pet name for AJ-P.

Shannon landed next. He seems to have followed the same exit route as Maltby and Martin over the Ijsselmeer and Helder peninsula, but he recalled he did not do so via the Moehne as the Operation Order required. He had an uninterrupted flight, according to Sumpter even at the coast. Three miles short of the North Sea, over the peninsula, Shannon took AJ-L up to 800ft and crossed the shore at almost 300mph in a fast dive. He landed back at base, 'terribly elated' and looking forward to the inevitable party, at 04.06 hours. One tiny hole in the fuselage had been caused by flak when crossing the Moehne Dam on the way in.

THE DAMBUSTERS: 'WAS THE RAID WORTHWHILE?'

Next to arrive was Gibson, who had flown from the Eder as ordered via the Moehne, where he observed that the river towards Neheim had swollen to 'several times its normal size'. Furthermore, the level of the water in the reservoir had dropped so dramatically that pleasure boats were stranded on the exposed shoreline mud. AJ-G followed the third exit route via Ahlen, Duelmen, Rees, Doesburg, Harderwijk, across the Ijsselmer and the Helder peninsula through a known gap in the defences near Egmond. Close to Hamm, the crew had seen an aircraft shot down and hoped that an enemy machine had fallen victim to flak. In reality, a Third Wave Lancaster had perished. Once over Germany, the rear gunner warned of a possible night fighter in pursuit and Gibson, like Martin, dropped to low-level and increased speed to 240mph. No threat did materialise, though. Fifteen minutes from the coast, Gibson unsuccessfully called Young via R/T. Like Shannon's, the Lancaster crossed the coast in a fast dive. To Gibson the North Sea looked 'beautiful ... perhaps the most wonderful thing in the world'. AJ-G landed at Scampton at 04.15 hours, having suffered three small holes in the tail.

After leaving the Eder, Knight's Lancaster reached the Moehne at 02.08 ½ hours, where the bomb-aimer, Johnson, like Gibson, remarked on the torrent of water surging down the river towards Neheim. Wireless operator, Kellow, was 'fascinated by the amount that the water in the reservoir had dropped'. When a solitary flak gun opened up, Knight took evasive action. After leaving the Moehne, flying at 220mph and a height of 100ft, he set off to follow the second exit route via Ahlen, Duelmen, positions 3 miles south-west of Haltern (51°43N 07°07E) and 1 mile north of Zutphen (52°10N 06°12E) to Elburg on the Dutch mainland 40 miles due east of the Helder peninsula. After flying over the Ijsselmeer, AJ-N crossed the Dutch coast at 02.59 hours, after which speed was reduced to 190mph. Over the North Sea, the aircraft climbed to 400ft and Hobday recorded 'nav lights on – nearing [English] coast'. AJ-N reached Scampton at 04.12 and landed at 04.20 hours.

Crew members remembered a relatively trouble-free flight. Johnson, the bomb-aimer, recalled, 'we flew very low and at maximum speed – independently and navigating ourselves mostly on close map reading'. However, the Lancaster did temporarily go off track between Zutphen and Harderwijk, there were some unpleasant flak bursts near Borken and, according to O'Brien, 'Fred Sutherland, our front gunner, blasted the engine of a train or freight train, which was stationary in small town.'

FIRST WAVE: MOEHNE AND EDER

The second incident reveals that luck had its place. 'We were flying very low during the return journey and at the Dutch coast the terrain rose under us. Les pulled up, over and down. On the sea side of this rise in the terrain and invisible to Les was a large cement block many feet high. This block passed under our tail not three feet lower. As the rear gunner, I was the only one to see it.' Fortunately, there were no further alarms. Hobday reflected: 'It turned out OK in the end and I was glad that we took the northerly route back [not the inward one] ... The navigation on the raid was tricky and the approach to the Eder, bearing in mind the requirements of height, speed and distance, needed a lot of skill, particularly on Les Knight's part.'

Five Lancasters of the First Wave had now returned safely to Scampton. Astell had been lost on the way to the Moehne, Hopgood at that dam. It would emerge that Young and Maudslay were shot down flying back from the Eder.

Harris, Cochrane and Wallis left Grantham at 04.00 hours on Monday 17 May, arriving at Scampton while the First Wave crews were being debriefed. Apart from the usual questions from an intelligence officer, each pilot had to complete a questionnaire about visibility at the target, rmp at which Upkeep was spun, particulars of the explosion and damage to the target, effectiveness of the system of control and value of the 100 per cent tracer ammunition used. Space was allowed for added comments.

Confirming that Young and Maltby had caused breaches at the Moehne, Gibson wrote: 'There are two holes in the dam.' Of the Eder, he recorded: '1st and 3rd [Shannon and Knight] hit 2nd [Maudslay] overshot.' He considered that VHF had proved a 'perfect' method of control and approved the use of 100 per cent tracer: 'Very effective against gun positions. No dazzle. Perfect for this job.' Martin agreed: 'Very good trip. Numerous searchlights and light flak positions north of the Ruhr against which gunners did wizard work. Rear gunner extinguished two searchlights. Front gunner shot up other flak posts and searchlights. Navigation and map reading wizard. Formation commander did great job by diverting the gun fire from target towards himself. Whole crew did job well.' About tracer, Martin felt: 'No trouble and slightly easier to aim.' He found VHF control 'excellent', and added: 'In two cases a second aircraft flew alongside the one bombing and machine-gunned ground defences on north side of objective'; reference to Gibson going in with Martin and Martin similarly helping Young.

Maltby thought: 'Good route, flak free and easy to map read'. Shannon was equally enthusiastic about the route, effect of tracer, VHF control and the overall plan. He believed that his Upkeep had 'made a gap 9 feet wide

THE DAMBUSTERS: 'WAS THE RAID WORTHWHILE?'

towards the east side' (right-hand flying towards the dam) and that the third aircraft (Knight's) had 'widened the gap'. He 'saw second aircraft overshoot'. Knight, though, proved less happy about the ammunition used: '100% tracer dazzled gunner but appeared to frighten searchlight and gun crews. Opinion of gunner – ordinary tracer would have caused greater accuracy because of reduced dazzle.' However, he considered: 'Routeing excellent. Reports from aircraft ahead re flak found to be very useful. Attack straightforward and as predicted. It was found possible to gain 1,000 feet easily after dropping the mine. Satisfied that the raid was successful.' In his log book, Shannon's bomb-aimer, Sumpter, wrote sparsely: 'Op No 14 via Holland to the Hun. Satisfactory attack on Eder Dam 18 miles west of Kassel. Average ht. 100 feet'. In his, Gibson entered: 'Led attack on Moehne and Eder dams. Successful.'

After debriefing, crews waited for others to return; Shannon's did so until after 07.00 hours. Wallis stayed up, too, until persuaded to go to bed in Group Captain Whitworth's house. As he did so, WAAFs were summoned from their quarters, the bar staff dispensed generous quantities of beer, which Gibson had instructed the adjutant, Humphries, to have ready, and a spontaneous party began in the Officers' Mess. When he returned, Flight Lieutenant J.C. McCarthy remarked on how discarded cans on the floor, 'gradually grew in quantity as each crew returned'. Such were the revels, that Pilot Officer Hobday admitted to regaining consciousness sunk deeply in an armchair at 13.00 hours on that Sunday. By then the toll of lost aircraft was known and the process of informing next of kin underway.

Chapter 9

Second Wave: The Sorpe

In the draft Order of Battle drawn up by Gibson on 12 May, the five aircraft bound for the Sorpe had been Pilot Officer Rice, Sergeant (since promoted Flying Officer) Byers RCAF, Sergeant (Flight Sergeant) Townsend, Sergeant (Flight Sergeant) Anderson and Pilot Officer Burpee DFM RCAF. They were designated Third Wave 'Target C only'. Their take-off times, 22.05–22.25 hours (at five minute intervals) overlapped with those of the Second Wave (three minute intervals), 22.21–22.36 hours. In the Op Order of 16 May, the Sorpe-bound aircraft were now the second wave and rescheduled to leave before the other two waves. The line-up and take-off intervals had also been changed. Three very experienced pilots, Flight Lieutenant J.C. McCarthy, Flight Lieutenant J.L. Munro and Flight Lieutenant R.N.G. Barlow, were now included.

The aircraft were to take-off individually aiming to cross the enemy coast at the Frisian Island of Vlieland, 120 miles north-north-east of the First Wave's Scheldt access route. They would initially fly almost due east to cross the Lincolnshire coast north of Skegness at Mablethorpe and rely on Gee fixes to navigate across the North Sea to make landfall. Crews were warned that Vlieland was low-lying and situated between the more prominent, heavily-defended Texel to starboard and Terschelling to port, the string of islands being north-north-west of The Ijsselmeer (Zuider Zee).

The Lancasters were due to cover the 228 miles from Scampton to Vlieland in 76 mins, flying at 180mph airspeed and a maximum height of 500ft, an altitude limit to be kept until the Ahlen turning point before the Moehne Dam, when up to 1,000ft was permitted. The last navigational check before the enemy coast, 5 miles north-north-east of Vlieland (53°20N 04°54E), would take the Lancasters over the narrowest part of the island. Crews were warned that 'VLIELAND is to be crossed at ZERO feet or as low as practicable'. They would make for Stavoren (52°53N 05°22E) on the eastern shore of the Ijsselmeer and the mainland, 36 miles way across the Afsluitdijk polder at its entrance; then fly parallel to the shore to Harderwijk (52°21N 05°37E) a further 30 miles and 13 minutes away. There the machines would turn inland to 1 mile north-east of Doesburg (52°02N 06°09E) 31 miles and 10 minutes and 20 seconds further on, before joining the First Wave route at Rees, 22 miles and 10 minutes and 20 seconds minutes distant. The aircraft would thereafter follow the revised First Wave route via Duelmen and Ahlen to the Moehne Dam, where they must 'keep sufficiently clear to avoid interfering with the aircraft attacking Target X'. Logs of First Wave navigators show that the amended leg of the route Rees to the Moehne amounted to 85 miles in 28 mins. The final 10 miles to Target Z (Sorpe) would take an estimated 3 minutes and 20 seconds. At the target, 'attacks are to be made from the lowest practicable height at a speed of 180mph IAS ... aim to hit the water just short of the centre point of the dam about 15 to 20 feet from the edge of the water'.

The first Lancaster to commence its take-off from Scampton to attack the German dams on the evening of 16 May 1943 was AJ-E (ED 927/G), piloted by Barlow, at 21.28 hours. Nothing more was heard from the aircraft, which failed to reach the target and was considered 'shot down'.

At 21.29 hours, Munro followed Barlow in AJ-W (ED 921/G). This aircraft, too, did not reach the Sorpe but survived. The navigator, Flying Officer F.G. Rumbles, noted that it set course for the target at 21.42 hours, 'drift nil' and the Lincolnshire coast was reached at Mablethorpe 'on track' at 21.54 hours, where it 'increases speed a little' to 175mph. Gee fixes over the North Sea confirmed that A-W remained on track, Vlieland being sighted at 22.56 hours and 'bomb fused'.

Bomb-aimer, Sergeant J.H. Clay agreed that 'take-off was smooth. The flight across the North Sea was uneventful and comfortable. Flying at such low altitude does not necessitate an addition to battledress, thick vest, long johns, two pairs of socks, two pairs of gloves, outer Sidcot [flying suit over uniform] and cap comforter tucked under my flying helmet, which I usually wore on 97 Sqn'. Clay recalled that, 'the sun had set when we reached the enemy coast but there was a little gloomy moonlight. I thought I saw someone to starboard skim the water and send up a plume of spray – it could have been Geoff Rice or Barlow or Byers' [probably Byers heading towards Texel]. AJ-W then ran into trouble, the official conclusion being that Munro's aircraft was 'damaged' by light flak crossing Vlieland at 22.57 hours. Apart from substituting the island further west, the front gunner Sergeant W. Howarth agreed: 'We had almost flown across the island of Texel when we were caught by light flak guns.'

SECOND WAVE: THE SORPE

His pilot attributed their misfortune to land-based flak firing from the port side. Years later, he reflected: 'I can clearly remember to this day seeing the breakers ahead of me and realising I would have to gain a bit of height to clear the dunes, which I did. I had just passed the crest of the dunes and was starting to lose a bit of height on the other side when a line of tracer appeared on the port bow and hit the aircraft between the engine and the rear gunner ... Bang! Hit by one shell'. A detachment of 3/Marine Flak 246 with 20mm guns stationed on the western end of Vlieland reported engaging 'several Lancaster bombers' between 22.57 and 23.40 hours that night. Feasibly, these gunners could have engaged AJ-W from the port side (as Munro recalled), while crossing Texel (if Howarth were correct) though this is pure speculation. There was another detachment, 4/Marine Flak 246 on the eastern end of Vlieland, and more likely that was responsible as Munro correctly crossed the island. Without doubt, though, as Howarth wrote, the aircraft was 'badly damaged':

> The intercom had been put out of action, also our VHF for communication with other aircraft in the wave; the master unit for the compass was destroyed and I believe that the tail turret pipes were damaged. This meant that we could not speak to each other in the plane – essential for calling out height and speed and direction in case of fighter attack. We could not speak to the other planes in the wave, and were left with one rather unreliable compass, and very little defence against fighters. By the time the damage was assessed, we were well into the Zuider Zee, and our pilot Les Munro decided we had little chance of success if we went on, and decided to turn for home.

Clay agreed with the extent of the damage, but attributed it to another source after clearing the Frisian Islands:

> Then we were over Vlieland into the Zuider Zee, when suddenly a flak ship opened up. None of us in the aircraft saw this vessel although we had, as was customary, been keeping a sharp look-out. We must have been a sitting target to the gunners below, a close target silhouetted against the sky. A hole was torn in the fuselage amidships, the master compass unit demolished and our intercom completely dead. Les kept

THE DAMBUSTERS: 'WAS THE RAID WORTHWHILE?'

on course for a while. Then Frank Appleby [flight engineer] passed a short note down to me. It said as far as I remember 'Intercom U/S – should we go on?' No doubt Les had been considering the position. I wrote, 'We'll be a menace to the rest.' Had it been a high-level operation there would have been time to make up some sort of signals between bomb-aimer, flight engineer and pilot, which may have worked. But on a quick moving low-level operation like this and with other aircraft in close proximity, Les could neither give nor receive flying instructions from the navigator nor bombing instructions from the bomb-aimer. A few minutes later, we altered course for home [and] so ended W for William's effort in respect of this particular raid.

No other crew member referred to a flak ship in the area nor do available German records mention one. Undoubtedly, however, at 23.06 hours the Lancaster began a reciprocal course for Scampton and almost certainly, although not recorded, came under fire from the island defences before gaining the safety of the North Sea. Rumble's log reflects none of this action, simply '23.06 a/c reciprocal DR compass MV gone. Flak. Intercom dead' and at 23.09 hours, 'a/c BASE'. 'Skipper informed bomb fused' was entered at 23.13 hours, followed by a series of Gee fixes with speed gradually reduced from 180 to 165mph. At 00.16 hours, the Lancaster crossed the coast at Mablethorpe again and flew west to touch down at Scampton at 00.28 hours; the first Chastise aircraft to return. At the very last minute, tragedy almost struck. Without means of communication, Munro flew straight in, unaware that another Second Wave early return was circling the base preparatory to landing and took evasive action to avoid a collision. In 1955, Munro reflected: 'I am one of the lucky ones. I always flew my lucky plane, W for William. I was bitterly disappointed, but I suppose that is why I am about to-day.'

In the Officers' Mess, the squadron engineering officer, Flight Lieutenant Caple, hearing the roar of engines recognised an early return and invited Humphries to go out to see the machine with him. The adjutant noted that the Lancaster was 'easily visible with landing lights blazing ... [but] much to our amazement we could also see shadowy figures running away from the machine'. Caple stopped a fleeing airman, who gasped that 'Flight Lieutenant Munro's ... just landed with his bomb still on and I think it's going to drop off.' Thoroughly alarmed, Caple turned the truck round

SECOND WAVE: THE SORPE

and raced back to the Mess. There he expressed his fear to Flying Officer Watson, the armament officer. Completely relaxed, Watson agreed to 'nip across and see what all the flap is about ... but I bet my lads have solved the problem already, and if they haven't, then you'd better duck'. Fortunately, the armourers, who had not fled, did have the matter under control. When Munro entered the Mess, Humphries observed that 'he was "hopping mad" with his bad luck'.

Pilot Officer V.W. Byers in AJ-K (ED 934/G) followed Munro down the Scampton runway one minute later at 21.30 hours. Like Barlow no further communication was established with this aircraft. The crew of Pilot Officer G. Rice's following Lancaster reported an aircraft flying at an estimated 300ft shot down 'off Texel' at 22.57 hours, which would later prove to be AJ-K; the first loss of the night.

'Chocks away' was recorded at 21.31 hours for Rice piloting AJ-H (ED 936/G), the fourth aircraft bound for the Sorpe. The machine crossed the North Sea in 'perfect conditions' and without enemy interference. Flying Officer R. MacFarlane, the navigator, noted that at intervals flame floats were dropped, which the rear gunner, Sergeant S. Burns, looked at through his reflector sight and confirmed no drift. Four minutes after Upkeep was fused, at 22.59 hours flying low Rice crossed 'the narrow part of the island without making the southerly turn as planned. I don't know how we achieved this, but we were dead on track. I was so low that I had to pull up over sand dunes'. A post-operational report confirmed that Rice's aircraft did not make the designated course adjustment at 53°20N 04°54E. Once clear of Vlieland, Rice climbed to confirm position, then sank low again to follow the briefed route. By now Gee had failed, as AJ-H flew towards the Afsluitdijk polder. Just short of it, the flight engineer noticed the altimeter reading zero and was about to warn the pilot, when Rice recalled 'we struck the sea and there were two distinct jolts in very rapid succession. The first was when the mine struck the sea, as it was the lowest part under the A/C, and the second was when the mine struck the tail wheel'. Panels in the main section of the fuselage buckled and water gushed over the navigator's charts. As Rice pulled up, water poured through the open bomb-bay and down the fuselage to swamp the rear turret, causing Burns to utter plaintively, 'Christ, it's wet at the back' (Munro's front gunner would later muse that 'my friend Michael was nearly drowned in the rear turret'). The flight engineer confirmed to the pilot, 'you've lost the mine'. The loose weapon had driven the fixed tail wheel into the fuselage and the chemical toilet forward of the rear turret, so Burns's cubby-hole was invaded by more than clear water. Rice would blame himself for not using the Aldis lamps to check height once he had regained low-level. He would, though, refute a subsequent impression that 'we lost two engines. Not so. All four continued to function beautifully throughout the whole trip'.

Patently, this crew's participation in the operation was over. After flying across the Afsluitdijk and into the Ijsselmeer, the full extent of the damage became evident. At precisely the time that Munro turned back beyond Stavoren, at 23.06 hours Rice made for home from higher up the Ijsselmeer. Without an effective rear gun, he was concerned about being shot down and ten minutes later flew out at low-level between Vlieland and Texel. He recalled that searchlights were playing across the gap, which he went under to avoid the accompanying flak. The Vlieland-West flak battery reported a Lancaster firing on it and destroying a pair of binoculars at 23.07 hours, which possibly is a misprint for 23.17 hours and would fit Rice's exit time. Without further incident, AJ-H made its way safely across the North Sea to reach Scampton.

Rice described what happened there: 'When we reached the circuit, I sent the flight engineer, Sergeant Smith, back down the fuselage to check the hydraulic system. He found we had lost most of the fluid, so I decided to use the emergency system, which was operated by an air bottle to lower the undercarriage. Previous experience of using this had shown that after the undercarriage had locked down, there was very little pressure fully to lower the flaps'. The wireless operator therefore warned the control tower, 'aircraft damaged – possibly no flaps'. Rice explained that this meant that, 'I would be some time before I attempted a landing, as the A/C was damaged and I might not be able to use the flaps and would require the maximum amount of landing run.' He circled at 1,000ft for 20 mins, while the emergency procedure was carried out. Then, 'I ordered the crew into their crash positions before landing, which meant that five of the crew sat with their backs to the main spar facing aft, and only myself and the flight engineer were up front during the landing'. So the rear gunner was not prised from his turret after the landing, contrary to later claims. As Rice prepared to put down, Munro without any means of communication flew in below him. He had rapidly to pull up to avoid an embarrassing and possibly fatal collision over the home base.

After circling once more and allowing Munro's aircraft to clear the runway, at 00.47 hours Rice at length 'did a wheeler', with the front wheels down and tail up. Once the aircraft had 'crunched down' on its tail fins, the pilot turned it off the runway and switched off. Scrambling out, Rice walked away 'thoroughly depressed'. The station commander, Whitworth, having driven out in a truck, found him, told him to get hold of himself and gave him a lift to debriefing. Despite being embarrassed at making 'a complete balls of things', Rice waited for other crews to arrive and noticed that Gibson's hair was plastered with sweat, even though he had flown in shirt sleeves. When he arrived from Grantham, Sir Arthur Harris on learning about the incident said to Rice, 'you're a very lucky young man'. There was an interesting postscript. 'Some time later, after de-briefing, a message was received from Flying Control, asking what I meant by saying I was going to land "without a clutch". Much leg-pulling ensued with the pretty LACW WAAF, who had taken the message!'

In a post-operational report, 5 Group briefly noted, 'aircraft hit sea and lost bomb load ... fairing retaining arm, tail wheel, hydraulics U/S'. British intelligence sources learnt that the Germans had recovered an intact Upkeep, and it was assumed that this was Rice's. In 1963, Wallis still thought so: 'We know that the bomb was wiped off through low flying in Zuider Zee was also recovered intact by the Germans.' Although in the vicinity after 90 secs, when the self-destructive fuse was set to activate, the crew of AJ-H did not observe an explosion. The back-up device must have been damaged during the unorthodox detachment, which might also be true of the hydrostatic pistols. However, a later British analysis concluded: 'The chances are weighed fairly heavily in favour of it landing in shallow water.' There were mud flats in the area with only some of the channels holding over 30ft of water. Hence the depth might not have been enough to activate the three hydrostatic pistols.

The first four Second Wave aircraft thus failed to reach their target, leaving Flight Lieutenant J.C. McCarthy and his crew to achieve success. From the outset, that task was not made easy. Scheduled to lead the wave, in the final checks on the hard stand immediately before take-off, AJ-Q (ED 915/G) on which the pilot complained he 'had spent a lot of loving care ... turned sour on me with a coolant leak on No 4 or starboard outer engine', so the machine could not fly that night. The reserve Lancaster, flown up from Boscombe Down by Commander Bergel that afternoon had been prepared as a reserve and been moved to outside of No. 1 hangar, as McCarthy later confirmed. B Flight aircraft were beyond the southern end of the south-north runway, which meant the crew had to haul themselves and their kit into a truck and dash off to claim it before anybody else – not without incident. As they left the aircraft, allegedly a parachute heaved out of the machine by the flight engineer caught on a hook and 'blossomed all over McCarthy on the ground'; reputedly, the pilot's own.

THE DAMBUSTERS: 'WAS THE RAID WORTHWHILE?'

When the crew members arrived at AJ-T (ED 825/G), time had allowed Upkeep to be hoisted into position but not the fitting of VHF radio nor the Aldis lamps. The bomb-aimer, Johnson, reflected that this would have created a major problem had the aircraft been diverted to one of the other target dams. In the chaos, he recalled that he had also left the triangular sight in AJ-Q. Fortunately, too, the crew was unaware of the potential problem with Gee, which LAC Munro hoped he had fixed. An important absence was quickly discovered: no compass deviation card, necessary for navigational accuracy. McCarthy was close enough to run to the flight offices in Hangar 2, where Flight Sergeant Powell gave him a blank card from the instrument section and another parachute. The deviation card had therefore to be filled in after the compass was swung with Upkeep in position, a process taking roughly forty-five minutes, which caused further delay.

So, instead of being in the van of the Second Wave, McCarthy took off at 22.01 hours, thirty-four minutes late and two minutes after the third section of the First Wave; the last of the initial fourteen aircraft, instead of the first. As he did so, his rear gunner Flying Officer D. Rodger reflected that their success and survival depended on close crew co-operation: 'Every operation was seven men against the Reich.'

According to the log of navigator, Flight Sergeant D.A. MacLean, the entire way to and from the target McCarthy flew at 100ft, for the initial 28 mins at 180mph, thereafter to the target at 200mph to make up lost time. The North Sea was crossed without incident, the position short of Vlieland (53°20N 04°54N) reached at 23.13.30 hours, Stavoren at 23.25.30 hours and 'bombs fused' [*sic*] at 23.31 hours, when MacLean appeared to get a Gee fix (the last) at 52°50N 05°31E. Harderwijk came up at 23.37.30 hours, Doesburg 23.49 hours, Rees 23.57 hours, Dulmen lakes 00.10 hours and Ahlen at 00.20 hours, where MacLean noted, 'WOP [wireless operator] fixing TR9 [radio] under my table'. At no point did he indicate enemy activity. AJ-T was at the Moehne at 00.27 hours and the Sorpe target 3 minutes later. The next entry read: '00.46 IAS 180 Ht 30ft bombs gone'. An interesting postscript to these entries was the belated revelation by Johnson, the bomb-aimer, that 'Len Eaton [the wireless operator] lost W/T shortly after take-off and Joe told him not to record this in his log book as strictly they ought to turn back'. As no R/T facility had been fitted, in effect AJ-T could communicate with no other aircraft, nor 5 Group in the absence of W/T. Another interesting issue is that the Lancaster took 7 mins, not 6 mins as with First Wave aircraft, from Ahlen to the Moehne Dam. This suggests that Second Wave aircraft adhered to the Operation Order point 1

SECOND WAVE: THE SORPE

mile east-north-east of Ahlen, not the amended one to the south followed by aircraft of the other two waves.

It would emerge that McCarthy was under the mistaken impression that those flying the more easterly route via Vlieland were doing so to distract night fighters from the First Wave, as he noted that 'in the slope of England the sun was just disappearing on the horizon'. In the bomb-aimer's compartment, Johnson was using the subdued amber light to check his map. After experimenting in training, he and MacLean had agreed not to join maps together and use a roller system. The navigator thought that 'dangerous', especially if the machine strayed off-track, when the maps would be useless. He preferred Johnson to use '½ in. folded maps' in succession.

Despite lack of note in the navigator's log, McCarthy mentioned a searchlight and two guns active on Vlieland. 'Very hot reception from the natives when crossed the coastline. They knew the track we were coming in on, so their guns were pretty well trained when they heard my motors. But, thank God, there were two large sand dunes right on the coast which I sank in between.' Johnson agreed that the aircraft was shot at 'going between two sand dunes flying across the narrow neck of the island'. Once over the mainland beyond Harderwijk, McCarthy used the shelter of hills and trees to escape the attention of the defences. He claimed that they evaded night fighters, which he 'could quite frequently see ... flying along at 1,000 feet above us', oblivious to the Lancaster 900ft below. They were 'baffled ... I don't think they expected us down there at all'. Rodger, the rear gunner, could not confirm these sightings: 'I did not see any fighters that night and there was no mention of them in our plane during the raid. You would expect these kind of reports from the air gunners, whose prime role was to search the sky at all times. However, it is possible that a pilot would notice them by chance.' Rodger did recall that he and the front gunner, Sergeant R. Batson, were 'busy'. At one point, Rodger had a lively exchange with a light flak gun, both gunners 'pumping away' until out of range, and occasionally a searchlight was doused; activity mentioned by Johnson as well. Rodger recalled another incident 'south of the Rhine' when inadvertently the Aldis lamps were switched on and there 'was an awful commotion up front, much yelling and swearing until they were turned off and we proceeded on our way'. When an 'innocent-looking train' loomed up, McCarthy said 'sure', after front gunner Batson asked permission to engage it. That was almost costly, as it turned out to be a flak train, which briskly returned fire, to inflict the only damage incurred by AJ-T that night: a cannon shell through

THE DAMBUSTERS: 'WAS THE RAID WORTHWHILE?'

the undercarriage nacelle. Bomb-aimer Johnson placed this incident close to the Moehne on the east-west railway line between Soest and Dortmund.

Johnson reflected that AJ-T saw the Moehne Dam beyond the equalising basin as it approached from the Soest direction over high ground short of the Guenne ridge. Under MacLean's direction, McCarthy then turned to starboard to pick up the Moehne river below the dam as it flowed towards Neheim. The Lancaster thus did not come under fire from any of the guns on or below the dam. In accordance with advice given to Satterly on 7 April by RAF Tempsford to fly alongside a river so that the pilot and map reader (bomb-aimer) could see clearly where they were flying, AJ-T followed the course of the Moehne alongside its starboard bank. That same communication had identified the need, if flying at low–level, for the map reader to be positioned in the nose of the aircraft and not to leave there 'unless absolutely necessary'. Short of Neheim, the aircraft altered course to port and picked up the Roehr River towards the Sorpe.

Although the dam itself was clear and as predicted there were no defences, thick mist had formed in the vicinity, and MacLean recalled difficulty in locating the target. The pilot claimed that only a yell of 'up' from the flight engineer prevented him from hitting water searching for it, which almost certainly involved the Roehr River on the approach not the dam's reservoir. McCarthy admitted to being surprised at no evidence of previous aircraft having attacked the target. The bomb-aimer agreed: 'We were puzzled to see nobody else there or evidence that there had been, even though we took off over half-an hour late. Nobody else arrived while we were there, even though five were briefed for the Sorpe.'

Approaching from the north-east, AJ-T flew round the reservoir towards the village of Langscheid from the south. As they circled over it, McCarthy pondered how to line up to fly along the top of the dam given the prominent church spire just short of it and steep hills at each end (308m west, 276m east) and uttered the immortal words, remembered by Sergeant Johnson: 'Jeez! How do we get down there?' It proved extremely difficult. Nine times, the bomb-aimer was not satisfied and refused to release Upkeep. 'There were', he recalled, 'two main reasons for this. Firstly, we had to familiarise ourselves with the target area and the method of attack. Secondly, it was extremely difficult to achieve the correct alignment and height simultaneously ... not only did we have the hills and trees to contend with but also a church steeple more or less in the direct line of approach'. Apart from the terrain, there were no Aldis lamps to establish height. After each

SECOND WAVE: THE SORPE

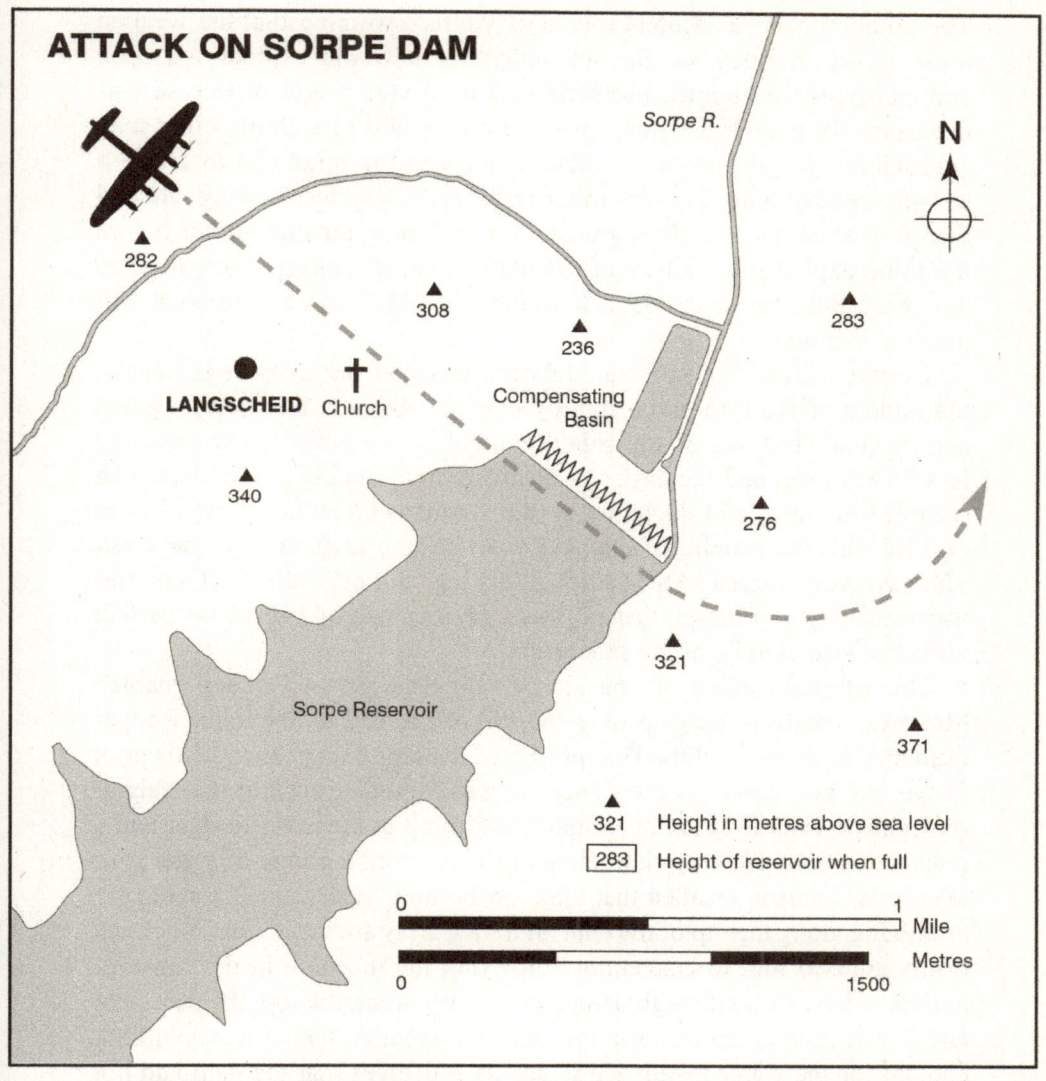

Sorpe Dam Attack. Overview of the reservoir, attack run and Langscheid village with its church spire.

abortive attempt, McCarthy pulled up over the far, eastern hill and circled to port to try again. Johnson recalled that his fellow crew members became increasingly restless. There were a series of disparaging remarks over the intercom, the most printable of which urged him to 'get that bloody thing out of here ... I had a feeling that these were aimed in my direction'.

THE DAMBUSTERS: 'WAS THE RAID WORTHWHILE?'

The bomb-aimer was acutely aware of Wallis's warning that the weapon must not be dropped too far out, otherwise it would explode too soon and endanger the aircraft. Furthermore, 'the lower height of release was necessary for greater accuracy (we had no method of sighting other than approximation), to prevent possible damage to the mine and to create a slower speed of entry into the water resulting in a slower sinking rate and therefore allowing a slightly greater "escape" time for the aircraft before the mine exploded'. Wallis had calculated that, if Upkeep were dropped 41ft from the core of the dam, it would roll 113ft before it reached 30ft depth to explode.

Eventually, on the tenth run, Johnson dropped the weapon as near to the middle of the dam as he could judge: 'I estimated the drop by guess and by God, God was on my side that night ... the lower we dropped the less forward run and the easier to estimate the dropping point.' MacLean recorded the release at 00.46 hours (the Germans 00.50 hours) at a height of 30ft with the nacelle of the port outer engine aligned with the crest. The navigator entered IAS 180mph in his log, and officially the Lancaster was travelling at 170mph ground speed on a course of 140°M in 'perfect visibility – no cloud – bright moonlight'.

The whiplash effect on the aircraft after release of Upkeep enabled McCarthy easily to pull up over the hill at the end of the dam, Rodger estimated to about 1,200ft. That prompted the rear gunner to urge his pilot to 'get the hell down' as the Lancaster was 'a sitting duck at this height' for fighters. Like O'Brien in Knight's rear turret at the Eder, Rodger had a grandstand view as, after 'a tremendous explosion' a plume of water rose skywards. Johnson recalled that the crew became 'really excited about the crumbling along the top of the dam' and McCarthy so 'vocal' that MacLean firmly advised him to concentrate on flying the machine in the cause of mutual safety. But, although damaged 15–20ft along the top, the dam held and it was time to make for home. Johnson recalled that 'we stayed long enough for the water to subside to satisfy ourselves that the dam had not been breached. Any water which we saw on the opposite side of the dam could only have been that which was flung over by the explosion'.

MacLean's log shows that at 00.51 hours, picking up speed to 200mph, AJ-T left the Sorpe, reached the Moehne three minutes later, Ahlen at 00.04 ½ hours, Duelmen lakes at 01.14 hours and Rees at 01.32 hours. From there, MacLean had not intended to follow any of the recommended exit routes, but to fly in reverse the inward track of the First Wave via Beek, 'Rosendale [sic]' and Southwold. However, it would become clear that

Right: Air Chief Marshal Sir Arthur Harris. (IWM)

Below left: Air Vice-Marshal the Hon R.A. Cochrane. (IWM)

Below right: Group Captain H.V. Satterly. (Satterly)

Roy Chadwick and Wing Commander G.P. Gibson. (Crown Copyright)

Barnes Wallis (left) and A.D. Grant, one of his research team. (Vickers)

Dr A.R. Collins. (Collins)

Spherical Form of Upkeep. (Vickers)

Dropping test at Reculver. (Vickers)

Balancing tests during development. H. Jeffree (left), one of Wallis's team. (Vickers)

Garston Moehne model. (Building Research Station)

Test model of Nant-Y-Gro Dam. (Road Research Laboratory)

Successful test on Nant-Y-Gro Dam. (Road Research Laboratory)

Crew of AJ-N. Pilot Officer L.G. Knight (centre). (IWM)

Flight Lieutenant J.C. McCarthy presented to the queen after the raid. (IWM)

Outside the Officers Mess with the king and queen on 27 May 1943. (IWM)

Type 464 (Provisioning) Lancaster. (IWM)

Gibson's aircraft with Upkeep. (Crown Copyright)

Large power station below Moehne Dam. (Ruhr Dams Association)

Eye-witness note of attack on Sorpe Dam. (Theunissen)

Large hill beyond Eder Dam. (Author)

Above and below: Moehne breach. (Ruhr Dams Association)

Above: Eder Dam (Collins)

Right: Sorpe Dam. (Crown Copyright)

Left: Flying Officer G. Rice: lost Upkeep on way to target. (Rice)

Below: Exposed scaffolding during Moehne repair. (Ruhr Dams Association)

SECOND WAVE: THE SORPE

AJ-T opted for a reciprocal of its own inward course. Doesburg was passed at 01.37 hours, Harderwijk at 01.46 hours, still flying at 200mph and 100ft, Stavoren 01.57 hours, 'wall' (Afsluitdijk) at 02.00 ½ hours and Vlieland at the estimated time of 02.06 hours. A series of Gee fixes took AJ-T across the North Sea at 190mph to Mablethorpe 15 miles north of Skegness and some 35 miles due east of Scampton at 03.08 ½ hours. The aircraft reached base at 03.18 hours and landed five minutes later.

The navigator's log recorded only the outline of an adventurous return flight. Approaching the Moehne on the reservoir side of the river to port, Johnson saw water surging along it towards Neheim. McCarthy exclaimed, 'Jeez, look at that'. Johnson recalled skirting the high ground adjacent to the western extremity of the dam and flying across the shattered wall. McCarthy turned to port beyond it towards Ahlen. Johnson confirmed that 'no flak opened up': two guns were out of action and the crew of the third was either surprised by AJ-T's direction of approach or temporarily fleeing the chaos. Leaving the Moehne behind, both the pilot and his bomb-aimer, in Johnson's words, were alarmed to see a well-defended town ahead 'with searchlights and flak to greet us'. Johnson believed that he 'must take some responsibility. Shouldn't have allowed us to be getting off track as we obviously did'. MacLean insisted that they were on course before it emerged that the Lancaster had strayed, according to Johnson, 'not simply over a railway yard, but the main marshalling yard at Hamm from which the armaments of the Ruhr were transported'. In the words of a later report, AJ-T was 'temporarily uncertain of position'; in a later broadcast, McCarthy claimed they were 'about 25 degrees off course to the left'.

Allegedly, the Lancaster pounded through the marshalling yards at 50ft, as a Canadian voice believed to emanate from the rear turret observed: 'Gee, at this height they don't need flak. All they need is to switch points.' Presumably, from the Sorpe to the Moehne had been flown with visual identification of landmarks; essentially following the Roehr and Moehne rivers. Thereafter, officially the aircraft had strayed off course due to 'trouble with compass'. Having extracted AJ-T from this 'temporary difficulty' and exasperated by the compass error, in McCarthy's words, they 'set course as route out and headed for the Zuider Zee'. Johnson was adamant that 'Joe was the one to sort out the situation'; he distinctly recalled exchanges between McCarthy and his navigator concluding with the pilot saying 'OK we'll go back the way we came in'. Although not recorded, like Leggo and Heal during the inward leg, MacLean must have worked out the extent of the compass error and made the necessary adjustment. McCarthy's decision to retrace AJ-T's inward flight could well have been influenced by the ebbing darkness and simplicity of following a proven route.

In his log MacLean made no mention of the unscheduled diversion, though he did show the Moehne Dam-Ahlen leg taking 10 ½ minutes not 7 minutes as on the inward flight. Just short of the Ijsselmeer, Rodger in the rear turret experienced 'the biggest scare of the whole trip', when a flak gunner managed to get the Lancaster in his sights even at such low level and at high speed. He feared that 'we would buy it' and kept thinking to himself, 'goin' to be the next one, goin' to be the next one'. Johnson, the bomb-aimer, recalled being fired on by flak over Vlieland. Like the preceding two Lancasters, Gee fixes were used to cross the North Sea, during which time Eaton finally fixed the W/T set. At 03.00 hours, a mere twenty-three minutes before landing at base, he could inform 5 Group that McCarthy's Upkeep had hit the Sorpe and caused a small breach.

The homecoming was not altogether straightforward. Johnson noted 'that all landings on grass airfields are bumpy, but this seemed particularly uncomfortable'. For, as McCarthy put down, the right wing sank low and the pilot controlled the aircraft with difficulty. Looking out to starboard, the flight engineer saw a flat tyre, and sitting uncomfortably close to the ground in the bomb-aimer's compartment, Johnson remarked that 'Joe controlled it [AJ-T] very well'. He discovered that, 'after going through the undercarriage nacelle, the shell had gone up through the roof by the navigator's head. Don could have been killed and if the shell had penetrated a fuel tank "woof" and Joe and his crew would have gone up ... But we got back and I count myself damned lucky to have survived'.

Responding to a post-war questioner, McCarthy admitted that flying an aircraft 'full of holes' on the way back was 'pretty cold'. After landing, the pilot 'taxied slowly to the point where the chief engineering officer took over and gave Joe a bollicking for getting his aircraft shot up'. No. 5 Group later summarised the operation: 'Compass slightly faulty having been swung with the bomb load. Bullet hole through the undercarriage which burst starboard tyre'. McCarthy, in answering the pilot's questionnaire, reported seeing the target clearly, with the moon to starboard and at that point visibility of 5 miles. Following the explosion, there was a 'half-circular swelling of water with wall of dam as diameter, followed by a spout of water about 1,000ft high ... crown or causeway of dam crumbled for a distance of about 15 to 20 feet'. He was not keen on the use of tracer by the gunners. McCarthy felt that it 'betrayed the position of aircraft to

SECOND WAVE: THE SORPE

searchlights and light flak en route' and, therefore, he was 'not in favour of 100% tracer ... Cannot say if a big breach in dam was made, but the raid seemed to be successful'. McCarthy concluded: 'Route out good and easily followed (blue). Return route (red 1) failed to find pinpoints because of faulty compass, so set course as route out and headed for the Zuider Zee'.

A hand-written report by Gibson confirmed that AJ-T had 'no VHF – no spotlight [*sic*] – and no deviation card', which as well as the compass swing, McCarthy would confirm in a post-war broadcast. Nevertheless, in 1978, Commander Bergel remained unsure about the card, implying that it might have been mislaid during the preparation process at Scampton:

> There is, to my mind, a considerable mystery about this, and the story of the navigation trouble that took McCarthy over Hamm on the way home ... from my experience in ATA, all compasses were swung and given deviation cards before they got to squadrons – either (as I think in this case) at the factory, or if not at MUs [maintenance units]. At either place they could not have been swung with bombs on board ... I agree that these Lancasters were very special, but after all the bouncing bombs must have been positioned as all bomb loads were positioned, right on the aircraft's Centre of Gravity, and therefore to all intents and purposes unlikely to have more of a major effect on the compass than the more normal bomb load had. I flew ED 825 without a bomb load and I am positive that if there had been the error that took McCarthy so far off course I would not have reached Scampton without noticing it.

Thirty years later, though, Bergel admitted 'a hazy recollection that the compass card was missing on my ferry flight'. Whatever the reason, there seems little doubt that the compass was swung at Scampton and that only AJ-T did so with Upkeep in position. So there could well have been a unique problem once it had been dropped.

More broadly and significantly, despite AJ-T's lone effort, the Sorpe Dam had not been breached. It was, Cochrane reflected, 'unlucky' that only 'one out of five' aircraft had got through. Five Lancasters of the Third Wave remained to complete the task.

155

Chapter 10

Third Wave: Final Chance

Once the last aircraft of the first and second waves (McCarthy's) had faded in the distance, crews of Third Wave Lancasters returned to the different mess ante-rooms or billeted accommodation. The scheduled take-off time of around midnight was, the Operation Order revealed, 'such that they may be recalled before crossing the enemy coast, if the 1st and 2nd waves have breached all the targets'.

The Squadron's Operations Record Book recorded: 'Each [aircraft was] detailed for one of the alternative targets [Lister, Ennepe and Diemel] and all [were] detailed to attack the Moehne and Eder dams in the absence of any direct orders in the air to carry on to the alternative targets.' Strangely, the Sorpe was not highlighted. However, as pilots Flight Sergeant K.C. Brown and Flight Sergeant W.C. Townsend confirmed, the crews were briefed about all six target dams. So they had a more complicated task than the first 14 machines. Townsend's front gunner, Sergeant D.E. Webb, reflected: 'The actual target would be given to us after take-off by W/T and we would be left to get to the Mohne Dam and set course from there to whatever target had been by then allocated to us. There were many alternatives ... [and] we would have to use our own judgement as to how to reach the designated target'. Responding to a post-war researcher, he drolly wrote: 'How nice if we had maps as good as those you have sent me.'

Brown, whose crew was the last to alight from the bus which carried three crews out to their aircraft, pondered that 'so many things were against you: low-level, at night, pylons, trees etc. The chance of coming back were much slimmer than on regular bombing. I thought we'd bought a one-way ticket.' As usual, he smoked two cigarettes before boarding and the navigator in Flight Sergeant Townsend's Lancaster, Pilot Officer C.L. Howard, completed his pre-operational ritual of walking round the aircraft twice.

Set to follow the inward route of the First Wave via the Scheldt estuary to the Moehne, these aircraft were due to cross the coast of the European

THIRD WAVE: FINAL CHANCE

mainland shortly after 01.30 hours, giving them little time to complete the operation in the short night allowed by Double British Summer Time. Like the Second Wave, they took off singly.

The first, AJ-C (ED 910/G) piloted by Pilot Officer W.H.T. Ottley, started to move down the runway at 00.09 hours on Monday 17 May. It would not come back. The 617 Squadron Operations Record Book noted: 'Missing, acknowledged the diversion to the Lister Dam, no further trace', and 5 Group: 'Believe Lister not attacked'. Members of crews following Ottley appear to have witnessed his demise. 'About half an hour' after crossing the enemy coast, Townsend saw 'a hell of a flash' to starboard short of the Ahlen turning point. His navigator, Howard, fairly accurately interpreted what he and his pilot saw: 'Ahead and to starboard searchlights broke out and an aircraft was coned at something over a hundred feet; more searchlights and lots of flak and a terrific explosion in the sky. It was one of ours; probably a little too close to Hamm, a heavily-defended rail centre, and too high.'

Independently, Brown recalled that an aircraft 'on my right, was hit and pulled up, his tanks exploded then his bomb – the whole valley was lit up in a bright orange'. He estimated the lost machine's position 4–5 miles north of Hamm and its height about 500ft. To some extent, W/T messages between AJ-C and Grantham shed a little more light on what happened. Once 5 Group established that the Moehne and Sorpe had been breached and no First Wave aircraft were available to move on to the Sorpe, difficult decisions had to be made. At this point, due to malfunction of the W/T set in McCarthy's aircraft, there was no evidence that any of the Second Wave had reached their target. At 02.30 hours, 5 Group called up AJ-C and a minute later sent 'Gilbert', meaning for this aircraft 'attack Lister Dam'. However, at 02.32 hours, this order was countermanded with 'Dinghy', meaning 'Eder destroyed attack Sorpe', and repeated at 02.50 hours. AJ-F, Brown's Lancaster, reported that the stricken machine seen by its crew had hit the ground at 02.35 hours.

AJ-S (ED 865/G), piloted by Pilot Officer L.J. Burpee, which began its flight from Scampton two minutes after Ottley at 00.11 hours, also failed to return. Officially, the machine was classified 'missing without trace'. However, its loss was also unwittingly witnessed by members of following crews. Brown's crew reported that over The Netherlands at 01.53 hours about ten miles ahead another aircraft exploded in mid-air and crashed in flames. The bomb-aimer, Oancia, had a clear view: 'The Lancaster ahead of us flew over a German airfield, was hit by ground fire, fuel tanks exploding and the ball of flame rising slowly – stopping, then dropping terminated by a huge ball of flame, as it hit the ground and the bomb exploded.' Brown recollected: 'As we turned on reaching the Dutch coast, I lifted the aircraft a bit and as the wing obscured my port side there was an explosion. We had noticed light flak off to our port but thought very little of it – then our tail gunner said "there was one hell of an explosion from back there". We did not know it was Burpee then'. In Townsend's Lancaster, trailing Brown, the front gunner, Sergeant D.E. Webb, simply reported 'a bloody great ball of fire' ahead and to port. Hence, 5 Group's messages at 02.32 and 02.50 hours ordering AJ-S to attack the Sorpe would go unacknowledged.

The third Lancaster in the final wave, AJ-F (ED 918/G), piloted by Flight Sergeant K.C. Brown, started its flight from Scampton at 00.12 hours. Brown was glad finally to be on their way. 'The worst period of any raid is the short time before take-off.' Heaving the heavily-laden aircraft off the runway proved nerve-racking. 'We had to use 2850 rpm and 9lbs of boost to keep the old girl airborne, so we didn't have much more for take-off.' Rather like the Battle of Waterloo for Wellington, 'it was a damned close run thing' to clear the perimeter fence. There was a stranger in the front turret. Sergeant Buntaine had reported sick and one of Pilot Officer Divall's crew, Sergeant D. Allatson, replaced him.

Like Sergeant G.L. Johnson, McCarthy's bomb-aimer, Oancia, favoured maps on which pencilled entry and exit routes were marked to assist identification of landmarks in preference to the roller system. 'The maps were folded in an orderly fashion and enabled me to know at all times our ground position with respect to the proposed route. Any variations would be passed on to Dudley [Heal, the navigator], who would quickly recalculate the headings to place us back on course.'

Due to the peculiar, low-level nature of the operation, Brown and Sergeant H.B. Feneron, the flight engineer, decided to split responsibility for forward vision: Feneron taking the starboard half, his pilot the port. Occasionally over the North Sea, Oancia glimpsed another 617 Squadron Lancaster briefly illuminated in the moonlight. Unlike Hobday, in Knight's aircraft, Heal found Gee transmissions blocked early on. As with First Wave machines flying the Scheldt entry route, AJ-F was off track at the Dutch coast, reached at 01.30 hours, and Brown needed to execute a succession of sharp turns. Heal realised that a 5 degree compass error existed and thereafter made the necessary adjustment in his calculations. Fifteen minutes later, 01.45 hours, 5 Group repeated Gibson's warning of flak near Duelmen at 51°48N 07°12E.

THIRD WAVE: FINAL CHANCE

Both Brown and Oancia remarked on the frequent need to pull up over power lines stretching between pylons and coping with pockets of flak and searchlights. Shortly after witnessing the crash near Tilburg, the gunners raked a steam train travelling right to left, which Feneron thought 'didn't do it any good.' Over Germany, Brown went so low that, when flying along a road, he saw enemy shells decapitating trees on either side without harming the Lancaster. As he put it: 'I chose to go down a road and German fire was knocking down tree tops along our path. We ran up to the front door of a castle – what a surprise – and I would like to visit there some day.'

Brown added: 'We saw another aircraft on our port side taking quite a beating and we thought he went down as well.' This might have been Townsend, who reported heavy flak opposition but survived. At 02.24 hours, shortly after leaving the Duelmen Lakes, AJ-F received 'Dinghy' from Grantham, acknowledged a minute later, and prepared to make for the Sorpe. Before the next turning point at Ahlen, the Lancaster ran into trouble from Hamm outer defences. 'They really peppered us,' the pilot wrote, 'yes, I was frightened but I was just too busy trying to survive to think much about it'.

Skirting the Moehne like McCarthy, as AJ-F neared its target the mist which hampered McCarthy's approach had thickened. Oancia recalled: 'All low lying areas were covered with a fog or mist leaving only the tops of the hills exposed and thus making a determination of the exact ground location impossible ... arriving at the Sorpe Dam vicinity to find the valley covered in dense fog – flying around in the general area and returning back to the area to find the Sorpe Dam clear.' Heal agreed that, after circling widely, the dam became visible nestling between its two hills. Like McCarthy, Brown was concerned about the position of the church spire and the need to pull up over the far hill, 'especially if we had to go round again with the mine still on board'. He appreciated, though, the absence of defensive fire.

Feneron, similar to Rodger in McCarthy's machine, worried about the appearance of night fighters when the aircraft surged over the distant hill. As Brown feared, Upkeep could not be dropped accurately on the first run and he had to circle to port to try again. During the third attempt, Brown explained that 'we went into a very deep valley before realising it and we almost bought stars ... We had a few loose incendiaries in the back of the aircraft, which we [thereafter] used to mark out a circuit. The Radio Op dropped them by hand as I called out – I timed the circuit which gave us some idea of where we were. I had done a similar thing at [RAF] Wigsley once before'. Years later, Oancia 'still vividly remembered ... dropping some incendiary bombs to locate a point advance of the bombing run thus

THE DAMBUSTERS: 'WAS THE RAID WORTHWHILE?'

being able to start our bombing run parallel to the dam, then diving over the first hill, to reach the required 60 feet altitude, at approximately the dam mid-point, dropping our Upkeep and climbing steeply to avoid crashing into the hill on the other side of the dam'.

As with Johnson before him, Oancia had difficulty in determining when to release Upkeep, though he did have Aldis lamps to help him. Eventually, on the sixth attempt, in bright moonlight and Upkeep not spinning, on a course of 130°M, groundspeed of 180mph and height of 60ft, Oancia released the weapon at 03.14 hours [Germans recorded 03.15 hours]. Brown reflected that 'we had stirred it [the Sorpe valley] up a bit'. As Wallis's weapon rolled down the sloping support, Brown had time to clear the far hill and bank to port before Upkeep exploded. 'After what seemed ages,' Oancia saw 'a large waterspout rise silhouetted against the moon and slowly fall back into the lake'. While the aircraft circled, Brown observed 'crumbling' along the top of the top of the dam, but no clear break. So at 03.23 hours, the wireless operator, Sergeant H.J. Hewstone, signalled that Upkeep had exploded in contact with the dam with 'no obvious breach'. An interesting postscript was provided by the navigator, Heal. 'I realised we were there for a long time, but I didn't see the attack or the incendiaries being used as I was busy plotting the way home.'

After the attack, Feneron recalled 'we didn't hang around too long' and flying back via the Moehne crew members were astonished at the devastation. Heal was summoned from his curtained cubby-hole to witness the flooded areas and, alarmed at the absence of recognizable landmarks, hurried back to his table to ensure the aircraft stayed on track. The flight engineer reported water 'spitting' out of two breaches in the dam wall and a single flak gunner opening up; the one on the eastern buttress. Brown sardonically observed: 'He was not firing after our departure. Mac [Flight Sergeant G.S. McDonald] our tail gunner really gave him hell.'

Oancia noted, less dramatically: 'We were surprised to see that the gun located on the dam was very active [and] that there was a gaping breach between the towers in the dam and the water pouring through the breach.' Almost certainly, McCarthy's previous flight from the direction of Neheim had alerted the gun crew to that line of approach.

The pilot noticed that in the reservoir, 'the water level had gone down considerably and there was a fast-flowing river below the dam' [the Moehne approaching Neheim]. Still concerned about night fighters, in Feneron's words, Brown 'got down low and turned on the taps'. Nevertheless, 'Hamm was where we encountered light and heavy flak.

THIRD WAVE: FINAL CHANCE

I had never known the Germans to put down low-level box flak as they did at Hamm. Two boxes were used, both were predicted on our track and airspeed and went off ahead of us.' Almost certainly, AJ-F escaped one of the strong outer protective belts of the railway centre's defences between Ahlen and Duelmen.

Brown added that, as he sped across enemy territory, he remembered passing 'right over' a 20mm flak battery, which his front gunner engaged: 'I could see our rounds striking one gun. I don't know if the crew were jumping off to escape, or if they were shot off.' Brown confessed, though, to continued fear of fighter interception particularly near the coast, which to his relief failed to materialise. However, the Lancaster very nearly perished as it sought the sanctuary of the North Sea. Beyond the Ijsselmeer, flying at 50ft on instruments, Brown prepared to cross the narrow Helder peninsula. Oancia wrote: '... as we approached the Don Helder Peninsula, tracer shells and searchlights [were] coming down on us, our front gunner returning fire causing the searchlights to momentarily waiver and Ken Brown, seeing a land wall directly ahead, climbing sharply over and diving down again on the North Sea side'.

Heal recorded that, with dawn breaking, he realised that AJ-F was slightly off track, but before he could correct the error, searchlights flooded the cockpit from both sides. He could not understand how Brown was able to see to fly the aeroplane. The pilot, Heal noted, put the nose down even lower and piled on maximum boost. His navigator had not appreciated that a Lancaster could fly so fast. Feneron confirmed Heal's impression. As Brown went lower and lower, the flight engineer crouched down hoping, as he put it, 'to melt into the floor', with shells shattering the cockpit perspex. Peering up to his left, Feneron saw Brown hunched over his instruments in those crucial, terrifying seconds. With the cockpit 'flooded in the glare from searchlights', Heal was amazed that his pilot could see to fly. Flak followed them, but Brown stayed at low level to frustrate the gunners. He sparsely recalled that 'the coast trouble was difficult because we had no horizon across the Zuider Zee and staying at 50ft was done on instruments – don't try it'.

After the immediate danger passed, with the sky now light and the enemy coast well behind, Feneron took over the controls as far as the vicinity of Lincoln. There, Brown slid into the pilot's seat for landing at Scampton at 05.33 hours. Feneron's gesture to kiss the ground on alighting did not seem extravagant. Even a cursory glance at the fuselage demonstrated that the crew was extremely lucky to return unscathed. A shell had exploded on contact with the starboard side, its shrapnel perforating the structure, which, Oancia observed, resembled 'a sieve'. According to Heal, 'the fuselage was stitched with holes'. Officially, there had been a 'cannon shell in fuselage starboard side'.

Answering the pilot's questionnaire, Brown described attacking the Sorpe with the moon to starboard and visibility 500 yards with 'missile dropped about 10 feet away from the dam about two-thirds of way across'. After the explosion, 'semi-circular swelling of water against dam followed by spout of water almost 1,000 feet high' followed by 'crumbling of crown of dam for about distance of 300 feet'. Brown, like McCarthy, reported ten circuits before release of Upkeep but Oancia would insist six and this is borne out by other reports. The pilot was not keen on tracer being used, 'very dazzling, ordinary night tracer preferred'. However, he admitted it 'appeared to have considerable effect on accuracy of searchlights'. Brown praised the planned routes and felt that his attack had been 'successful', despite the target being 'difficult to attack because of hills and trees on both ends'. His comments and the observations of his crew about the scene at the Moehne, which they 'went to have a look at' on the way back, were to some extent at odds with other reports. He confirmed, like Feneron and Oancia, that there were 'two large breaches close together ... about a quarter width of space between the two towers [with] water pouring through both gaps and shooting well out before falling in two powerful jets. The valley seemed to be well covered with water'.

He added that 'front gunner reports a third breach beyond the tower on the north-west end of the dam. Breach about half the size of the other two. Water pouring through'. These observations were made roughly three hours after the dam was breached and would be supported by no other surviving aircraft. When AJ-F returned to the Moehne, it seems inconceivable that the two adjacent breaches made by Young and Maltby would not have been joined as the force of escaping water washed away the remaining section in between. Nor is there any evidence of major, structural damage elsewhere on the dam. It seems highly likely, therefore, that the crew fleetingly saw water washing round the remains of the destroyed power station and the large detached turbine later depicted on reconnaissance photos. Nevertheless, the extent and intensity of the damage had been reinforced.

Reflecting afterwards, Brown mused: 'I remember Essen, Berlin and other targets. This one we didn't expect to get back, but we sure as hell expected to drop our bomb in the right place – you don't forget this target was in the middle of fog.'

Many years later, he dined with the German fighter ace, Adolf Galland, and raised with him the lack of fighter activity during the operation. Galland

THIRD WAVE: FINAL CHANCE

replied that 'one would have to be stupid to attempt fighter intercepts of aircraft operating at low level at night'. General Josef Kammhuber, creator of the defensive line bearing his name which coordinated flak, searchlights, radar units and night-fighters to protect Germany against aerial attack, independently supported Galland. 'The night-fighter force could not come to grips with the attackers since it was an attack at the lowest level, and their targets [617 Squadron Lancasters'] could not be picked up by the radar, hence they offered no prey to the night-fighters.'

The fourth Third Wave Lancaster (ED 886/G), piloted by Flight Sergeant W.C. Townsend, had begun its take-off run two minutes behind Brown at 00.14 hours. Pilot Officer C.L. Howard, the navigator, did not look forward to this exercise with such an heavy load: 'I had visions of the bumpy [grass] take-off causing the lights under the fuselage to be shaken loose so that instead of being 60 feet above the ground we would finish up 60 feet underneath it. Fortunately, my fears were not realised and we set course for Southwold on a beautiful full moonlight.' Unknown to him, Townsend had similar qualms. Gradually, 'semi-stalling', he 'just' hauled AJ-O into the air, his impression being through the perimeter hedge rather than over it. The front gunner, Sergeant D.E. Webb, thought it 'a good job we had a [grass] runway to bump off'. Howard confirmed that 'Charlie Franklin our bomb aimer assisted with the navigation from a map on two rollers, which I think was a very good idea. I had a map and used it to pinpoint our combined observations, which I believe worked well'.

The flight across land to the North Sea was uneventful. The Aldis lamps were duly tested and 'found correct as far as we could judge'; though Howard retained a nagging suspicion that during take-off they might have become misaligned. The navigator recollected: 'There was no wind and the moon shining on the water made a beautiful picture, one which since that night I have not regarded as romantic or even a beautiful sight.' Howard noted that, because of the staggered take-off times, 'we didn't see much of the other four'. As AJ-O approached the Dutch coast, flak could be seen rising away to port; possibly Burpee in trouble. Turning correctly near the tip of Shouwen Island in the Scheldt estuary, Townsend crossed the enemy coast at 01.31 hours. 'The land below', he observed, 'was clearly seen, peaceful with no sign of war'; an idyllic scene, which soon changed. Even at 100ft, the pilot reflected the flight was about to turn 'very, very nasty'.

At 01.45 hours, as 5 Group re-broadcast Gibson's warning of trouble near Duelmen, the Lancaster ran into a concentration of searchlights and flak. Such was the cacophony, that Howard wondered whether he would ever see his home at Perth, Western Australia, again. But Townsend 'threw that heavily-laden Lancaster around like a Tiger Moth and we flew out of it'. Howard could not fathom how one of the wings did not strike the ground and, despite these violent evasive manoeuvres, the aircraft remained 'dead on track'.

Flight Sergeant G.A. Chalmers, the wireless operator, listened to messages from the other aircraft as he stood 'watching history from the astrodome, although everything happened so quickly [at 100ft] that incidents came and went almost before the mind could appreciate them – flat meadows sped past as we thundered over Holland and Germany, a fiery glow, followed by the familiar black-streaked mushroom as an aircraft fell to light "ack-ack"'. Townsend recalled turning for 30 seconds at one stage to avoid a flak concentration, and actually like Brown flying below the level of the trees in a forest fire-break, which his wireless operator confirmed: 'We attracted some attention when we attempted to cross a canal, as suddenly ack-ack was turned on us. We did a quick about turn. Looking out I could see tree tops and realised we were circling a forest. Some debate took place about the best method of approach and the considered opinion was "head down, keep low and go on through". It worked and we were safely through with the ack-ack all round us'. At 02.22 hours (received at 02.24 hours), 5 Group signalled the Lancaster to attack the Ennepe Dam, repeated four minutes later and again acknowledged.

On the Duelmen-Ahlen leg, away to starboard, 'searchlights and lots of flak and a terrific explosion in the sky' unknowingly indicated Ottley's loss. AJ-O reached the Ahlen turning point towards the Moehne unscathed and, shortly afterwards, the rear gunner, Sergeant R. Wilkinson, extinguished two searchlights. According to Howard, about 20 minutes after receiving the target message, the bomb-aimer reported a large lake below, which the navigator declared, 'nonsense, there's no lake here'. Emerging from his curtained position, Howard saw 'a great stream of water rushing out of the breach in the dam and rolling down the valley below the wall'. Soberly he reflected that it was 'a horrifying, frightening sight'.

'We set course for the Ennepe over wooded, valley-marked country with little or no features to map read. We were frequently diverted from the dead reckoning track I had set by the moon shining off what appeared to be water in some of the valleys – it was actually mist rising in them and the moon's beam made it look like water.' In its search, AJ-O flew close to the Sorpe, which probably gave rise to the German report of another aircraft in the vicinity other than McCarthy and Brown. During briefing, there had been

THIRD WAVE: FINAL CHANCE

photographs and maps, but no model, to show the location and outlay of the Ennepe and in the misty conditions it proved difficult to locate: Howard found it 'smaller than the Moehne, though tempting enough'. Townsend recalled circling the murky area cautiously in an eerie silence and Webb a mid-air crew conference to confirm the location. Fortunately, flak stationed there earlier in the war had been removed.

Apart from difficulty in lining up the attack run, the spinning Upkeep caused a pronounced shudder. Three times the bomb-aimer felt unable to release the weapon and the pilot circled to port for another attempt. Howard did not enjoy the experience. 'With the aircraft shaking horribly with six tons of bomb revolving underneath, I had to lean in the blister on the starboard side and guide Bill [Townsend] to the correct height with the two lights.' Howard could see little of the terrain, but to starboard he glimpsed the outline of a large house on the skyline.

On the fourth run on a reported bearing of 355°M and a groundspeed of 220mph, at 03.37 hours Upkeep was dropped. Circuiting to inspect the result, the crew saw a circle of water spread outwards from the point of explosion to strike the dam. Howard recorded that, 'a mass of white water shot into the air: it settled and we saw the dam wall intact'. Webb, in the front turret, felt enormous relief that the job was done for he, too, recalled they had been warned about having to return if they failed to attack successfully. Almost immediately, a dense mist settled over the reservoir. Howard recalled that 'we waited around, circling it [reservoir] for some time expecting at least one other of the reserve aircraft to appear, but none did ... The moon was going down on one side and the sun was rising on the other' as the Lancaster left the area. At 04.11 hours, the wireless operator, Chalmers, signalled to Grantham that Upkeep had exploded 50 yards from the Ennepe Dam with no apparent effect. Officially, 'contact believed as ripples seen against the dam'. Different reports would refer to the 'Ennerpe', 'Enerpe' or 'Ennipe', clearly minor typing errors. But some would refer to an attack on the 'Schwelme' dam.

Howard wrote:

> We turned for the Moehne – found it, and stared amazed at the drop in the water level on the banks of the lake – and still the water gushed in a white stream down the valley ... the track home was more northerly than the one in ... a feature that terrified us all was the electric power lines; in that part of Germany they were prolific and hard to see even in the

approaching dawn. More than once our speed – we had now piled on the power until we were flying at 270mph – enabled a last minute jump as it were to get over the damn things. I remember looking back at the country – no doubt sure of our position for a few minutes – and seeing a miasma rising from the ground looking to me after the events of the night like all the evil in the world manifesting itself.

As on the inward track, the pilot described the flight as 'very nasty', and put the Lancaster 'right on the deck'. He had never flown so low before even in training and he retained only a patchwork memory of figures either waving or lying flat. With the rays of the sun beginning to penetrate the eastern sky, Townsend was acutely aware of the lone machine's vulnerability to enemy gunners. In the mixture of darkness and light, Webb found power lines difficult to spot. Townsend agreed that his flight engineer, Sergeant D.J.D. Powell, put on maximum power to achieve 240–270mph, and the pilot also recalled that 'many a last minute jump' was necessary 'to get over those damn things [power lines]'.

Townsend planned to follow the second exit route via Ahlen, 1 mile north of Zutphen (52°10N 06°12E) and a headland west of De Lemmer (52°50 N 05°33E) on the Ijsselmeer. Instead of crossing the Helder peninsula, though, he now intended to 'sneak between the islands of Texel and Vlieland'. Once into the North Sea, AJ-O would pick up the designated Gee locations. Howard explained how this scheme was disrupted. As the Lancaster approached the Frisian Islands, 'a heavy flak gun opened up on us; no doubt even at our low level we were seen, as the sun by now had risen and showed us clearly over the calm water. Being a heavy flak gun, it could not depress too much, so the German crew lowered it as much as possible and skipped the shells on the water towards us (as we had just done something similar against the dams, I thought it hardly cricket!). We turned back towards Germany and luckily got out between Vlieland and Terschilling without interference'.

Similarly, Townsend and Chalmers both realised that some of the shells actually dropped short and bounced over the aircraft, and the wireless operator agreed with Howard: 'The fact that we were so low saved our bacon'. Townsend recalled rapidly turning to starboard parallel to Vlieland, then port again, as Howard revealed, before slipping out between the eastern end of that island and Terschelling.

Once clear, the crew could relax. Of these hair-raising minutes, Chalmers simply wrote: 'I well recall the opposition we met at Texel, which forced us to turn back and sneak out higher up the Frisians.' Webb, in the front turret, held that the aircraft 'dodged Texel' and went out between it and Vlieland, as shown in Air Vice-Marshal Cochrane's report of 7 June 1943. Officially enemy searchlights caused the diversion. Further confusion occurred in retrospect, when a post-operational report maintained that AJ-O had missed a turning point at Elburg (52°28N 05°50E). Cochrane's report suggests that AJ-O might have turned to starboard before the Zutphen point and thus effectively flown northwards parallel to the planned route. This meant that it turned before the designated point 52°50N 05°33N to take the aircraft across the Isselmeer to reach the Helder peninsula. An illustration in Cochrane's report shows a strange starboard turn over the peninsula to take the Lancaster directly north across its tip to fly parallel to Texel and exit through the gap with Vlieland. That does not fit in any way the account involving the bouncing shells and dodging Texel recollected by Townsend, Chalmers and Howard. Nor does it equate with a post-operational pencilled summary by Gibson, who agreed that Townsend had 'turned round at Texel to dodge' defences. Made aware years later of the assertion that Elburg had been missed, Howard strongly disagreed: 'We missed no turning points'. Moreover, 'I still maintain that we flew between Vlieland and Terschelling – can you argue with official records?' He added another note of mystery: 'My log book shows 00.07 as take-off time though I cannot remember if we were first off.' Of that night, Howard reflected: 'As a crew we had flown together for nearly a year over Germany and Italy: I could ask for none better.'

Sergeant G. Kraft, pilot of a Messerschmitt Bf 110 from IV/NJG 1 based at Leeuwarden, on the Dutch mainland east of Vlieland, who had shortly after midnight been deployed vainly for 105 minutes searching for hostile aircraft, was 'specially scrambled' again at 04.29 hours on 17 May to the neck of the Helder peninsula and once more fruitlessly orbited at 6,000m. Neither he nor his radio operator, Eric Handke, glimpsed anything in 'excellent visibility'. Later, Handke learnt that the enemy aircraft for which they were searching had flown out 'north-west over Texel/Vlieland'. He reflected that, not only the low altitude but the fact that it 'had changed its course from west to north-west probably saved it from being shot down'. The timing and location strongly suggests that Handke was referring to Townsend's Lancaster and perhaps provides more evidence that AJ-O did exit between Texel and Vlieland, not Vlieland/Terschelling.

Meanwhile, once clear of the enemy coast, the crew's troubles were not over. An oil gauge (later found to be faulty) indicated malfunction of one engine, which Powell shut down. Webb believed that a 'Mayday' call was made. Townsend kept low over the North Sea and did not use the IFF equipment. This led to a colourful legend that two Spitfires were scrambled to intercept an enemy intruder; not supported by available evidence.

In broad daylight, Townsend approached Scampton, where a swarm of figures poured out of a wide variety of buildings to greet him. The pilot failed to distinguish himself. With oil from the front guns smearing the windscreen and forced to peer out of the quarterlight, he landed downwind into the sun on three engines and admitted to bumping 'an awful number of times – it seemed like twenty-four'. But, at 06.15 hours on Monday 17 May 1943, he had brought back AJ-O safely. Webb, the bomb-aimer, reflected that 'we had fought our way in and fought our way out'.

Thoroughly exhausted and irritated by the crowd pressing towards the ladder leading from the crew exit, Townsend pushed past a braided figure at its foot. In answer to his query, the pilot rasped, 'wait until de-briefing'. Presumably, Air Officer Commanding-in-Chief Bomber Command was not amused. Preceding Townsend, the wireless operator, Chalmers, had been altogether less abrasive. 'I was first out of the aircraft to be met by Air Chief Marshal Harris, Air Vice-Marshal Cochrane and Group Captain Charles Whitworth and at the shock of seeing them I nearly fell over in shaking their hands. They told me we were the last aircraft to land and congratulated me on my Morse, which was easily read by them.'

Years later, Webb recalled the night's drama: 'The fact is that if I had not "borrowed" an extra 1,000 rounds for each gun and rearmed while flying I would have had no ammunition for the return trip. The other fact is that if it had not been for the absolutely superb flying that Bill [Townsend] put in, simply by going lower and lower, we could not have survived. It is as simple as that. I still remember vividly some of those power cables and pylons'. Webb paid further tribute to his pilot and crew. 'Bill was at all times dedicated to the one and only thing, to get there and put the bomb in the right place no matter what the opposition. Anything else would be unthinkable, and that went for all of us.'

He explained the origin of his extra ammunition. 'We could not get from RAF sources the tracer we wanted (one that would burn from the gun barrel to impact) and it was made up for us by the Ordnance Corps, and only delivered on the morning of the 16 May.' Writing in 1981, Webb had just returned from Italy on a commercial jet through 'what the pilot called "severe turbulence"', which caused several passengers to be sick. 'They

THIRD WAVE: FINAL CHANCE

can have no idea of the throwing about that used to take place during a wartime flight and in our case with only 50 feet under the wingtip.'

In answering the pilot's questionnaire, Townsend reported that the Ennepe had been 'sighted by profile of hills' and that the attack had been executed 'running into the moon in half-light reflected on mist and water' with visibility '3/4 mile approximately' after 'three dummy runs'. 'Explosion occurred approximately 30 seconds after release' after one bounce of the spinning Upkeep. Townsend confirmed that 'a high column of water and dirt' had been thrown up as Upkeep exploded short of the target with 'circle afterwards meeting dam', though there were 'no signs of damage'. Of tracer, he concluded, 'has a good deterrent effect on flak ... no trouble with dazzle or stoppages and very encouraging to crew'. However, he complained that contrary to briefing information, 'the island in the centre of the lake is actually joined to the spit'. Before attempting to attack the dam, he 'circled several times having difficulty with drifting mist and dazzle from moon'. Townsend concluded sharply: 'Considered timing too late as we were still over Germany in daylight'. So, on the homeward flight, 'kept the aircraft right on the deck and cruised at about 240, [and] this appeared to fox the defences'.

As well as Harris and Cochrane, Wallis attended the debriefing of AJ-O's crew and asked: 'Did you notice the relative positions of the explosion and the wall of the dam?' Webb, who had the clearest view, confirmed Townsend's report that the circle of disturbed water was bisected by the dam. 'He seemed satisfied by that'. Webb, like his pilot, had acid words for the planners. 'We did not take off till after midnight. If ever there was an ill-conceived idea it was this. We took off three hours after the first wave, to fly over the same route and to bomb the same targets. It was hardly surprising that we were expected all the way there and back.'

Behind Townsend, Flight Sergeant C.T. Anderson, had begun his operation from Scampton in AJ-Y (ED 924/G) at 00.15 hours. That Lancaster would also survive but in much different circumstances. Like other Third Wave aircraft, it flew in via the Scheldt estuary, but its times of crossing the coast and subsequent flight over enemy territory are unclear. At 02.28 hours 5 Group contacted AJ-Y and a minute later sent 'Dinghy', which directed the aircraft to the Sorpe. Two other Air Ministry documents indicate that, previous to this order, the aircraft had been destined for the Diemel. However, off track, uncertain of position, with the rear turret out of action and dawn rapidly approaching, Anderson 'realised we could not reach the target in time so turned back' to follow the inward route via the Scheldt; the only aircraft to do so that night.

THE DAMBUSTERS: 'WAS THE RAID WORTHWHILE?'

At 04.23 hours, Sergeant W.D. Bickle informed Grantham, 'returning to base unsuccessful', and at 05.30 hours AJ-Y landed with Upkeep still on board. At debriefing, Anderson thought the use of tracer proved 'very satisfactory – no dazzle and continuous line very helpful and apparently scaring to the enemy'. He then explained his aborted operation. 'Unable to find lakes near Duelmen. Mist in valleys made recognition difficult and about five minutes before Duelmen we were forced off our track by searchlights, being at that time unable to shoot at them owing to stoppages in rear turret. Realised we could not reach target in time so turned back at 3.10 hours bringing the mine back.'

Messages between Grantham and Third Wave aircraft suggest that initially 5 Group planned for Brown and Burpee to attack the Sorpe, Townsend the Ennepe, Anderson the Diemel and Ottley the Lister. Hence all six target dams would be covered. Anderson and Ottley were redirected to the Sorpe, in addition to Burpee. These three would replace the hoped-for trio from the First Wave to fulfil Cochrane's intention of ideally sending eight Lancasters to the Sorpe.

Townsend's was the last of the nineteen Chastise aircraft to come back. Three – Munro, Rice and Anderson – returned without attacking a target, of the sixteen others eight were lost, in Sergeant Heal's studied understatement, 'an awful lot'. In the Sergeants' Mess, ACW2 Morfydd Jane Gronland and the other waitresses, were called together. 'Our WAAF sergeant entered and addressed us: "I must tell you now the very sad news that of our nineteen aircraft only eleven have returned" ... We all burst into tears'.

Eighty miles south of RAF Scampton, that night Lieutenant A.R. Collins, camouflage officer of the 4th Battalion, the Middlesex Home Guard, was on duty at Hatton Grange, in north London, which would become Heathrow airport. The man, who had carried out tests for Wallis on model dams at Harmondsworth and Garston as well as the Nant-y-Gro in Wales, looking up at 'the beautiful moon in a clear sky', speculated: 'I wonder whether they've attacked the dams'.

Chapter 11

The Story Unfolds

At 08.00 hours on Monday 17 May 1943, at RAF Scampton Leading Aircraftman Munro and other maintenance staff:

> assembled at the hangar to pick up our equipment and fan out to the various aircraft. Quite frankly, it struck us how quiet it seemed to be at the dispersal points. We finally discovered one or two in the north-east corner of the field next to the bomb-dump. It was as if these aircraft had managed to land and had their motors cut as soon as they reached the perimeter track. These same aircraft had flak holes through the fuselage of such a size that you could put your fist through them. The tractors were hitched up and these were hauled back to their hard standing.

Looking at the number of empty hard stands, he could scarcely credit the extent of the losses. As maintenance personnel laboured to repair the damage that day, 'the vacuum in which we were operating soon was filled by the announcement that someone had heard on the radio about the raid'.

Those in the permanent buildings of the base, like Leading Aircraftman Drury, learnt via the station tannoy: 'To us at Scampton, it appeared to be the biggest thing the RAF had done.' Among the aircrew, McCarthy's bomb-aimer, Sergeant S. Oancia, became acutely aware that thirteen fellow Canadians had been lost (Fraser's survival being unknown). Fellow Canadian Flying Officer D. Rodger, equally upset, balanced loss of so many countrymen with realisation that the operation had proved 'a good show'. Flight Sergeant L.J. Sumpter felt both a sense of relief and anti-climax that the training objective for his aircraft had been achieved 'in half a minute'. Having flown from Scampton to RAF Ringwood, Roy Chadwick reached his Manchester home shortly after 07.00 hours, as his elder daughter, Margaret, was leaving for work. 'It was a great success, but a great many young men died,' he told her.

THE DAMBUSTERS: 'WAS THE RAID WORTHWHILE?'

When the member of Wallis's Vickers staff and interloper at the final briefing, Herbert Jeffree, woke he remembered that some aircraft had landed with Upkeep still on board and feared, like the adjutant Humphries after Munro's early return, that if mishandled they could obliterate the airbase. He was alarmed that armourers might not know how to deal safely with the fuse mechanisms. One hundred yards short of one aircraft, he saw ground crew working on it. Should he crouch, flee rapidly or advance sedately? He reasoned that, if the weapon exploded, whatever he did would not save him, so opted for a dignified approach. Like the armament officer, Watson, in response to Humphries earlier, he was assured that the matter was well in hand. Jeffree could therefore enjoy a leisurely breakfast before setting off by train for home.

Wallis was less relaxed. He was unable to come to terms with the heavy losses, which he had not foreseen. Air Vice-Marshal Cochrane, 5 Group commander, found him 'quite inconsolable' and unwilling to accept his argument that 'the percentage losses' in the context of achievement were acceptable. Twenty years later, Wallis abruptly responded to a questioner on the subject, 'I don't want to talk about it.' In 1989, a scientist closely involved with RAF operations during the Second World War, Professor R.V. Jones, wrote: 'I can still see him standing in the hall of the Athenaeum [Club], his hands clenching so hard that his knuckles were white, and then [saying], "after the Dams Raid I swore I would never risk another pilot's life again"'. Mary, Wallis's elder daughter, felt sure her father would 'not have set the whole raid in motion, if he had realised so many young men would go'. As AJ-W's pilot Flight Lieutenant Munro put it, 'Barnes Wallis didn't think of losses, only the perfection of the weapon to do the job.' His query to Collins, 'was the raid worthwhile?', centred on loss of the fifty-three aircrew.

During the morning of 17 May, Wallis mingled with survivors – Shannon found him 'distraught' – and after lunch left with Major Kilner for the Vickers-Armstrongs factory at Castle Bromwich before visiting the Air Ministry in London at 20.00 hours and eventually reaching his Effingham home at 22.30 hours.

At Scampton that morning, publicity photographs were taken, including one of Wallis with senior officers and surviving pilots outside the Officers' Mess. Once this ritual finished, Gibson turned to dealing with the early returns. The damage to Munro's Lancaster and his inability to complete the operation were self-evident. But after the last camera clicked, he and Rice sat down with their backs against the Mess wall. The pilot explained his mishap with Upkeep, and Gibson readily understood: 'Bad luck. I almost did the same myself. It could have happened to anybody.' He was less

THE STORY UNFOLDS

sympathetic towards Flight Sergeant Anderson. He and his crew, whose flight in Squadron records was classified 'aborted' in contrast to 'early return' of Munro and Rice, were posted back to 49 Squadron.

Meanwhile, Humphries supervised the melancholy task of contacting next of kin by telegram. This would be followed by personal letters signed, and in some cases amended, by Gibson; a process, which lasted almost three days. When the scale of the losses became clear on the Monday morning, Humphreys recalled: 'I returned to the Mess in a daze. I had to send fifty-six telegrams to next-of-kin. Fifty-six letters to write regretting ... Eight messages to the Air Ministry, followed by eight circumstantial reports ... When I arrived in the office ... Flight Sergeant Powell, Corporal Munro and Sergeant Heveron, plus our small staff were all there waiting for me to start the day's unpleasant task.' Powell recalled that one of his more disturbing tasks was to gather the belongings of non-survivors ready for the separate Committees of Adjustment for officers and NCOs.

Hence, shortly after midday on 17 May, in Chichester, Mrs E. Tees received her priority telegram: 'Regret to inform you that your son Sergeant F. Tees is missing as a result of operation on night 16/17th May 43 letter follows please accept my profound sympathy = OC 617 Squadron.' Four days later her personal letter arrived, dated 20 May addressed to 'My dear Mrs Tees' and signed 'Yours very sincerely Guy Gibson'. Like all official records, it wrongly placed Tees in the front turret of AJ-C. In expressing 'sincere sympathy' and informing her that her son's belongings would be forwarded 'through normal channels in due course', Gibson attempted to hold out hope: 'It is possible that the crew were able to abandon the aircraft and land safely in enemy territory, in which case news will reach you direct from the International Red Cross Committee within the next six weeks. The captain of your son's aircraft was an experienced and able pilot, and would, I am sure, do everything possible to ensure the safety of his crew'.

On 1 June, came a standard communication from the Air Ministry Casualty Branch stating that 'enquiries have been set in hand through the Red Cross ... If any information regarding your son is received by you from any source you are requested to be kind enough to communicate it immediately to the Air Ministry. The Air Council desire me to convey to you their sympathy in your present anxiety.' Shortly afterwards, Mrs Tees received notification from her son revealing that he was alive, which prompted her to contact the Air Ministry. On 7 July, she received a formal response from the Casualty Branch addressed to 'Madam' and signed, 'I am, Madam, your obedient servant'. The writer referred to 'your letters [sic] of recent date' and noted that 'official confirmation had not yet been received in this office' that Tees was a PoW. 'Would you therefore be good enough to forward to this Department the card you have received from your son, in order that he may be reclassified as "prisoner of war". The card will be returned to you as soon as it has received attention.' The style was in keeping with bureaucratic practice, but scarcely a warm, sympathetic reply to a distraught mother.

Doris Fraser similarly received a telegram at her home in Doncaster informing her that Flight Sergeant J.W. Fraser was missing, followed by a letter from Gibson dated 20 May. In the latter, Gibson wrote: 'The circumstances which led to the aircraft's failure to return are most unlucky. The aircraft dropped its load with great precision on the target, and then was subjected to intense fire from the ground. The port engine was seen to catch fire, and the pilot climbed to 1,000ft, and after that nothing more was seen of it'. As in his letter to Mrs Tees, Gibson held out hope that the crew of AJ-M had manage to escape, 'in which case news will reach you direct from the International Red Cross Committee within the next six weeks ... The captain of the aircraft, Flight Lieutenant Hopgood DFC was one of my most outstanding pilots,' he added, before concluding: 'If there is any way in which I can help you, please let me know.' On 29 June, Doris Fraser received a Red Cross card from her husband, dated 3 June, 'telling me he was safe and well'.

News of the operation spread quickly. Dr Collins, who had been on Home Guard duty during the night, was at Boscombe Down and did not learn about the outcome until he returned home in late afternoon. When his wife told him about the announcement on the radio, he admitted to being 'very excited that they'd pulled it off'. That was how Molly Wallis learnt that the months of experiment, persistence and dedicated effort by her husband, had come to fruition and Eve Gibson heard of her husband's achievement. 'I knew very little about the whole operation,' Mrs Gibson recalled in 1980, 'and only learned about it from the news on the radio the day after it had taken place, when I was working in a camouflage factory on the third floor of a London store.' She was amused to discover that press representatives mistook her for Gibson's step-mother, 'about my age and working as a telephonist'.

The wife of Sergeant G.L. Johnson who was serving at RAF Hemswell, learnt in a peculiar way. The evening after the raid, her husband was in a bus taking her back to her own base north of Lincoln and she heard people talking about the operation. She asked George what that was all about and he rather sheepishly admitted 'I was on that raid'. Gwyneth was not amused, being 'rather annoyed that I hadn't told her before'.

THE STORY UNFOLDS

The BBC used an Air Ministry communiqué to reveal details of the operation in its lunchtime bulletin. Listeners learnt that, 'in the early hours of this morning Lancasters of Bomber Command, led by Wing Commander G.P. Gibson DSO DFC, attacked with mines the dams of the Moehne and Sorpe reservoirs ... [which] store 2/3rds of the water capacity of the Ruhr basin'. Reconnaissance photos revealed 'that the Moehne Dam had been breached over a distance of 100 yards and that the power station below had been swept away'. The Eder Dam, 'which controls the headwaters of the Weser and Fulda valleys and operates several power stations was also attacked and reported breached ... [with] the river below [the dam] in full flood'. Noting that 'the attacks were pressed home with great determination and coolness in the face of fierce resistance', the announcer concluded solemnly with 'eight of the Lancasters are missing'.

Cochrane had been quick to register his formal approval. At 08.30 hours on 17 May, he despatched a lengthy, personal message to Gibson: 'All ranks in 5 Group join me in congratulating you and all in 617 Squadron on a brilliantly conducted operation. The disaster which you have inflicted on the German war machine was a result of hard work, discipline and courage. The determination not to be beaten in the task and getting the bombs exactly on the aiming point in spite of opposition has set an example others will be proud to follow.'

Air Officer Commanding-in-Chief Coastal Command, Air Marshal J.C. Slessor, who in 1938 at the Air Ministry had been involved in the infancy of the dams' concept, sent a brief, but expressive, telegram: 'Well done Scampton. A magnificent night's work.' A signal from the Chief of Air Staff (Portal) in Washington read: 'Heartiest congratulations to you [Harris] and all Bomber Command on the outstanding recent successes against Germany. In particular please tell the special Lancaster unit of my intense admiration for their brilliant operation against the German reservoirs last night.'

Lord Trenchard telegrammed Harris: 'Many congratulations on destruction of dams; it is splendid. Please congratulate Gibson and all concerned from me. Wonderful work of Bomber Command is being recognised by all now.' Gibson's reaction is unknown to a personal message from 137 Squadron at Manston, referring to his mishap after watching one of the Reculver trials: 'Many congratulations on your success. The Squadron has new Maggie ready for pranging.'

At 17.30 hours on Monday 17 May, Deputy Prime Minister Clement Attlee, chaired a meeting of the War Cabinet at 10 Downing Street. The Vice Chief of the Air Staff, Air Marshal Sir Douglas Evill, reported on 'the

THE DAMBUSTERS: 'WAS THE RAID WORTHWHILE?'

principal events of the week ... On the previous night an attack, which had been planned for some time, had been made on three of the most important dams in the Ruhr [*sic*], the Moehne Dam, the Eder Dam and the Dam on the River Sorpe. These attacks had been most successful.' The Secretary of State for Air, Sir Archibald Sinclair, then circulated reconnaissance photographs of the damage. After further discussion, 'the War Cabinet asked that their congratulations on this operation should be conveyed to the squadron concerned and to such other persons concerned with the preparations as the Secretary of State for Air and the Minister of Aircraft Production, in consultation, might select'. Later that evening, Evill summarised the encouraging results, including two breaches in the Moehne comprising a gap of 30 yards, in a personal cypher message to Portal in Washington. Sinclair subsequently appeared in the *Movietone News* account of the operation shown on cinema screens declaring: 'Bomber Command struck last night a big blow of a new kind at the source of German war power.'

Wallis was not forgotten. Although he had congratulated him in person earlier that day, Cochrane wrote to Wallis more formally on 17 May: 'Before reaching the end of this somewhat long but exciting day I felt I must write to tell you how much I admire the perseverance which brought you the astounding success which was achieved last night. Without your determination to ensure that a method which you knew to be technically sound was given a fair trial we should not have been able to deliver the blow which struck Germany last night'. Harris wired: 'We in Bomber Command in particular and the United Nations as a whole owe everything to you in the first place for the outstanding success achieved.' Gibson assured Wallis that, 'all my pilots and I are honoured that we had the opportunity to take part in the last great experiment which has proved all your theories.'

A postscript to Monday 17 May was added by Bob Handasyde. After flying a Mosquito in Highball trials from RAF Manston, he took modified Lancaster ED 817 to Scampton prior to attending a Squadron party at Woodhall Spa. During the journey by coach to that event, Flight Lieutenant D.J. Shannon proposed to Section Officer Ann Fowler. She would later recall having accepted on the understanding that he shaved off his moustache.

Wallis received a swathe of personal letters, telegrams and phone messages from a wide range of Service and civilian authorities and individuals. Three, he later reflected, gave him special pleasure. Sir Henry Tizard wrote: 'Taking it all in all, from the first brilliant idea, through the model experiments and the full scale trials, remembering also that when the sceptics were finally convinced you had to work at the highest pressure to

THE STORY UNFOLDS

get things done in time, I have no hesitation in saying that yours is the finest individual technical achievement of the war.'

Roy Chadwick sent a disarming and generous tribute: 'It was a great pleasure for me to have helped you in some small measure and I shall always remember this particular operation as an example of how the Engineers of this country have contributed substantially towards the defeat of our enemies.' Chadwick's elder daughter, Margaret, recalled that her father often referred to the conflict being 'an engineers' war' and would have been proud that two of his grandsons joined that profession.

Interestingly, in his diary on 15 May 1943, Josef Goebbels wrote that, in the opinion of the physicist, Professor Karl Ramsauer, in physical science the British and Americans had 'completely eclipsed' their German counterparts. Goebbels therefore observed: 'As a result, the Anglo-Saxon powers are very superior to us in the practical application to warfare as the result of research in physics. That is noticeable both in air and submarine warfare.'

Thirdly, Wallis recalled his special delight at a telegram received from his elder daughter, Mary affectionately known as 'Wiggy', who had witnessed the marble experiment in the garden of the family home in Spring 1942 and was at boarding school near Salisbury: 'Hooray Wonderful Daddy!'

Wallis would painstakingly reply to every message, though to Air Vice-Marshal F.J. Linnell, former Controller of Research and Development at the Ministry of Aircraft Production, he revealed irritation: 'I do hope that next time you will give us a little more time to do the job, as at the moment I feel as though I could not survive another effort at the same pressure.' To others, positive letters more accurately represented the tone of his response and his gratitude to all those who had helped and supported him during the difficult pre-operational period as in this example:

> To you [Chadwick] personally, in a special degree, was given the making or breaking of this enterprise. For if at that fateful meeting in CRD's office on the 26 February you declared the task impossible of fulfilment in the given time, the powers of opposition were so great that I should never have got instructions to go ahead. Possibly you did not realise how much hung on your instantaneous reaction, but I can assure you that I very nearly had heart failure until you decided to join the great adventure. No-one believed that we should do it. You yourself said it would be a miracle if we did, and I think the whole thing is one of the most amazing examples of team work and co-operation in the whole history of war.

THE DAMBUSTERS: 'WAS THE RAID WORTHWHILE?'

He also responded to a letter from the Avro chief test pilot, Captain H.A. 'Sam' Brown, who had carried out some of the decisive trials at Reculver. 'A great part of the credit is due to you and I have been seeking an opportunity to tell you once more how deeply we appreciated the courage and skill with which you demonstrated the possibilities of the Lancaster on its initial trials. Everything depended upon Avro's and I feel that a tremendous debt is owed to Mr. Dobson [managing director], Chadwick and yourself for the courage and vision which you all showed in tackling what must have seemed an almost hopeless task.'

In writing on 21 May to Group Captain Whitworth, who had found him distraught on the morning after the operation, he expressed 'my very deep gratitude for all you did for us during the past eventful week-end. Your thoughtful hospitality was of immense help at a time of considerable strain'. He went on:

> I was very deeply impressed by the whole spirit of the Station under your command ... it is difficult for a civilian to understand how the formation, organisation and training of a squadron for such special work could possibly have been done in the very limited time available ... on the 26th February there had not been so much as pencil put to paper ... [yet] on the 16th May you were able to deliver this astounding attack ... The courage and gallantry of the air crews is beyond praise ... May I add my very sincere sympathy for the losses which you have sustained.

To Cochrane, Wallis wrote further:

> It is impossible to find words adequately to express what one feels about the air crews. The gallantry with which they go into action is incomparable. While the older generation of Air Force officers may not be called upon to carry out actual attacks in person, the spirit of their juniors must proceed from their thought and training, and in praising your crews I would like to add the thanks which I feel are due to you as one of the senior officers of the Air Force, for the outstanding generation of pilots which your example and training has produced. Will you please accept the deepest sympathy of all of us on the losses which the Squadron has sustained.

THE STORY UNFOLDS

> You will understand, I think, the tremendous strain which I felt at having been the cause of sending these crews on so perilous a mission, and the tense moments in the Operations Room when, after four attacks, I felt that I had failed to make good, were almost more than I could bear; and for me the subsequent success was almost completely blotted out by the sense of loss of those wonderful young lives. In the light of our subsequent knowledge I do hope that all those concerned will feel that the results achieved have not rendered their sacrifice in vain.

Amid the mass of congratulatory messages arrived a stern warning by teleprinter from Sir Charles Craven, Vickers-Armstrongs' chairman: 'I must impress on you the fact that 'Upkeep' is just as secret now as it ever has been, and will continue to be' (details were not officially released until 24 January 1963). To underline Craven's warning, three days later Wallis was made aware that Air Commodore Bufton was already considering more targets for it in Germany. He himself would shortly afterwards raise with the Director of Bomber Operations the possibility of attacking important dams in Italy with Upkeep.

By 18 May, the press had access not only to Air Ministry communiqués, but interviews with unidentified air crew. Some correspondents were misled by the cover story agreed by the Air Staff in advance. The *Daily Express*, in drawing on this delightful fiction, explained: 'Meanwhile Gibson flew up and down alongside the dam to draw the fire of the light anti-aircraft guns emplaced on it. Guns were poking artfully concealed out of the slots in the walls'. The *Daily Mail* was one of the papers to reproduce before and after reconnaissance photos of the Moehne with the caption: 'The Smash-Up. RAF Picture Testifies to Perfect Bombing'. Accompanying sketch maps depicted the localities 'Devastated – By Water'. One showed the area between the breached Moehne and the Rhine River, optimistically claiming that fifteen industrial centres in the Ruhr, including large conurbations like Duisburg and Duesseldorf, had been swamped. A second covered the region below the Eder Dam showing the effect on the Fulda and Weser rivers. Interruption had been caused to the passage of large vessels between Bremen and Bremerhaven, those of up to 350 tons on the long stretch Muenden to Bremen, 'smaller craft' between Muenden and Kassel and barges thereafter to the region of the Eder Dam. Readers of this publication were assured that 'two mighty walls of water were last night rolling irresistibly down the Ruhr and Eder valleys. Railway bridges, power stations, factories, whole villages

THE DAMBUSTERS: 'WAS THE RAID WORTHWHILE?'

and built-up areas were being swept away ... No man-made defence can stand in their way'. The air correspondent, Colin Bednall, concluded: 'It is quite impossible to predict where the damage will end ... the devastation done to Germany's war machine has probably only just begun.'

Despite the Air Ministry's attempt to restrict access to information about the raid, *The Times* printed lengthy interviews with survivors. 'A flight lieutenant' (Martin) was quoted: 'I was able to watch the whole process. The wing commander's load was placed just right and a spout of water went up 300ft into the air. A second Lancaster attacked with equal accuracy, and there was still no sign of a breach. Then I went in and we caused a huge explosion up against the dam. It was not until another load had been dropped that the dam at last broke. I saw the first jet very clear in the moonlight. I should say that the breach was about 50 yards wide'.

Another pilot spoke of 'jets of water hurtling out horizontally at least 200ft'. A third (Maltby), elaborating his post-operational debriefing questionnaire answer, explained: 'When we attacked you could see that the crown of the wall was already crumbling. There was a tremendous amount of debris at the top. Our load sent up water and mud to a height of 1,000ft. The spurt of water was silhouetted against the moon. It rose with tremendous speed and then fell gently back. You could see the shock wave at the base of the jet.' Harris was also quoted: 'We had high hopes but the immediate results of breaching the dams were far beyond our expectations.'

The following day, the *Daily Mail* published more photos of destruction under the headlines, 'Heart of Ruhr Flooded', 'Three Great Rivers are Rising Swiftly; Waters Sweeping Kassel', '100-Miles Wave'. 'Third Great Dam Now Tottering ... May Burst at Any Moment' held out hope that the Sorpe would soon collapse. On 22 May, *Illustrated London News* printed a double-page spread entitled, 'A Titanic Blow at Germany: RAF Smash Europe's Mightiest Dams' with dramatic photos accompanied by an article based upon the pre-arranged, official cover story. A week later further illustrations and photos enhanced the story under the caption: 'RAF cameras record the Dam-Breakers harvest of destruction'.

The associated article declared: 'No matter to what lengths Nazi propaganda may go to minimise the results of this catastrophe that has befallen the industrial Ruhr, they cannot explain away such scenes as are revealed in these pictures'. On 26 May, *Punch* contributed a light note with a cartoon, 'The Song of the Ruhr', showing three sirens perched on rocks wielding megaphones as floodwaters swirled past them, and its next edition included the witty offering: 'It is suggested that any further leaflets dropped by the RAF on the Ruhr should be folded in the form of paper boats.'

THE STORY UNFOLDS

All the publications made use of the photographic results of PRU flights flown by Spitfires of 542 Squadron from RAF Benson in Oxfordshire. Two on 14 and 15 May had been instrumental in the decision to launch Operation Chastise. Scarcely an hour after Flight Sergeant Townsend landed the last Lancaster to return from the raid at Scampton, on 17 May a patently disenchanted Flying Officer F.G. Fray took off for yet another excursion to the Moehne: 'That Damn Dam!', he scrawled in his log book. More soberly he recorded: 'After a very early call, I struggled into the air at 07.30hrs ... Crossed in Ijmuiden and when 150 miles away from the targets saw floods stretching towards Ruhr. Did two runs, when saw two hostiles approaching from NE. Beat it for base and landed 11.05hrs with the news and amidst a vast concourse of people.' Flying Officer G. Searle followed him into the air at 09.10 hours and landed at 12.40 hours after a less successful flight and, incidentally, illustrated how difficult it had been for crews to identify their targets at low-level at night in an area speckled with lakes and reservoirs. 'I too was called early and leapt into the air about an hour after Gerry [Fray] bound for the same targets. All went well until I was within sight of my first target and then a couple of trails appeared coming my way. I did three short runs over where I thought the dam was and then s/c for home with the trails getting much nearer. Unfortunately, my guess was wrong and I had only photographed a severely submerged marshalling yard.'

Flights on the following days also had mixed fortunes. On 19 May, Sergeant T.P. Turnbull 'flew up in clear air over the [Sorpe] dam, which was still unbroken', but two days later Fray was frustrated. Heading again for the Ruhr, he encountered 'cloud at 21,500 over Zuider Zee and bags of cirrus, so turned for base and landed at 12.45 after a Joe trip'. Flying Officer G.W. Puttick, sent to the Ruhr and Kassel, demonstrated how the vagaries of the weather could affect the success of a PRU operation:

> Off from base at 18.30 and flew to Cassel [*sic*] area via Zuider Zee. At first could not find Cassel through cloud and mist. Was fortunate enough to find the Eder Dam and so found Cassel from there. I made three runs, on second flak appeared. I made an attempt to find Sorpe Dam and other parts of the Ruhr, cloud and fog obscured both. My first indication of the Ruhr was a burst of flak. Low on petrol put down at Bassingbourn (22.30). Took off in Oxford flown by American crew at midnight, but missed Benson and had to land at Lyneham. Reached base at 04.15 on 30th. Very poor quality photos after all that.

THE DAMBUSTERS: 'WAS THE RAID WORTHWHILE?'

Not all the reconnaissance photos were disappointing. A restricted Air Staff analysis of the results on 24 May, 'Evidence in Camera', showed 'almost 200ft' of damage to the crown of the Sorpe over which 'water appears to have run down the face of the dam and carried earth from the dam into the Compensating Basin'. It did not, though, encourage speculation that seepage through a crack in the core, leading to collapse of the structure, had occurred; wisely, as it transpired. This was based on PRU flights on 17 and 19 May, which RAF Medmenham concluded showed 'two points where explosions have taken place.' However, 'the structure of the dam was not sufficiently damaged to cause complete destruction, and the latest photograph shows what may be work in progress on some sort of repair'. A photo of the Eder, taken thirty hours after the breach, revealed a gap of 180ft through which water was still flowing, with extensive damage to houses, bridges, electrical installations and 'at least 200 yards' of the river bank at Affoldern evident below. On the morning after the raid, the level of water in the reservoir had dropped an estimated 75ft, approximately 'a loss of 7/8 of the maximum capacity of the lake'.

In his 'fortnightly summary to 1200 23 May 1943', presented to the War Cabinet on 3 June, Sir Archibald Sinclair, Secretary of State for Air, referred to 'the outstanding operation during this period [being] the great attack on the Moehne and Eder dams'. He confirmed that Young and Maltby had breached the Moehne. Five aircraft attacked that dam, three of which 'achieved no immediately visible result but undoubtedly loosened the masonry'. However, 'the fourth and fifth caused adjacent breaches estimated to cover 150 feet of the dam'. Two aircraft also hit the Sorpe, which 'belonged to the Ruhr system, but was of different construction'. There, 'the intention was to cause leakage on a sufficient scale to force the Germans to empty the reservoir in order to effect repairs. It is clear that some leakage was caused, but it is not yet known whether the enemy can make good the damage without wholly or fully emptying the reservoir'. He referred to reconnaissance photos that showed power stations, roads and bridges being inundated and destroyed. 'Taken together, [this] would constitute a disaster of considerable magnitude, even if no other factors were involved', such as 'the loss of animal life' and the impact of flooding on 'agricultural land'. He continued: 'Most important of the immediate consequences were that the success of the operation added very materially to the atmosphere of general disaster and panic in the Ruhr and helped to spread it over other parts of Germany.'

Sinclair concluded his optimistic assessment with a summary of reports from Switzerland: 'The weakening of German production power is resulting in improvisation and disquieting special measures, which are felt not only by Party Leaders and factory managers, but by German citizens.' Specifically, absence of spare parts would mean 'a very long delay before factories can recover'.

Bomber Command Operations Record Book recorded: 'On 20th May the King received in audience at Buckingham Palace Air Chief Marshal Sir Arthur Harris, Air Officer Commanding-in-Chief, Bomber Command, and expressed his personal congratulations on the Command's recent brilliant exploits, particularly on the outstanding success of the raid on the German dams.'

Reflecting the mood of the moment, five days after the operation Wallis wrote to B.A. Duncan at Vickers-Armstrongs, Chester: 'I feel that a blow has been struck at Germany from which she cannot recover for several years.' In Parliament, Rear-Admiral Sir Murray Sueter a First World War naval aviator exclaimed: 'We are ... grateful to the Secretary of State for Air and the Under-Secretary and the Commander-in-Chief Bomber Command for organising the great air attack that resulted in our gallant pilots breaching the Ruhr dams [*sic*], as we read in the press to-day.' In early July, the Ministry of Economic Warfare believed that the Eder Dam could not be repaired before the autumn rains and therefore the valley below would be swamped.

The international impact was widespread and politically significant. The operation was lavishly praised in Canada, Australia and New Zealand whose air forces had together provided 43 of the 133 aircrew involved and, not least the USA, which provided one pilot serving in the RCAF. There it was timely as the American and British Combined Chiefs of Staff were meeting in Washington to shape the course of future strategic planning. On 17 May, that body formally 'took note', when Portal 'outlined Operation "Upkeep" [*sic*] and the results that it was hoped had been obtained'. The following day 'Admiral Leahy, on behalf of the US Joint Chiefs of Staff, offered Sir Charles Portal congratulations on the success of the RAF force in this operation'.

On 18 May, American public interest was stirred by *The New York Times* quoting Reuter's correspondent in Berne, Switzerland:

> The RAF has secured another triumph. With unexampled daring, skill and ingenuity it has blasted two of Germany's important water dams which are vital parts of the whole industrial and transportation system of West Germany and has therefore delivered the most devastating single blow dealt from the air ... All Americans will join with Sir Archibald

THE DAMBUSTERS: 'WAS THE RAID WORTHWHILE?'

> Sinclair in congratulating Wing Commander G.P. Gibson on his feat and mourn with him the loss of eight aircraft and their gallant crews in the enterprise.

That same day, an American radio announcer declared Operation Chastise 'one of the most daring and devastating raids of the war'. Also reporting from Berne for C(olumbia) B(roadcasting) S(ystem), Howard Smith declared that floods from the Moehne and Eder breaches had 'already inundated 54 towns and villages in the Ruhr leaving some 50,000 families homeless'. The first 'packed' refugee trains had left the area 'for the protectorate of Bohemia'.

These reports formed an encouraging backcloth for Winston Churchill's address to a joint session of Congress on Wednesday 19 May, of which Reuter's special correspondent wrote: 'Mr Churchill's speech to the US Congress has been hailed as one of the most masterly and important of his career.' Operation Chastise proved especially timely, for on 18 March Field-Marshal Sir John Dill, Chief of the British Joint Staff Mission in Washington, had reported American doubts about concentrating aerial strength in Europe rather than the Far East. Furthermore, at the current Trident conference Churchill faced naval pressure to reduce commitments in the Atlantic and, more generally, questions were raised about the wisdom of British strategy in the Mediterranean. So in Churchill's speech to Congress, after paying tribute to the invaluable contribution and achievements of American forces to the wider Allied war effort, he focused on the bombing campaign against the German homeland, which the 8th USAAF had joined in January 1943; 'round the clock', US by day, RAF at night.

'The condition to which the great centres of the German war industry, and particularly the Ruhr, are being reduced is one of unparalleled devastation. You have read of the destruction of the great dams which feed the canals and provide the power to the enemy's munition works. That was a gallant operation, costing eight out of nineteen Lancaster bombers employed, but it will play a very far-reaching part in reducing the German munitions output ... Wherever their centres exist or are developed, they will be destroyed.' He pledged British support for the United States, even if the European war should end before that in the Far East, by attacking the Japanese munition centres.

The occupied countries of Europe were not forgotten: the RAF dropped leaflets illustrating the success of the operation. Apart from the striking PRU before and after photos, diagrams similar to those published in the

THE STORY UNFOLDS

national press showed extensive flooded areas below the dams together with lengthy explanations of the operation. French readers of *Le Courier de l'Air Illustre, apporte par vos amis de la RAF* learnt that this raid constituted 'one of the greatest successes of the RAF', that Lancasters had dropped 'mines of more than 7,000 kilos on the dams, which served the war industries of the Ruhr'. Breaches of nearly 100m had been caused in the Moehne and Sorpe and a similar one in the Eder, 'which controls the flow of the Weser and Fulda rivers ... The attack, pressed home by determined men fully aware of the dangers which faced them, has resulted in material destruction of factories, which will be further increased by the loss of water when the floods abate.'

One illustration similar to that published earlier in the *Daily Mail*, headed '*Repercussions sur L'Industrie Allemande*', depicted devastation following 'the breaching of the Moehne Dam ... to power stations supplying energy to a chain of industrial towns in the Ruhr'. *De Vliegende Hollander*, dated 22 May, dropped over The Netherlands contained similar material and another, 26 January 1944, contained an article 'How we destroyed the Dams'. Post-war Colonel A.P. de Jong of the Dutch Ministry of Defence observed: 'These leaflets did create an immense impression among the Dutch people and stiffened the resistance approach. It [the raid] was generally considered as a major victory by the RAF on the road to our liberation.'

Meanwhile, at home, official recognition of the crews' achievements abounded. On 18 May, Cochrane visited Scampton to convey his formal thanks to the whole squadron, after which aircrew survivors went on a week's leave, ground crew three days' with half going immediately, the others on their return. All 617 Squadron members were, therefore, due back by Wednesday 26 May.

Returning to his Effingham home on 25 May, following three frustrating days in Scotland working on the troublesome Highball intended for use by Mosquitoes against the German battleship *Tirpitz*, Wallis discovered a letter from Cochrane dated two days previously inviting him to spend the following night at Grantham. 'Their Majesties are visiting Scampton on Thursday 27 May, and they have expressed a desire that you shall be present.' Such was the pressure of work that, having read the letter over breakfast following an overnight train journey from Glasgow, he was at Weybridge by 10.00 hours to deal with modifications to the Highball Mosquito and in the afternoon at Burhill in connection with the design of the B.3/42 (Windsor) aircraft. Following a similar programme at the two sites on 26 May, he left Effingham at 16.15 hours, an hour later was with

THE DAMBUSTERS: 'WAS THE RAID WORTHWHILE?'

Bufton at the Air Ministry and reached Cochrane's Lincolnshire home at 20.00 hours. He was, therefore, in ample time for the next day's royal visit.

That could not be said of Pilot Officer G. Rice, who stayed overnight with friends in Nottingham and reached Scampton at 11.00 hours on 27 May, alarmed to find 'a tremendous flap going on'. Technically, he had overstayed his leave and was relieved to encounter a relaxed OC. 'Good job I'm in a good mood', Gibson told his errant pilot. Rice was further relieved to discover that one of his crew had remembered to secure a lunch ticket for him. Leading Aircraftman Victor Gill, the maintenance mechanic, granted only three days leave was less fortunate. He did not begin his journey to a remote village in north Devon until late on the afternoon of 18 May. Gill recalled overstaying his leave to attend a dance and his offence being compounded by the fact that the local taxi driver, set to take him to the station, had run out of his official supply of petrol. On return to Scampton that excuse was 'deemed too feeble' and he found himself confined to barracks for fourteen days.

King George VI and Queen Elizabeth arrived at 13.00 hours on 27 May to inspect raid survivors drawn up in their crews, with one exception each captain in front with his feet brushing a neat, white line. Flight Lieutenant W.C. Townsend was indisposed, so his Australian navigator, Pilot Officer C.L. Howard, took his place. When newsreel footage of the event was eventually shown in cinemas in his home town, Perth, his wife Marjorie admitted to having 'dragged my friends round them all to see Lance on screen'. Reporters and cameramen recorded the scene for newspapers, magazines and journals. The tall American Flight Lieutenant McCarthy was prominent with his twin shoulder flashes 'Canada' and 'USA'. This was Flight Lieutenant Shannon's 21st birthday and readers learnt that the King had encouraged him to celebrate accordingly. In reality, despite the careful preparation, administrative snags did occur. The King and Queen inspected the crews in turn and each had a helpful escort to present individual crew captains. To his, and their amusement, Wallis found himself in the procession of worthies to whom they were introduced. King George was accompanied by Gibson, Whitworth and Cochrane, who knew the personnel; Queen Elizabeth by an officer unfamiliar with them, which caused some embarrassment. He contrived to get both the names and background of some individuals wrong. Pilot Officer Knight was introduced as 'a newcomer', which prompted the Queen to enquire whether he was 'settling down nicely'. Flight Lieutenant Munro was loath to let an inaccurate introduction pass: 'Munro's my name.'

THE STORY UNFOLDS

Following the inspection and prior to a buffet lunch, the King was photographed looking at pre-operational maps and being briefed on the raid by Gibson. The Squadron's Operations Record Book recorded that the King and Queen inspected aircrew personnel, visited the crew room and 'the Squadron Commander reconstructed by models the operation against the German Dams'. The King was also shown two designs for the 617 Squadron crest and asked to choose one. The first depicted a hammer parting chains representing Europe with the motto 'Alter the Map'. The second, which the King preferred, showed a broken dam with a flash of lightning and the words *'Apres Moi le Deluge'*. Nobody seemed concerned that this was a corruption of the reputed words of Madame de Pompadour, Louis XV's mistress, *'Apres nous le deluge'*.

The buffet lunch, which followed, meant that the food was not served and legend has it that nobody could begin until the royal family had collected their meal. At one stage, Barnes Wallis supposedly found himself beside a bemused Queen Elizabeth faced with a large, uncut cheese and nonplussed. In answer to her anguished query, he purportedly said: 'Take a knife, Your Majesty'.

Newspapers on 28 May would carry extensive coverage of the royal visit to the Squadron at 'an air station in the north of England' together with multiple photos. *The Daily Telegraph*'s front-page featured a prominent shot captioned: 'He [the King] is seen laughing with Wing Comdr Gibson who for his leadership has been awarded the V.C.' The recommendation for that, and other awards listed in the article, had been forwarded by Whitworth to HQ 5 Group on 20 May and passed rapidly up the line. Under the heading 'Particulars of Meritorious Service', Whitworth noted of Shannon's crew: 'With great skill and determination they succeeded in dropping their mine in exactly the right position ... I strongly recommend that the excellent work of this crew be recognised by the immediate award of the Distinguished Service Order to Flight Lieutenant Shannon and of the first bar to the D.F.C. to Flying Officer Walker, and of the Distinguished Flying Medal to Flight Sergeant Sumpter.'

Telegrams of congratulation were despatched to all the recipients signed personally by Harris on 23 May; that to Flying Officer H.S. Hobday typically reading, 'My warmest congratulations on the award of your Distinguished Flying Cross.' When he opened his wire revealing award of the DFM, Sergeant D.E. Webb suspected an elaborate joke as he himself had the reputation for being a prankster. Having rung Scampton for confirmation, 'I nipped into a shop round the corner for a ribbon and put it up'. Sergeant

THE DAMBUSTERS: 'WAS THE RAID WORTHWHILE?'

D.P. Heal 'couldn't believe it', when he opened his telegram at the Gosport home of his parents. Also having checked with Scampton, that evening he and his father celebrated at the British Legion club. In company with other local newspapers focusing on residents' achievements, *The Hampshire Telegraph and Post* would publish a photo of Heal in describing the award to its readers.

In his log book, Gibson wrote, 'Awarded V.C. 23 May 1943'. Replying to the Warden of his old school, St Edward's in Oxford, praising the execution and outcome of the operation following press reports, he wrote: 'P.S. Was awarded the V.C. yesterday'. Early notification allowed those decorated to wear the appropriate ribbon for the royal visit.

Thirty-four of the 77 aircrew, who returned, were decorated: 19 RAF (including one Australian, Martin), 7 RCAF (including the American McCarthy), one RNZAF and 7 RAAF. Of these, apart from Gibson, 5 received the DSO, 4 a Bar to the DFC, 10 the DFC, 2 Conspicuous Gallantry Medal (Flying), one a Bar to the DFM and 11 the DFM. Pilot Officer G.A. Deering flew as a Flight Sergeant on the operation not knowing that he had been commissioned, but was awarded the DFC (an officer's decoration). Flight Sergeant D.A. MacLean had been similarly promoted. When the adjutant, Humphries, noticed that he had been awarded the DFM, he asked the Canadian whether he should press on his behalf for it to be changed to a DFC. 'Hell, no', came the steadfast reply. Another Canadian, Flight Sergeant K.W. Brown, was officially commissioned on 16 April 1943, but not notified until later and wrote: 'To the best of my knowledge I was the only officer to receive the CGM [Conspicuous Gallantry Medal]'. On 15 May, Flight Lieutenant R.N.G. Barlow had learnt about the award of the DFC, which in the event he would never receive. Also lost on the night, Flight Lieutenant W.H.T. Ottley would never know that his DFC for previous service had been promulgated on 16 May.

The decorations were formally presented by the Queen, the King being in North Africa, on the morning of 22 June at Buckingham Palace; following a somewhat chaotic railway journey to London from Scampton and an evening of prior celebration later described by Humphries in print. Gibson's flight engineer, Sergeant J. Pulford, was absent ill and would receive his DFM from the King in November. Sergeant Webb reflected that he believed the Queen had been persuaded to conduct the ceremony in the King's absence, 'because nobody could guarantee that this lot would be around when he got back'. He also revealed that, after Gibson, the Squadron recipients were decorated in alphabetical order regardless of their award.

THE STORY UNFOLDS

At the same ceremony, Roy Chadwick received the CBE for his services to aviation and Gibson a Bar to the DSO in addition to the VC to make him the highest decorated RAF officer.

That evening, A.V. Roe and Co. Ltd., manufacturers of the Lancaster, sponsored a dinner at the Hungaria Restaurant in Lower Regent Street 'to celebrate decoration of members of 617 Squadron RAF'. On the menu card appeared 'Damn Busters', which looked like a splendid pun, until reference to the 'Rhur Dams' rather suggested a printing error. Among those present were the adjutant, Humphries, and 'Chiefy' Powell, from Vickers-Armstrongs chief designer, Rex Pierson, Sir Hew Kilner and Wallis. Before and after photographic reconnaisance photos of the Moehne were on display. Gibson was snapped signing his name on a photo of the breached dam in the gap, to which the signatures of other survivors were added. This illustrated an account of the celebration in the *Daily Mirror* the following morning.

'The dam-busting boys of the RAF had a stag party in the West End last night' with Gibson the guest of honour. 'Only women at the party were the waitresses – proud to serve dinner to the crews and ground staffs of the famous 617 Squadron. 'Well, chaps', said the VC, 'we have had a lot of praise but this raid was not carried out by one man. It was carried out by a lot of people working hard'. A fusing link from the Upkeep dropped by Gibson was auctioned for the RAF Benevolent Fund and bought for £30 by T.O.M. Sopwith, the famous aeroplane designer and Avro director.

On 24 June, Wallis could write: 'The shores of the empty reservoir are now adorned by the signatures of the other members of the crews and this picture will form a historical record of this outstanding accomplishment on the part of the RAF.' Having left the Hungaria restaurant with them two days earlier, in retirement the photo signed by Gibson and one of the Moehne before the attack would adorn the wall of his study in the Effingham family home.

After the Buckingham Palace ceremony photographers produced group photos, some of individuals and others with their families, which accompanied lengthy articles in the following day's newspapers. The *Daily Sketch* appears to have originated 'dam-busters' in its edition, which described the events of the previous day. 'Never before has a Queen Consort presented medals to British war heroes. It was a memorable scene as Queen Elizabeth stood alone on the dais in the Throne Room'. The *Daily Mirror* quoted Gibson: 'I'm very glad to get that over though the Queen was most charming. She told me the King regretted that he could not be there.' On the

THE DAMBUSTERS: 'WAS THE RAID WORTHWHILE?'

other side of the Atlantic, *The New York Times* printed a photo of McCarthy with an expansive account of his participation in the raid.

The citation for Gibson's VC, published in *The London Gazette* on 28 May, began: 'Under his inspiring leadership, this squadron has now executed one of the most devastating attacks of the war – the breaching of the Moehne and Eder dams. The task was fraught with danger and difficulty.' It went on to detail Gibson's own attack at the Moehne, direction of other aircraft there and at the Eder. The 617 Squadron Operations Record Book would note that, somewhat belatedly, on 9 July 'the whole of the Squadron personnel were photographed this afternoon'.

In his foreword to the May edition of *V Group News*, Cochrane used 'the destruction of the dams' to urge greater accuracy in the Battle of the Ruhr. 'Unfortunately a number of bombs are still falling, 2, 3 and 5 miles from the aiming point and this is delaying the victory.' The publication illustrated the breach in a dam under the heading 'Dam-ping Their Ardour':

> Half a dozen major bomber raids could probably not have effected the results caused by 617 Squadron ... As summer progresses factories will have insufficient water and nothing the Germans can do will be able to make good the shortage this year. Even if repaired, the dams will take two seasons to fill ... As a consequence of this master-stroke of strategy in the Ruhr campaign there will also be such subsidiary diversions as the de-pollution of filter beds and the re-building of roads. But the main result is undoubtedly further paralysis of the area of Germany and an addition to the atmosphere of panic and gloom.

Independently, Pilot Officer I. Whittaker, Martin's flight engineer, held that 'this raid was a great milestone, which represented a professional advance in achieving precision, a new plateau of expertise'. This, he emphasised, had been achieved in the Ruhr, 'a frightening place to fly over'.

In its 1943 edition, *The Annual Register* would declare Operation Chastise: 'The most sensational air exploit of the month [May] – and perhaps of the war.' Writing to Barnes Wallis on 2 August 1946, Group Captain Whitworth would echo this sentiment: 'In my opinion, it eclipses practically any other single event of the war.'

Chapter 12

Impact – Germany

Unteroffizier Karl Schuette, Luftwaffe NCO in charge of the 20mm flak gun on the right-hand (eastern) tower at the Moehne, revealed that the gunners on the dam were trained to deal with aircraft approaching from the north (air side) not across the reservoir. When the Lancasters overflew the dam from that direction and disappeared to the south, Schuette assumed that they were using the reservoir as a navigational aid. Hence the gun crews failed to detect Gibson's low-level approach during his initial dummy run, but were ready for the subsequent attacks as their weapons had a 360° all-round capability.

There had been ample notice of danger. Inhabitants of nearby Guenne reacted to an alert at 23.30 hours on 16 August, with some, not all, taking to the shelters. In the power station beneath the dam wall, the duty policeman, Oberwachtmeister (NCO) Wilhelm Strotkamp, informed the engineer-in-charge (Klemens Koehler) of the air-raid warning, then went outside the building. When aircraft subsequently flew so low over the dam that he could see them clearly, he rushed back to tell Koehler. As the attacks developed, Strotkamp took refuge in a slit trench on the wooded slope at the eastern end of the dam. Realising that the machines were attacking across the reservoir, he scrambled further up the bank. From there, he witnessed the attacks and the destruction of the power station, but did not attempt to phone his superiors in Soest until the breach occurred.

Bezirks Oberleutnant der Gendarmerie Hilse, chief of police at Soest, recorded that during the night of 16/17 May 1943, 'I observed enemy aircraft flying from north to south over the town. After a time I saw in the direction of the Moehne Lake the anti-aircraft artillery firing.' He rang the police station at Guenne to be told that the dam was under attack but unbroken. Having alerted Reg. Oberinspecktor Junghoelter of the regional council, he set off by car for the Moehne. Reaching it at 01.08 hours, he found 'the dam already damaged'. Hilse's timings were then awry.

THE DAMBUSTERS: 'WAS THE RAID WORTHWHILE?'

He claimed that 'the warning service Arnsberg had transmitted an alert at 00.20hrs ... At 00.21 hrs the power station was struck and at 00.42hrs the dam broke'. Hilse added that 'the official on duty' had reported the breach to Junghoelter. Reflecting post-war on the sequence of events, Dr Ing Koenig supported other reports that a warning had been given long before 0020 hours. 'Between 00.15 and 00.20hrs, Gibson and his group reached the Moehne reservoir. By this time the alarm had been raised and flak installations on the towers of the dam were manned.'

By the time Hilse reached the Moehne Dam, the guardroom was in chaos: 'The furniture was turned upside down by the atmospheric pressure [blast] and no connection could be established by phone.' So he settled himself in the adjacent Hotel Moehneterrassen, which had a functioning communications system. He noted that the relevant entry in the guard book read: '16–17 May 43. At about 00.20hrs an enemy air-raid took place on the dam and the power station. The raid was executed by several enemy aircraft. The power station was completely destroyed, and the dam so heavily damaged between the two towers that the water poured out with a terrific force into the lower valley'. A report from the regional centre of Arnsberg on 24 June 1943 would confirm that the direct line from the Moehne to Soest had been so damaged that contact was re-established via the Koerbecke railway telephone system.

A police reservist named Hannermann was in his flat at Koerbecke, when the attacks took place and swiftly set off for the dam on his motor cycle. Quite how much he saw is debatable, for he revealed that his account was 'the result of the investigations I then made as the competent Gendarme'. Its inconsistencies indicate the confusion of the moment. According to him, the Moehne guard received warning of impending danger at 00.10 hours. Shortly afterwards, three aircraft attacked the flak positions and 'at the same time the lock-house of the first-tower was hit by a bomb'. As the gunners fired on these aircraft, a four-engine bomber flew over the reservoir at a height of 10m towards the middle of the dam. All three guns on the dam focused on it. 'Just before' the double torpedo net, which was 25m from the wall, 'the bomber dropped a special bomb', which produced 'a 10 metre high whirlpool' dragging the net to the dam and exploding there. As a result of blast, the guns posted on both towers were displaced from their rests and put out of action. The dam still held, even though water was seeping through two cracks in it and, with smoke pouring from its tail, the aircraft flew on to crash near Ostoennen.

Three other aircraft then 'started a second raid': the power station sustained a direct hit and 'the electricity stored in the batteries was

IMPACT – GERMANY

suddenly set free in a gigantic light reflex similar to lightning which probably doubled the effect of the explosion. It is to be supposed with all probability that at the same time a bomb had struck the dam in the middle for it broke'. The surge of water 'about 6000 cu metres per second, swept away all the buildings standing below the dam'. Another observer in Guenne quaintly described the impact of Hopgood's Upkeep: 'Then the power station flies into the air'.

Hannermann claimed that at 02.30 hours, 'several aircraft' appeared, attacked the flak positions and in the process set Farmer Nettlebeck's farm alight. This must have been Lancasters returning from the Eder from which four set out around 02.10 hours. Shannon recalled by-passing the Moehne, but Gibson wrote about circling twice and Hobday (Knight's navigator) of flying via it, though neither recorded engaging flak. It is likely that Young followed orders to return via the dam and, possibly, Maudslay's damaged machine, also, slightly earlier. One flak gun was certainly active and Guenne schoolboy, Karl Heinz, held that the three in the meadow resumed firing after the initial raid, the crews presumably returning once the level of water settled short of that position. Strangely, Hannermann mentioned that, 'this time, too, one aircraft showed smoke and landed near Hamm'; obvious reference to Ottley's totally unrelated demise.

Despite his insistence that he witnessed the sequence of events distinctly in 'very clear moonlight', another observer, Kleeschulte, gave a further garbled account of the attacks at the Moehne between 24.00 and 01.00 hours on 17 May 1943. 'About three to four aircraft were flying for a while in the vicinity of the Moehne barrage. One aircraft, which was brightly illuminated crossed directly above the Moehne Lake several times while the anti-aircraft artillery posted on the dam was firing at it. When after a few loops the aircraft flew directly upon the dam the anti-aircraft suddenly stopped firing.' Kleeschulte maintained that 'these observations could easily be made from this place'.

'A few minutes later this office was rung up by the Gendarmerie official who is living directly on the Moehne Lake, who informed that in his opinion the dam must be hit because the water in the lake was visibly diminishing.' Initially, due to phone lines either being destroyed or engaged, this could not be confirmed by the Guenne station, but eventually 'the catastrophe' became clear. 'A gap of about 80 metres in length and about 20 metres in depth' in the dam wall was noted. 'Through it the water masses of the Moehne Lake, which at that time was full to the edge, poured into the valley inundating it.'

THE DAMBUSTERS: 'WAS THE RAID WORTHWHILE?'

The power station engineer Klemens Koehler recalled an air-raid warning from 'the observers on the Bismarck Tower' at 00.20 hours, which seems odd as Martin reached the dam at 00.15 hours and other evidence, not least from Strotkamp, put the alert before midnight. Koehler confessed to concern, because the reservoir was only 6 million cubic metres short of maximum capacity and any damage to the wall could prompt a catastrophic flood. For that reason, he and other engineers had repeatedly called for reduction of capacity to 80 million cubic metres. Not mentioning Strotkamp's second warning, he recalled that his fears were raised when he heard aircraft approaching from the north and promptly phoned his superiors at Neheim and other depots of the United Westphalian Power Stations organisation only to be brushed aside.

Koehler then went to the door of the building, which he explained stood on the edge of the equalising basin in the shadow of the dominating dam and separated from it by a 50-yard wide herbaceous border. He could see nothing of what was happening over the reservoir, but was aware of heavy gunfire before an aircraft flew across the wall in a hail of shells and he heard an explosion. Like the duty policeman, he fled up the bank to a position where he had the two towers, power station and reservoir in sight. He saw Hopgood's burning aircraft disappear to the north and realised that the enemy had 'launched several bombs into the lake in front of the wall'. He claimed that two gunners were blown off 'the towers' – though other accounts mentioned just the left-hand (western) one – and lay wounded on the roadway. The remaining guns on the wall and in the meadow beneath Guenne continued 'firing like mad'. 'Now I saw the catastrophe coming without being able to do anything to help my cousins and nephews who live near the sawmill on the lake below (all six were drowned), nor forester Wierleuke with his thirty paying guests on holiday, nor the people of Neheim, Niederensee and Himmelpforten ... And down there in Neheim, they had answered my warning with "Don't tell us any fairy tales"'.

He claimed to have seen fine sprays of water spurting through cracks in the dam wall before the breach occurred. Twenty years later, Koehler's son, Eberhard, repeated in more detail the decisive incident. 'From the direct hit of this bomb great cracks were caused in the dam, one could clearly see the water trickling out and a loud hissing noise was heard similar to that from a steam engine.' Marks on surviving buildings in Guenne suggest that the immediate level of the water before it escaped into the Moehne valley reached roughly 7m above ground level. The three flak guns, although below the main ridge, were on a slight rise on the eastern side of the equalising basin. Situated as they were beneath the towering dam wall, it seems likely that initially the crews fled to higher ground as the water gushed out of the widening gap above them; regaining their posts as it settled.

The Luftwaffe NCO on the eastern tower, Karl Schuette, perhaps naturally as he was under fire, gave some additional information to these various accounts without providing persuasive clarity. 'I stood behind the gunner' making adjustments as necessary to the elevation and lateral bearing of the barrel. 'We fired whatever the gun would give. The shells whipped into the face of the attacker.' He, like Hannermann, insisted that those on the dam were only alerted of impending danger 'shortly after midnight' and that the flak guns engaged the first aircraft at 00.20 hours, which might be when Sumpter was reporting Shannon's Lancaster being 'hosepiped'. There seems to be no acknowledgement of Gibson's dummy run and implicitly Schuette's gun did not fire on his actual attack. Scheutte claimed to have missed 'the first attack ... as it was at such a low level', but 'saw an explosion short of the dam wall'. He held that his gun scored direct hits on the second aircraft (Hopgood's). He confirmed that when Upkeep demolished the power station, 'huge chunks of masonry were thrown in the air', which put the gun on the western tower out of action and fits with Koehler's testimony. Each gun had a crew of six and the uninjured members, with their weapon out of action, carried spare ammunition across the roadway on top of the dam to the eastern tower. Indirectly, Schuette underlined the accuracy of the Lancasters' gunners, when he admitted that his crew had to take cover as the attacking aircraft flew between the towers.

After the power station had been destroyed, two aircraft attacked, the higher one with what Schuette believed were navigation lights on. This was Gibson going in with Martin, whose bomb, Schuette confirmed, exploded near the far side of the dam. Such had been the rapid, continuous fire that the gun barrel had to be changed 'regularly' due to excessive heat. Smoke from the burning power station and spray from exploding bombs (the spouts reported by Lancaster crews) reduced visibility and further hampered the gunners.

The next attack (the fourth in reality) saw three aircraft, two with lights on flying higher than the centre one: Gibson and Martin with Young. Schuette placed this at 00.45 hours, when his gun jammed and the crew were reduced to firing rifles at the attackers. With two guns on the dam now out of action, only the one on the eastern buttress beyond the towers opened up against Maltby, although the three close to Guenne were then still active.

THE DAMBUSTERS: 'WAS THE RAID WORTHWHILE?'

Schuette recorded that the enemy aircraft left the area at 00.55 hours, but mentioned one subsequently being engaged between 03.00 and 04.00 hours. This would seem to support the report of Flight Sergeant Brown's crew that AJ-F was fired on at the Moehne on the way back from the Sorpe. Despite the incident involving the gunners on the western tower, no serious injuries were suffered by Leutnant Jorg Widmann's command. He would receive an Iron Cross 1st Class for the action that morning; each gun commander (including Schuette) being awarded an Iron Cross 2nd Class.

On 6 July, in Berlin, Hermann Goering chaired a Luftwaffe conference at which Oberst Dietrich Schwenke presented a flawed account of the attack on the Moehne, yet again demonstrating the disarray caused among the defenders. 'The first bomb made no impression on the dam, fell short of the dam and broke into pieces there. The flak gunners had seen all of this imperfectly: they were very excited. The second bomb exploded. We don't know if at the net or at the wall; at all events it didn't break the dam. The third bomb penetrated the wall. The fourth attacked, but when it saw the water was flowing out, it flew over the dam without dropping its bomb.' When those at the meeting pointed out that other reports did not coincide with this version of events, Schwenke became angry: 'There is no doubt ... There were four aircraft and altogether there were nine attacks. A bomb was not dropped on each attack: in all there were only three. That's absolutely certain.'

A more comprehensive 'secret report on air attack on the Moehne and Sorpe dams' was circulated on 30 September 1943 by Dr M. Pruess, Superintendent of Works for the Ruhr Valley Dams Association (Ruhrtalsperrenverein or RTV), who had himself reached the breached Moehne in the early hours of 17 May.

He opened: 'As a result of my inspection of Air Zone VI records in Muenster and of personal discussions with the OC of the A.A. Battery (3/840) operating on the Moehne dam wall, the occupants of the left hand sluice tower and the controllers of the Moehne and Sorpe dams, with members of the police target guard of the Moehne Dam and others living in the Moehne Valley, I forward the following report on the course of the attacks'.

Despite the broad spectrum of sources, however, his conclusions too were in places confused. Pruess agreed that visibility was good in the bright moonlight and held that '5–20 hostile aircraft circled at high altitude over the Duessseldorf-Essen-Duisburg area, obviously as a feint for the proposed attack on the dams.' They provided a diversion from two groups of four to five aircraft approaching from Holland, which 'shortly after midnight', flying between Muenster and Dortmund, made for the Moehne region. These attacking aircraft flew at low altitude round the northern edge of the Ruhr defences, descending to 'tree top level' to avoid heavy flak batteries. The six 20mm guns at the Moehne had greeted the approaching aircraft with 'barrage fire', having been alerted to their imminent arrival by the authorities at Hamm. 'Three were stationed in the meadow below the dam wall and the other three were stationed on the wall itself. One of the latter was located on each of the upper platforms of the sluice towers and the third at the right hand extremity [when looking down the valley] on the overflow where the wall surface had been suitably extended.'

The officer-in-charge of the 3/840 flak battery at the Moehne, Leutnant Jorg Widmann, reported 'about twelve single attacks', although bombs had not been dropped each time. This demonstrated that the flak gunners had, indeed, been confused by the tactics of Gibson and Martin. 'When approaching the dam wall from the water side, the aircraft kept to the right bank and suddenly appeared hedgehopping over the last wood clearing in front of the dam with the result that the line of approach as seen from the wall surface was very short. We may add that since then this wood clearing has been guarded by A.A. guns.' Pruess, therefore, agreed that the attacking aircraft kept to the right bank (eastern sleeve distinct from the Heve western sleeve) of the reservoir and that they 'suddenly appeared' over the tree-covered spit of land between the two rivers. He observed that 'all the aircraft flew through the barrage and destructive fire of the A.A. batteries with great determination'.

'According to observations by numerous people', the first bomb exploded in front of the protective torpedo nets short of the dam face, which fairly accurately describes Gibson's attack. Damage to the left-hand (western) floating fender indicated that the bomb exploded on the shore side of the tower. However, he then placed Martin's third attack as the second. This bomb exploded near the left-hand bank of the reservoir 80–100m from the dam face. Unaware of Upkeep's tendency to veer to port, Pruess speculated that the Lancaster released its bomb too close to the wall and at an angle to it. When the reservoir drained, parts of it were discovered close to where the left bank had collapsed over a significant distance. Following the explosion, water surged over the far left of the dam wall, causing the crew on the adjacent tower to fear that the dam had been breached.

Pruess's third attack was, in reality, Hopgood's: 'approached the exact centre of the wall, but clearly released the bomb too late. It went clear over the top of the wall and fell into the overflow pond situated below the dam wall. This caused the destruction of a power plant built right across the valley about 40m from the open side of the wall and it blew up with a large sheet of flame. Simultaneously, the electric current failed over the whole valley area'. Blast from the explosion 'caused the roof of the left-hand [western] sluice tower to collapse and blew the gun posted there from the flat roof ... Thereupon, the crew left the tower to assist the gun crew of the right-hand [eastern] sluice tower in carrying ammunition. The gun crew were still able to proceed by way of the undamaged roadway of the centre portion of the wall to the right-hand tower'.

Shortly after this exercise had been completed, a fourth aircraft attacked, releasing its bomb 'a few metres from the centre of the wall ... [and] after a dull explosion, which did not appear to be particularly heavy, the wall between the two towers collapsed and water poured into the valley'. Pruess described only four attacks, which suggests that this was Young's, with Maltby's not included as the dam had already been breached. However, Pruess insisted that 'a total of three mines was dropped on the water side of the Moehne Dam', indicating that the attacks of Young and Maltby were somehow conflated. He explained that 'experimental borings of the wall proved that, as opposed to the Eder, the horizontal cracks at the breach only extended a few metres from the edge of the breach ... The Moehne wall has on its water side a flat earth layer up to about half the height of the wall which clearly proved very effective'. Pruess agreed that 'when the large mine bombs were released the machine lifted sharply'.

He seems also to have confused part of the evidence from Hannermann and Schuette. 'Scout planes' appeared low over the Moehne Dam at 02.45 and 03.24 hours. Their machine-guns engaged the flak guns and with incendiaries set fire to a barn in Guenne.

The Pruess report provides more evidence of the disruption to the administrative system caused by the attacks on the Moehne Dam. It goes some way to explaining why night–fighter training continued at nearby Werl airfield with no attempt to douse the runway lights nor to engage the raiders. No night fighters were scrambled because none had been requested. Given that Gibson's wave was in the vicinity for roughly 45mins, the reported failure of the telephone system combined with the disorganisation discovered by Oberleutnant Hilse appear to be the reason. Surviving records suggest that Widmann, commander of the flak contingent, was unable formally to report the breach and associated damage until an hour after the action. This would be approximately when Hilse discovered

IMPACT – GERMANY

intact communications in the Moehneterrassen hotel. Only on receipt of Widmann's report could the area commander order troops to the Moehne and set about officially informing a wide range of Nazi party, government and military authorities of the raid.

Rescue teams converging on the Moehne and Ruhr valleys encountered scenes of devastation only partly exposed in the RAF reconnaissance photos. The defenders of the Moehne Dam might have escaped loss, but that was not true of inhabitants in the area, nor was the farmer's burning barn the sole example of physical devastation. The witness named Kleeschulte recorded that, apart from the power station, many buildings in the valley 'were either destroyed or heavily damaged. Eight dwelling houses and a few other buildings heavily damaged'. Like the policeman Hannermann, he put the death toll in Guenne at 30. At the dam itself, the torpedo nets had been dragged through the breach and were stranded on the western side of the equalising basin, the 20-ton turbine from the power station stranded on the eastern side. From the 132.2 million cubic metres of water in the reservoir, 116 million cubic metres poured through the gap within twelve hours, burst across the equalising basin and created a torrent through the narrow valley carrying the Moehne river to its junction with the Ruhr river at Neheim.

The draining of the Moehne reservoir, reported by Kleeschulte, meant that feeder pools like those at Koerbecke and Delecke were emptied so rapidly that retaining banks were severely damaged. District authorities in Soest would demand 1 million Reichsmarks for repairs in those areas of the Moehne and Ruhr valleys under their jurisdiction as a result of 'the catastrophe'. The W. Broekelmann Aluminium Works at Neheim-Huesten was but one of many individual factories to list detailed damage to its facilities caused by 'the great catastrophe'.

Communities in the Moehne valley below the dam were also devastated. The power station engineer, Koehler, claimed when the breach occurred, a motor cyclist vainly tried to beat the flood before it reached Niederensee. At Himmelpforten, like inhabitants in Guenne, several had failed to take refuge in shelters and, once the flood water began to sweep through, the local priest, Father Berkenkopf, rushed to the parish church desperately to ring the bell in warning. It would seem that those near the Moehne had been alerted to impending danger by authorities in Soest, whereas Neheim at the junction of Moehne and Ruhr rivers relied on Arnsberg, which according to one report did not issue a warning until 00.50 hours. Officially, the wave of destruction reached the town, eight miles below the dam, 'at about 0055', which is patently wrong; '01.10' in another summary more likely in the light of Maltby's testimony. McCarthy's Lancaster returning from the Sorpe observed flood water surging out of the equalising basin in the direction of Neheim shortly before 00.54 hours.

Marks left on trees indicated that in places the wave reached 15m, and witnesses estimated that it had been 2m above the height of bridges swept away in its wake. Many foreign labourers were allocated to work in Neheim's twelve armament-related factories. One local source declared that heavy loss of life among them occurred because the commandant of the camp, where many were housed, supposedly mistook the roar of the approaching torrent for a train on the disused Moehne-Neheim railway. The different details surrounding events at Neheim underline yet again the mayhem caused on the night.

A pamphlet published in Neheim-Huesten in 1958, added a further dimension of regret. 'If the police in Neheim had only listened to the [unidentified and untimed] private telephone warning and given it credit and immediately warned the population of the impending danger, it is highly probable that many human lives would not have been lost and they would have been spared much sorrow ... The official warning system broke down, partly owing to faulty reasoning, and partly from negligence.' Of the impact on the area, the writer dramatically explained: 'In a few minutes the peaceful valley countryside of the Moehne and the Ruhr was transformed into a raging deluge in which the sleeping or startled human beings, bellowing cattle, numerous houses and valuable property fell a sacrifice.'

L.J.H. Hoesen, a Dutch conscript worker, fortuitously survived the deluge. He was with other forced labourers in sleeping quarters on the top floor of a factory overlooking the river, when the warning sounded. Post-war he recorded his experience:

> I remember well that the night was a beautifully clear moonlit one. The air-raid alarm sounded between 00.30 and 01.00. I raced out of the factory and outside, on the left, there was a reinforced concrete bridge spanning a small river. A large group of people stood there together and I joined them. In the distance I heard the dam anti-aircraft defences having a go. I also saw and heard the planes. I clearly remember they had powerful lights and they were flying very low. There was a tremendous din of machine-gun and anti-aircraft gunfire. Suddenly I heard an appalling loud explosion followed shortly by a violent rushing sound. I stood there for a moment until I realised that the dam had broken.

IMPACT – GERMANY

A moment later, I saw in the distance a dark grey 'something' coming towards us. I then shouted, 'run, run up the hill', but the people just stood there. I ran off with a Belgian named Rene. I was about 100 metres above the bridge when, turning round, I saw that the water, with tremendous force, had swept away the bridge with all the people on it. At the same moment there was a tremendous spark: the power station had also been washed away, with houses and streets.

Hoesen concluded:

I sat all night on the hill until the Green Police took me off to the other side in the morning in an assault boat. I then joined up with the work parties clearing up and I also had to identify the bodies of my young workmates. The factory was for the greater part destroyed (we were forced labour, employed by the Broeckelmann Neheim-Huesten factory). I was then billeted with some townsfolk until I obtained three days special leave and went home to Holland. When I got home, I went underground until the liberation.

Hoesen's account of the devastation in Neheim suggests that the municipal authorities were justified in referring to 'terrible chaos'.

In April 1943, Peter Theunissen, a 29-year-old Dutch conscript had been sent with two others from the town of Boxmeer to a factory in Hachen, north of the Sorpe Dam and 8km from Neheim, where three more from his home town like Hoesen were deployed to a factory there. Theunissen recalled what happened on 17 May:

That morning we heard that the Moehne Dam had been destroyed. Towards midday we went to Neheim where we found a ghastly situation. Our three fellows from Boxmeer together with many more had been drowned. On the banks of the Moehne there was much destruction: factories, houses, bridges. One bridge had been swept bodily 150 metres downstream. Railway waggons were overturned by the rails. Things lay everywhere: household implements, trees, dead deer; the streets thick with layers of mud. We spoke to a Dutchman, who stood on the bridge but managed to climb up a hillock before the water reached it [almost certainly Hoesen].

THE DAMBUSTERS: 'WAS THE RAID WORTHWHILE?'

We then went to the churchyard and spoke to an SA man on duty. The dead were brought in by lorry, identified and buried together according to their nationalities. There was no trace of our Boxmeer friends: it was thought that they still lay under the ruins of the factory.

He added that, 'the small village of Guenne lay fairly close to the Moehne Dam and it caught the first rush. It was rebuilt after the war'.

The water, which poured out of the Moehne Reservoir and down the valley to Neheim, then undulated westwards through the Ruhr Valley towards the river's junction with the Rhine. On the way, it swamped adjacent towns, giving rise to the RAF reconnaissance photos and optimistic press sketches of lasting, widespread destruction. As at Guenne, a warning had sounded at 23.30 hours in Wickede, beyond a large bend in the Ruhr River. But with no aircraft activity apparent, many did not seek refuge in a shelter. Those that did were misled by a 'fire horn' at 01.40 hours warning of immediate danger believing it to be the 'all-clear'. Heavy loss of life therefore occurred. In addition, 161 houses were damaged or destroyed, six factories similarly affected, railway and road bridges in the area badly damaged. Surrounding farmland was strewn with fallen trees and domestic debris from the town. All gas and electricity supplies were cut off.

Dr Ing K.W. Koenig, who would be become the 'Civil Engineer responsible for the reconstruction of the Moehne Dam', held that 'the water works in the upper Ruhr valley were extensively damaged. Water purifying plants were covered with thick layers of mud, and water works were put out of commission as far along the valley as Witten'.

Clemens Mols, in the post office at Wickede, confirmed the 23.30 hours warning and that shortly afterwards he received another by phone that aircraft were flying low at the Moehne. He therefore went to the window with his wife to look towards the distant dam. He could hear, but not see, the action. 'Suddenly, an immensely loud detonation was heard and I saw in the direction of the Moehne Lake a huge column of water or smoke soaring.' He heard more explosions and, after a while, 'over the warning line aircraft were reported over the Eder Lake and no more mention of the Moehne', so he went to his neighbour's house, where the family was in the cellar, and told them that all was now well and that they could go to bed. Returning to the post office, he heard the telephone ring. Arnsberg post office told him to get out of the house because a flood had reached Vosswinkel, only 5km away and was advancing rapidly. After vainly trying to reach other houses by phone, as the air grew damp and 'a sulphurous vapour cloud' rose from the bath in the cellar, Mols slammed the door and rushed upstairs. He noticed 'a short distance from the railway bridge a goods train was standing. We could see from the window how the valve of the engine let steam escape with a loud wheezing', as the water level rose. A lorry trailer floated by as the lower floor of the house was swamped. When dawn came, Mols realised that the heavy engine and part of the railway embankment had been washed away, the rails deposited in a meadow. Two years afterwards, he recalled, agricultural land 'was still deserted'. An unidentified witness remembered that 'by 8am the water had subsided and I came down from a tree'. Another, named Hoberg, claimed that in half an hour the water rose 7m, with small houses being swept away, but by 09.00 hours the torrent had abated so that inhabitants could walk through the streets deep in mud.

On the night, further west, the flood (almost 4m higher than the previous record flood of 1890) reached Froendenberg, 25km from the Moehne at 03.00 hours. At Hagen, 65km from the dam, it exceeded the former maximum by 2m. Several pumping stations were put out of action in the valley, so urban concentrations like Bochum and Dortmund were without water. A large power station at Herdecke (132,000kW capacity) 60km below the Moehne lay under 2m of water. The torrent took six hours to reach the junction of the Ruhr and Rhine rivers, 148.5km from the Moehne, where it remained 4m above normal twenty-five hours and thirty minutes after the breach. Not until midday 17 May, did the outflow from the reservoir slow to a trickle.

Writing post-war, Professor Dr Ing Otto Kirschmer believed that 'the damage caused was very great ... houses built on lower ground levels were destroyed or damaged up to a distance of about 65km downstream; up to 50km downstream all bridges were destroyed'. He explained, too: 'As the Moehne reservoir was the main source of the water supply of the Ruhr valley, the consequences of the breach of the dam wall was grave ... numerous towns, e.g Hamm, Hagen, Bochum and Dortmund, were without water.'

Long before then, a vast array of military, police and paramilitary personnel, supplemented by civilian rescue organisations and volunteers plus schoolchildren bussed in from the surrounding area, had swung into action. One schoolchild vividly recalled being taken by bus to Niederensee and seeing old people sitting on top of a house with water lapping their feet. At first light, gun crews at the dam set about removing the rubble from the roadway on the crest. The western tower had been virtually destroyed,

THE DAMBUSTERS: 'WAS THE RAID WORTHWHILE?'

Schuette's gun on the eastern one required repair, confirming his claim and that of Hannermann and Brown's crew, that only one flak gun on the dam wall remained active after Young's attack. In addition, the disorder in the guard room identified by Hilse together with damage to the military living quarters and storage facilities had to be dealt with. Further afield, over 2,000 military personnel and civilians concentrated in the Ruhr Valley between Neheim and Wickede. On 5 June when the Dutch conscript, Peter Theunissen, obtained permission to travel back from Hachen close to the Sorpe Dam to The Netherlands, the railway system was so disrupted that he had to make a lengthy diversion.

By mid-June, the scale of destruction caused by the breaching of the Mohne Dam had become clear. The total of dead and missing, comprising Germans and foreign labourers, amounted officially to 1,294. Apart from extensive damage to urban and rural properties, 125 factories were either damaged or destroyed, 4,043 hectares of arable land, meadows and pasture rendered useless or damaged, 6,316 cattle and pigs destroyed, forty-six road and rail bridges either destroyed or needing extensive repair. This was in addition to a swathe of power stations, pumping stations, water and gas supply facilities affected to a varying degree of severity.

A similar sequence of events had unfolded at and around the Eder Dam. As at the Moehne, enemy airmen often used the surface of the reservoir as a navigational aid, so no particular concern occurred when aircraft were heard shortly after 01.00 hours on 17 May. Karl Albrecht, engineer in charge of the two power stations beneath the dam wall, was on duty and 'thought at first that the bombers would only fly over the lake as had happened before. The glistening surface of the water was easily identified from above and must have often served as a navigational point'.

His recollections, voiced post-war, were confused with no clear time frame. He claimed that he was unaware of danger until the explosion of a bomb damaged the wall and the northern building power station. This is not the area, where Shannon's Upkeep hit the dam and seems to refer to Maudslay's attack. However, Albrecht did not mention any of the attacking aircraft, the direction of their flight nor fate, presumably because, being inside or close to one of the stations on the air side of the wall, he did not actually see the attacks develop. He seems to have been in the southern station, when what he assumed was the second bomb (clearly Knight's) detonated:

'I was actually on the steps of the engine room, when a dull thud occurred. I had the feeling as if the construction rocked and was about to collapse ... I groped my way through the darkened rooms, as from above stones began to crash through the roof and water to come in. We [he and other engineers] managed to clamber up the steps onto the slope and reach the dam wall. I saw the breach, which was becoming increasingly wide and through which water was pouring with great force into the valley.'

Another close-quarter witness was an official, August Rubsam, who was flung several metres by the blast from Knight's Upkeep. Once he recovered his composure, he realised he must inform his superiors at the authority's headquarters in Hannover-Muenden that the dam had been breached. Stranded north of the rupture, though, he was helpless as all telegraph and telephone links in the vicinity had been severed: 'There was no alternative but to ask a passing motorcyclist on his way to Waldeck from there to inform the administrative authority, and officials arrived at the dam soon after dawn.' People living in the small community of Hemfurth close to the river below the dam as it curled towards the equalising basin, unable to see what was happening over the reservoir, stood outside their houses, puzzled as aircraft cleared the dam and circled the adjacent hills. One witness reported seeing a figure poke his head out of a cockpit, another that two explosions occurred close together [Shannon and Maudslay] almost half an hour after the first sound of aircraft was heard. He added that 'an awful commotion' followed the third explosion 'at about 02.00'.

A post office worker at Bad Wildungen, 7km south-east of the Eder Dam, heard the air-raid warning followed by the sound of aircraft engines. Fearing that the Mauser small-arms factory on the Netz-Buehlmen road might be the target, he alerted the flak battery there only to learn that the aircraft had passed over. He, therefore, like so many others went outside and from afar watched hostile aircraft circling without realising that the dam was under threat. Then, 'I saw a high spiteful, green flame rise up and shortly afterwards an explosion, followed by a din like the distant, muffled sound of a railway engine.' Hearing the phone ring, he went back in time to see the post master pick it up and hear: 'Edersee here, the dam is broken. I ...' The instrument went dead and all attempts to reconnect with the Edersee community abutting the southern end of the dam failed. So the Bad Wildungen post master began contacting other villages in the Eder Valley and, in doing so, saved many lives. He instantly rang Affoldern on the edge of the equalising basin, whose post master exclaimed: 'Almighty God! Is it true? We've heard the noise ourselves.' Within 'a few minutes' every community as far as Fritzlar, had been contacted with the warning: 'Tell the Burgomeister [mayor], sound the tocsin [alarm]. It must be sounded immediately.'

THE DAMBUSTERS: 'WAS THE RAID WORTHWHILE?'

Christian Kohl, in Hemfurth beneath the dam wall, recalled that 'we had hardly reached a safe height, when all the houses in the path of the raging torrent were swept away ... With a colossal din, the upper part of Hemfurth's suspension bridge, a robust iron structure, was swept away by the flood and broke asunder'. Lieschen Paar, living on the outskirts of Affoldern, recalled:

> We didn't really believe in an attack on the dam ... [but] I ran into the village, because my father had seen a bright light, and met a soldier who told me that the water was coming. My parents ran out, meanwhile I went [upstairs] to get grandfather up quickly and heard a sound which made me run downstairs again. It was no longer possible to get out of the house, because the water kept the doors shut. So I ran up to the attic with grandfather. From there we looked out. At first the outhouses, then the houses in the village, were swept away. We passed the whole night in anxiety. In the morning, I saw a rubber dinghy travelling towards Mehlen and Herr and Frau [Mr and Mrs] Koetter, whose house was destroyed and who were above clinging to the ruins of the chimney, to rescue them. We were rescued towards midday by another boat.

It emerged that the Eder Dam had suffered damage from all three Upkeeps. Eyewitnesses in Edersee reported that Shannon's not only destroyed steps to the landing stage at the southern end of the dam, but also cracked the wall itself. As well as the adjacent power station, property in the village was affected by the blast, the parapet of the dam and the roadway along its crest damaged. Because the bulk of Maudslay's had gone upwards, mainly the pavement on the air side of the roadway above the tenth overflow outlet and the parapet on each side of the road had been affected. Knight had left a V-shaped breach slightly to the south [right] of centre with 'a radius of 25m' or, in another report, 'a semi-oval breach of 70m wide and 22m deep'. 'Cracks and loosened spots' beyond the breach were evident together with lengthy horizontal fissures. At the bottom of the breach, the wall was 18m thick and thus some 30,000 tons of the dam had been lanced from the structure.

Professor Dr Ing Kirschmer, who put the first attack at 01.20 hours, also analysed evidence of the effect on the Eder area from the breach 'near the left-hand tower'. Noting that, when full, the reservoir covered 11.7km, he emphasised that the dam (built 1908–13) not only protected the lower valley from flooding but increased 'the water flow of the Fulda and Weser rivers and the Mittelland canal in order to improve navigation in these rivers and the canal'; further justification of the stated reasons for this attack. He also outlined associated power facilities: 'At the bottom of the dam are two power stations, Hemfurth I of 15,000 kW capacity, and Hemfurth II with 17,000 kW capacity ... There is also a pumped accumulation plant in Hemfurth with a peak power output of 115,000 kW, supplied by four turbines, and below the dam at the equalising pool [near Affoldern] there is a small power station with a single turbine of 2,560 kW capacity.'

At the time of the attack, the reservoir contained 202.4 million cubic metres of water and 154.4 escaped during approximately 48hrs, due to a slower rate of outflow than at the Moehne through a smaller breach. The speed and depth of the flood, although noted briefly as 12m high and 8m wide, was on average considerably less than below the Moehne, because the bulk of the valley was wider. So, the water spread further laterally, and few communities in the Eder, Fulda and Weser valleys escaped. At Hannover-Muenden, 94.4km from the Eder, although the flow was believed a third of that in the Ruhr Valley, it was 7m deep. On 18 May, a photographer snapped milk being delivered by rowing boat at Karlshafen, 139km below the Eder. The effect of the tidal wave was felt at Interschede, near Bremen, 425.6km from the breach.

As in the Moehne and Ruhr valleys, a rescue operation swiftly got underway. SS Colonel Burk recorded his reaction to the scene: 'The first impression of damage is devastating. The affected population have lost their houses. It is impossible to form any kind of picture of the casualties.' It gradually became clear that 50 hectares of fertile fields had lost valuable topsoil and vast areas had been strewn with shingle and scree to a depth of 2m. A large quantity of cattle had been lost, irrigation networks, pumping and electricity facilities had been extensively affected, including the four power stations close to the Eder. A wide variety of vessels had been stranded on the banks and the bed of the Eder reservoir drained; landslides had occurred in four places where the bank collapsed. Anglers discovered that virtually the whole of the fish stock (originally installed in 1935 to boost food supplies) had been lost. On learning about this, an unsympathetic 617 Squadron wireless operator expressed satisfaction that 'we'd deprived the Germans of their fish and chips'. Of the 3.3km long equalising basin between Hemfurth and Affoldern, only 500m of the banking remained unscathed.

THE DAMBUSTERS: 'WAS THE RAID WORTHWHILE?'

Kirschmer supplied more detailed information:

> The sluices of seven accumulation lakes between Gunterhausen and Hannover-Muenden were completely filled up with sand and partly undermined. The flood water started an intensive earth movement in the Fulda and the movement of 30,000 cubic metres of earth by dredging operations was necessary to re-establish the conditions as they existed before the breach in the dam occurred. The earth movement continued in the Weser from Hannover-Muenden onwards and this necessitated further dredging operations involving about 5,000 cubic metres of earth. About 1,000 groynes were also destroyed in the Weser and the river banks of the Weser and Fulda were seriously damaged; about 5½km of bank protecting structures had to be rebuilt in the Weser alone.

Due partly to the comparatively slow escape of the water from the Eder reservoir, the wider nature of the valley and rapid alerts initiated by the Bad Wildungen post master, the loss of life was put at forty-seven.

There was little recorded local reaction and scant collateral damage at the third dam to be attacked. Dr Pruess's report of 30 September also covered the Sorpe and, once more, his witnesses presented a distorted picture. The account of McCarthy's attack, at about 00.45 ... from an approximate height of 20 metres' against a dam 'not protected by flak or balloon barrage' was reasonably accurate. 'The aircraft flew several times across the dam wall in the direction of the earth dam and did not release a heavy mine till the tenth run. This forced a bomb crater on the water side of the earth wall close to the water line covered by only three metres of water with the result that, since it blanketed the explosion only to a minor degree, this explosion took an upward direction and threw up a column of water to a height of 150–200 metres.'

His account of Brown's attack was neither clear nor accurate. 'For the second attempt on the Sorpe Dam two aircraft appeared, both of which attempted to locate the damaged spot with their searchlights, and later during the fifth run, one aircraft dropped a second mine close to the first point of impact.' Like the first mine it 'only formed a small crater which was prevented from extending across the dam by the concrete wall, which was stripped on the water side to a depth of several metres but remained undamaged'. The mythical second aircraft does seem to have been Townsend en route to the Ennepe Dam.

Peter Theunissen, the conscript working in Hachen, recollected: 'It so happened that both factories where we worked were sited downstream of a dam ... From Hachen, we could see the Sorpe Dam. On the night of 16–17 May we were wakened by a tremendous din. We looked through the window and saw a four-engine aeroplane flying very low towards us. It banked, turned sharp left and disappeared from view behind a hill known as "Angel Mountain". We were sure it was making a forced landing'. Post-war, he described his experiences that night in detail to his young family (his daughter subsequently corresponded with Flight Sergeant Brown's flight engineer, Basil Feneron), indicating that he had witnessed at least some of the action at the dam. 'Those fellows weren't afraid. They were dare-devil. They had to wait and see if another run to the target was required.' In his written account of that night, he recalled: 'The first explosion I still remember very clearly', which suggests together with the fact that he was woken by the low-flying aircraft, that the Lancaster he saw so clearly was McCarthy's. He claimed that 'the Sorpe Dam was considerably damaged ... [and] when we tried to go and have a look at it, it was forbidden. You'd be guilty of spying. By then the repairs were well on the way'. He explained that 'a few days later [after the raid] military transport brought in barrage balloons, torpedo nets and smoke dischargers for the Sorpe Dam. The smoke dischargers were set off by a light beam and thus, in the shortest of time, visibility was virtually nil'.

In his official report, Pruess concluded that the blast of the Upkeeps of McCarthy and Brown had caused some structural damage to the pumping station on the edge of the compensating basin beneath the dam and to some houses in the vicinity. On the dam itself, two craters were located 30m apart and 3m below the water level. The explosions had sent water 150–200m into the air, their downward effect being 'damped by the material of the rubble dam'. Although Pruess maintained that both craters were 'small'; another German estimate thought them to be '12m deep' and a third '8m in diameter by 4–5m deep'. Pruess insisted that the structure had 'remained undamaged', but admitted that the concrete central wall on the water side had been stripped 'to a depth of several metres'. Walking through the inspection tunnel at the base of the dam after the attacks, RTV staff found no evidence of seepage, but viewing the structure externally agreed with Koenig that 70m of the crown had been torn away. It would cause the level of water in the reservoir to be lowered for necessary repairs.

Post-war, Albert Speer recalled: '... [at] the Sorpe Valley reservoir, they did achieve a direct hit on the centre of the dam. I inspected it that same day. Just a few inches lower and a small brook would have been transformed into a raging river, which would have swept away the stone and earthen dam'. Presumably, he meant that if Upkeep had exploded deeper in the water, less of the blast would have gone fruitlessly skywards. Professor Dr Ing Otto Kirschmer agreed that, 'it was very fortunate for Germany that this earth dam did not collapse at the same time as the breach of the Moehne gravity dam occurred ... as the resulting damage to the Ruhr valley would have been very grave indeed'.

Dr Ing Koenig, who would be prominent in repairs to the Moehne Dam, was an eye witness to events during the early hours of 17 May. He was staying that night with friends in Balve, close to the Sorpe, and was woken by an air raid warning. He dressed and 'went into the street ... There we saw the light of star shells on the horizon and heard a loud explosion'. He reflected that 'this must have come from the first attack on the Sorpe reservoir [McCarthy's] ... [and] afterwards the silence seemed intensified'. This is the only reference to 'star shells' or any similar illumination during either attack on the Sorpe. Koenig and his hosts went back to bed until 'later that night' he was roused by 'a state emergency call' on the telephone. The Moehne Dam had been attacked and he was to go there immediately.

'Shortly afterwards', the burgomeister collected him by car with the aim of going via the Sorpe Dam. 'On our way to the Sorpe, we had to turn off the headlights of the car several times as a bomber flew low over us: we had the impression that the pilot was searching for his target ... while we were just over two kilometres from the reservoir, there came the second air attack on the dam.' On reaching the Sorpe, he estimated that 'roughly one third – about 70 metres – of the crown of the dam had been torn away'. He joined the RTV officials in their inspection. 'Together we walked through the internal inspection tunnels, which run the length of the dam at its base, to check for water seepage but did not detect any serious damage.'

'At about 4am', he left to drive alone to the Moehne, but was slowed 'by a number of vehicle convoys – army, fire service and other emergency services ... I tried to imagine what might have happened at the Moehne: perhaps torpedoes had been used to breach the dam'. Koenig was unable to use the Delecke bridge 'and I had to make a detour via Koerbecke. Light fog lay over the valley. I could see no water. I stopped and noticed that the reservoir, as far as I could see, was empty. I realised that something terrible must have happened. Driving on, I saw, at the last moment, that the road had been broken away, caused by the water pressure in the smaller reservoir to the right of the road which had been able to empty as quickly as the main reservoir'.

Eventually he got through to the dam 'at around 5am' to see 'an enormous breach in the wall between the towers from which masses of water were still pouring – rushing and foaming into the valley'. Koenig noted that the level of water in the reservoir had been 'almost at its highest'. 'The main power station had disappeared completely. Instead there was a large expanse of water, a great section of the broken wall, torn torpedo netting and buoys. The first rays of sun shone through the fog – it was a picture of devastation which I shall never forget.'

'At about 5.30am', he met Dr Pruess and 'we estimated the remaining water in the Moehne reservoir to be approximately 25 million cubic metres. In just over 5 hours 110 million cubic metres had gushed through the breach. Pruess realised that the flood would surge westwards from Neheim along the Ruhr River to its junction with the Rhine. Along that stretch were three smaller reservoirs, Baldeney, Hengstey and Harkort. The first had already been drained to deter enemy aircraft from using it as a navigational aid and Pruess 'immediately' ordered the other two to be emptied and this, Koenig claimed, significantly reduced the torrent beyond them. Nevertheless, 'the enormous damage in the valley of the Ruhr ... demanded an extraordinary effort in the employment of people and machines', with 'emergency services and volunteers working day and night'.

As notification of the attacks reached responsible authorities in Germany, reaction was indeed swift. Albert Speer, Reich Minister for Armaments and Munitions, was roused from his bed in Berlin with the 'most alarming [news] ... in the early hours of the morning' that the Moehne Dam had been breached, its reservoir 'emptied' and, that 'three other dams' had been attacked. He quickly made arrangements to fly to the affected region in a Fiesler Storch light communications aircraft. Shortly after dawn, he landed at Werl airfield close to the Moehne, having overflown the dam, where 'the power plant at the foot of the shattered dam looked as if it had been erased along with its heavy turbines'. He was in no doubt that the enemy bombers had 'tried to strike at our whole armaments industry by destroying the hydroelectric plants of the Ruhr'. The spectacle of the black and white

THE DAMBUSTERS: 'WAS THE RAID WORTHWHILE?'

carcasses of cattle scattered across the flooded terrain impressed, but did not unduly worry, him. Apart from the more important industrial impact, his immediate fear was that a follow-up raid would be mounted while the defences were in disarray. He therefore called immediately for flak guns to be deployed to all important dams without delay.

Speer spent two days touring the affected areas by car, concentrating on the Ruhr-related dams, and concluded that 'the electrical installations at the pumping stations were soaked and immobilised and the water supply of the population was imperilled'. Later, he explained the details of his inspection exercise. At Dortmund on 18 May, he met officials responsible for water, electricity and gas supplies, as well as four regional Nazi party leaders (gauleiters). That evening, he despatched a provisional plan of action to Hitler. Practically, he set in motion priority arrangements to bring into the affected areas experts from throughout Germany to restore utility services and he confiscated necessary machinery from distant factories 'regardless of the consequences' to short-term requirements elsewhere. He aimed to have normal water supplies restored 'within a few weeks'. Forty-eight hours after the raid, Hitler approved the withdrawal of Organisation Todt (OT) workers from building the Atlantic Wall. Speer's office diary recorded that 'within a few days over 7,000 labourers' were deployed to assist the clearing-up process and to help the rebuilding process at the damaged dams and in the valleys below, as well as urban concentrations like Kassel and Dortmund; another indication that the dramatic sketches, which appeared in the British press, were not altogether fanciful. A further 20,000 labourers were to swell the repair force 'as soon as possible'. Speer ordered the Inspector General for Water and Energy to carry out a thorough investigation and report on measures to ensure the future supply of domestic and industrial water supplies together with the associated drainage system.

Speer flew back to Berlin on 20 May, not having visited the Eder Dam or the damaged area below it, although he flew over them on the return flight. On arrival in the German capital, he assured Joseph Goebbels that on closer inspection the damage was not so disastrous as first thought. He hoped to have the armaments industry in the Ruhr in half production at the beginning of the next week (24 May), just seven days after the raid, and in full working order by the end of that week. Highly impressed Goebbels wrote in his diary: 'Speer is truly a management genius'. Neither he nor Speer acknowledged that to achieve these feats elsewhere routine industrial output and special projects like the Atlantic Wall would haemorrhage men and equipment.

IMPACT – GERMANY

The Physical Institute of Goettingen University, in recording seismographic readings during the night of the raid, noted seven, which represented the reported attacks on the gravity dams, with the exception of Hopgood's. His Upkeep detonated above the ground so that its impact did not show, and similarly the two at the Sorpe, where the bulk of the explosive effect went upwards. Significantly, the reading recorded for Knight's Upkeep known to have decisively breached the Eder Dam was 0.2mm, the same as that for Young.

Different military sources sought to minimise the impact of the damage and, at the same time, over-estimate the number of enemy aircraft involved while underlining the success of defenders. The High Command of the Armed Forces (OKW) issued a communiqué from 'The Führer's Headquarters' on 17 May: 'Weak British flying formations entered the area of the Reich last night and dropped a few bombs in specially planned locations. Two reservoirs were damaged and due to the resulting escape of water heavy losses were caused among the civilian population'. However, 'eight of the attacking planes were shot down'. Although acknowledging that the Moehne and Eder dams had been 'badly damaged', the Sorpe had allegedly not been hit. The Naval Staff claimed that 'seven' aircraft had been accounted for by flak, but then parted company with reality. During the night of 16–17 May, '180–190 planes' had operated over German-occupied territory, '70 of which flew over the Reich. Fifty aircraft in two waves attacked a number of dams. The Moehne dam and a section of the Eder dam were severely hit. The power plant at the Sorpe was damaged. The Bever dam remained undamaged'; the significance of this assertion becoming clear later. A supplementary assessment emphasised that 'the raiders flew in in a low-level attack and were not detected either by plane reporting [visual identification] or night-fighter controlling equipment [radar]. Only one of the attacked valley dams was protected by light anti-aircraft fire'.

The Nazi Party newspaper, *Voelkischer Beobachter*, having on 18 May quoted the OKW communiqué from the previous day, two days later attempted to quell panic. Relying on information from military sources, it maintained that: 'The losses among the civilian population ... the damage and injury caused by the floods were happily not so great as were at first feared ... Emergency help and assistance' had proved highly effective.

Chapter 13

Significant Outcomes

Speer's tour of the affected areas led not merely to a clearing-up process, but positive efforts both to repair and protect the dams. His call for deployment of strong military defences was rapidly heeded. Even so, on 30 May 1943, Hitler complained to him that sufficient flak batteries were still not in position. The Ruhr, Hitler stressed, was the centre of the armaments industry and all aspects connected with that must be guarded as a matter of priority. This resulted in comprehensive defences being allocated to all the 617 Squadron target dams and others which were not. In co-operation with Heinrich Himmler, Speer had also to devise a warning system for every important dam, not simply those attacked during the night of 16–17 May.

The full range of passive measures was not quickly completed, though, resulting in prolonged diversion of resources from other commitments. At the Moehne, doubts were expressed about sinking a 500m-long barrier of wooden fascines to protect the dam wall and, instead, Inspector Schmitz of the Luftwaffe Board of Works agreed that a series of floating wooden deflectors would suffice. So 44 linked to 398 buoys were installed over the winter. The amount of water in the reservoir caused controversy, too. The RTV decided that the maximum level would be 208.50m, which Dr Pruess protested would reduce capacity by 47 million cubic metres, but he was overruled by 'higher authority'. In the reservoir a third torpedo net, 400mm thick and 650m long, was installed 6m behind the existing double nets (each 100mm thick) between them and the wall. Closely-spaced pieces of timber, supported by floats anchored to the face of the dam angled at 45°. and weighted by ballast, comprised additional deflectors beneath the surface.

The civil engineer, Dr Ing H.W. Koenig, recorded that above the reservoir 'an aerial apron' was strung between the banks attached to 90m high steel pylons. It comprised 'a light steel net – in which were small bombs – suspended between the pylons so that any attacking aircraft would inevitably have to fly into the net'. Nor was the air side neglected.

SIGNIFICANT OUTCOMES

Anti-rocket and anti-bomb netting was supported by struts attached to, and jutting out from, the dam wall.

Manning of the array of searchlights, balloons, flak guns and smoke canisters together with troops to deter sabotage or parachute operations amounted to an estimated 1,000–1,500 men. Some were rapidly deployed, as archival photos confirm, but correspondence between the RTV, Heinrich Butzer Company and Organisation Todt casts doubt on the nature of the defences in place by October 1943. Extensive exchanges during the opening months of the following year, not least over the torpedo nets and underwater deflectors, strongly suggest that the full breadth of static defences was not in position until May 1944.

At the Eder, elaborate precautions were also taken. Two flak batteries each with twelve 20mm guns (some Vierling four-barrelled), one battery of four 37mm guns and two batteries each of two 88mm weapons were amassed. In addition, there were a battery of six rocket-launchers, multiple large and small searchlights and 48 balloons. A special contingent controlled 500 smoke pots capable of creating a thick smoke-screen and a company of Landesschuetz (local defence) riflemen were on hand to deal with parachutists. Altogether, 1,300–1,500 first- and second-line troops were committed to defence of this dam. Similar defences to those at the Moehne in and above the reservoir were installed. Eleven 10 x 20m wooden stakes, attached to buoys and angled into the reservoir, were sunk immediately in front of the dam wall and 50m from it were three rows of 3m deep torpedo nets attached to more buoys. A row of six mines was sunk 250m from the wall and 480m from it, and 90m high pylons were erected on high ground each side of the reservoir between which was slung a cable, 50–100m above the water at its lowest point, to which contact mines were attached to counter low-flying aircraft. Three further rows of mines attached to buoys were sunk 550m, 1,100m and 1,350m from the dam wall, each mine 1,000kg and electronically operated by water turbulence caused by an aircraft flying at 80–100m. During the night of 8–9 July 1944 a heavy thunderstorm activated some of the mines, which led to minor damage to the dam.

Parallel to deployment of these defences, repairs to the three damaged dams got underway. The civil engineer, Koenig, recorded the Moehne breach as 76 x 22m. The Road Research Laboratory scientist, Dr A.R. Collins, was reluctant to ascribe this to adjacent breaches by Young and Maltby, seeking to prove that the Moehne structure was inferior in strength to that of the Eder, where the gap was smaller. Post-war he contended that 'a fifth aircraft claimed a hit and a second breach, but there is no certain physical evidence to support this'. In his report of 30 September 1943, Dr Pruess summarised the extent of the damage at the Moehne, which supported Koenig's figures. 'An approximately rectangular wedge of 76 metres broad and of an average depth of 20–22 metres was broken away. The wall was approximately 17 metres thick at the base of the breach. Approximately 12,500 cu. metres of masonry were washed away at the breach. As the Moehne wall was built in a steep curve the section which was destroyed exerted a strong downward pressure on adjoining wall sections, and this pressure caused further considerable damage.' This meant that 'an additional 6,800 cu. metres of stone work were removed with a result that 19,500 cu. metres of wall needed replacing.'

Although the RTV (Ruhrtalsperrenverein/Ruhr Valley Dams Association) had technical responsibility for the reconstruction, Speer put Koenig in charge of the labour force at the Moehne and Sorpe dams. The Organisation Todt (OT), he explained, 'was the only one in Germany which had available sufficiently large resources of people, machines and building materials. It had been founded [pre-war under Fritz Todt] for the construction of the West Wall [Siegfried Line] and was an enormous organisation with engineers, experts of every kind and labourers drawn from firms, local authorities, engineering bureaux etc. During the war, it was made responsible for extending the [defensive] Atlantic Wall. Developed with a military structure, the Organisation Todt had its regional headquarters for the Ruhr at Heidhausen near Essen, offices for the middle and upper Ruhr area at Hagen and a local section office at the Moehne reservoir. That the RTV exercised 'the technical responsibility for the reconstruction of the dam' caused administrative friction. The Organisation Todt considered the RTV 'interlopers'.

The priority was to repair both dams before the winter rain, the initial target at the Moehne being reconstruction 'up to the overflow crown' by October. Aware of this 'extremely short construction time', the OT 'proposed to fill the breach in the dam with concrete which their experience, particularly with the Atlantic Wall and other fortified walls, had led them to believe would be suitable'. To the RTV this was 'absolutely unthinkable'. It insisted on the reconstruction being 'exactly as before and with the same material, i.e. quarry stone, as such an enormous cement in-filling would produce unacceptable forces within the wall. With backing of the Reich Ministry for Food, Agriculture and Forestry which was also responsible for water management throughout Germany', the RTV's view prevailed. Koenig admitted that this created

SIGNIFICANT OUTCOMES

for the Organisation Todt 'the undoubtedly difficult task of obtaining thousands of tons of sound quarry stone and many quarries over the whole area were used. Skilled labour was an even greater problem and large areas of Europe were searched for workers experienced in building with stone'. Koenig noted that the bulk of the foreign labourers came from France, The Netherlands and Italy.

At the Moehne, Koenig estimated that approximately 1,600 conscript foreigners, exclusive of specialist quarry workers, were involved in the repair work, which was directed on the spot by the Heinrich Butzer Company from Dortmund. Work went on without pause seven days a week. Koenig explained that remaining parts of the wall each side of the breach had to be cleared and secured, before 'the shafts' could be tackled. 'Under the stress of the fracture these had been torn along their entire length, from top to base ... Special permissions [sic] and authority for the work had been given and all trains transporting materials for the work had priority over all others.' Both the Moehne and Eder dams were repaired with 'cyclopean rubble masonry of the same type as the original construction' and the cracks were sealed by a pressure grouting system. On the air side of the Moehne, a deep hole had been scoured as water flowed through the breach and possibly weakened the heel of the dam. A huge block of some 13,000 cubic yards (10,000 cubic metres) was inserted.

Speaking in 1983, Koenig recalled that on 24 September 1943, six days in advance of the target, the wall had been repaired 'up to the overflow crown and a few days later the road built along the top'. Speer recorded that this work was completed by 2 October. The following day, he travelled to the dam to congratulate all concerned on their remarkable achievement and attend a celebratory ceremony together with party officials from the surrounding area. During the proceedings, he recalled, a phone call from Hitler was received. Koenig estimated that, overall, 2,800 workers had been specifically devoted to the Moehne repairs, which were completed in 78 days. He also reflected that 'it was surprising at the time – and for me still is today – that during the entire period of reconstruction there were no more allied attacks on the dam'. Only occasionally did the work force have to take cover when an air-raid warning sounded, but no direct attack ever developed.

The breach at the Eder measured 60m wide and 22m deep. Philip Holzmann AG from Frankfurt-am-Main was appointed main contractor for the reconstruction, its work force enhanced by OT conscripts. A light railway delivered material to the foot of the wall and cranes hoisted it to the top, so that the gap was closed by the end of September. Fortunately, the administrative authority at Hannover-Muenden recorded, the two power stations and the banks beside them had held during the raid, the machinery within damaged, but not destroyed. The contractor confirmed that masonry each side of the breach was loosened and contained fissures, and that only 17m of the wall beneath the breach remained intact. Similar to the Moehne, a 12m deep hole had been scoured out of the rocky sub-soil, in this case on the reservoir side, to present an additional problem.

Further to work on restoring the dam wall, below it Heinrich George, deputy manager of a road construction firm in Arolsen, used 100 'Ostarbeiter' (conscript labourers), housed in a tented complex, to supplement staff repairing a 14km stretch between Hemfurth and Geismar. George confirmed that six bridges between Hemfurth and Wegen-Wellen had been swept away to be replaced by wooden structures and not permanently rebuilt until after the war. Correspondence between Philip Holzmann and the OT confirmed that the elaborate system of planned defences was not fully in place before May 1944.

The RRL scientist, Dr A.R. Collins, wrote that 'in September 1945, [Dr] Glanville and the author inspected the Moehne and Eder dams and had a discussion with the engineer who supervised the repair work on the Moehne, which he said was completed in six months. From the information obtained from him and from inspection of the dams, it was concluded that the breach in the Moehne was about 240ft wide at the crest and 200ft wide at the bottom and the depth was about 55ft. At the Eder the equivalent dimensions were 210, 140 and 180ft. These figures were, however, for the size of the breaches when they were repaired and include those parts removed by scour and in any trimming undertaken during the repair work. On a basis of the weight of explosive used in Upkeep, the linear scale of both attacks was slightly more than three times that of the test on the Nant-y-Gro Dam from which it was forecast that the breaches would be 180ft wide at the crest and 48ft deep. If some allowance is made for scour and trimming and some inaccuracy in the depth at which the bombs exploded, the agreement between the model and the full-scale results appears to be good. It was also consistent with the experience of RRL in respect to other structures which had shown that the extent of the damage tended to increase with scale'.

Controversially, he concluded: 'In view of this agreement, it seems unlikely that there was a second effective hit on either dam.' Collins

SIGNIFICANT OUTCOMES

formalised his findings in a RRL report, 'Inspection of the Moehne and Eder Dams, September 1945', dated April 1946.

Repairs at the Sorpe were more superficial. Nevertheless they entailed lowering the water level and arrival, noted by the Dutch conscript Peter Theunissen, of 'twenty-four barrage balloons, torpedo nets and smoke dischargers'. One of the other dams on the Dambusters target list was the Ennepe. Flak guns, smoke canisters, balloons and an anti-torpedo net were installed there. Directly in front of the dam wall was a tree-covered spit of land. Again, as at the Moehne, the trees were cut down and flak guns, now with a clear field of fire, positioned there. Writing to Wallis in 1945, Cochrane suggested that Operation Chastise had an unexpected effect, when 9 Squadron dropped 12,000lb Tallboy deep-penetration bombs on the Sorpe Dam on 15 October 1944. 'It now appears that our first method of attack did not provide the cratering required, whereas the second attack would have succeeded if they had not lowered the water level.'

A further legacy of the raid caused consternation both sides of the North Sea. When Pruess circulated his report in September 1943, he noted: 'The nature of the bombs has been already established from an aircraft which crashed on the lower Rhine on its way in': Barlow's missing Lancaster. Wallis revealed, 'I knew that they had every detail of the bomb since MI5 quoted figures to me received from Germany immediately after the raid and asked if they did refer to this special store, but I had always imagined that in this case the particulars were obtained from the Zuider Zee specimen [Rice's Upkeep]'.

Nine days after the breaches occurred, 26 May, German Naval Headquarters in Berlin signalled subordinate commands: 'In a successful attack on dams the British used 4-ton mine-bombs with 2.6 tons of explosive, hydrostatic and time fuses, dropped in low-level flight. Effective even at a considerable distance (400 metres) from the object'. 'Locks, moles, etc ... especially U-boat bases were therefore at risk' and defensive measures were to be put in place forthwith. Separately, the Luftwaffe was required to ensure protection of 'the most important dams in Upper Italy ... against air attack'.

By the beginning of July, full details of Upkeep, its operation and installation in the aircraft, together with extensive, accurate drawings (although the belt from Upkeep to the small motor was horizontal), were available in a document entitled *Britische Rotations-Wasserbombe 3900kg*. A preliminary, illustrated summary had been in circulation since ten days after the operation. Because 'Mark XIV 1729' appeared on one of

THE DAMBUSTERS: 'WAS THE RAID WORTHWHILE?'

the hydrostatic pistols and existence of the Mark XIV depth charge was known, the Germans concluded that Upkeep was a revolving depth charge. This was more accurate than the British contemporary use of 'mine' or popular conception of a 'bouncing bomb'. Specialist examiners worked out that there were three hydrostatic pistols (each with '1820g Tetryl') and another (1,255g Tetryl) as a back-up if the other three failed to function. The latter they thought would activate 15–30 secs after release, so that the aircraft was not threatened by its detonation.

The analysis concluded that the weapon had been 'dropped from a low-flying aircraft in advance of the target and set to explode at a predetermined depth', but did not appreciate that it had ricocheted across the water. It was cylindrical, 1,270mm in diameter and 1,530mm long with a charge of 2,600kg. Although Field-Marshal Erhard Milch, the Reich's Air Inspector General, allegedly believed it was forward spun, the report held that Upkeep had been back-spun to give the unusually-laden machine stability before its release. Fortunately for the allies, cautious scientists insisted on thorough testing of the findings, which frustrated German development of a similar weapon.

Even more detailed knowledge, not only of the weapon but of the method of delivery, identity, training and Scampton location of the named responsible unit (617 Squadron), was revealed in a report drawn up for the Reich Minister of Aviation and C-in-C of the Luftwaffe on 19 June. The Germans believed that the pilot was responsible for 'height and direction', the flight engineer 'throttle and airspeed', the wireless operator 'supervising the motor which rotated the bomb and ensuring the correct rpm' and the bomb aimer 'the accurate release of the weapon'. They did not appear to know the navigator's role or details of the Aldis lamp arrangement and concluded that 'the hydraulic motor must be started 5–6 minutes before reaching the target' to acquire either 380rpm or 400–500rpm. The attacking speed had been 260mph (420kph)and height of release 60ft (18.25m).

A sketch of the plywood, triangular sight including measurements was referred to and its relation to the width of the towers at the Moehne (given here as 620ft – 'about 195m'). Release of the weapon seemingly occurred at 900ft (about 275m) from the dam wall. The report confirmed that specially-modified Lancasters had been used. It made clear, also, that the nature of pre-operational exercises and that dropping of cement-filled ('Zementbombe') practice weapons had occurred. Preparations ('Vorbereitungen') were believed to have taken about one year.

Without appreciating the full extent of their knowledge, realisation that the Germans not only had discovered the secrets of Upkeep, but were

SIGNIFICANT OUTCOMES

developing the long-range, heavy load capacity Heinkel He-177 which might carry a German version of it against British dams, brought a flurry of anxious activity. Vulnerability of water supplies to sabotage or attack by parachutists had, shortly after war began, led to large reservoirs and dams being protected by a combination of police, Home Guard and, in some cases, regular troops.

After the Dams' Raid, even before news that the enemy had recovered an Upkeep intact seeped through, allocation of more elaborate arrangements was set in motion. On 27 May, Captain H.H. Balfour, Under Secretary of State for Air, alerted the Secretary of State, Sir Archibald Sinclair, to a complaint made by the MP for Edinburgh North, Alexander Erskine-Hill. During the week end after Operation Chastise, he had discovered that 'several vital dams' were vulnerable to air attack. Loch Ericht, a crucial source of supply for the Scottish Power Co., he found guarded by four policemen. Destruction of Laggan Dam, he maintained, would put British Aluminium 'out of operation'. The authority responsible for the Caban Coch Reservoir near Rhyader in Wales, whose disused off-shoot the Nant-y-Gro Dam had featured heavily in Wallis's experimental work, independently expressed its concern that this dam might become a target.

The Ministry of Home Security had already registered alarm on 24 May. Two days later, the Anti-Aircraft Sub-Committee of the Chiefs of Staff Committee discussed the defence of eleven major dams, including the Howden and Derwent used during pre-operational training for the raid, the Laggan and Caban Loch, as well as the Queen Mary, near Brooklands, over which the embryo Upkeep had been spun in December 1942. On 3 June, Dr T.R. Merton chaired an *ad hoc* committee of the Ministry of Home Security, attended by Lord Cherwell. The minutes noted: 'It is known that the enemy already have some information about "Upkeep". Although it is not improbable that all the projectiles reaching Germany exploded, yet it must be assumed that the enemy has pieced together much of the story by examining the Lancasters that were lost.'

Much the same scope of defences placed around German dams and reservoirs was contemplated: mines attached to light cables strung across the water, barrage balloons, sloping, horizontal and vertical barriers in advance of a dam wall, searchlights, smoke canisters and anti-aircraft guns. Three days afterwards, the Director of Flying Operations (DF Ops) at the Air Ministry concluded that Loch Ericht, highlighted by Erskine-Hill, needed no enhanced defence as its natural position rendered it safe from aerial attack. The very next day, in his report on Operation Chastise,

THE DAMBUSTERS: 'WAS THE RAID WORTHWHILE?'

Air Vice-Marshal Cochrane pointed out that searchlights at the German dams could have frustrated the attacking aircraft. On 10 June, DB Ops reported that the Admiralty, again like the Germans, favoured placing minefields 300–400 yards from vulnerable dams and revealed that twelve (not eleven) locations were now on the priority list. These included 'five Sheffield lakes', which together would be allocated twenty four 40mm anti-aircraft guns and forty-two searchlights.

Merton's committee met again on 23 June noting that it was preparing an inter-departmental report for the Anti-Aircraft Sub-Committee on the assumption that some form of aerial attack could be expected 'within three months' of Chastise. It observed that 'immediate protection' had been given to 'important targets', but that 'permanent counter measures' were absolutely necessary. 'Dazzle and smoke' had now overtaken minefields and barriers as the preferred method of defence. On 1 July, an Admiralty proposal for floating masts to support cables was rejected in favour of a heavy cable with secondary wires and attached explosive devices slung between two towers on the banks of a reservoir. The Derwent Valley Waterworks, in particular, supported this arrangement. Notwithstanding this proposal, 5,000 men and women of 57 Anti-Aircraft Brigade were deployed to cover the Howden, Derwent and other Sheffield reservoirs, together with anti-aircraft guns and searchlights. The associated smoke screen system, 'with 30,000 generation points built right up in the hills' would allegedly obscure the valleys in five minutes. A special 'dams breached' siren was installed, in case of enemy success, linked to a designated evacuation programme.

Behind the moves to protect British dams lurked not only fear that the Germans would exploit knowledge of Upkeep, but that they did indeed have the means to deliver such a weapon. On 25 June, Wallis received details of the He-177 and a warning of concern that the Dornier Do-217 bomber could be modified. Hence, he began to examine the proposed methods of defence. On 9 July, he forwarded his conclusions to Sydney Barratt, who had been involved in the development stages of Upkeep, at the Ministry of Aircraft Production. Wallis queried the worth of the pylon-wire or boom systems as they would be easily detected by reconnaissance aircraft. 'The only effective form of defence is powerful dazzle with or without the addition of smoke ... Permanent dazzle lights in concrete emplacements with bullet-proof glass screens would be quite feasible, practically indestructible and brought into action at a moment's notice'; a 'dazzle and daze' option. He suggested that the effectiveness of searchlights be tested 'on a site such as the Staines [Queen Mary] reservoir or elsewhere', a proposal not apparently pursued.

SIGNIFICANT OUTCOMES

In February 1944, the concept of defensive barriers was again raised, leading Wallis to point out that this system had been rejected the previous year on the grounds that it could be destroyed by a mine thereby leaving clear access to the target dam.

In the event, no German threat did materialise. The He-177, dismissed by Field-Marshal Milch as a 'dead racehorse', never became fully operational and the Do-217 was not modified to carry such a heavy load. Experiments based on evolution of an Upkeep-style weapon, involving a different principle of ricochet, were pursued but ultimately failed in November 1944. Nevertheless, in the months after Chastise the vulnerability of British dams seemed real and the defensive measures put in place fully justified. Operation Chastise, in this respect, had prompted both the UK as well as Germany to take similar, defensive precautions.

There were wider diplomatic consequences, as well. Not only was the outcome of Operation Chastise welcomed in the USA, British Commonwealth and the occupied countries of Europe, but also in the USSR. On 30 March, Churchill had informed Stalin that, in order to support the allied advances in North Africa and to prepare for the invasion of Sicily as a preliminary to an assault on the Italian mainland, Arctic convoys would be temporarily suspended. The naval escorts were required in the Mediterranean. He assured the Soviet leader that, as compensation, the bombing of Germany would be escalated. It seemed to work. Early in May, the press published the text of a communication from Stalin to Winston Churchill: 'Every blow delivered by your Air Force to the vital German centres evokes a most lively echo in the hearts of many millions throughout the length and breadth of our country'. In the wake of the Dambusters Raid, the Soviet leader sent special appreciation, which was soon followed by a more tangible request.

British military representatives in Moscow signalled that Soviet naval authorities were seeking full details. 'They are showing great interest in this operation and are possibly contemplating something similar.' Unenthusiastically, the First Sea Lord, Admiral of the Fleet Sir Dudley Pound, feared 'possible grave danger to security', but Air Marshal Sir Douglas Evill, Vice Chief of Air Staff, acknowledged that 'the Germans know a good deal already' and pointed out that Upkeep was not Highball, as yet unused. On 7 June, in principle, the Chiefs of Staff agreed to respond positively to the request, a decision formalised on 11 August. No. 30 Mission in Moscow was advised: 'You should make the greatest possible capital out of our handing over this important and highly secret information.' In doing so, the Air Ministry was aware that for some time the Soviets had been seeking advice 'on air matters', Anglo-Soviet relations would benefit and, not least, the prestige of the RAF be enhanced.

In the short-term, more targets for Upkeep were actively sought. On 30 May, Air Vice-Marshal Saundby discussed breaching the bank of a long-standing target, the Dortmund-Ems canal. An Air Staff appreciation shortly afterwards identified three stretches suitable for attack and added a fourth priority target, the Rothensee Ship Lift. This apparatus enabled vessels to reach Berlin via the Elbe River from the Mittelland Canal without 'an enormous diversion'. All these targets required dropping Upkeep on land, where forward spin would be preferable. So, on 2 June, Flight Lieutenant D.J. Shannon flew Gibson's Chastise Lancaster (ED 932/G) to Farnborough for RAE staff to modify the spinning mechanism. Two days later, watched by Wallis and RAF staff officers, he dropped Upkeep spinning at 500rpm from 100ft at 230mph on the Ashley Walk Bombing Range near Fordingbridge in the New Forest. Shannon recalled that, 'it hopped in front of me like a bloody great kangaroo', its initial bounce 30–40ft and range achieved in excess of 1,000 yards. Inevitably, after release the aircraft travelling faster passed over it and was 'peppered' with stones. Similar trials were carried out on 9 June and 'Mr Wallis expressed himself entirely satisfied at these tests'.

The previous day, 8 June, Air Vice-Marshal N.H. Bottomley, Assistant Chief of the Air Staff (Ops), chaired an Air Ministry meeting attended by Ministry of Aircraft Production and Bomber Command representatives as well as Wallis to discuss target options. This was followed, on 1 July, by another under Air Commodore Bufton, which widened the scope with Italian targets now under consideration. Hence, on 6 July, Wallis submitted to Bufton a detailed appreciation of the Janisokoski Power Plant, recommending that an attack be 'directed at the central line of the Power Station ... the vulnerable width is well within the degree of line accuracy attained in the practice attacks at Reculver and probably in the actual attacks on the Moehne and Eder dams'.

Pilot Officer G. Rice, who had lost his Upkeep on 16 May off the island of Vlieland, found himself involved in more forward-spinning trials at the Aeroplane and Armament Experimental Establishment, Boscombe Down. Nothing came of the target plans nor the modified method of delivering Upkeep, even though Wallis revived the Italian project with Bufton early in 1944. He contended that failure to attack any of the '100 Italian dams ... threw away an early chance of victory ... If only Bert Harris had been a bit more flexible'. He regretted that Upkeep performed only 'one wonderful feat'.

SIGNIFICANT OUTCOMES

Chastise did have a more successful spin off. On the morning after the raid, Cochrane assured Wallis that Harris was now prepared to consider the idea of a 'big bomb'. Wallis graphically recalled another approach. 'Sir Wilfrid Freeman, the Chief Executive of the Ministry of Aircraft Production, asked me if I remembered my mad idea of a 10-ton bomb ... I said "Yes, indeed, Sir Wilfrid, I do". "Well", he said, "how soon can you let me have one?" I said ... "five months if I have all the labour available in Sheffield"'.

The meeting on 8 June, chaired by Bottomley, therefore discussed 'the deep penetration bomb producing a camouflet effect'. This would lead in the first place to a scaled-down 12,000lb version of the 10-ton bomb (codenamed Tallboy) and, ultimately, Grand Slam (22,400lbs). Tallboy was first used against the Saumur railway tunnel two days after D-Day in June 1944 to prevent enemy reinforcements reaching the battlefront, then against V-weapon sites including that of the V-3 long range cannon. It was used to sink the battleship *Tirpitz* and attack the Sorpe Dam. Grand Slam was dropped on the Bielefeld railway viaduct in the closing stage of the war as part of the thrust to dislocate industrial traffic within Germany. Cochrane and Wallis, not unreasonably, believed that these successes were a major contribution to Allied victory and without the achievements of Operation Chastise would not have been possible.

As Wallis wrote: 'It [Chastise] tended to establish in the minds of the C-in-Cs such as Sir Arthur Harris and the CE [Chief Executive of the MAP] Sir Wilfrid Freeman an impression of the rightness of the lines on which I argued my "Notes on means of attacking"'. In a post-war description of his work at this time, he added a colourful anecdote. Freeman had phoned Sir Charles Craven to tell him that Wallis had been given 'unlimited priority' to proceed with development of 'the 10-ton bomb'. 'When I visited his [Craven's] office an hour later I was greeted by a shout of, "what the hell do you want the use of twenty thousand men in Sheffield for?" Wallis added: 'We set to work, working 70, 80 and even 90 hours a week.'

For many years after the war, one specific aspect of the operation irked Wallis. In 1963, he wrote: 'I am, for scientific reasons, very anxious to get some reliable confirmation that only one bomb was responsible for the destruction of the Moehne Dam.' He related the gist of a conversation that he had with the proprietor of the adjacent Seehof Hotel, when visiting the area in April 1945. 'As far as I could make out from his voluble German, the first four bombs either did not reach or passed over the dam, and it was the last one which actually brought about the breach.' He added that 'the hotel proprietor described one bomb as running to the side of the lake [Martin's]'.

THE DAMBUSTERS: 'WAS THE RAID WORTHWHILE?'

Wallis knew that the author, David Irving, had interviewed a 'German attendant who was in the drainage tunnel running along the base of the dam at the time the attack was made. He escaped from this subterranean tunnel owing to the fact that the breach did not go down sufficiently deep to cut it, and he was able to escape.' The attendant claimed that, although 'in the drainage tunnel during the whole of the attack, he heard only one explosion'. This, Wallis felt, supported the contention that the first Upkeep to hit the dam destroyed it.

As a postscript, he admitted to being 'highly amused' to find that a contemporary article in the German publication *Die Welt* had ascribed the design of the bomb, which had breached the Moehne and Eder dams, to 'Professor Jeff'. 'It suddenly struck me that in his book *Enemy Coast Ahead* ... Guy Gibson states that he is only allowed to refer to the persons concerned in this raid as "Mutt" and "Jeff" [characters in a series of animated films]. Now "Mutt" is, of course, the late "Mutt" Summers the test pilot and "Jeff" is myself ... to whom he [the author of the article] had given the honorary rank of "Professor"'. At the time of writing, Wallis evidently did not know that Dr Pruess in his report of 30 September 1943, after describing the early attacks and that they had not damaged the structure of the wall, concluded that 'the last mine [Preuss's fourth] which exploded close to the centre of the wall was able to cause the breach without previous serious damage having been sustained by the wall as a whole'.

An unrelated, confusing issue directly connected with Operation Chastise post-war was highlighted by Pilot Officer C.L. Howard, Flight Sergeant Townsend's Australian navigator. Faced with conflicting evidence, he queried: 'Did we bomb the wrong dam?' The War Diary of the German Naval Staff (Operations Division) recorded that the Bever Dam had been attacked without effect and Pruess in his 1943 report wrote: 'At the same time as the Sorpe Dam attack, the Bever Dam was attacked. Only one mine was dropped and fell about 800 metres from the dam wall in the middle of the reservoir and did no damage.'

No known German source mentioned an attack on the Ennepe Dam that night. Subsequently, in reply to an enquiry, the *Wupperverband* authority responsible for the Bever, explained that the remains of the mine there were recovered short of the contemporary structure and close to the position of an old dam, rather like the Nant-y-Gro superseded by enlargement of the reservoir 1935–8. Cochrane's post-operation report was among several documents apparently to equate an attack on the Ennepe with a Schwelme Dam: 'his [Townsend's] target was at SCHWELME beyond the SORPE

SIGNIFICANT OUTCOMES

target'. The *Ennepe Wasserverband* later insisted that during the whole of the war only one bomb dropped in the vicinity of this dam; 350m short of the wall 'in the wood on the side of the dam' and not in the reservoir itself.

There was an eye witness to an attack on the Bever Dam in the early hours of 17 May 1943. Paul Keiser, a 19-year-old soldier on leave, was woken at around 03.00 hours at his home nearby by the sound of a low-flying aircraft. He hastily dressed and went outside to investigate. He recalled:

> The aircraft made several approaches always from an easterly direction towards the west. It turned away over the dam to begin its attack profile in the same direction no higher than 100 metres in bright moonlight [and] dropped its weapon. There was a big explosion and a great pillar of flame in a column of water. The aircraft then flew an identical pattern over the spot at which it dropped the weapon, lifted over the dam wall and flew off in a westerly direction.

This puts Kaiser's location east of the reservoir, which in reality ran north to south, with the dam at its southern end. The Ennepe Dam authority separately maintained that a German in that vicinity remembered an aircraft 'circling ... for almost ¾hr' at roughly 03.00 hours but heard no explosion, which chronologically would fit with Kaiser's memories.

These recollections seem to confirm Webb's memory of an aerial conflab and Townsend's of difficulty in finding the target. Moreover, Townsend was right to complain that illustrations used at briefing showed an island short of the dam wall, whereas there was actually a spit of land. That was only 300m from the face of the dam and its two towers, making the release of Upkeep at 450 yards from it in direct line highly improbable.

That AJ-O attacked the Bever Dam, not Ennepe Dam, has therefore to be considered. Webb recalled the navigator, Howard, spotting 'a manor house' to starboard of the attack line over the reservoir, but the *Ennepe-Wasserverband* was adamant that no such building existed at the Ennepe. The wireless operator, Flight Sergeant G.A. Chalmers, believed that the Lancaster attacked 'an earthen dam'. The Bever was of earth construction like the Sorpe; the Ennepe a concrete, gravity dam.

Five miles from the Ennepe adjacent to Hueckswagen on the Wupper river, the Bever was located in a similar, confined setting. In advance of the dam were three tree-covered spits of land. The final 1,200m to the target ran over the central one (336m) and a narrow gap between that to right (310m) and left (313m). Kaiser's evidence and Townsend's answer to the post-operational questionnaire suggest this line of attack. Townsend complained of 'running into moon in half-light reflected on mist and water', which was inconsistent with attacking at 355°M. At the Bever, the moon's azimuth was 242° and altitude 16°05. Moreover, a substantial building to starboard of an attacking run, roughly 750m from the reservoir in the area of Mickenhagen, might well have been 'Lance's manor house' recalled by Webb.

Being an earth dam, the Bever had no towers on it. However, roughly 500m apart at its extremities and immediately behind the crest were two identical storage buildings. The towers at the Ennepe were slimmer than at either the Moehne or Eder and at briefing crews would have been alerted to the difference. In the moonlight, the Bever structures could feasibly have been mistaken for them. If the bomb-aimer used the setting for the Ennepe towers, that would explain why Upkeep fell 800m from the dam wall. Writing to Wallis on 30 March 1943, the Admiralty scientist, Dr E.C. Bullard, had predicted that 'the waves from an explosion will, of course, spread in a circle till they meet the edge' of a lake. This would justify observations of the crew as well as the official conclusion 'ripple against the dam'.

Townsend reported three runs on the target and another after release of Upkeep. It seems likely that the aircraft had also circled before deciding this was its target, which would fit Keiser's account. The only firm contrary evidence is the assertion that the attack occurred on a bearing of 355°M, whereas analysis of information concerning the position of the moon, Townsend's report that AJ-O attacked running into it, examination of a map of the area and the location itself suggests rather an approach at about 210°M. This points to the Bever Dam.

Howard's astonishment and positive reaction to the bearing query and subsequent detailed examination of the surviving evidence indicate that he had no inkling of a target issue. Townsend's dismay at the inaccuracy of the briefing map supports the view that the crew of AJ-O believed that the information that they had been given was not wholly accurate. In retrospect, Webb seemed justified in complaining that the planners had not paid enough attention to the Ennepe, Lister, and Diemel dams. He recalled, too, that no photos of the Ennepe had been used at briefing, only in his opinion inadequate maps and diagrams. The location of the Ennepe and Bever dams were both at the extremity of a narrow reservoir set in tree-covered hills. Use of 'Schwelm' or 'Schwelme' dam in post-operational summaries and in Bomber Command ORB does perhaps imply that bombing of the Bever, instead of Ennepe, was recognised but obscured. Schwelm was a town

SIGNIFICANT OUTCOMES

approximately 6 miles north-west of the Ennepe and 10 miles north-north-west of the Bever.

Emphatically, no criticism should be levelled at the crew of AJ-O for the evident sequence of events which has unfolded. Despite, as its front gunner pointed out, having been provided with limited visual details and hampered by mist-covered valleys in the vicinity, it made determined and prolonged efforts to locate its target; confirmed by different German witnesses. As a result, Townsend found his lone Lancaster perilously still over hostile territory as dawn approached.

Indirectly, AJ-O's experience underscored the highly unusual navigational issues faced by all Operation Chastise crews carrying out this unique, low-level raid deep inside enemy territory at night.

Chapter 14

Missing Aircraft

Air Vice-Marshal Cochrane's report, dated 7 June 1943, shows how the sparse information available then led to misleading conclusions about the fate of some of the missing aircraft. AJ-B (Astell) was 'thought' to have been brought down by light flak 8 miles north-west of Dorsten at 00.15 hours. AJ-E (Barlow) or AJ-K (Byers) had 'possibly' been the victim of light flak, while flying at 300ft off the island of Texel at 22.57 hours. AJ-S (Burpee) was 'thought to have exploded' in mid-air in the Tilburg area at 01.53 hours.

Another aircraft had come down near Hamm at 02.35 hours. The defences of the railway centre were so extensive that it might have turned '2½ mins too early' short of Ahlen on the last leg to the Moehne. This could, though, have been a First or Second Wave aircraft returning from the Moehne, west of the designated course. Illustrating the complete fog of misunderstanding about this incident, alternatively Cochrane suggested that, having attacked the Sorpe, the Lancaster could have been making straight for Ahlen and 'cut the corner at Target X'. Either AJ-K or AJ-E was 'thought' to have attacked the Sorpe, and the crash could have involved one of those; that not lost off Texel.

What actually happened to seven of the missing aircraft, Hopgood's loss having been witnessed and recorded accurately by other crews at the Moehne Dam, became clearer as evidence from Germany and The Netherlands emerged post-war.

The identity of the aircraft seen by Pilot Officer G. Rice's crew to crash at 22.57 hours on 16 May off the Frisian Islands was confirmed as the Lancaster of Pilot Officer V.W. Byers (AJ-K, ED 934/G). The body of the rear gunner, Flight Sergeant J. McDowell, 'was found floating in the Waddenzee (Vliestroom near buoy no. 2) on 22 June 1943 between Harlingen and the isle of Terschelling'. Caution about locating the precise position of the aircraft's loss was advised by a later assessment: 'The period between the crash of the aircraft and the finding of the body is so long, over a month, that it is quite impossible to give any indication of the position of the crash. The effect of the wind on the upper layers of the sea is very great and not always in the same direction as the wind.' One Dutch summary recorded: 'During the night of 16/17 May 1943, Lancaster ED 934 K (for Kathy) was shot down by flak when it was flying on a level of 450 feet over the heavy [sic] defended isle of Texel instead of the isle of Vlieland, and crashed into the Waddenzee', the stretch of water south of the Frisians and east of the Ijsselmeer. Post-war the Dutch Ministry of Defence officer, Colonel A.P. de Jong, quoted another document, whose author also evidently had access to RAF records: 'Lancaster ED 934 'K' shot down in the Waddenzee, a few miles east of Texel Island. Made landfall at coast of Dutch Frisian Isles too far south. Flew over heavily-defended island of Texel instead of planned Vlieland. German heavy naval flak batteries opened fire and could not miss the aircraft. Batteries at Texel were 1 and 3/Mar Art 201 (1st and 3rd Battery of Naval Artillery Battalion 201) and 3/808 (3rd Battery of Naval Artillery Bat. 808)'.

De Jong added that the crash position was 'some 18 miles west of Harlingen' and that MacDowell's body had been 'buried at Harlingen Cemetery afterwards'. Writing in 1980, he added, 'the remaining six crew members are still listed as "missing at sea". In the months following the crash, several unidentifiable remains were found and buried as "unknown airmen". Identification Impossible'. The German flak units 1 and 3/Marine Artillery 201 and 3/808 stationed on Texel, noted by de Jong, were officially credited with destroying the machine, which had undoubtedly crashed into the Waddenzee at 22.57 hours west of Harlingen; independent confirmation of AJ-H's contemporary observation. 5 Group had suggested the aircraft might have flown too high 'to get a coastal pinpoint' having crossed Texel west of the briefed route either because it was 'south of the track from base or had altered course too soon from position 53 20- 04 54'; indisputably, though, the first loss of the night.

Lancaster AJ-E (ED 927/G), piloted by Flight Lieutenant R.N.G. Barlow, was heading for the Sorpe Dam in the Second Wave too. Slightly confusing evidence of its demise would emerge. The aircraft unquestionably crashed 5km east-north-east of Rees near Haldern at 23.50 hours, suggesting that it was fatally damaged either short of the Rees turning point or was slightly off-track on the way from Rees to Duelmen. The British thought it had been 'shot down', but a German report, based on eye witness accounts claimed that it hit high-tension wires running roughly north west/south-east parallel to a railway line and that no flak was in that area. Another enemy report held that, after striking the wires, the pilot tried to make a forced landing, but the Lancaster exploded on impact and killed the entire crew. In order, the three reports possibly describe the actual sequence of events: hit by flak, struck high tension wires and attempted landing.

For the British, there was an unfortunate postscript. One eye witness recalled that the aircraft 'hit the top of a 100,000 volt electricity pylon and crashed into a field', adding that a large object detached to roll 50m away. Upkeep failed to detonate, presumably because the self-destructive mechanism had been damaged either by flak or when the Lancaster struck the pylon, as it seems to have been released before contact with the ground. The local community believed it to be an extra fuel tank and the mayor of Haldern had his photo taken beside what he thought would be an addition to local fuel supplies. After removal to a secure location by Bomb Disposal Squad I/VI from Duesseldorf, its true nature, as confirmed in Pruess's report, became apparent and full details of Wallis's weapon were rapidly worked out by German scientists.

Apart from Hopgood, three First Wave aircraft failed to return, the first being Flight Lieutenant W. Astell's Lancaster AJ-B (ED 864/G). There is no doubt that it crashed close to the village of Marbeck, 30 miles east of Rees on the revised inward route to Duelmen at 00.15 hours. The bodies of the crew were subsequently buried in the cemetery at Borken, north of Marbeck, and reinterred post-war in the Reichswald War Cemetery. To the south of Marbeck, the Raesfeld village museum would mount a photographic display of the crash site highlighting images taken on 17 May.

Air Vice-Marshal Cochrane's summary of the operation quoted information from Knight's crew. 'AJ-N at 100ft 8 miles NW Dorsten saw an aircraft dead astern shot at from the ground and returning fire – followed by an explosion on the ground'; 'probably' B/617.

Years later, Flight Sergeant R.T.G Kellow, Knight's wireless operator, recalled more fully what he had observed looking back from the astrodome: 'I saw Astell go down. As No 7 and No 9 (us) crossed the centre of the drome, we were fired at by gunners on either side of the drome and two trails of tracer bullets crossed behind us. However, Astell was now late following a few minutes behind us and was caught in this cross fire, hit and crashed.' In a further conversation, he added that he had seen the Lancaster burst into flames and explode on the ground. Cochrane estimated that the aircraft was two miles behind AJ-N when fired on. Kellow's recollections married to the contemporary reports seem conclusive, especially when linked to Gibson's words in *Enemy Coast Ahead* concerning the inward flight. 'Once we went over a brand-new aerodrome which was very heavily defended and which had not been marked on our combat charts'.

Referring to available German records post-war, the RAF Air Historical Branch found no enemy airfield, temporary or permanent, in that area. Moreover, Gibson appears to associate the airfield with the flak concentration, which he identified, close to Duelmen, beyond Marbeck. In the same passage, Gibson erroneously and colourfully described the fate of Astell (whom he named); '... out to the left. He got blinded in the searchlights and, for a second, lost control. His aircraft reared up like a stricken horse, plunged onto the deck and burst into flames.' AJ-G had broadcast a warning of the flak concentration near to Duelmen at 00.11 hours, four minutes before AJ-B was lost roughly 25km (12 miles) west of that spot. In correspondence after the raid with Astell's family, Gibson explained that he had not seen the aircraft after take-off and, by implication, was therefore relying on the information from others; in effect, Knight's crew.

It is just possible that Gibson conflated two incidents and that he had encountered the airfield mentioned by Kellow, but no other aircrew flying that night at the time or later referred to such a hostile position and it was not mentioned by Cochrane. The comment that Astell was 'out to the left' and Cochrane's that AJ-B was 'dead astern' are self-evidently contradictory. Local school teacher, Martin Drescher, recorded that an aircraft flew low over houses close to Reasfeld, 6km south of the crash site. Anni Reining, the maid in a farmhouse adjacent to the crash site, recalled that the second aircraft came from the same westerly direction 'but nearer to us'. A schoolboy, B.J. Sieling, immediately west of where Astell crashed, could not 'be certain whether one or more planes were overhead'. Collectively, this suggests that although in sequence, the three aircraft were not together; and 'dead astern', therefore, puzzling. Quite possibly, the aircraft close to Raesfeld was Maudslay, the second nearer to Marbeck Knight and Astell's was to its left (as Gibson claimed) on a track due east of Westerborken. This would be consistent with the vic-3 having become dispersed and is not inconsistent with Sutherland's claim that contact had been lost with Maudslay.

There are further complicating factors, though. AJ-N's rear gunner, O'Brien, wrote and when questioned again confirmed that, 'I would not say we saw Bill Astell's aircraft'. The navigator, Hobday, was more expressive: 'Astell's unfortunate fate was very quick. As for crossing the "airfield" firing at gun positions – a lot of hooey'. Interestingly, four minutes after leaving Rees to fly eastwards towards Duelmen, Sergeant V. Nicholson

THE DAMBUSTERS: 'WAS THE RAID WORTHWHILE?'

(Maltby's navigator) in the second section of the First Wave ahead of Knight, recorded taking evasive action due to flak in the Dingden area. Hobday did not record a similar diversion, yet there is a three minute time lag between his projected and actual arrival time at the Duelmen lakes. At 00.09 hours (5 mins after leaving Rees) Hobday noted a Gee fix, which put AJ-N north of the briefed track with the entry 'A/C Pos C ', which implied changing course towards Duelmen, reached at 00.19 hours. Perhaps Knight, like Maltby, avoided the flak at Dingden.

Speculation, based on the conflicting accounts from other crew members, does not explain Kellow's graphic portrayal of AJ-N, AJ-Z and AJ-B encountering flak short of the site where Astell crashed. So, on this evidence, the precise circumstances leading immediately to Astell's loss remain doubtful.

Details of the crash itself are much clearer. After the war, several people in the area recorded their memories of that night, particularly two close eye witnesses; farmer Tueckling and Anni Reining, the maid of a neighbour on whose land AJ-B crashed. Following an air-raid warning, Anni and 'old Herr Thesing' stood outside their farmhouse looking southwards towards the Ruhr in anticipation of another aerial attack on that industrial complex. They and Tueckling were therefore surprised by three aircraft in succession approaching from the west at an unusually low altitude, initially believing them friendly. All agreed that there was no sign of fire as the third clipped the top of trees before striking a 'high tension cable pylon', taking the 'top off'. It then burst into flames either immediately or, more likely, shortly after hitting the ground, when ammunition began exploding. According to Tueckling, 'a fiery red kind of ball rolling away from the front of the aircraft' travelled 'for about 80 metres', followed by 'a very loud bang and the whole area was lit up'. Seemingly, as with Barlow, Upkeep had been deliberately released before an attempted landing or been torn free by impact with the pylon. Tueckling's main concern was that the commotion 'caused our horse and foal to bolt and they both disappeared through a gap in the fence'.

In daylight, he discovered a 12m wide crater where the bomb had detonated and that over about 3km 'roofs were covered in earth and most windows and doors were blown in'. Another witness in a village almost 4km west of the crash site and a fourth in Raesfeld 6km south recalled houses being shaken both by the low-flying aircraft, 'the noise certainly was deafening', and after Upkeep's explosion, 'vibrations shook the house and I felt the shock waves in the air'. Both Tueckling and Thesing's

MISSING AIRCRAFT

maid separately recorded a peculiar survival. Close to the crater stood a statue of Joseph with the baby Jesus in his arms. 'This wasn't touched at all. It didn't even lose a finger'. Anni Reining claimed that, although a searchlight in Marbeck vainly attempted to locate the low-flying aircraft, no flak responded in the immediate locality. Interestingly, the civil engineer, Dr Ing H.W. Koenig, responsible for repairing the Moehne Dam, reflected that two of the attacking aircraft hit 'high tension cables' before crashing, presumably relying on reports about Barlow and Astell.

The Lancaster of Squadron Leader H.E. Maudslay (AJ-Z, ED 937/G) was the second uncertain loss from Gibson's First Wave. An immediate 5 Group post-operational report concluded: 'Missing believed damaged by own store, which had hit parapet and detonated instantaneously. Spoken to by R/T afterwards and heard once when he sounded very weak. Not heard after that.' Speculation that the aircraft crashed at the Eder Dam, blown up by its own Upkeep, proved false, even though the commercial film depicted it. Writing to Dr Collins, the RRL scientist in 1972, Wallis still believed: 'One of the two lost on the dams was destroyed by his own bomb, which owing to being dropped too late, struck the dam immediately below the aircraft and exploded on impact, thus eliminating the delay provided by the time to sink to the depth required to fire the hydrostatic pistols.'

Flak records would reveal that the aircraft survived another three-quarters of an hour to crash 2km inside the German/Dutch border at Klein Netterden, 3.5km east of the defended, industrial port of Emmerich on the Rhine at 02.36 hours on 17 May, a gunner being decorated for shooting it down. The whole crew was killed, their bodies being initially buried in the military section of Duesseldorf North Cemetery and post-war reinterred in the Reichswald Forest War Cemetery. Reports of a weak R/T transmission after the detonation of Upkeep, noted by crew members in other Lancasters, already suggested survival. After Wallis's weapon had been dropped, it would have slowed over the water as Maudslay's machine lifted sharply. The faint nature of the response to Gibson's enquiry about the aircraft's state would be explained by damage, though not fatal, from the aerial blast. There was, too, the W/T message to Grantham at 01.57 hours, seven minutes after the attack on the Eder was officially recorded. That no further contact via R/T was made may be explained by Maudslay flying low beyond the surrounding hills as, in strict accordance with pre-operational orders, he made his way back to England after completing his attack.

Post-war, Knight's bomb aimer, accepting that AJ-Z had survived there, undertook further research on events at the Eder, particularly 'the

THE DAMBUSTERS: 'WAS THE RAID WORTHWHILE?'

mysterious flash-explosion which at the time we thought was Maudslay crashing into the high ground facing the dam ... The bomb definitely landed on the top of the dam causing extensive damage to the parapet walls and upper structure ... There were immediately on the land side of the dam an electricity generating station and, more importantly, some very high pylons carrying high voltage current. These could conceivably have been damaged or cables brought down by large pieces of masonry dislodged by the premature explosion'; a reasonable conclusion.

Maudslay seems to have been following Exit Route 1 via Rees, where a starboard adjustment towards Doesburg was needed. Either the aircraft was to port of this north-north-east track or, with AJ-Z badly damaged, the pilot had decided to make directly for the coast and unfortunately ran into the fatal flak near Emmerich.

Gibson tried in vain to contact Squadron Leader H.M. Young (AJ-A, ED 877/G) on the way home, and this aircraft, too, was lost without trace until details of its end emerged post-war. Young had probably followed orders in flying to the Moehne from the Eder and then along exit route 3 via Rees, Doesburg and Harderwijk aiming to cross the tip of the Helder peninsula approximately 20 miles north of the port of Ijmuiden. At 02.58 hours, gunners stationed near Castricum-aan-Zee, above Ijmuiden on the coast, reported shooting down a Halifax over the North Sea after it crossed the peninsula. The tail configuration of the Lancaster and Halifax ('Lancaster low, Halifax high') were similar and could be confused even by experienced gunners from behind. The whole area was heavily defended as Ijmuiden contained U-boat pens, ironworks and a valuable harbour; 3 and 4/ Marine Flak 246, 2, 4 and 6/Marine Artillery 808 and 8/Flak Abteilung 45 claimed to have fired on the aircraft which crashed into the sea near Castricum. Officially, it was 'shot down off the Dutch North Sea coast north of Ijmuiden' and its destruction credited to 'the flak batteries of Ijmuiden' by the German High Command. Bodies were washed up between 27 and 30 May along a 15 mile stretch of the shore from Wijk-aan-Zee to Bergen-aan-Zee, north of Ijmuiden.

The circumstances in which two Third Wave aircraft were lost also became clearer post-war, in the case of one incontrovertibly through a survivor. The Operation Order had specifically warned crews to avoid German-occupied airfields at Eindhoven and Gilze-Rijen in The Netherlands and Lancaster AJ-S (ED 865/G), piloted by Pilot Officer L.J. Burpee strayed off track fatally there. Colonel A.P. de Jong, the Dutch Ministry of Defence officer, summarised official records:

MISSING AIRCRAFT

This Lancaster apparently flew a few miles too far north to be able to avoid the heavily defended area of the important Luftwaffe base Gilze Rijen. This airbase was housing major units of KG2 (Do-217 bombers, Bf-110 night fighters and Bf-109 day fighters). Close to 02.00hrs the aircraft approached the dense defences of the airbase and could not possibly get through undamaged. The first impression of the loaded Lancaster, crashing on important key facilities of the base were that the RAF had carried out one of the most successful pinpoint target attacks of WWII, destroying several ops buildings in the centre of the airbase quarters. Such was the violence of the explosion, that only three of the crew could be positively identified in the shattered remains of the aircraft.

More details were contained in the reports of Dutch eye witnesses. One saw the aircraft switch on its landing lights, a standard Luftwaffe practice, in an attempt to fool defenders into believing it to be friendly. In vain, as another Dutch observer recalled: 'An aircraft approaches from the West at very low altitude and tries to break through the light flak barrage between Molenschot and Gilze-Rijen. It seems to be caught by searchlights. Then a fierce spreading red light becomes visible: the aircraft is on fire and crashes at the airfield amongst the buildings and hangars. A most terrific explosion follows. The explosion continues to burn quite fiercely for a time, much ammunition explodes time after time and a smokepile climbs to 1,000 feet'.

After consideration, later he wrote: 'We fear [it] is an Avro Lancaster. According to reports from people of the air base it was a four-engine aircraft.' The closest account of Burpee's fate came from a Ju88 wireless operator in Staffel E/NJG2 stationed at Gilze Rijen and he strangely ascribed AJ-S's loss to a searchlight. Alerted by reports of enemy aircraft in the vicinity:

we had our ears cocked into the night and we heard a plane flying towards the airfield from the west. The flak batteries at the edge of the airfield didn't open fire. I saw a searchlight beam suddenly come on and catch a four-engine plane, which couldn't have been more than 20 metres up ... The searchlight was located between our command post and the hangar and the beam caught the bomber more or less horizontally ... [it] grazed across the top of some trees, tearing a great path through the woods before crashing into an empty, rectangular-shaped

MT garage ... another 100 metres [and] he would have literally rammed the searchlight tower. The plane caught fire and a few seconds later there was a deafening explosion. The blast was so strong that I and other aircrews standing about 700 to 800 metres away on the other side of the airfield were almost knocked over.

At dawn, it became clear that the aircraft was 'a total wreck. All that was left was the rear turret and tail unit and this was more or less intact. All the crew had been killed'. Herbert Scholl added: 'No one could find out why the airfield flak hadn't opened fire. It was certainly not every day a plane was brought down by a beam of light like that one at 2am on that morning'.

A third Dutch observer noted in his diary: 'During the night [16–17 May] the activities were like mustard with the coffee in the moonlight. During the whole night British fighter bombers ... were interfering with the air base defences. One of the low flying aircraft found its end there'. He recorded 'very strong' fire from light flak and machine-guns and from heavy batteries at Klein-Tilburg and Nerhoven, supported by searchlights, between 23.30 and 03.00 hours. At about 01.30 hours, shortly before Burpee's fatal error, another aircraft was fired on by light flak at Moleschot and Nerhoven. Presumably this was one of the intruders, which inadvertently fore-warned the defences before Burpee's approach.

Reports from the crew of AJ-F suggest that Burpee, aware that he was off track, had climbed to establish position. One German document specifically stated that at 02.00 hours, AJ-S crashed on the edge of Gilze-Rijen airfield, demolishing kitchens, offices, ablutions and a large number of other buildings. An estimated 1.5 million guilders-worth of damage was caused. A PRU photo taken in September 1943 would show a crater where the aircraft hit the ground and allow photographic interpreters to trace 'the track of AJ-S as it sliced through the trees to crash on the barracks'.

German records show that Pilot Officer W.H.T. Ottley's Lancaster AJ-C (ED 910/G) crashed at Boselagerschen Wald in Heesen on the northern outskirts of Hamm and south-west of Ahlen. It appears to have been roughly 1.5 miles south of the amended track to the Ahlen turning. More details of the loss emerged, when the only survivor, Sergeant F. Tees, returned from captivity in 1945. He was able to correct an error in 617 Squadron's Operations Record Book and the published Official History: 'To put some of the records straight, I was in the rear turret not as is seen in print the front'; which allowed him to survive.

MISSING AIRCRAFT

Over the North Sea, Tees and the navigator, Flying Officer J.K. Barrett, used flame floats to establish drift, and the flight was uneventful until the Scheldt estuary, though a few searchlights and desultory flak there 'hardly worried' the crew. Tees did recall 'firing away' at isolated searchlight and flak positions as the Lancaster flew deeper into enemy territory. He thought that the machine was about 15 mins short of the dam, when the wireless operator said, 'Moehne gone' and almost immediately over the intercom he heard 'we go to …', when there was 'a hell of a commotion'. AJ-C was bathed in searchlights, a barrage of flak struck the aircraft and Tees realised the port wing had been hit as he lost hydraulic power for his turret, while flames began to stream past him.

He distinctly recalled Ottley saying, 'sorry boys we've had it'. Like Burcher at the Moehne, Tees' parachute was inside the fuselage, but he had no means of getting at it. '… at nought feet on three engines and burning well, you don't have a chance to use parachutes, you go into the deck with what I believe to be one hell of a crash'. For him 'everything went blank'. Tees regained consciousness on the ground, badly burnt, to spend the rest of the war either in hospital or a prisoner-of-war camp. Later analyses suggest that there were two explosions: the petrol tanks in the air and Upkeep on striking the ground. It seems likely that Tees and his turret were blown from the aircraft after the second one. Dryly he reflected, 'other raids had been more fun'.

In captivity, he would spend several weeks in different hospitals before being sent to a 'Lithuanian border camp'. As Soviet troops advanced in 1944, the prisoners were handcuffed and 'put in the bowels of a ship by the propeller shaft', as the ship sailed westwards in the Baltic Sea 'dodging mines and Russian submarines'. Just after it docked, American bombers appeared and, when the raid finished, still handcuffed the prisoners were locked into cattle trucks at the railway station. Eventually, they reached Silesia, 'where we were doubled up a hill in great heat at bayonet point and left in a vorlager [wired camp] without water for ten hours'. Over that Christmas, in a permanent camp, suffering from meningitis, his life was saved by 'a dedicated British doctor'. Shortly after he recovered, between January and May 1945 the prisoners were marched backwards and forwards across Germany alternately avoiding the advancing Soviet and Allied armies. At first, Red Cross parcels sustained them, but they were soon reduced to foraging for food.

At one stage, Tees recalled being housed in a marquee in northern Germany. On 1 May, 'a jeep liberated us and I grabbed the nearest pistol determined to shoot one of the guards. But I could only find a dog, so

THE DAMBUSTERS: 'WAS THE RAID WORTHWHILE?'

I shot that'. Now free, the prisoners commandeered a German bus ('drive or hang') and made their way to an airfield at Celle, where 'we forced our way onto a Dakota, having convinced the crew, wrongly, that we'd all been deloused'. He eventually reached his home in Chichester, Sussex, to find that his mother had been killed, when the crew had baled out of a damaged aircraft, still with its bombs on board, which demolished the laundry where she worked. Tees discovered, too, during his captivity, he had been progressively promoted to Flight Sergeant and Warrant Officer.

The location of the burial sites of lost members of the crews from the missing aircraft are held by the Commonwealth War Graves Commission. The five from Flight Lieutenant J.V. Hopgood's Lancaster are interred at the Rheinberg War Cemetery in the Ruhr, 15 miles north of Krefeld and 8 miles south of Wesel. The entire crews of Squadron Leader H.E. Maudslay, Flight Lieutenant W. Astell, Flight Lieutenant R.N.G. Barlow and six of Pilot Officer W. Ottley are buried in the Reichswald Forest Cemetery, close to the German-Dutch border, 3 miles south-west of Cleves (Germany) and 6.25 miles from Gennep (The Netherlands). The crew of Squadron Leader H.M. Young are interred in Bergen General Cemetery in The Netherlands at Bergen-aan-Zee, 27 miles north-north-west of Amsterdam, close to Alkmaar, on the Helder peninsula. Post-war, the carillon of a rebuilt church in Bergen-aan-Zee would be inscribed with the names of AJ-A's crew and rung once a year, on Liberation Day. When members of 617 Squadron Aircrew Association visited Bergen in 1975, the carillon played 'God Save the Queen'. The body of Flight Sergeant J. McDowell, the only one recovered from Pilot Officer V.W. Byers's aircraft, is interred, as shown in Dutch reports, in Harlingen General Cemetery in Friesland on the shore of the Waddenzee, The Netherlands. The remaining six of the crew are commemorated on Runnymede Memorial in Englefield Green, near Egham, Surrey. Pilot Officer L.J. Burpee and his crew are in Bergen-op-Zoom War Cemetery, 23 miles north-north-west of Antwerp, close to the Scheldt estuary.

Thus, although, the crash sites of the lost aircraft have been confirmed through evidence, which has emerged post-war, the precise circumstances leading to some of the losses remain in doubt.

Conclusion

Some Answers

Air Vice-Marshal S.O. Bufton, successively Deputy Director of Bombing Operations and DB Ops at the Air Ministry during the build-up to Operation Chastise, emphasised that 'the Dams' attack fell within the remit of the Casablanca Directive of 21 January 1943, which established the aims of the Anglo-American Combined Bomber Offensive against Germany. This entailed 'the progressive destruction and dislocation of the German military, industrial and economic system, and the undermining of the morale of the German people to a point where their capacity for armed resistance is fatally weakened'.

Criticism levelled at the operation has asserted not only that it failed to achieve these objectives, but was badly planned and effectively pointless. In 1972, the British journalist, Bruce Page, penned an article, 'How the Dam Busters Courage was Wasted', exclaiming:

'The truth about the Dams Raid is that it was a conjuring trick, virtually devoid of military significance ... Wallis's "skipping bomb" was just a gimmick ... the story of the raid is one of sloppy planning, narrow-minded enthusiasm and misdirected courage.'

Six years afterwards, a Cambridge academic, Dr Ian Hutchings, wrote: 'The dams raid ... had scant effect on German war production and morale; the influence of the ricochet bomb on the imponderable sum of war was negligible'. Air Vice-Marshal Cochrane declared such allegations 'disgraceful'. Nevertheless, they and other even more fundamental censures do warrant scrutiny.

Undoubtedly, the physical damage caused by Operation Chastise failed to match extravagant portrayals of widespread, lasting destruction penned prior to the raid and in its euphoric aftermath. The rationale behind the decision to go ahead on 26 February 1943 was demonstrated by Air Chief Marshal Sir Charles Portal's contemporary reference to an appreciation, 'The Economic and Moral Effects of the Destruction of the Moehne Dam

THE DAMBUSTERS: 'WAS THE RAID WORTHWHILE?'

and the Added Effects which will result from the Destruction at the same time of the Sorpe and Eder dams', credited to the 'Office of Scientific Advisers to the War Cabinet'. It held of the Moehne, that the 'direct effect of escaping water ... [would be] great enough to cause a disaster of the first magnitude', severely affecting Industry, Transportation, Domestic Water Supplies and Morale. Destruction of the Sorpe, in addition to the Moehne, would 'produce a paralysing effect upon the industrial activity in the Ruhr and would result in still further lowering of morale'. There was a less damaging prediction for the Eder: 'destruction of this dam would be spectacular, [but] economic effects would be problematical'.

In March 1943, Air Vice-Marshal Bottomley referred these conclusions to the Ministry of Economic Warfare (MEW) for an 'authoritative opinion', provided on 2 April 1943 by Mr O.L. Lawrence. His response was equivocal. There would 'not necessarily' be 'a large or immediate' effect on industrial and household water supplies, which in the Ruhr relied on 'underground water-bearing strata, supplemented by colliery water, water pumped from the Rhine and water drawn from the Emscher river and canal system'. The main purpose of the Moehne Reservoir was 'to maintain the level of these underground supplies through conserved rainfall'. It was not, therefore, possible to envisage that 'a critical shortage of water supplies in the Ruhr would be a certain and inevitable result of the destruction of the Moehne Dam'. Lawrence agreed, though, that a simultaneous, successful attack on the Sorpe 'would be worth much more than twice the destruction' of the Moehne.

Emphasising that the Eder Dam had no connection with the Ruhr, he too was lukewarm about the outcome of its destruction. There might be an impact on 'agricultural land' and 'possibly the low lying districts of Kassel'. 'Probable destruction' of four power stations below the dam, albeit not of 'major economic importance', would likely cause 'a useful measure of interference' with the Preuessenelektra supply system.

About the effect on morale, Lawrence was considerably more positive. Devastation below the Moehne and Eder would be 'witnessed by thousands'. 'Whatever the facts', he believed that 'alarmist rumours about lack of drinking water, disease and lack of fire-fighting capability would spread ... [and] exceptional opportunities would be presented for successful measures of political warfare.'

Nonetheless, expectations of catastrophic physical damage persisted, although Dr Hutchings's negative assertions of 'scant effect' and 'negligible influence' are debatable. The raid did have a debilitating impact, particularly

SOME ANSWERS

during the succeeding months of 1943 at a critical stage of the war. Albert Speer's office diary revealed that 'the temporary failure of pumping stations had led to a noticeable decrease in gas production by the coke works. The major consumers could be supplied with only 50 to 60 per cent of their needs'. Waterworks at Neheim, Huesten and Herdecke below the Moehne were among several, once repaired, to offer only a 'tolerable' supply. The level of water thereafter held in the Moehne, Eder and Sorpe reservoirs was reduced, thus lessening their output.

Despite failure drastically to affect the Mittelland Canal, serious disruption of the movement of military supplies, notably from the Kassel armament factories, transported via the waterways below the Eder Dam occurred for some time. Speer's office diary shows that repairs to the banks of the Fulda and Weser rivers were not completed until October 1943. Nor did agriculture escape. Heinrich George, the construction company official working on roadways there, held that floods in the Eder Valley carried away so much top soil that farmland could not be satisfactorily tilled. Similarly, Klesschute, a witness at the Moehne, reflected: 'The fields in the valley below will yield no crops for many years owing to the inundation'. If the physical repercussions of the Dams' Raid were not extreme, they were by no means insignificant.

Withdrawal of a division's worth of first-class troops destined for active service to man equipment at the target and other such vulnerable dams was decidedly not 'negligible'. Neither was the deployment of flak guns, including the dual-purpose 88mm, balloons and smoke canisters, which otherwise could have been used to defend urban and industrial concentrations or sent to the battlefront. There was, too, assignment of over 30,000 labourers and specialist tradesmen, some for a prolonged period, to carry out repairs on the damaged dams and throughout the affected areas and to install additional protective devices over the winter 1943–44.

The precise effect on morale is more difficult to judge in the broader context of the aerial bombardment of Germany. Sir Arthur Harris maintained: 'There is little doubt that the destruction of the Dams had an enormous moral effect on the Germans', which Joseph Goebbels appeared to acknowledge. On 18 May 1943, he wrote: 'Naturally the gauleiters in all gaus [regions] in which there are dams that have not yet been attacked are very much worried, since the anti-aircraft measures there are quite inadequate.'

This diary entry acknowledged that, 'the attacks of British bombers on our dams in our valleys were very successful. The Fuehrer is exceedingly

THE DAMBUSTERS: 'WAS THE RAID WORTHWHILE?'

impatient and angry about the lack of preparedness on the part of the Luftwaffe'. In 1954, Hans Rumpf, former Inspector-General of Fire Prevention in the Ruhr, believed that, in the wake of the attack, 'confidence in the air defences suffered a new heavy blow'. Reflecting once more on the short- and long-term effects of the Dams' Raid in 1979, Speer recalled that, when he reported in person to Hitler following his visit to the affected region, 'details of the damage contained in my report on the situation ... made a deep impression on the Führer. He kept the documents with him'. Hitler quickly displayed his concern publicly. During a strategic conference attended by Field-Marshal Wilhelm Keitel and Major-General Walter Warlimont on 19 May, he referred to 'this disaster in the west'. Hitler expressed particular dismay about interruption to the supply of self-propelled guns, so necessary to replace losses in North Africa and on the Eastern Front. To his irritation, Warlimont suggested that the results of the raid might not be so severe as at first thought. Hitler brusquely replied: 'That may be so in the three summer months. If a dry year occurs, it will be catastrophic. If we encounter a year when the Ruhr has no water, can we survive?'

The planning and execution of RAF bomber operations were the responsibility of Service personnel preoccupied with the day-to-day fighting of a global war and aerial defence of the homeland. They had to be convinced that Wallis's extraordinary weapon was not simply the product of a fertile imagination. Harris admitted to being wary of 'many crackpot schemes peddled to Bomber Command' over the previous three years and, to him, initially this was yet another pipe dream; Page's 'gimmick' and 'conjuring trick'. To protagonists of the idea, the Moehne gravity dam offered the graphic means of gaining the attention of hard-pressed decision-makers. However, it is inescapable that the narrow concentration on one attractive target did bypass a more exhaustive examination of the whole range of prospective targets and the means of destroying them.

This particularly applies to the Sorpe Dam. Speer contended that failure to disable it allowed its water supply to 'plug the gap that summer'. Without the output from the Moehne and Sorpe reservoirs, other Ruhr sources would have produced only '16% of the necessary amount of water'. Astonishingly, in 1979, he went further in declaring that were the Sorpe Dam breached, 'the war would have been finished earlier'. Independently, Professor Dr Ing Otto Kirschmer, in claiming that destruction of the two dams would have been 'very grave indeed', implied much the same. Overall, Speer believed that the operation had been 'spectacular' and the German government

SOME ANSWERS

'concerned', but without breaching of the Sorpe, the operation could not be termed 'a very great success'.

The irony is that from the genesis of the proposal to bomb the dams, the Sorpe Reservoir had been recognised as the second most important source of water for the Ruhr. The adjacent dam's different construction, though, posed a seemingly insuperable challenge. In reflecting that Wallis had never mentioned it during the model experiments, Dr Collins remarked: 'I was, in fact, surprised to hear that the Sorpe had been attacked and a little irritated, because we could easily have made some model tests which I am sure would have made the attack more successful'. Speer and Kirschmer indirectly confirmed the validity of the pre-war assertion that destruction of the Moehne and Sorpe dams would fundamentally, if not fatally, undermine industrial capacity in the Ruhr, recognised by the CAS's marginal comment during early discussions concerning the Moehne: 'What about the Sorpetal'?

On 18 March 1943, the committee chaired by Air Vice-Marshal N.H. Bottomley to oversee the project, reflecting earlier opinions, concluded of the Sorpe: 'We have ruled [it] out as being unsuitable for attack, for tactical and technical reasons'. The Moehne was more important and more suitable for attack, and 'its destruction would have far-reaching effects on the enemy's war economy'.

However, although not evidently a primary consideration, during the planning process, the Sorpe remained on the target list. At a meeting attended by Wallis on 5 May, Cochrane maintained that 'the method of attack against this dam was simple and should prove effective'. Wallis agreed that there was a 'very good prospect' that this 'would bring about its destruction'. He had previously proposed a right-angle approach as at the other targets in 'Air Attack on Dams', while Cochrane initially favoured cratering the top of the dam so that water would wash over and erode the structure; first proposed in July 1938 by Squadron Leader C.G. Burge to the Air Ministry's Bombing Committee. The tactic of flying along the crest to release Upkeep appears to have been a late development.

Harris was never convinced, recalling that, once alerted to the Sorpe as a target with Upkeep, he held out little hope of success. In his post-operational report of 7 June 1943, Cochrane maintained that 'immediate results' were not expected. 'The intention was to crack the centre watertight concrete core so as to start a leak which might [sic], in time, destroy the dam or at the least force the enemy to empty the reservoir to repair the damage.' Disingenuously, the Operation Order referred to 'specially trained crews' being directed to the Sorpe, whereas the composition of the Second Wave had not been finalised before 13 May. Crew members of the two Lancasters which attacked the dam and two others forced to turn back due to damage were adamant that they followed the same training programme as the rest of the Squadron. No distinct exercises associated with the Sorpe took place. Need for a clear, persuasive argument to secure Service executive support, which involved principally the Moehne, lies behind the belated revival of active interest in the Sorpe Dam. Cochrane then hoped, ideally, that eight of the initial 14 Lancasters would attack it.

Acknowledging the soundness of targeting the Ruhr dams, Speer emphasised that to allocate part of the limited force to the Eder was 'a waste ... A single mistake which puzzles me to this day ... [is that] they divided their forces that same night to destroy the Eder Valley dam, although it had nothing to do with the supply of water to the Ruhr'. Once the case for attacking gravity dams gathered pace pre-war, the Eder became a prime target. Questioning its inclusion in the list of Chastise targets, foreseen in the Bomber Command appreciation of 17 July 1939, overlooks one major argument for attacking any of the dams. Flooding after a breach would effectively strike several other designated targets below them. Speer conceded that important aircraft and submarine component factories were at Kassel, which became targets from the origin of the RAF's bombing campaign; June–July 1940 being attacked seven times. Rumpf agreed that the Eder Reservoir supplied water for such plants, besides keeping up the level of the Eder, Fulda and Upper Weser rivers, topping up that of the Mittelland Canal in dry periods and providing important hydro-electric power stations with regular supplies.

There is no doubt, therefore, that the Eder Dam was a credible target. The pivotal question is to whether it should have featured in this operation, given that the declared aim was to neutralise the Ruhr industries and such a small force was made available.

Positive conclusions about the achievements during the early hours of 17 May 1943 avoid the basic question about such an onerous task being allocated to 20 Lancasters. Bufton referred to 'an awful lot of damage for a few aircraft'. Twelve years later, Rumpf reflected that the Dams' Raid 'represented its [RAF's] biggest and most impressive success ... carried out by precision bombing of a high order'. Speer admitted, 'that night, employing just a few bombers, the British came close to a success which would have been greater than anything they had achieved with a commitment of thousands of bombers'.

At the time, Goebbels wrote: 'We must therefore record the absurd fact that ten planes could drive 15 to 18 million people out of their beds.'

SOME ANSWERS

However, Speer's parallel doubts about the wisdom of dividing a limited force to attack such a wide range of targets remain relevant. The number of aircraft was not based on a study of how many would be needed to achieve success, but willingness to make available a limited number of 'precious' four-engine bombers from the assembly line; the original 30 being reduced to 23, three of those for trials. Admittedly with twin-engine bombers and different types of weapon, Portal's 1940 proposal envisaged 12 aircraft attacking the Moehne alone. Finch Noyes' plan the following year proposed 16 and, notably, anticipated losses, early returns and failed attacks. In his letter to Winterbotham on 12 February 1943, even with Upkeep superseding the earlier weapons, Wallis wanted 30 aircraft to attack the five Ruhr dams then under consideration: six to each target 'to make certain'.

It is, therefore, difficult to escape the impression that for Operation Chastise insufficient attention was paid to how many aircraft should be committed to the intended seven targets or to cater for failures either to reach the target area or to bomb accurately.

After highlighting the Moehne, the Operation Oder explained: 'The additional destruction of one or more of the five dams in the Ruhr area would greatly increase the effect ... Target Z [Sorpe] is the next in importance'. In the event, roughly half (11) of the force attacked four dams in individual totals, 5 (Moehne), 3 (Eder), 2 (Sorpe), 1 (Ennepe). Of those which failed to attack any target, two returned early through damage, one aborted and five were shot down. Under the pressure of conducting a major bombing campaign against Germany, Harris regarded the Dams' Raid as part of the Battle of the Ruhr and integral to the allied bombing campaign against Germany; Portal's exhortation to 'bust the dams' is in that context, too.

Disquiet about the operational plan came from an unlikely quarter: Sir Barnes Wallis. Almost thirty years later, to the Road Research Laboratory scientist, Dr Collins, he wrote: 'I can't understand why dummy raids and Window were not used to divert attention from the actual dambuster aircraft. My own belief has always been that had the dambuster aircraft had fighter escort, plus dummy raids, plus Window the losses would have been reduced to these two'; assuming Maudslay and Hopgood were lost at a dam. Window was not deployed until July 1943 and diversionary fighter attacks ('dummy raids') were actually mounted to distract enemy defences. In May 1943, a long-range fighter escort at night would have been both impracticable and, even if possible, have nullified the plan to infiltrate a small force. The Operation Order emphasised: 'The whole essence of this operation is surprise'.

THE DAMBUSTERS: 'WAS THE RAID WORTHWHILE?'

Failure to mount follow-up raids has particularly attracted critical comment from different quarters. Wallis could not understand why, during the months of repair work to the breached dams, 'an attempt to break down "the false work" had not been attempted'. Speer, too, felt that '... the British air force missed its second chance. A few bombs would have produced cave-ins at the exposed building sites, and a few more bombs could have set the wooden scaffolding blazing'.

Hans Rumpf agreed: 'What was surprising was that the Bomber Command made no attempt to interfere with the repair work on the dams'. Quite apart from the powerful range of weapons immediately allocated to defence of the Moehne, Eder and Sorpe dams, to obtain the necessary precision achieved on 17 May 1943 had involved a prolonged struggle to devise a workable low-level method of attack. The pinpoint accuracy required could not be attained with either HE or, particularly, incendiary bombs from a high altitude; a low-level operation under the circumstances would be suicidal.

However, evidently further action after successful breaches was never seriously considered. Cochrane thought it 'unreasonable' to anticipate the work being completed so quickly. But that, seemingly, was not the primary reason for lack of a follow-up plan. Writing in *V Group News* in May 1943, the Air Officer Commanding 5 Group asserted that, even if the dams were repaired, it would take 'two seasons' to refill the reservoirs.

Over the years, the morality of the Dams' Raid has been queried, on the grounds that it did little more than kill some 1,300 civilians including over 400 foreign forced labourers. A German contributor to a 70th anniversary radio programme specifically condemned it as 'a war crime'. In conversation, Air Vice-Marshal Bufton conceded that The Casablanca Directive was an operational plan, but pointed to the RAF's declared commitment to the Rules of Air Warfare laid down at The Hague Conference of 1922–23. On 14 October 1932, the Air Ministry indicated that it intended to abide by the outcome of the proceedings, which referred to 'a military objective' being a target whose 'destruction or neutralisation' would constitute a military advantage. A subsequent publication, 'Bomber Command' (1941), underlined that 'the rules for aerial warfare were drawn up at The Hague in 1923 ... [and were] adopted as a basis' for the RAF's bombing campaign from the outset. Specific reference was made to Article 24 of the relevant protocol, which laid down that 'targets directly concerned with the prosecution of the war might legitimately be attacked. Considerations of humanity therefore could not constitute a legitimate reason for never attacking land targets'. These were

SOME ANSWERS

defined as 'factories constituting important and well-known centres engaged in the manufacture of arms, ammunition or distinctively military supplies, lines of communication or transportation used for military purposes'.

The objectives of the dams' operation were centred on German war production and set within these parameters. In 1938, the Bombing Committee of the Air Ministry believed that 'reservoirs and dams' supplied the means of production for 'the industrial energy system'. Two years later, Air Chief-Marshal Sir Charles Portal's proposal to attack the Moehne sought to bring 'the industrial activity of the Ruhr ... to a standstill' and Finch Noyes similarly aimed to 'disorganise its industry'. In setting up Squadron X, Air Vice-Marshal R.D. Oxland asserted that destruction of the Moehne Dam 'will have serious consequences in the neighbouring industrial area'. After the raid, Churchill informed the American Congress that the reservoirs provided 'power to the enemy's munition works', leaflets dropped on occupied countries focused on 'the material destruction of factories' and the Secretary of State for Air declared that 617 Squadron had struck at 'the source of German war power', something recognised by Hitler to Speer. Significantly, pre-war the responsible German official, Justus Dillgardt, feared that breaching of 'the large dams in southern Westphalia' would result in 'the entire industrial area' below being 'completely paralysed'.

In *Enemy Coast Ahead* Gibson stressed: 'We had merely destroyed a legitimate objective so as to hinder the Ruhr Valley output of war munitions. The fact that people were in the way was incidental.' Patently, civilian casualties should never be considered simply 'incidental'. However, historically, they have constituted the unavoidable consequence of armed conflict and, notably from May 1940, bombing operations putting non-military personnel at risk were conducted by all major combatants in the Second World War. The Dams' Raid did not target people.

Spring 1943 was an anxious time for the Allies. German aircraft were still bombing Britain ('Night Sirens in London again' captioned an article in one newspaper, which covered the Dams' Raid), heavy loss of merchant ships in the Atlantic gravely threatened supplies of food and military hardware from overseas, the Soviet advance into eastern Europe following the survival of Stalingrad had not yet gained momentum and, after the fall of Singapore, Japanese forces were steadily advancing on India through Burma. North Africa had just been cleared of Axis troops, but the European mainland, dominated by Germany, must still be invaded.

In the UK, reconnaissance photos released to the press of the breached dams and destruction caused by the subsequent escape of water from their reservoirs provided a morale boost to a war-weary population. Hitherto, the only photos of air raids on Germany were images of smoke-filled areas under a headline like that in the provincial publication, *Exeter Express and Echo,* on 22 January 1943: 'Germany Bombed Again'. The historian John Terraine observed, 'Guy Gibson's Dams Raid is a prime example of a brilliantly executed alternative'.

Sir Robert Saundby, in pointing to the lengthy build-up to the operation, rightly emphasised that Wallis did not originate the concept. Yet, without him, the raid could not have been mounted in May 1943 and conceivably never at all. As his nephew, Robert McCormick, put it: he provided 'a brilliant answer to a contemporary problem'. Nor should the full extent of Gibson's contribution be underestimated. Award of the VC acknowledged his bravery and directional skills in leading the crews into action. Behind that feat, lay the achievement of preparing a new squadron, which did not finalise its composition for three weeks, to carry out such an unparalleled, testing operation in under two months. He did so, while travelling to a succession of high-level planning meetings, liaising with scientists like Wallis over the detailed delivery of Upkeep and observing multiple, development trials; all outside the normal responsibility of an operational squadron commander.

Navigator Pilot Officer C.L. Howard recalled: 'My memory places Guy Gibson as the outstanding figure. Though we did not see a lot of him, he seemed to set a standard of perfection in all our training and the final preparation. It's called leadership – how do you define it?' Flight Lieutenant D.J. Shannon, AJ-L's pilot, and Pilot Officer I. Whittaker, Martin's flight engineer, were among the 617 Squadron members to echo Howard. Gibson's forthright manner and insistence on strict discipline did not, though, meet with universal approval especially from NCOs: air gunner, Sergeant F. Tees, held that 'he demanded rather than commanded respect' and navigator, Sergeant D.P. Heal, considered him 'cocky'.

Gibson's duty was to be efficient, not popular. Three days before he took command of his previous squadron, No.106, Bomber Command issued a directive, 'Discipline', which pinpointed 'such matters as the giving and acknowledging of salutes in the approved manner, deportment, clean and properly worn uniform, correct in every detail, and insistence upon an unfailing observance of smartness, [which] helps to eradicate a "go as you please" mentality'; the blue print for Gibson's style of command. 'Chiefy' Powell insisted that 'he never bawled out anybody, who didn't deserve it'.

SOME ANSWERS

Timing is crucial. Peter Lewis, reviewing a biography of Gibson in 1994, wrote: 'In recent years the effects of the dam bust on German war production has been questioned or pooh-poohed, but its theatrical propaganda effect was immense at the moment when a British blow against occupied Europe was badly needed'. On the 50th anniversary of the operation, navigator, Sergeant Heal, agreed. 'It came at a time, when the country needed it. We were not getting anywhere. Nothing seemed to be changing – bombers going over every night, and the Germans were not surrendering'.

Group Captain Sir Douglas Bader recollected: 'I well remember the destruction of the Moehne and Eder dams while I was in a prison camp. It had an enormous effect on the Germans and the opposite effect, of course, on the prisoners-of-war'. Flight Sergeant J.W. Fraser, who escaped from Hopgood's burning aircraft at the Moehne Dam, also learnt of the raid's effect while in captivity. One of his interrogators told him that 'this raid had accomplished as much as one hundred normal air raids ... That made me feel pretty damned good'.

Commenting on the operation in 1993, himself a decorated Second World War bomber pilot, Marshal of the Royal Air Force Sir Michael Beetham observed: 'It was a great bonus to the British people. You have to have hope and they were looking for good news.' As a 1943 intelligence officer, Flight Lieutenant G.E. Pine, succinctly recalled, 'we did need it', and Sergeant D.E. Webb held: 'If we did nothing else, we gave people in this country a lift.'

The Road Research Laboratory scientist, Dr A.R. Collins, agreed that 'the attack was certainly a boost to morale in Britain', but believed, too, it enhanced 'its reputation in other countries, especially as a demonstration of imagination and ingenuity'. The capacity to devise and develop Upkeep to attack such precise targets underlined the creativity of British engineering; a reprise of exchanges between Wallis and Chadwick. A domestic bonus was the enhancement of Wallis's reputation and support for the development of his 12,000lb Tallboy and Grand Slam (the original 'big bomb'); Harris's pink elephant.

However, conclusions about this operation must inevitably involve more than assessment of its significance for the home front. Undoubtedly, under the daily pressure of co-ordinating an allied bombing campaign on Germany and aerial protection of the United Kingdom, shortcomings in the planning, conduct and, to some extent, rationale behind the project can be discerned in retrospect. These perceived drawbacks have tended to influence judgement about the effect of Operation Chastise.

THE DAMBUSTERS: 'WAS THE RAID WORTHWHILE?'

Evidence of allied success in Europe and further afield on land, at sea and in the air, despite the recent triumph in North Africa, was unquestionably scarce in May 1943. Sir Michael Beetham and the intelligence officer, Flight Lieutenant Pine, were right to emphasise the hope this raid generated during the uncertain middle period of the Second World War. Despite the colourful hyperbole of an over-excited publicity machine (Lewis's 'theatrical propaganda'), the repercussions of the Dambusters Raid in the USA, USSR, Commonwealth, occupied territories of Europe and within Germany are well documented. Interviewees and correspondents on both sides of the conflict, who have contributed to this volume, reinforce that reality.

In the contemporary context, nationally and internationally, Operation Chastise demonstrably had extensive political, social and military impact, thus generating a justifiably positive response to Wallis's query, 'was the raid worthwhile?'

Acknowledgements

I am deeply indebted, in particular, to Sir Barnes Wallis and Dr A.R. Collins for their invaluable time and patience in providing a deep insight into the background to the attack on the German dams in May 1943 and for permission to use the material they have provided.

The staff of the following libraries and archives have been extremely helpful and I am most grateful to them:

Albert F. Simpson, Historical Research Center, Maxwell Air Force Base, USA
Bundesarchiv-Militaerarchiv, Freiburg, Germany
Brooklands Museum, Weybridge, Surrey
Canadian Forces Records Centre, Ottawa, Canada
City of Birmingham Public Libraries
Commonwealth War Graves Commission, Maidenhead, Berkshire
Department of Aviation Records, RAF Museum, Hendon
Department of Defence (Air Force Office), Canberra, Australia
Doncaster Metropolitan Borough Council
Ennepe-Wasserverband, Gevelsberg, Germany
Essex County Record Office
Exeter City Library
Gemente Harlingen, The Netherlands
Imperial War Museum: departments of Documents and Photographs
Institution of Civil Engineers
Leicestershire Record Office
Lincoln Public Library
Ministry of Defence, Air Historical Branch
National Archives, Kew
Portsmouth City Library
Rhyader Public Library

THE DAMBUSTERS: 'WAS THE RAID WORTHWHILE?'

Royal Aircraft Establishment
Royal Military Academy, Sandhurst
Ruhrverand und Ruhrtalsperrenverein, Germany
Severn-Trent Water Authority
Sheffield City Library
South Yorkshire County Record Office
Transport and Road Research Laboratory, Crowthorne, Berkshire
Wupperverband, Wuppertal, Germany
617 Squadron Museum

I readily acknowledge permission to use the information which they have provided and I thank, too, the Controller of Her Majesty's Stationery Office for permission to reproduce photographs and to quote from records under Crown Copyright; the Imperial War Museum for allowing production of photographs and documents held there; the Bundesarchiv-Militaerarchiv, Ennepe-Wasserverband and Ruhrverband and Ruhrtalsperrenverein in Germany, British Aerospace and the Officer Commanding 617 Squadron for similar permission. The John Oxley Library, State Library of Queensland, Australia, has kindly given permission to quote from the papers of Flying Officer C.R. Williams.

I am extremely grateful to the following for supplying photographs, illustrations and sketches: R. Burton, Dr A.R. Collins, E.C. Johnson, G.L. Johnson, S. Oancia, L. Sumpter, F. Tees and Sir Barnes Wallis.

Many of those directly involved in Operation Chastise gave generously of their time to meet or correspond and have given permission to use the information that they have supplied:

Marshal of the Royal Air Force Sir Arthur Harris, Air Chief Marshal the Honourable Sir Ralph Cochrane, Air Vice-Marshal S.O. Bufton and Air Vice-Marshal H.V. Satterly.

617 Squadron aircrew, who flew on the operation: K.W. Brown, G.A. Chalmers, J.H. Clay, H.B. Feneron, R.E. Grayston, D.P. Heal, H.S. Hobday, C.L. Howard, W. Howarth, E.C. Johnson, G.L. Johnson, R.G.T Kellow, D.A. MacLean, S. Oancia, H.E. O'Brien, G. Rice, D. Rodger, D.J. Shannon, T.D. Simpson, L.J. Sumpter, F.E. Sutherland, F. Tees, W.C. Townsend, D.R. Walker, D.E. Webb, I. Whittaker.

Other contemporary service personnel at RAF Scampton: Dr M.W. Arthurton, Mrs E. Bark, Mrs M.J. Brooks, J. A. Bryden, A. Drury, V. Gill, Reverend C.D. Hulbert, H.K. Munro, G.E. Powell, Mrs A. Shannon (née Fowler).

ACKNOWLEDGEMENTS

Combined Operations: Lord Louis Mountbatten; Ministry of Aircraft Production: Sir Benjamin Lockspeiser, N.E. Rowe; Vickers-Armstrongs: N.W. Boorer, A.D. Grant, H. Jeffree, R.C. Handasyde, W.E. Startup; Royal Aircraft Establishment: C.W. Shaw, S. Wright.

The following provided considerable assistance, often of a technical nature: Herr G. Aders, H. Archer, Group Captain Sir Douglas Bader, J.V.D Banham, N. Barfield, D.R. Barraclough, D.M. Bennett, Flight Lieutenant T. Bennett, Herr K. Bischof, Wing Commander G.A. Bone, B. Broad, R. Burton, E (Roy) Callow, Group Captain G.L. Cheshire, Oberstleutenant J. Damm, Herr H. Diener, Heer H.B. van den Dool, Mrs M. Dove, Mevr H van Els-Theuissen, Professor M.R.D. Foot, Major M. Foster RE, H. Hamer, Herr E. Handke, M.B. Illiot, D. Irving, Squadron Leader T.C. Iveson, K.W. Jones, L.B. Jones, Professor R.V. Jones, General J. Kammhuber, Herr P. Keiser, A.A. Lowes, Dr and Mrs J. McCormick, Dr R. McCormick, R.S. McLaren, A.J. (Bill) Newman, G.C.S. Oliver, Dr R. Owen, Mrs P. Podmore, F. Rayment, A.J.W. Scopes, H.E. Scrope, Dr M.R. Stopes-Roe, B.W. Wallis, C. Wallis, Herr A. Speer, J.R. Tate, Wing Commander J.C. Weller, J. Wickens, Dr N. Young.

My special gratitude goes to Andrew Panton for allowing me access to his more recent research connected with the operation.

Appendix A

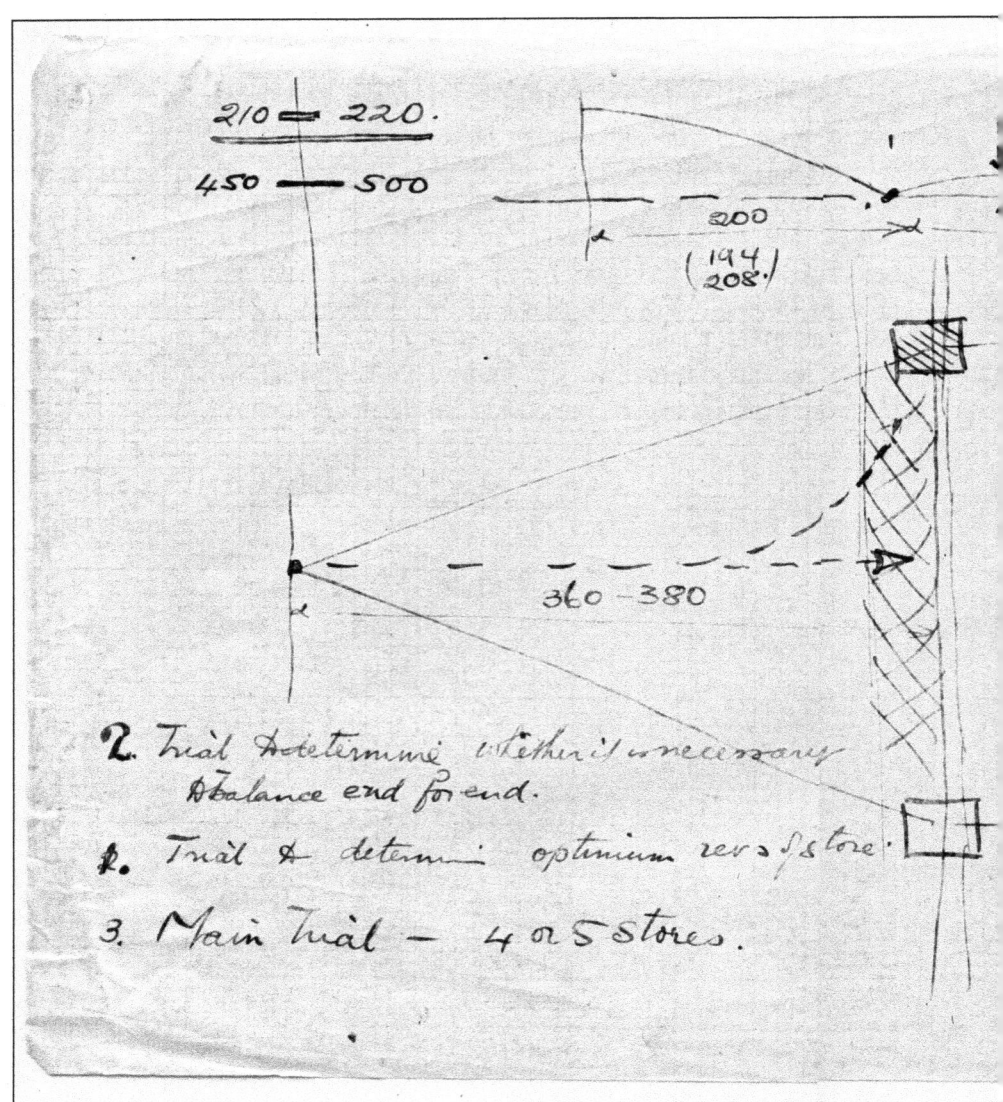

APPENDIX A

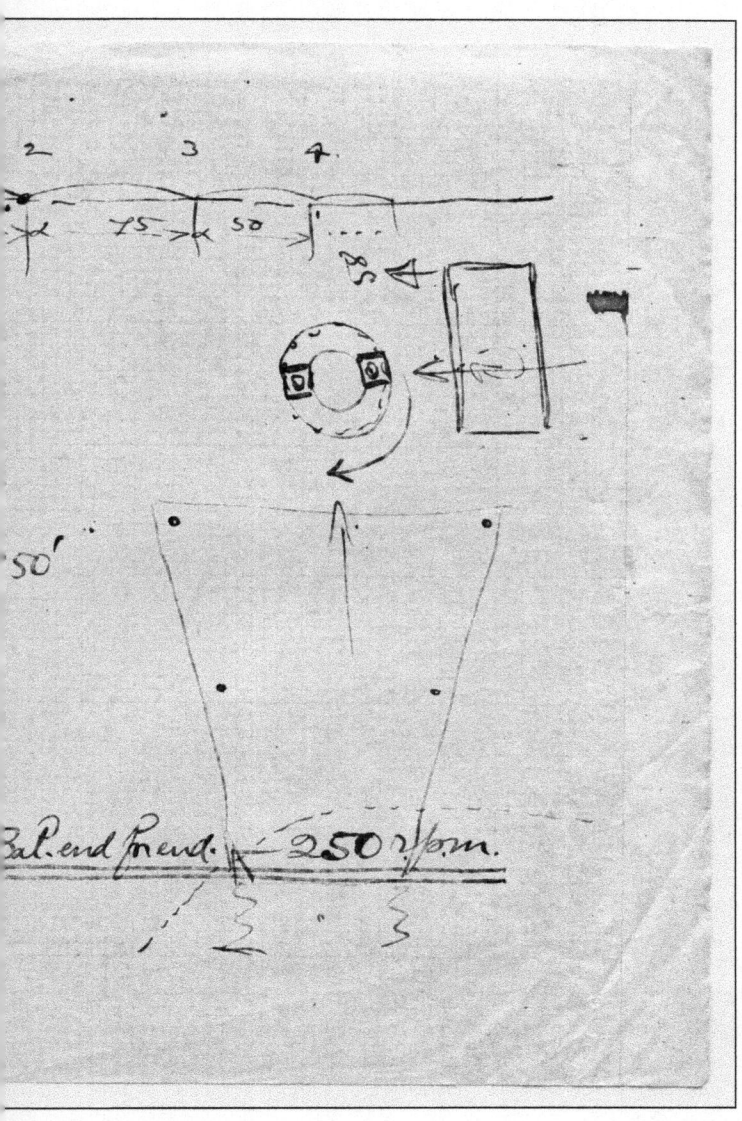

Release of Upkeep. Preliminary working details sketched by Barnes Wallis. Top left (above) proposed ground speed on release (below) distance of release from target. Top right number of bounces after release and distance from target. Centre calculation of release point between towers 750ft apart on dam and early spherical form of Upkeep back-spun at 250rpm.

THE DAMBUSTERS: 'WAS THE RAID WORTHWHILE?'

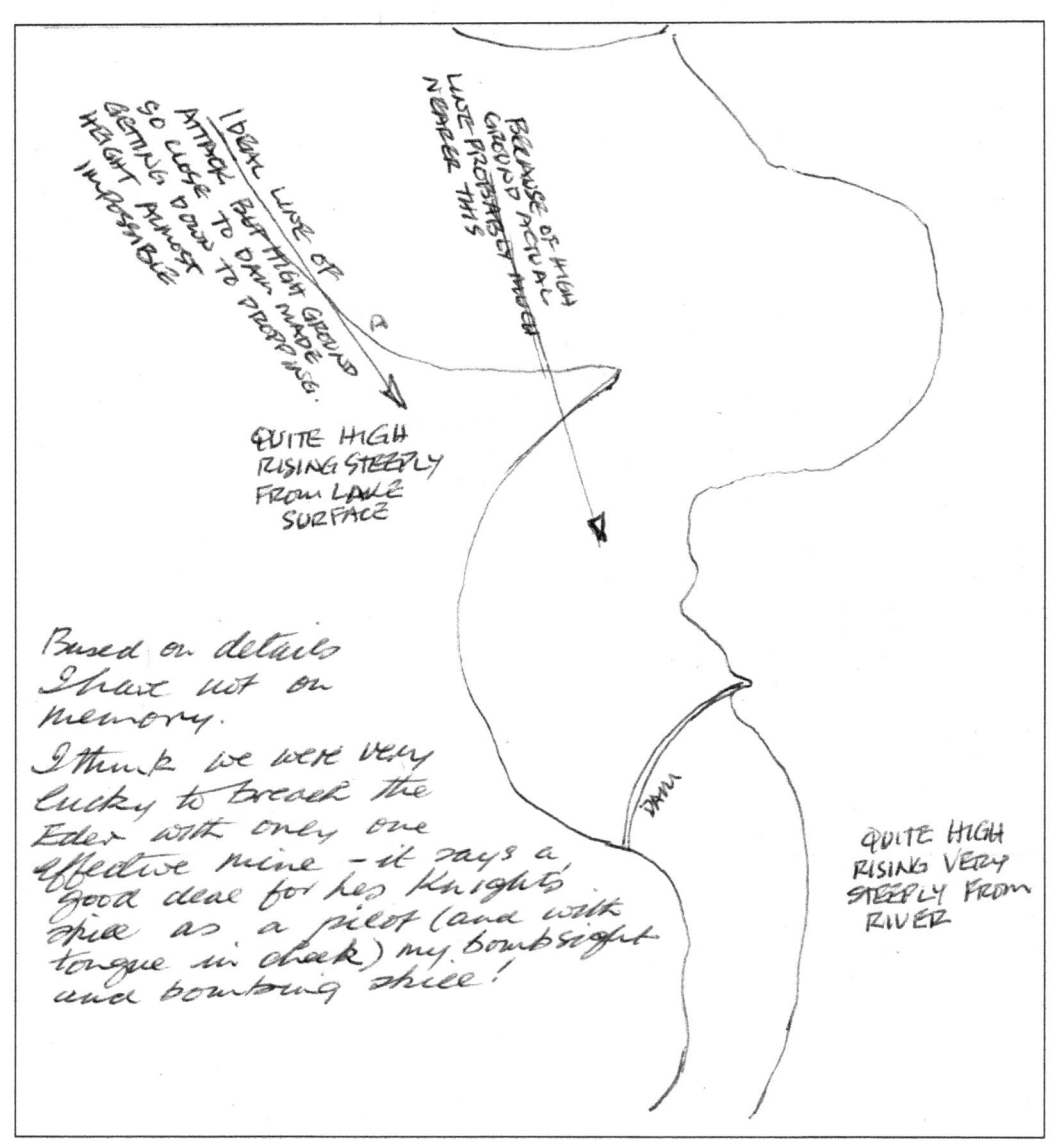

The Eder Dam. Sketch with explanation of AJ-N's successful attack by its bomb-aimer, Flying Officer E.C. Johnson.

APPENDIX A

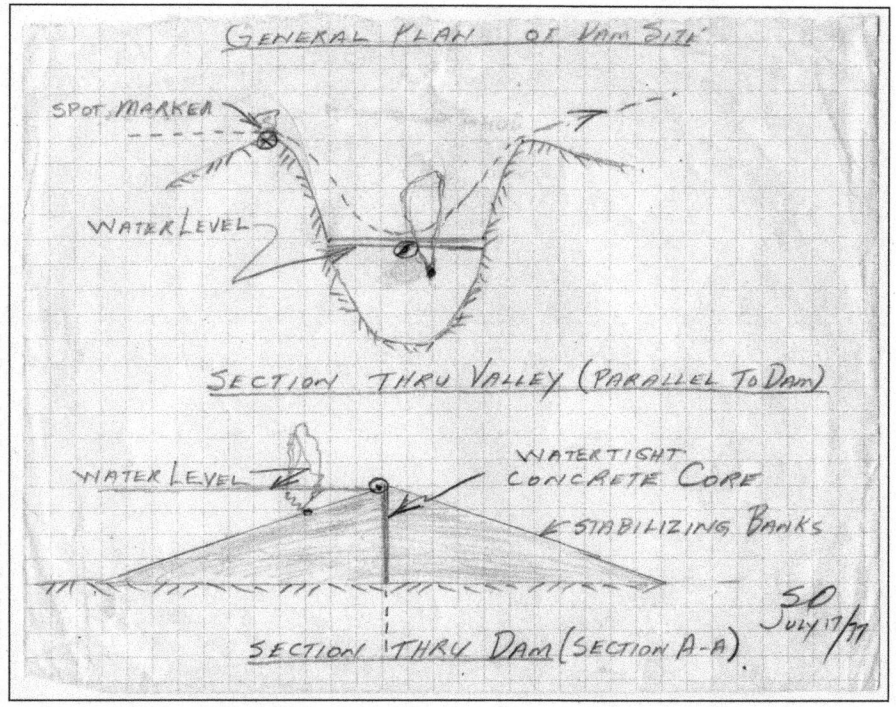

The Sorpe Dam. Sketches by Sergeant Steve Oancia, bomb-aimer of AJ-F, (top) aircraft attack line (bottom) cross-section of dam.

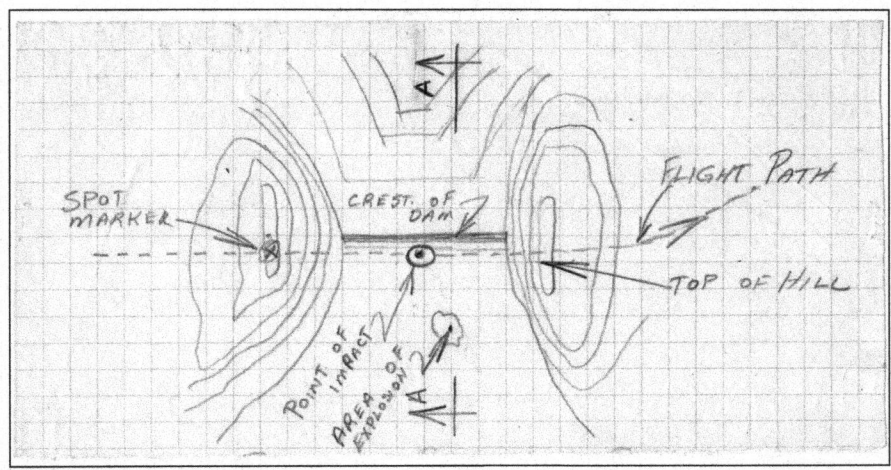

The Sorpe Dam. Release point of Upkeep from Flight Sergeant K.C. Brown's Lancaster illustrated by the bomb-aimer, Sergeant Steve Oancia.

Appendix B

                                          Albury Heights
                                          White Lane
                                          Guildford
                                          Surrey GU4 8PR

                                   Telephone 0483 504488

                                     15th March 1994

Dear Dr. Sweetman,

     Thank you for your letter of 8th March. Rather than you coming here, I think the best thing is for me to tell you the story in a letter and when you have digested it, if there are any further points you wish to raise, give me a ring.

     I was Experimental Manager at that time and was involved in some of the development work for the bomb. In the very early stages, I rigged up a catapoult on the lake at Silvermere in Cobham, which fired balls; so far as I remember, they were a bit bigger than a billiard ball.

     Wallis was convinced that it needed top spin; as an enthusiastic bowler of leg breaks, I knew that it did not, and I arranged the catapoult in such a way that the balls could be fired with either top spin, no spin, or back spin; I knew from my experience of the "flipper" that back spin would prove to be best, although Wallis was quite adamant that it would not.

                                                  contrinued......

APPENDIX B

> Albury Heights
> White Lane
> Guildford
> Surrey GU4 8PR
>
> Telephone 0483 504488
>
> - 2 -
>
> I recall the balls with top spin did not bounce at all; those with no spin bounced five or six times, and those with back spin up to 15 times.
>
> The only credit I got for this amazing discovery was that Wallis, in a subsequent report, ascribed the decision to advice which he had received from "a county cricketer of his acquantance". I may say that was the closest I got to being one!
>
> I hope this is of some help.
>
> Yours
> George Edwards
>
> Dr. J. Sweetman
> Department of defence & International Affairs

Opposite and above: Letter from Sir George Edwards. Experimental Manager at Vickers-Armstrongs, Weybridge, in 1943 explaining how back-spinning of Upkeep evolved.

THE DAMBUSTERS: 'WAS THE RAID WORTHWHILE?'

FROM
MARSHAL OF THE ROYAL AIR FORCE, SIR ARTHUR T. HARRIS, BT. GCB. OBE. AFC. LLD.

THE FERRY HOUSE,
GORING ON THAMES,
RG8 9DX.

5.8.81

Dear Dr Sweetman

Many thanks for yr letter of 4th. I will be very interested to read yr book when it comes out. I was against Wallis' "bouncing Bomb" originally, but I had not then heard it was for the Dams;! I had been told by Wallis' himself, that it was for attacking Battleships!! & I was damned if I would have my pilots out-Kamikazeing the Kamikazis!! Quite apart from the fact that obviously a battleship under weigh would be a mile away by the time a bomb had hit it, bounced back, ~~enter~~ sunk 20 feet or more crawled underneath & finally exploded!!!! Only then did Wallis say it was also for attacking the Dams — & produced photos of his ~~~~ working model of the whole Idea in action!! It was then that I immediately told him that I would raise a special Squadron of thoroughly experienced

***Above and opposite*: Letter from Sir Arthur Harris.** Explaining his contemporary reaction to Barnes Wallis's proposal.

APPENDIX B

Warriors, who had finished a whole tour of operations, & put Gibson in command of it.

That was my "negative reaction" reinforced by the proven fact that bombs could deal with Battleships without suicide squads!! as they did! Bombs destroyed twice as many as the Navy did!

I knew, & asserted from the start, that the Sorpe Dam was the wrong construction to collapse from the bouncing bomb, but there was a faint chance that it might start a leak, crack the concrete "blade", & then escaping water might do the rest.

I cannot stop you writing a biography but I cannot help you because I am under contract for one already written & not to appear until I've departed because I cannot longer take the inevitable mound of work that would follow its production.

warm regards y[ou]rs sin[cerely]
Arthur T. Harris

THE DAMBUSTERS: 'WAS THE RAID WORTHWHILE?'

S E C R E T

Headquarters, No. 5 Group,
Royal Air Force,
St. Vincents,
Grantham, Lincs.

RAC/DO/1/Air.

17th May, 1943.

Dear Wallis,

Before reaching the end of this somewhat long but exciting day I feel I must write to tell you how much I admire the perseverance which brought you the astounding success which was achieved last night. Without your determination to ensure that a method which you knew to be technically sound was given a fair trial we should not have been able to deliver the blow which struck Germany last night.

2. I spoke to the Commander-in-Chief about your other project and he expressed the greatest interest. He asked if you would send him as soon as possible a copy of any papers bearing on the problem and when I suggested that you might come down in person to explain what you had in mind he said that this would be an excellent idea. I suggest, therefore, that you should get in touch either with him or with the Deputy Commander-in-Chief, Air Vice-Marshal R. H. M. Saundby, who also knows of the project.

3. If you want a trial there should be no difficulty in dropping the projectile which you have at Weybridge.

Yours Sincerely,
R.A. Cochrane

B. N. Wallis, Esq.,
c/o Messrs. Vickers Armstrong Co. Ltd.,
WEYBRIDGE.

P.S. Since writing this I have heard the result of the full photographic cover. What a disaster.

Letter from Air Vice-Marshal the Hon R.A. Cochrane. To Barnes Wallis in the immediate aftermath of the raid.

APPENDIX B

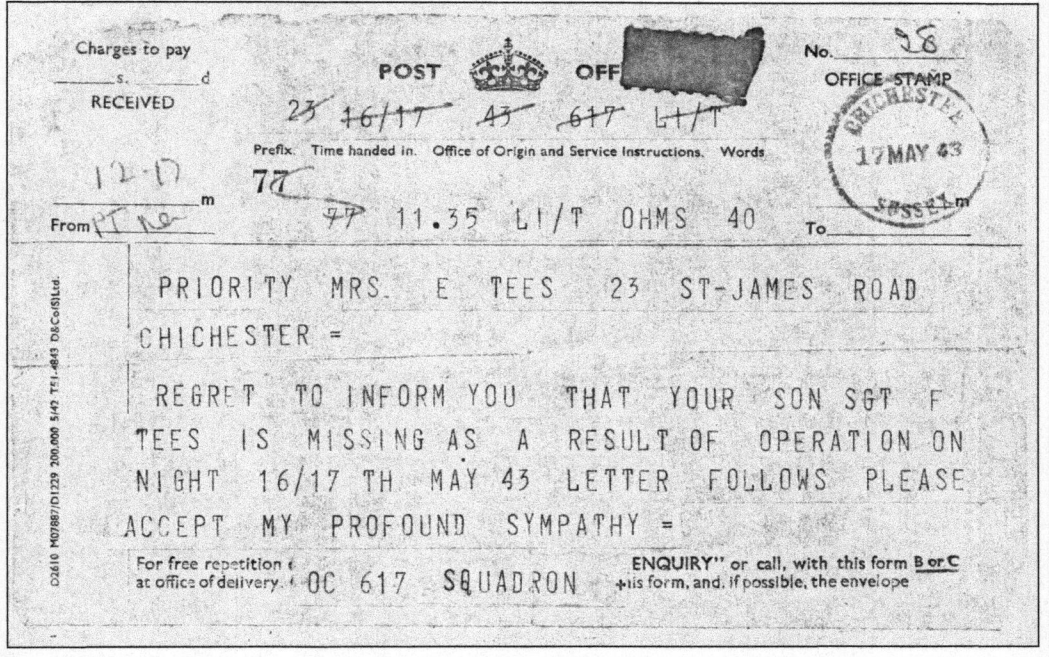

Telegram to Mrs Tees. From RAF Scampton on 17 May 1943, informing her that her son was missing in action.

THE DAMBUSTERS: 'WAS THE RAID WORTHWHILE?'

> **KEEP YOUR MOVEMENTS SECRET**
>
> R.A.F.
> May 20th. Scampton.
>
> My Dear Mr Wallis,
>
> Now that the floods are subsiding and the tumult dying down (Vait for the Scope) I've at last found time to drop you a line.
>
> I'm afraid I'm not much of a letter writer but I would like to say just this. The weapon that you gave us to deliver worked like a dream and you have earned the thanks of the civilized world.
>
> All my pilots and I are honoured that we had the opportunity to take part in the last great experiment which has proved all your theories.
>
> And now, I think you need a holiday.
>
> Best Regards to Mutt, Shorty and Handy
>
> Yours Sincerely,
> Guy Gibson
>
> WRITE ON BOTH SIDES   IT'S A WARTIME ECONOMY.

Letter from Wing Commander Guy Gibson. To Barnes Wallis on 20 May 1943 in the wake of Operation Chastise. 'Mutt, Shorty and Handy' were the Vickers test pilots Summers, Longbottom and Handasyde.

APPENDIX B

> F TEES
> 65, STATION Rd
> LETCHWORTH
> HERTS
> SG6 3BJ
>
> 27/5/77
>
> Dear Dr. Sweetman
> with regards to your letter yes I did fly with Bill Ottley, and we were shot down by light flack on the way to its dams, to get some of the records straight I was in the rear turret not as is seen in print, the front, also at rooftop feet on three engines and burning well, you don't have a chance to use parachutes, you go into the deck with what I believe to be one hell of a crash.
> If you think a chat will help, I've no doubt that it might be arranged some time, but as I'm not on the phone it would mean further correspondance
> Yours Sincerly
> Fred Tees

Letter from Sergeant Fred Tees. Survivor of AJ-C being shot down, confirming in rear, not front, turret.

THE DAMBUSTERS: 'WAS THE RAID WORTHWHILE?'

From Sir Barnes Wallis. APRIL 1972
[V-A = Vickers-Armstrong]

My dear Collins,

Being able, now that I am living on a pension, to afford my old Secretary for only 3 hours a week, has slowed up my rate of answering correspondence to an almost dead stop; and I must apologise very sincerely for the corresponding delay in answering your letter & fascinating enclosure of 27th March. But here are notes on some of the points that I have noticed:—

1. p.4. You refer to the Building Research Station, & on p.5 to the Road Research Laboratory (R.R.L.). My memory — probably defective — only recalls dealing with the latter, of which Dr Glanville was the Director. On p.6. you are back to B.R.S. again.

2. At the bottom of p.6 I think you should treat me in the same way as you have Glanville & Stradling, ie. Mr (now Sir) Barnes Wallis.

***Above and opposite*: Extracts from letter by Sir Barnes Wallis, April 1972.** Written to Dr A.R. Collins, the Road Research Laboratory scientist responsible for the model tests commenting on a draft article by Collins, highlighting the pivotal question as to whether the raid were worthwhile and noting that to perform properly Upkeep had to strike the water horizontally.

APPENDIX B

release range from about 650 yards to about 450 yards. And the cylinder had a further great disadvantage in that while a slight degree of roll on the aircraft at the instant of release had no perceptible effect on the directional accuracy of the run, the result of roll on a cylinder was disastrous in that one end striking the water before the other, caused the cylinder to run on the arc of a circle.

This unfortunate effect accounts for so many of the stores hitting the bank at the side of the reservoir.

p. 16. Was the raid worthwhile. Only 2 aircraft were lost on the actual site of the dams, the other 6 being shot down by coastal defences. I cannot understand why a number of dummy raids + window were not mounted at the same time, to relieve the concentration on the actual dambuster aircraft. And one of the 2 lost on the dams was destroyed by his own bomb, which owing to being dropped too late, struck the dam immediately below the aircraft, & exploded on impact, thus eliminating the delay provided by the time to sink to the depth required to fire

Bibliography

Barnes Wallis Papers

When studied, these were together at Sir Barnes Wallis's home in Effingham, Surrey. They have since been relocated to Churchill College, Cambridge, and the National Science Museum. They contain minutes of relevant Highball and Upkeep meetings, whether Wallis was present or not, together with pre- and post-raid photos and interpretation reports plus a large amount of correspondence with ministries, firms and individuals. Sketches, copious notes and diagrams in his immaculate copperplate script and a vast number of German documents (some translated, some not) concerning the construction and function of target German dams as well as assessments of damage after the attacks on them are included. A scrapbook of press cuttings associated with Operation Chastise has also survived.

Cherwell Papers, Nuffield College, Oxford

They demonstrate the breadth of Cherwell's influence during the war years and contain details of the many extraordinary and often bizarre schemes submitted to him. There are copies of correspondence with Wallis.

Imperial War Museum

(a) **Milch Papers**. They include details of a conference on 25 May 1943 to discuss defensive measures to be taken after the Dam's Raid and of another gathering on 1 June 1943, at which the General Staff requested a copy of the report on the Chastise aircraft, which crashed on the Lower Rhine and from which Upkeep was recovered.

BIBLIOGRAPHY

(b) **Speer Collection**. Interrogation of Speer after his capture in 1945 and Speer's own reports on allied bombing of Germany.

National Archives, Kew

Air 2	4967 Citations and Awards
Air 4 37	Wing Commander Gibson's log book
Air 6 63	Air Council Minutes, January–December 1943
67	Conclusions of Air Council Meetings, July 1940–December 1943
Air 8 1102	May–September 1943, protection of dams and reservoirs in the United Kingdom
1234-6	February 1943–May 1945, possible use of Highball and Upkeep
1237	March 1943–October 1944, Highball and Upkeep progress reports
1238	March–April 1943, economic effects of the destruction of German dams
1239	July–August 1943, Soviet request for Chastise info.
1458	Correspondence of Air Staff and Naval Staff, February 1943–March 1945
Air 9 96	1938–40, War Plans
102	Attacks on German War Industry (WA 5)
214-6	Joint Planning Staff, 1941–43
Air 10 3395	Operational Numbers of Bomb Targets in Germany (SD 226)
Air 14	
22 91938	Bombing Committee Minutes
595	Operation Chastise
717	April 1943–October 1944, Operations of 617 Squadron
790	June 1942–April 1945, Operational Research Committee
817	July 1940–June 1941, Attacks on German reservoirs and dams
840	Operation Chastise
842	Operation Chastise
844	Operation Chastise
1195	December 1941–July 1943, Bomber Command operations final report
1385	January 1942–October 1943, analysis of night photos

2036	Operation Chastise
2060-1	1943–45, further trials with Upkeep
2062	April 1943, operational role of 617 Squadron
2087-8	Operation Chastise
2144	November 1942–October 1943, No. 5 Group Intelligence Diary
Air 19 304	1941–43, publicity in USA
383	Attack on Ruhr Dams, including interpretation reports
Air 20 2617	Chiefs of Staff papers, Highball and Upkeep
Air 24 205	Bomber Command Operations and Administration, January-December 1943
252-5	Appendices to 205 above, February–May 1943, including intelligence reports
Air 27 538	57 Squadron Operations Record Book
2017	542 Squadron (PRU) Operations Record Book
2021	542 Squadron B Flight Operations Record Book
2128	617 Squadron Operations Record Book
9156	Citations and Awards
Air 28 682	RAF Scampton Operations Record Book
AVIA	15 384, 1001, 2340 MAP files
Cab 23	3, 13, 16, 44B War Cabinet minutes
Cab 65 34	1 April–29 June 1943, Conclusions of War Cabinet meetings
37-8	11 January–30 June 1943, Confidential annexes to Cabinet meetings
Cab 66 36-7	April–June 1943, War Cabinet memos
Cab 69 2	War Cabinet Defence Committee (Ops), 1941
5	War Cabinet Defence Committee (Ops), 1943
8	War Cabinet Defence Committee (Ops), Secretary's standard file, 1943
Cab 79 10-1	Chiefs of Staff Committee minutes
26-7	Chiefs of Staff Committee minutes
88	Chiefs of Staff Committee, Secretary's standard file, 1943
Cab 80 27-8	Chiefs of Staff Committee memos
39	Chiefs of Staff Committee memos
Cab 99 22	Trident conference, British Chiefs of Staff and Combined Chiefs of Staff meetings, Washington, USA
DEFE 2	Investigations into the demolition of dams and Operation Cornet
WO 208 3262	Operation Cornet
WO 216 133	May-Dec 1943, Mission No. 30 in Moscow

BIBLIOGRAPHY

Bundesarchiv-Militaerarchiv, Freiburg, Germany

E 2024 and 204/1	Documents concerned with the interruption of water supplies following the breaching of the Moehne Dam and their restoration together with sectional and construction drawings of the dam
RL 199/3 and 203/4	Progress of repair work on the Moehne Dam
RL 200/61	Effect of breaching of the Moehne Dam on waterworks
RL 200/62-3	Details of defensive measures taken at the Moehne Dam and other similar dams, 1943–44
RM 122/v.M/1309/83077	Relevant flak records

Wasser-und-Schifffahrtsamt, Hannover-Muenden, Germany

17 July–30 November 1943, weekly reports of rebuilding at the Eder Dam
27 July 1943, report on repairs to electricity supplies
January 1950, report on 'The War Damage to the Eder Dam and its repairs', by the senior administrator and construction adviser to the *Wasser-und-Schifffahrtsamt*
Text of lecture at the *Technische Hochschule*, on the damage to, and rebuilding of, the Eder Dam

Department of Aviation Records, RAF Museum, Hendon

B 689 Hand-written note by Dr Norman Davey, formerly of the BRS, Garston, dated May 1980
DC 72/28 Instructions for the fitting of spotlights to Type 464 (Provisioning) Lancaster
DC 74/144 Various German eyewitness accounts and summaries of the course, damage and wider impact of the attack on the Moehne Dam
Drawings of the modifications required to a Lancaster III for this operation and copies of German documents analysing Barlow's crashed aircraft (AJ-E) and its Upkeep, together with a copy of the cross-sectional diagram of the Moehne Dam used by Wallis to brief 617 Squadron crews

THE DAMBUSTERS: 'WAS THE RAID WORTHWHILE?'

Other German Archives

The *Ennepe Wasserband*, Gevelsberg, *Ruhrverband und Ruhrtalsperrenverein*, Essen, and *Wupperverband*, Wuppertal, Germany, hold records and certain eye witness accounts.

Miscellaneous Data

Albert F. Simpson Historical Research Center, Maxwell Air Force Base, USA:
HQ VIII Bomber Command, Narrative of Operations, 15–17 May 1943
HQ VIII Fighter Command, Weekly Intelligence Summary, 16–22 May 1943
Hansard Parliamentary Debates, 389 and 390 HC Debates Fifth Series
Herr Albert Speer: Office Diary (1943) pp. 63-4, 99, 154-5, Vol 45
617 Squadron RAF: Chastise navigator's logs: A-J G (partial), AJ-H, AJ-J, AJ-N, AJ-P, AJ-W

Published Books (London, unless otherwise stated)

G. Aders	*History of the German Night-Fighter Force 1917-1943* (Eng trs 1978)
M. Balfour	*Propaganda in War 1939-1945* (1979)
P. Brickhill	*The Dam Busters* (1952)
G. L. Cheshire	*Bomber Pilot* (Mayflower ed. 1979)
R.W. Clark	*Tizard* (1965)
C. Cruickshank	*The Fourth Arm, Psychological Warfare 1938-1945* (1977)
C. Eade (ed)	*The War Speeches of the Rt Hon W S Churchill, ii,* (1952)
H. Euler	*Als Deutschlands Daemme Brachen* (Stuttgart, 1976)
S. Finn	*Lincolnshire Air War 1939-1945* (Lincoln, 1973)
A. Galland	*The First and the Last* (Eng trs, 1955)
G.P. Gibson	*Enemy Coast Ahead* (Pan ed, 1955)
W Green	*Avro Lancaster* (1959)
W.K. Hancock	*Statistical Digest of the War* (1951)
Sir Arthur Harris	*Bomber Offensive* (1947)

BIBLIOGRAPHY

M. Hastings	*Chastise* (2019)
O.F.G. Hogg	*The Royal Arsenal, ii* (1963)
J. Holland	*Dam Busters* (2012)
P. Huskinson	*Vision Ahead* (1949)
D. Irving	*The Rise and Fall of the Luftwaffe* (1973)
R.V. Jones	*Most Secret War: Britain's Scientific Intelligence 1939–1945* (1978)
W.J. Lawrence	*No. 5 Bomber Group RAF 1939–1945* (1951)
L.P. Lochner (ed)	*The Goebbels Diaries 1942–3* (Westport, Connecticut, USA, 1970)
W.N. Medlicott	*The Economic Blockade*, ii (1959)
G. Pawle	*The Secret War* (Corgi ed, 1959)
M.M. Postan, D. Hay and J. D. Scott	*Design and Development of Weapons* (1964)
D. Richards	*Portal of Hungerford* (1977)
H. Rumpf	*The Bombing of Germany* (Eng trs, 1975)
J.D. Scott	*Vickers – A History* (1962)
A. Speer	*Inside the Third Reich* (Eng trs, 1977)
	Spandau Diaries (Eng trs, 1976)

United States Strategic Bombing Survey (Overseas Economic Effects Division) The Effects of Strategic Bombing on the German War Economy (1945)

W. Warlimont *Im Hauptquartier der deutschen Wehrmacht 1939-1945* (Frankfurt-am-Main, 1962)

C. Webster and N. Frankland *The Strategic Air Offensive against Germany* (the official history) i, ii, iv (1961)

Articles and Pamphlets

Anon, Die Nacht als die Daemme brachen, *TWS Stimmen,* Ig *17,* 1968

Lord Baker, William Henry Glanville, *Biographical Memoirs of Fellows of the Royal Society,* Vol 23, (December 1977)

British Intelligence Objectives Sub-Committee, German Experimental Work on the Attack of Reinforced Concrete by Explosives and Projectiles and Inspection of the Moehne and Eder Dams, (unpublished, September 1945)

A.R. Collins, Dam Busting the 'uncivil engineering' behind the famous wartime raid, *New Civil Engineer,* (May 1972)

A.R. Collins, The Origins and Design of the Attack on the German Dams by D.R. Collins (unpublished draft, 1981)
Department of Scientific and Industrial Research, Building Research 1940–1945 (1948)
Department of Scientific and Industrial Research, Wartime Activities of the Road Research Laboratory (1949)
R. Goeoeck, Als die (Eder) Sperrmauer Brach (Korbach und Bad Wildingungen, 1974)
I. Hutchings, Bouncing Bombs of the Second World War, *New Scientist*, (8 November 1979)
O. Kirschmer, Zerstoerung und Shutz von Talsperren und Daemmen, *Schweizerische Bauzeitung*, Ig 67 (1949)
H.W. Koenig, Instandzetung der Sorpetalsperre zur Besichtigung von Kriegsschaeden, (Hamburg, 1961)
J.D. Lewin, German Dams Attacked Successfully, *Engineering News Record*, (New York, 17 June 1943)
Ministry of Information, Bomber Command (1941)
Ministry of Information, Over to You, broadcasts by the RAF, (1943)
W.G. Ramsey, The Ruhr Dams Raid, *After the Battle, No. 3*
B.N. Wallis, Dambusting Weapon, *Air Clues* (May 1963)
B.N. Wallis, The Man and His Bomb: the Dambusting Weapon, *Aerospace Historian* (1973)

Newspapers and Periodicals

Aerospace Historian
After the Battle
Air Clues
Annual Register
Daily Express
Daily Mail
Daily Sketch
Daily Telegraph
Express and Echo, Exeter
Evening News, Portsmouth
Evening Standard
Hampshire Telegraph and Post
Illustrated London News

BIBLIOGRAPHY

Lincolnshire Echo
London Gazette
New Civil Engineer
New Scientist
New York Times
Observer
Star, Sheffield
Sunday Express
The Times
Western Telegraph

Glossary

AA	Anti-aircraft gun(s)
AAD	Aerial or Air Attack on Dams (Committee or Wallis's paper)
A and AEE	Aeroplane and Armament Experimental Establishment Boscombe Down
ACAS (I)	Assistant Chief of the Air Staff (Intelligence)
ACAS (Ops)	Assistant Chief of the Air Staff (Operations)
ACAS (TR)	Assistant Chief of the Air Staff (Technical Requirements)
ACM	Air Chief Marshal
Adm	Admiralty or Admiral
Air Cdre	Air Commodore
AJ	617 Squadron's code
AM	Air Marshal
Amatol	Explosive
AOC	Air Officer Commanding
AOC-in-C	Air Officer Commanding-in-Chief
AP	armour piercing (bomb)
API	Air position indicator
ATA	Air Transport Auxiliary
AVM	Air Vice-Marshal
Avro(s)	A.V. Roe and Co. Ltd.

GLOSSARY

Baseball	Version of 'bouncing bomb' planned for a motor torpedo boat or gun boat
BC	Bomber Command
Brig	Brigadier
BRS	Building Research Station, Garston
BST	British Summer Time
Capt	Captain
CAS	Chief of the Air Staff
CCS	Combined Chiefs of Staff
CE	Composition explosive or Chief Executive
Chastise	operational code name for Dams Raid
C-in-C	Commander-in-Chief
CID	Committee of Imperial Defence
CIGS	Chief of the Imperial General Staff
CO	Commanding Officer
Col	Colonel
COS	Chiefs of Staff or Chiefs of Staff Committee
Cpl	corporal
CRD	Controller of Research and Development, Ministry of Aircraft Production
CSRD	Chief Superintendent of the Research Department, Woolwich
D Arm	Director or Directorate of Armament Development, initially Air Ministry, then Ministry of Aircraft Production
DBST	Double British Summer Time
DB Ops	Director or Directorate of Bomber Operations, Air Ministry
DCAS	Deputy Chief of the Air Staff

DCSRD	Deputy Chief Superintendent of the Research Department Woolwich
D/CRD	Deputy Controller of Research and Development, Ministry of Aircraft Production
D/D Arm D	Deputy Director of Armament Development, Ministry of Aircraft Production
D/DB Ops	Deputy Director of Bomber Operations, Air Ministry
D/DSR	Deputy Director of Scientific Research, Ministry of Aircraft Production
deg(s) or °	Degree(s)
D/F	Direction finding
DF	Ops Director or Directorate of Flying Operations, Air Ministry
DI	Daily inspection
DMWD	Director or Directorate of Miscellaneous Weapon Development, Admiralty
D/R	Dead reckoning
DSIR	Department of Scientific and Industrial Research
DSD	Director or Directorate of Staff Duties, Air Ministry
DSR	Director of Scientific Research, Ministry of Aircraft Production
DTD	Director or Directorate of Technical Development, Ministry of Aircraft Production
E	East
ENE	East-north-east
ETA	estimated time of arrival
F/E	Flight Engineer
Fg Off	Flying Officer
Flak	German anti-aircraft guns

GLOSSARY

Flt Lt	Flight Lieutenant
F/Sgt	Flight Sergeant
GCI	Ground controlled interception
Gee	Navigational aid
Glycol	Coolant liquid
Golf Mine	Code name of all version of the 'bouncing bomb'
GP	General purpose (bomb)
Gp Capt	Group Captain
HCU	Heavy Conversion Unit
HE	High explosive or high explosive bomb
Highball	Code name for smaller 'bouncing bomb' destined for use against enemy shipping
HQ	Headquarters
ICI	Imperial Chemical Industries Ltd
IFF	Identification Friend or Foe airborne device
Intercom	Communication system within an aircraft
kilo	Kilogram
km	Kilometre
kph	Kilometres per hour
kW	Kilowatt
LAC	Leading Aircraftman
LACW	Leading Aircraftwoman
Lt Cdr	Lieutenant Commander
LMF	Lack of moral fibre
M	Magnetic bearing
m	Metre
mag	Magneto or magazine
MAEE	Marine Aircraft Experimental Establishment

Maj	Major
MAP	Ministry of Aircraft Production
met	Meteorological
MEW	Ministry of Economic Warfare
mm	Millimetre
mph	Miles per hour
MRAF	Marshal of the Royal Air Force
N	North
NAAFI	Navy, Army and Air Force Institutes
NCO	Non-commissioned officer
NE	North-east
NNE	North-north-east
NNW	North-north-west
NPL	National Physical Laboratory, Teddington
NW	North-west
OC	Officer Commanding
OKW	Oberkommando der Wehrmacht: High Command of three German armed forces
Op	Operation
ORB	Operations Record Book
OT	Organisation Todt
OTU	Operational Training Unit
PE	Plastic explosive
Plt Off	Pilot Officer
PPS	Parliamentary Private Secretary
PRU	Photographic Reconnaissance Unit
RAAF	Royal Australian Air Force
radar	Radio detection and ranging

GLOSSARY

RAE	Royal Aircraft Establishment, Farnborough
RAF	Royal Air Force
RCAF	Royal Canadian Air Force
RDF	Radio direction finding (radar)
RDX	Research Department Explosive
rev(s)	Revolution(s)
RN	Royal Navy
rpm	Revolutions per minute
RRL	Road Research Laboratory, Harmondsworth
R/T	Radio-telephone
RTV	Ruhrtalsperrenverein/Ruhr Valley Dams Association
RNZAF	Royal New Zealand Air Force
S	South
SAP	Semi-armour piercing (bomb)
SASO	Senior Air Staff Officer
SE	South-east
Sec Off	Section Officer
Sgt	Sergeant
SOE	Special Operations Executive
Sqn	Squadron
Sqn Ldr	Squadron Leader
SSE	South-south-east
SSW	South-south-west
Store	Bomb or aerial mine
SW	South-west
Torpex	Underwater explosive
Upkeep	Code name for version of 'bouncing bomb' carried by a Lancaster

U/S	Unserviceable
USAAF	United States Army Air Force
VHF	Very high frequency
VSG	Variable-speed gear
W	West
WA	Western Air Plan
WAAF	Women's Auxiliary Air Force
Wg Cdr	Wing Commander
WO	War Office or Warrant Officer
W/Op	Wireless operator
W/T	Wireless telegraphy

Index

(Ranks at time of operation)
Abberton Reservoir (Colchester Lake), 89–90, 96 110
Admiralty Mine Dept., Havant, 10
Aeroplane & Armament Experimental Establishment, Boscombe Down, 10, 26, 51, 59, 96, 111, 147, 174, 224
Air Bases;
  Brooklands (Vickers, Weybridge), 21–2, 32, 76, 100
  Eindhoven (Luftwaffe, Neths), 120, 123, 236
  Gilze-Rijen (Luftwaffe, Neths), 120, 236–8
  RAF Bradwell Bay, 27
  RAF Manston, 27, 29–31, 33, 58–9, 76, 87–91, 96, 112–13, 175–6
  RAF Ringwood, 118, 171
  RAF Scampton, 57, 59–61, 63–5, 68–72, 76–9, 81, 84, 86–8, 90, 92–3, 96, 98–100, 103, 106, 110–12, 118, 121, 129–30, 136, 138–9, 141–2, 144–6, 153, 155, 157–8, 161, 168–72, 175–6, 181, 185–8, 220
  RAF Warmwell, 22, 24, 26, 28
  Werl (Luftwaffe, Germany), 121, 198, 211
Aircraft;
  Lancaster Mk I, 24–5, 27–9, 31–2, 38, 41–2, 44–8, 50, 57–8, 95
  Lancaster Mk III (464 Provisioning), 33–4, 53–60, 62, 76, 80, 82–3, 86–7, 97, 109, 110
  Messerschmitt Bf 110, 167, 237
  Miles Magister, 'Maggie', 75, 175
  Mosquito, 20, 25, 27–8, 47–9, 76, 91, 94, 96, 176, 185
  Wellington, 5, 9, 13, 19–22, 24, 26–9, 100, 158
Air Attack on Dams Committee, 35–8
Aldis Lamps, 62, 86–8, 119, 121, 125, 127, 134, 146, 148–9, 150, 160, 163, 220
Anderson, Flt/Sgt C.T. (617), 141, 169–70, 173
Andrade, Prof E.N. da C., 35–6
Arthurton, Fg Off M.W. (Scampton MO), 77, 89–90, 93, 95, 112
Astell, Flt Lt W. (617) 63, 66, 74, 100, 113, 120–2, 128, 130, 228

Bader, Gp Capt Sir Douglas, 251
Baker, Gp Capt J.W., 41–2, 45, 50
Barlow, Flt Lt R.N.G. (617), 70, 83, 90, 94, 99, 116–17, 141–42, 145, 188, 219, 230–31, 234–5, 240
Barratt, S., 15, 49, 222
Beaverbrook, Lord, 9–10, 37
Bennett, Plt Off T., 92
Bergel, Cdr H.C., 111–12, 147, 155
Bever Dam, 213, 226–9
Big Highball (Upkeep), 41–2
Blackett, Prof P.M.S., 18–19, 57
Bottomley, AVM N.H., 4, 27, 43–4, 56, 91, 97, 224–5, 242, 245
Brennan, Sgt C. (617), 77, 127–8
Brennan, C.E., 81, 118
British dams' defence, 220–23
Brown, F/Sgt K.W. (617), 65, 68, 77, 90, 99, 101, 110, 113, 115, 156–64, 170, 188, 196, 204, 208–209
Brown, Capt H.A. 'Sam' (test pilot), 27, 31–2, 59, 178
Bryden, Cpl J. (617), 85, 109, 117
Buckley, Fg Off J. (617), 115, 134
Bufton, Air Cdre S.O., 8, 20, 27, 39, 45, 60, 94, 97, 102, 179, 186, 224, 241
Bullard, Dr. C., 57, 228
Burcher, Plt Off A.F. (617), 115, 126–8, 186, 239
Burge, Sqn Ldr C.G., 2–3, 245
Burpee, Plt Off L.J. (617), 70, 82, 89, 93, 97, 114–15, 139–40, 142, 186, 217, 228–30, 232–3
Byers, Plt Off V.W. (617), 74, 96, 99, 141–42, 145, 230, 240

Caple, Flt Lt C.C. (617), 118, 144
Casablanca Directive, 241, 248

Chadwick, R., 27, 49–50, 53–4, 57–60, 81, 118, 171, 177–8, 189, 251
Chalmers, F/Sgt G.A. (617), 68–9, 83, 110, 114, 164–8, 227
Chambers, Fg Off L. (617), 99, 128–9
Cherwell, Lord, 10, 20, 40–3, 47, 51, 221
Churchill, Rt Hon W.S., 10, 41, 136, 184, 223, 249
Clay, Sgt J.H. (617), 60, 67–8, 72–3, 79, 82–3, 88, 114–15, 142–3
Cochrane, AVM The Hon R.A., 8, 20, 47, 50, 57, 61–5, 73, 76, 82, 85, 88–92, 99, 100–101, 104, 109, 114, 130–1, 135, 139, 155, 167–70, 172, 175–6, 178, 185–6, 190, 219, 222, 225–6, 230, 232–3, 241, 245–6, 248
Collins, Dr A.R., vii, 10–15, 17–20, 31, 39, 49, 52, 56, 58, 60, 113, 129, 170, 172, 174, 215, 218, 235, 247, 251
Combined Operations, 46
Cottam, Warrant Off A.P. (617), 132–3
Craven, Sir C., 49–51, 54–6, 179, 225

Dann, Wg Cdr C.L., 61, 86, 127
Davey, Dr N., 12
Deering, Plt Off (617), 69, 125, 188
Dillgardt, Herr J., 3, 249
Divall, Plt Off W.G. (617), 70, 90, 94, 158
Douglas, AVM W.S., 2, 4
Dove, Mrs M., 81, 118, 225

INDEX

Drury, LAC A., 80–1, 130, 118, 171
Dunn, Wg Cdr W.E., 99–100, 110, 130

Earnshaw, Fg Off K. (617), 115
Eaton, F/Sgt (617), 148, 154
Edwards, G.R.E. (later Sir George), 8, 16–18, 59
Elworthy, Gp Capt S.C., 44
Evill, AM Sir Douglas, 97, 175–6, 223
Experimental sites;
    Building Research Station, Garston, 11–14, 35, 170
    Chesil Beach, Dorset, 21–8, 30, 40, 43, 47, 64
    Foxwarren (Vickers facility), 16, 32, 57
    Nant-y-Gro Dam, Wales, 13–14, 20, 38, 170, 221, 226
    National Physical Laboratory, Teddington, 18–20, 23, 37, 39, 41, 43, 47, 57
    Porton Down, 26
    Reculver Bay, 27–8, 30–3, 58–9, 76, 87, 89, 93–6, 111–13, 129, 175
    Road Research Laboratory, Harmondsworth, 10, 13–14, 19, 31, 37, 39, 46, 56, 170, 215, 218, 247, 251
    Silvermere Lake, 16–18, 32

Feneron, Sgt H.B. (617), vii, 111, 115, 158–62, 209
Finch Noyes, Wg Cdr C.R., 4–6, 14–17, 247, 249
Fowler, Sec Off A. (617), 90, 97, 115, 176

Foxlee, Fg Off B.T. (617), 78, 120
Fraser, F/Sgt J.W. (617), 74, 86, 127–8, 132, 171, 174, 251
Fray, Fg Off F.G., 178–9
Freeman, Sqn Ldr C.T., 54, 56
Freeman, ACM Sir Wilfrid, 55, 225

Galland, Gen A., 162–3
Gammon, T., 7, 42, 56, 59
Garro-Jones, G.M., 37–8, 52
Gibson, Wg Cdr G.P. (617), vi, 48, 57, 60–78, 80–4, 86–7, 89–91, 93–6, 99–105, 109, 113, 115–16, 119–22, 124–34, 136–41, 147, 155, 158, 163, 167, 172–6, 179, 184, 186–93, 195, 197, 198, 224, 226, 232–3, 235–6, 249–51
Gibson, Mrs E., 90, 174
Gill, AC V. (617), 63, 78, 102, 109, 117, 186
Gillan, Sec Off F. (617), 76, 90, 97, 118
Glanville, Dr W.H., 10–15, 24, 49, 56, 218
Goebbels, J., 177, 212, 243, 246
Goodale, Fg Off (617), 70, 132
Grant, A.D., 19, 22–3, 30, 32–3, 42, 59
Grayston, Sgt. R.E. (617), 88, 94, 111, 114, 123
Gronland, ACW M.J. (617), 71–2, 117, 170
Guenne, 108, 124–5, 128, 150, 189, 191–5, 198–9, 202

Hague Conference (1922-3), 248
Handasyde, Capt R.C. (test pilot), 7, 22, 25–9, 31–4, 94, 112

Hannermann, Herr, 192–3, 195, 198–9, 204
Harlingen, 230–1
Harris, ACM Sir Arthur, 44–9, 56, 61–2, 64–5, 85, 99, 130–1, 136, 139, 147, 168–9, 175–6, 180, 183, 187, 224–5, 243–5, 247, 251
Hay, Flt Lt R.C. (617), 76, 89, 99–100, 123, 128
Heal, Sgt D.P. (617), vi, 65, 77, 110, 118, 153, 158–62, 170, 188, 250–1
Hemfurth, 109, 205–207, 218
Heveron, Sgt J. (617), 71, 173
Hewstone, Sgt H.J. (617), 65, 160
Highball, 42–6, 49, 53, 63, 91, 94, 96–8, 176, 185, 223
Hilse, Oberleutnant, 191–2, 198, 204
Hitler, A., 17, 212, 214, 217, 244, 249
Hobday, Fg Off H.S. (617), 66, 86, 94, 101, 110–111, 121–5, 130–34, 138–40, 158, 187, 193, 233–4
Hoesen, L.J.H., 200–201
Hopgood, Flt Lt J.V. (617), 70, 74, 77, 86, 90, 94, 100–101, 115, 119, 124, 126–8, 130, 139, 174, 193–5, 197, 213, 230, 232, 240, 247, 251
Howard, Plt Off C.L. (617), 69, 74–5, 87, 91, 110–11, 156–7, 163–7, 184, 186, 226–8, 250
Howarth, Sgt W. (617), 67, 77, 85, 142–3
Humphries, Flt Lt H.R. (617), 73, 102, 109, 116–18, 140, 144–5, 172–3, 188–9

Huskisson, Air Cdre P., 4, 35, 37
Hutchings, Dr I., 241–2
Hutchison, Flt Lt R.E.G. (617), 116, 120, 126, 129–31, 135

Institution of Civil Engineers, 8, 10

Jeffree, H., 16, 19, 23, 25, 27, 32, 34, 57, 59, 61, 112–13, 117–18, 172
Johnson, Fg Off E.C. (617), 60, 86, 113, 123–4, 131–34, 138, 233–4
Johnson, Sgt G.L. (617), 67, 70, 74, 84–5, 111–14, 116, 148–54, 158, 160, 174
Jones, Prof R.V., 172
Jong, Col A.P. de, 185, 231, 236

Kammhuber, Luftwaffe Gen J., 163
Kassel, 2, 109, 140, 179–81, 212, 242–3, 246
Keiser, Herr P., 227
Kellow, Sgt R.G.T. (617), 66–7, 123, 133–5, 138, 232–4
Kilner, Maj H., 7, 26, 42, 49, 56, 189
Kirschmer, Prof Dr Ing O., 203, 206, 208, 210, 244–5
Kleeschulte, Herr, 193, 199, 241
Knight, Plt Off L.G. (617), 66–7, 86, 88, 94–5, 101, 111, 113–15, 121–5, 130–35, 138–40, 152, 158, 186, 193, 204–206, 213, 232–5
Koehler, Herr K., 3, 191, 194–5, 199
Koenig, Dr Ing K.W., 192, 202, 210–11, 214–17, 235
Kraft, Luftwaffe Sgt G., 167

INDEX

Lawrence, O.L., 242
Leggo, Flt Lt J. (617), 99–101, 119–21, 136, 153
Linnell, AVM F.J., 20, 41–3, 45–6, 49–50, 58, 175
Lockspeiser, B., 8, 41–6, 49–50, 59, 61–3, 87–88
Longbottom, Sqn Ldr M.V. 'Shorty' (test pilot), 28–30, 32–4, 76–7, 94–5, 98, 112
Ludlow-Hewitt, ACM Sir Edgar, 2, 4, 245

MacLean, F/Sgt D.A. (617), 113, 115, 148–54, 188
MacNeece- Foster, AVM W.F., 58
Maltby, Flt Lt D.H. (617), 67, 95–7, 121–22, 124, 129–31, 136–7, 139, 162, 180, 182, 195, 198, 200, 215, 234
Martin, Flt Lt H.B. (617), 68–70, 73, 78, 90, 94–5, 99–100, 102, 113, 116, 118–22, 124, 127–30, 136–9, 180, 188, 190, 194–5, 197, 225, 250
Maudslay, Sqn Ldr H.R. (617), 70, 83, 87, 90, 95–6, 100, 111, 116, 122–4, 131–34, 139, 193, 204–206, 233, 235–6, 247
McCarthy, Flt Lt J.C. (617), 67, 70, 73–4, 77–8, 82, 84–5, 111–12, 115, 140–41, 147–60, 162, 164, 186, 190
McDowell, F/Sgt (617), 230, 240
Minchin, Sgt J.W. (617), 127
Ministry of Aircraft Production, 7, 10–11, 15, 20, 23, 25, 27, 30, 32, 35, 37, 41, 43, 49, 51, 53, 55, 57–8, 61, 87, 94, 17, 222, 224–5

Ministry of Home Security, 8, 10, 46, 221
Mittelland Canal, 3, 6, 40, 104, 207, 224, 243, 246
Mountbatten, Lord Louis, 46–7
Munro, Flt Lt J.L. (617), 67, 70, 72–3, 77–9, 82–3, 85–6, 90, 94–6, 101, 111–13, 116, 141–46, 170, 172, 186
Munro, LAC H.K. (617), 71, 78–9, 110, 148, 171

Neheim, 108, 138, 150, 153, 160, 194, 199–202, 204, 211, 243
Neheim-Huesten, 199–200
Newman, A.J. 'Bill', 11–12
Nichols, Sgt L.W. (617), 27, 131
Nicholson, Sgt V. (617), 121–2, 124, 129, 136, 233

Oancia, Sgt S. (617), 65, 77, 82, 110, 157–62, 171
O'Brien, Sgt H.E. (617), 67, 111, 114–16, 122–3, 132–6, 138, 152, 233
Oliver, G.C.S., 88–9
Operation Order B.976, 92–3 (draft), 100–105, 112, 120, 137, 148, 156, 245, 247

Paar, Fraeulein L., 206
Peirse, AM Sir Richard, 6
Pidcock, Air Cdre G.A.H., 37, 43
Pierson, R.K. 'Rex', 7, 9, 189
Pine, Flt Lt G.E., 251–52
Portal, ACM Sir Charles, 4–6, 45–9, 55, 58, 60, 97, 136, 175–6, 183, 241, 247, 249

Pound, Adm of the Fleet
    Sir Dudley, 46, 96, 223
Powell, Sgt D.J.D. (617), 166
Powell, F/Sgt G.E. 'Chiefy' (617),
    71–3, 78, 101–103, 109, 117,
    148, 173, 189, 250
Pruess, Dr M., 196–8, 208–209,
    211, 214, 216, 219, 226, 232
Pye, Dr D.R., 10, 35–7

Rayment, F., 19
Renouf, Rear Adm E. de F., 19–20,
    22–3, 27, 37–8, 46, 49, 56, 77
Rodger, Fg Off D. (617), 148–9,
    152, 154, 159, 171
Rice, Plt Off G. (617), 66, 70, 73,
    77, 83, 85, 90, 110, 115, 141–2,
    145–7, 170, 173, 186, 224, 230
Rowe, N., 7–8, 20, 30–2, 51, 54
Royal Aircraft Establishment,
    Farnborough, 8, 27, 53, 56, 59,
    62–3, 87
Royal investiture, 187
Royal visit to Scampton, 186–8
Rubsam, Herr A., 205
Rumbles, Fg Off F.G. (617), 82, 142
Rumpf, Herr H., 244, 246, 248

Satterly, Gp Capt H.V., 73–6,
    84, 91–5, 99–100, 103, 110,
    131, 150
Saundby, AVM R.H.M.S., 6, 31,
    44–5, 47, 91, 224, 250
Scrope, H.E., 9, 14
Shannon, Flt Lt D.J. (617), 69–70,
    78, 85, 94–6, 100, 114–16,
    121–2, 124–5, 127, 130–34,
    137–40, 172, 176, 186–7, 193,
    195, 204–206, 224, 250

Schuette, Unteroffizier K., 191,
    195–6, 198, 204
Significant Route Locations;
    Ahlen, 120–22, 124, 136, 138,
        141–2, 148–9, 152–4, 157,
        159, 161, 164, 166, 230, 238
    Beek, 120, 122–3, 152
    Duelmen Lakes, 120, 122–4,
        136, 138, 142, 148, 152,
        158–9, 161, 163–4, 168, 170,
        231–4
    Hamm, 120, 124, 138, 153–5,
        157, 159–61, 193, 197, 203,
        230, 238
    Luedinghausen, 120, 122
    Marbeck, 232–3
    Rees, 120–24, 138, 142, 152,
        229, 231–4
    Scheldt estuary, 75, 119, 122–3,
        156, 158, 163
    Soest, 121, 150, 199
    Terschelling island, 141,
        166–7, 230
    Texel island, 118, 141–46,
        166–7, 229–30
    Vlieland island, 75, 141–43,
        145–6, 148–9, 153–4,
        166–7, 231
Simpson, F/Sgt T.D. (617), 68,
    90, 94, 99–100, 113, 119–22,
    127–30, 136
Sinclair, Sir Archibald, 182,
    184, 221
Slessor, AM J.C., 4, 175
Sorley, AVM R.S., 39, 41–6
Special Operations Executive, 47
Speer, Herr A., vii, 3, 210–12, 214,
    216–17, 243–9
Stewart, Maj O., 9, 39

INDEX

Stone, Sgt A.J.B. (617), 130–1
Stradling, Dr E.R., 10, 13
Summers, Capt J 'Mutt' (test pilot), 21–7, 29, 31, 47–8, 74, 76, 100, 137
Sumpter, F/Sgt L.J. (617), 60, 69–70, 82–3, 85–6, 95, 110, 122, 124, 127–31, 133–34, 140, 171, 187, 195
Sutherland, Sgt F.E. (617), 123–4, 133–5, 138, 233
Sutton Pippard, Prof A.J., 10, 21

Taerum, Fg Off (617), 119–20
Target Dams;
    Diemel, 6, 40, 100, 109, 156, 169–70, 228
    Eder, 2–3, 6, 12, 36, 40, 55, 92, 97, 108–110, 123, 130–40, 156–7, 168, 175–6, 179, 181–5, 190, 193–4, 198–9, 202, 204–208, 212–13, 215, 217–19, 224, 226, 228, 235–6, 242–3, 246–8, 251
    Ennepe, 6, 40, 108, 110, 156, 164–5, 196, 219, 226–9, 247
    Henne, 6, 13, 40, 100
    Lister, 6, 40, 111, 156–7, 168, 228
    Moehne, 2–6, 9, 12–13, 33, 35–6, 40, 44, 46–7, 55, 58, 60, 64, 92–3, 96–7, 99–101, 104–6, 108–10, 113–14, 119, 121–133, 136–42, 148, 150, 152–4, 156–7, 159–60, 162, 164–5, 175–6, 179, 181–2, 185, 189–94, 198–204, 207, 210–11, 213–20, 224–6,
228, 230, 235–6, 239, 241–9, 251
    Sorpe, 1–2, 6, 13, 25, 33, 36, 39–40, 48, 75, 92–4, 104–106, 108, 110, 114–15, 136, 141–42, 145, 148, 150, 152–60, 162, 164 169–70, 175–6, 180–82, 185, 196, 200–201, 204, 208–210, 213, 216, 219, 226, 230–1, 242–8
Taylor, Prof G.I., 10, 30–1
Tees, Mrs E., 173–2, 238
Tees, Sgt F. (617), 67, 83, 111, 173–4, 238–40, 250
Theunissen, P. 201, 209, 219
Tilburg, 120, 159, 230
Tirpitz, 20, 96, 110, 185, 225
Tizard, Sir H., 13–14, 18–20, 36–8, 49, 176
Townsend, F/Sgt W.C. (617), 68–9, 74, 78, 83–4, 88, 94, 96, 110–111, 114–15, 141, 156–9, 163–70, 181, 186, 209, 226–8
Training Locations;
    Abberton Reservoir (Colchester Lake), 89, 96, 111
    Eyebrook Reservoir (Uppingham Lake), 88, 90, 96, 111

Upkeep, 27, 32–4, 42–5, 49–50, 52–60, 63–4, 76–8, 80, 82, 87–8, 91, 93–5, 96–9, 101–106, 109, 113–16, 122, 125–34, 139, 145, 147–8, 150, 152, 154–5, 159–60, 162, 165, 169–70, 172, 179, 183, 189, 193, 195, 197, 204–206, 209–10, 218–24, 227–8, 232–35, 239, 245, 247, 250–1

Verity, Sqn Ldr C., 41
Verschoyle, Flt Lt D., 47

Wainfleet bombing range, 78, 82, 87, 90, 136
Walker, Fg Off D.R. (617), 86, 124–5, 127, 130, 132, 187
Wallis, B.N. (later Sir Barnes), vi–vii, 7–10, 13–60, 62–3, 65, 86, 95–6, 100–101, 109, 112–14, 116–18, 129–32, 139–40, 147, 152, 169–70, 172, 174, 176–9, 183, 185–7, 189–90, 187, 219, 221–6, 228, 232, 235, 241, 244–5, 247–8, 250–2
Wallis explanatory papers:
Air Attack on Dams, 31, 33, 38–9, 41, 44, 245
A Note on Attacking the Axis Powers, 9, 35
Spherical Bomb-Surface Torpedo, 18
Wallis B.W., 7, 17
Wallis, Mrs M., 174
Wallis, Miss M., 16, 170, 175
Watson, Plt Off H. (617), 91, 102, 118, 145, 172

Webb, Sgt D.E. (617), 68, 82, 88, 111, 114, 118, 156, 158, 163, 165–6, 167–9, 187–8, 227–8, 251
Whittaker, Plt Off I., (617) 68, 70, 88, 91, 102, 116, 128, 136–7, 190, 250, 254
Whitworth, Gp Capt J.N.H. 'Charles' (CO RAF Scampton), 64, 70, 82, 84, 86–7, 91, 93, 96, 99, 101–102, 140, 146, 168, 178, 186–7, 190
Williams, Fg Off C.R. (617), 70, 83, 116
Wilson, Flt Lt H.S. (617), 94, 96
Winterbotham, Gp Capt F.W., 8, 10, 16–18, 20, 24, 31–2, 37–8, 41, 45, 49, 52, 55, 247
Woolwich Arsenal, 2, 10, 52–3
Wynter-Morgan, Gp Capt W., 27, 31, 33, 52–4, 56

Young, Sqn Ldr H.M. (617), 63, 66, 70, 74, 87, 90, 95, 100, 102, 121–2, 129–31, 139, 162, 182, 193, 195, 198, 204, 213, 215, 236

Dear Reader,

We hope you have enjoyed this book, but why not share your views on social media? You can also follow our pages to see more about our other products: facebook.com/penandswordbooks or follow us on Twitter @penswordbooks

You can also view our products at www.pen-and-sword.co.uk (UK and ROW) or www.penandswordbooks.com (North America).

To keep up to date with our latest releases and online catalogues, please sign up to our newsletter at: www.pen-and-sword.co.uk/newsletter

If you would like a printed catalogue with our latest books, then please email: enquiries@pen-and-sword.co.uk or telephone: 01226 734555 (UK and ROW) or email: Uspen-and-sword@casematepublishers.com or telephone: (610) 853-9131 (North America).

We respect your privacy and we will only use personal information to send you information about our products.

Thank you!